Early Praise for *Merchants of Light*

Merchants of Light is a clarion call to reclaim the universal, unitary, and boundless state of conscious awareness that has periodically surfaced in the human evolutionary journey. If we are to survive the materialistic nightmare that currently threatens our existence on Earth, our choice is clear: awaken or perish. That's the grim news. The good news, as Kovács shows, is that the awakening has already begun. This splendid book is a *tour de force*, an infusion of wisdom capable of changing the direction and fate of our species.

— Larry Dossey, M.D. Author, *One Mind: How Our Individual Mind Is Part of a Greater Consciousness and Why It Matters*

A rich and valuable immersion in sacred consciousness as it stretches back over millennia. Here are the spiritual secrets that the priests of the patriarchy and their drive for power have tried to repress, but which we urgently need at this present moment of evolutionary crisis. *Merchants of Light* reconnects us to this essential shamanic-mystic wisdom, and shows how it can make a vital contribution to heal and transform our dying world. This is an important book that can expand our understanding of spiritual consciousness.

— Llewellyn Vaughan-Lee, Ph.D. Sufi teacher and author, *Spiritual Ecology: The Cry of the Earth*

Betty Kovács' *Merchants of Light* is a magnificent masterpiece of illumined scholarship and the exquisitely written distillation of a lifetime's experience of revelation and grace. It is essential reading for all seekers on all paths and most especially for all those who are beginning to understand the tremendous secret at the heart of the dark night of our time—that this chaotic, terrifying ordeal we are now living through is the ordained birthing ground of a new, empowered, embodied, divine humanity. There is nothing like this book and reading it will change your life, renovate your hope, and inspire you to grow deeply in vision so as to step up humbly to the great work ahead. Buy this book, read it many times, and give it to everyone you know.

— Andrew Harvey, Poet, mystical scholar, spiritual teacher, Founder and Director of Institute for Sacred Activism, author, *Return of the Mother*, *Radical Passion*, and *Turn Me to Gold*

In *Merchants of Light*, Betty Kovács combines extensive historical scholarship with personal memoir to show how we lost the knowledge of our immortality and divinity and how we are reclaiming it today. A moving and compelling account that taught me many things. Vital reading in the century where we either transform ourselves or perish.

—Christopher Bache, Ph.D. Author, *Diamonds from Heaven* and *Dark Night, Early Dawn*

The intuition of there being an embracing, underlying "cosmic" consciousness has accompanied the development of all the great civilizations. Betty Kovács undertakes to trace this deep consciousness in the interest of bringing to us the light that it can provide in our increasingly dark and un-illuminated age. Her book deserves to be read both for its intrinsic interest, and for the light it promises to convey to us.

—Ervin László, Ph.D. Author, Systems Theorist, Founder of the Club of Budapest, twice Nobel Peace Prize nominee

Those who are dismayed and depressed by the state of today's world could do no better than read *Merchants of Light*. This historical panorama asserts that humankind has the resources to participate in its own evolution, thanks to the ancestral wisdom that has survived in the Hermetic Arts, Alchemy, Kabbalah, Mystic Christianity, and shamanism worldwide, in spite of its repeated repression by both Church and State. Dr. Betty Kovács' well-researched book is a wake-up call for the human species to tap into these primordial creative energies of love, following millennial-old technologies. This is a compelling vision, and one that can be actualized and embodied before it is too late.

—Stanley Krippner, Ph.D. Co-author, *Personal Mythology*

Merchants of Light is an exceptional book! Betty Kovács brilliantly weaves together the history of shamanism, mysticism, and science to show how they reveal the blueprint of our evolution. This book is filled with such a wealth of information, layers of wisdom, and moving personal visions that it will be returned to again and again to find new inspiration!

—Sandra Ingerman, M.A. Award winner, author of 12 books on shamanism, including *Soul Retrieval* and *The Book of Ceremony: Shamanic Wisdom for Invoking the Sacred in Everyday Life*

Plotinus said that remembering is for those who have forgotten. In this book of breathtaking scope and depth, Betty Kovács reminds us of our inherent divine identity and how the mystic-shamanic tradition of gnosis has been repeatedly submerged and repressed in Western culture, resulting in a devastating loss of soul and heart.... If we have created our current world, we can recreate a new one together that truly integrates heart and head, feminine and masculine, love and wisdom.... I urge people to read this profound and moving book and become part of this contemporary Renaissance, the fulfilment of our deepest longings for wholeness and cosmic consciousness.

—David Lorimer, Programme Director, Scientific and Medical Network (UK), Editor, *Paradigm Explorer*

Merchants of Light is a brilliant *tour de force* through 40,000 years of human evolution. This is a wonderful and heart-opening book, a guide for awakening the soul of the world.

—Barbara Hand Clow, Author, *Awakening the Planetary Mind* and *Alchemy of Nine Dimensions*

Progressive thinkers such as Dr. Betty Kovács believe that we have an obligation to focus on the evolution of consciousness and the gifts that our ancestors have been waiting for us to open. Many of these ancestors were skilled mystics, visionaries and scientists who have sought to bring a cosmic consciousness back into our awareness. We are currently at a precipice, and our fall can be prevented only if we pay attention to the psychic blueprint that has been laid out beneath our feet.

—Robert Ginsberg, Vice-President and Co-Founder of Forever Family Foundation

Betty J. Kovács' outstanding book sheds new light on the ancient and authentic wisdom of humankind and reveals this wisdom's significant influence upon the survival of our species.

—Györgyi Szabó, Ph.D. Dean of Graduate Studies at Ubiquity University

Merchants of Light

Merchants of Light

THE CONSCIOUSNESS THAT IS CHANGING THE WORLD

Betty J. Kovács, Ph.D.

Foreword by Anne Baring

Claremont, California

Copyright © 2019 by The Kamlak Center

All rights reserved. This publication may not be reproduced, stored in a retrieval system, or transmitted in whole or in part, in any form or by any means, electronic, mechanical, photocopying, recording, or otherwise, without the prior written permission of the publisher, except for excerpts that fall under the provisions of "Fair Use" under United States Copyright Law. Permission to use quotations and images from other sources that were incorporated into this publication must be obtained directly from the original source. For further information, write to the publisher.

The Kamlak Center
112 Harvard Avenue #23
Claremont, California 91711-4716

www.kamlak.com

Cover Art: Maiden with the Holy Grail at the Castle of Corbin, Copyright © 1917 by Arthur Rackham, from *The Romance of King Arthur and His Knights of the Round Table* by Alfred W. Pollard (1917).

Cover Design by Carl D. Galian
Interior Design by Anita Jones, Another Jones Graphics
Index by Kate Mertes

DISCLAIMER
Neither Betty J. Kovács nor The Kamlak Center shall have liability or responsibility to any person or entity with respect to any loss or damage caused, or alleged to have been caused, directly or indirectly, by the information in this book. If you do not agree to be bound by the above, you may return the book to the publisher for a full refund.

ISBN 978-0-9721005-5-7 paperback

ISBN 978-0-9721005-6-4 e-book

Library of Congress Control Number: 2018962777

Publisher's Cataloging-In-Publication Data
(Prepared by The Donohue Group, Inc.)

Names: Kovács, Betty J., author. | Baring, Anne, 1931- writer of supplementary textual content.
Title: Merchants of light : the consciousness that is changing the world / Betty J. Kovács, Ph.D. ; foreword by Anne Baring.
Description: Claremont, California : The Kamlak Center, [2019] | Includes bibliographical references and index.
Identifiers: ISBN 9780972100557 (paperback) | ISBN 9780972100564 (ebook) | ISBN 9780972100571 (Kindle)
Subjects: LCSH: Consciousness. | Spiritual life.
Classification: LCC B808.9 .K63 2019 (print) | LCC B808.9 (ebook) | DDC 153--dc23

Printed on acid-free paper

Printed in the United States of America

Grateful acknowledgment is made to all copyright holders for permission to reprint previously published material contained in this work.

The author and publisher acknowledge permission to reprint the following excerpts:

Approximately one hundred and nineteen (119) words from *The Myth of the Goddess* by Anne Baring and Jules Cashford (Viking, 1991). Copyright © Anne Baring and Jules Cashford 1991.

Christmas: The Original Story by Margaret Barker. Copyright © Margaret Barker 2008. Reproduced with permission of Society for Promoting Christian Knowledge (SPCK) through PLSclear.

The Masks of God: Occidental Mythology by Joseph Campbell. Copyright © 1991, Digital Edition, Copyright © 2017, Joseph Campbell Foundation (jcf.org). Used with permission.

Prolegomena to the Study of Greek Religion by Jane Ellen Harrison. Copyright © Princeton University Press 1991. Republished with permission of Princeton University Press. Permission conveyed through Copyright Clearance Center, Inc.

Symbols of Transformation: An Analysis of the Prelude to a Case of Schizophrenia, Volume 5 of *The Collected Works,* by C.G. Jung. Copyright © Bollingen Foundation, Inc. 1956. Republished with permission of Princeton University Press. Permission conveyed through Copyright Clearance Center, Inc.

The Structure and Dynamics of the Psyche, Volume 8 of *The Collected Works,* by C.G. Jung. Copyright © Princeton University Press 1969. Republished with permission of Princeton University Press. Permission conveyed through Copyright Clearance Center, Inc.

The Collected Works by C.G. Jung. The First Complete English Edition of the Works of C.G. Jung. Copyright © 1973 Routledge. Reproduced by permission of Taylor & Francis Books UK.

The Secret Life of Bees by Sue Monk Kidd. Copyright © 2002 by Sue Monk Kidd Ltd. Used by permission of Viking Books, an imprint of Penguin Publishing Group, a division of Penguin Random House LLC. All rights reserved. Any third party use of this material, outside of this publication, is prohibited. Interested parties must apply directly to Penguin Random House LLC for permission.

The Secret Life of Bees by Sue Monk Kidd. Copyright © 2003 by Sue Monk Kidd. Reproduced by permission of Headline Publishing Group.

The Sacred Embrace of Jesus and Mary by Jean-Yves Leloup published by Inner Traditions International and Bear & Company, Copyright © 2006. All rights reserved. http://www.Innertraditions.com Reprinted with permission of publisher.

Every effort has been made to trace the copyright holder for the following publication. The publisher is willing to rectify any omissions in future editions.

Alvin Boyd Kuhn. *Who is This King of Glory? A Critical Study of the Christos-Messiah Tradition*. Bensenville: Lushena Books, 2006.

Foreword

When, in 2003, I wrote the Foreword to Betty Kovács' book, *The Miracle of Death*, I knew that I had encountered the work of a woman of profound insight and intelligence that was forged in the fiery crucible of tragic personal experience. Her revolutionary theme was that for each one of us, life was eternal; the finality of death was an illusion.

Now, sixteen years later, she has given us a second book, this time exploring the many different factors in the fields of both religion and science that have prevented us from accessing this realization and living our lives in full awareness of it. At a time when the most powerful nations of the world have lost touch with their soul, are failing to safeguard the life of the planet and are seeking world domination in rivalry with each other, the fortuitous appearance of this second wise and wonderful book comes as a great blessing and a priceless gift.

In clear and uncompromising language and drawing on innumerable historical facts, she has restored to us what has been lost or denied for so many centuries: the knowledge that, contrary to what we have been told by both religious belief and scientific materialism, we are immortal, divine and creative beings. Even more importantly, she also reveals in great detail how the 'shadow' or unconscious power-driven aspect of our psyche has seized control of the way governments conduct their relations with each other, leading the world towards catastrophe of one kind or another: the catastrophe of climate change or the catastrophe of nuclear or biological war.

"What we are witnessing," she says in her concluding chapter, "is the full-blown pathology of the Western worldview." She describes in great detail how this pathology came into being, what sustains it and what can challenge and transform its domination of world culture. She also describes the tragic story of how the shamanic peoples who retained the ancient knowledge of caring for the earth and staying in touch with the cosmos were despised, reviled and subjected to the conquest and control of the white settlers of their domains and the forcible imposition on them of the settlers' religion. And she shows how this genocide was supported by several papal bulls from the Vatican.

However, a major part of her study is the twentieth century discoveries of shamanic cultures that form the roots of Western civilization and reveal our human ability to experience cosmic consciousness. "We are now," she states, "reclaiming the sacred knowledge of how we evolve. We are realizing that the true role of civilization is to discover and nurture this knowledge. Our ancestors understood that *civilization* cannot develop unless it is rooted in the power of the heart to give birth to a *feeling world*. They knew that without feeling, we cannot bring *justice* into being. And they understood that *without the inward journey to develop soul, creation cannot continue to unfold*. The message is clear: without the creative energy of love, we cannot create a true civilization. And when we cannot create, we destroy."

In this final chapter she describes how she discovered that our planet is surrounded by a Net or Web of Light that has been recognised by scientists as well as by ancient cultures. To lift ourselves out of the darkness we have brought into being, we need to "open our hearts, focus on a nodal point in the net of light and allow that light and love to flow through us, into the earth, and around the world. We might not even feel the energy at first, but eventually we will. Those who love are doing this whether they are conscious of it or not. When we love, we attract the light of love everywhere, and the power of love distils darkness into light.... It appears that now we all need to focus that love by *consciously* connecting with the nexus points in the great net of light, *consciously* grounding that light in the earth beneath us, and then *consciously* sending that light around the world."

Quantum Physics has shown us that every atom of life in the entire universe is connected with every other atom and that light is the foundation of the quantum vacuum or zero-point field. "Our every thought, feeling, and act, whether constructive or destructive, sends ripples throughout the entire universe and is reflected in all the jewels of this divine net. This is the wisdom of Indra's cosmology, quantum physics, and modern visionaries. *We are creative beyond anything we have ever allowed ourselves to imagine*. Our ancestors knew this, and they wanted us to have the sacred knowledge that we are immortal, divine, and *creative*. This is the fruit from the Cosmic Tree of Life. Once we know this, we know we *can* create a loving and peaceful world."

To have brought all the information in this book into an accessible and understandable form is the achievement of a lifetime, requiring years of search and scholarly research that have been enriched by unusual personal experiences of the change of consciousness now being orchestrated by the universe on behalf of our precious planet—a change of consciousness that requires the assistance of as many people as possible in the shortest possible time.

Anne Baring, Ph.D. (Hons)
Winchester, England

M.A., University of Oxford. Honorary Degree of Doctor of Philosophy in Wisdom Studies, Ubiquity University, The Wisdom School. A Jungian analyst and author and co-author of seven books, including *The Myth of the Goddess: Evolution of an Image* (1991) with Jules Cashford; *Soul Power* (2009) with Dr. Scilla Elworthy; and her most recent book, *The Dream of the Cosmos: A Quest for the Soul* (2013). Her website is www.annebaring.com.

Acknowledgments

I wish to express my gratitude to those persons who read individual sections or the entire manuscript and offered valuable suggestions: Dr. Anne Baring, for her editorial skills and knowledge of myth and history; Dr. Jill O'Hora, Jane Hallinger, Jan Sutherland, Patricia Savoie, Jacqueline Sullivan, Reverend Dr. Susan Chamberlain, Jill Raiguel, Reverend Dr. Christopher Rubel, Alicia Otis, Camille Bertolet, and Dr. Rae Ballard for their various perspectives on the material; Douglas Hamilton, for consistently supplying me with information on new archaeological discoveries of prehistory; and special thanks to Robert and Phran Ginsberg, founders of the Forever Family Foundation, for their work in bringing together scientific and experiential knowledge of the continuation of consciousness after physical death, for their friendship, and for their support of *The Miracle of Death, Merchants of Light,* and the work of The Kamlak Center.

I will never be able to adequately thank Kimberly Saavedra, Director of The Kamlak Center and my friend, editor, and publisher, who has read and reread every word of the text, discussed with me every idea in the book from every possible perspective, has offered valuable suggestions throughout the years of writing, has gracefully secured copyright permissions for quoted material and images, has painstakingly checked each footnote and every entry into the bibliography, and has sensitively and professionally seen this book through the entire publishing process. Without her expertise, the manifestation of this work would not have been possible. I am deeply grateful for her loving and total commitment to this project.

A Note to the Reader

It is my hope that, as you read about the new discoveries of our deep roots in the historical shaman-mystic-scientist cultures, you will be as amazed as I have been with the radically different vision of our past—and ourselves—that they offer us. The destructive and now discredited worldview of the West has blinded us to the reality of a vast, creative universe and our role in it. It has denied and repressed our evolutionary potential for Cosmic Consciousness. But Cosmic Consciousness is our true heritage, and this is the *Gift* that our ancestors are now returning to us.

This ancient and new consciousness is cosmic *and* personal. That is why this book includes scholarly material and scientific evidence as well as my own personal experiences. The unity of the cosmos requires the unique and personal creativity of each of us. We are all on a personal *and* cosmic journey that is a collective, cooperative, and ongoing process.

During the years that I taught mythology and symbolic language, the students and I made surprising and exciting discoveries, but we were all left with many questions. I will always be grateful to those students for their interest and commitment to discovering the interconnecting patterns that lay hidden in the symbolic systems of the myths, fairy tales, and archaeological images of our past.

When the deaths in my family occurred, I retired and entered a decade of intense inner experiences, some of which I wrote about in *The Miracle of Death: There is Nothing But Life* and others I write about in this book. These experiences helped me to understand on a much deeper level what I had been teaching for so many years. I then plunged into more years of research. Gradually, a startling picture of our past began to emerge. I am grateful for the scholars and visionaries whose work has made this picture possible. I am also grateful for those scientists whose work in quantum physics provides a scientific understanding of the legacy of our ancestors.

To summarize briefly, this book tracks the existence of a consciousness that is capable of relating to both the visible and invisible dimensions of reality. By at least 40,000 BCE our ancestors had developed symbolic language and various shamanic techniques to trigger altered states of consciousness. Some of these ancestors achieved great skill as visionaries, mystics, and scientists, while others, it is not known how many, achieved the ability to experience Cosmic Consciousness. Since this evolutionary consciousness activates the whole mind and is centered in the heart, it creates a feeling and just world.

This new consciousness appears to have first emerged in the Cave cultures in Europe and in the San Bushmen cultures in Africa. Among a few surviving San Elders in Africa, the ability to experience and transmit Cosmic Consciousness continues to this day. In the West, this consciousness continued to exist among the Megalithic Builders; in Neolithic Old Europe; in the shaman-mystic-scientist culture of Egypt; in the shaman-mystic culture of First Temple Judaism; and in the Presocratic shaman-mystic-scientist tradition of Anatolian Greeks. It is *this* ancient tradition that carries the blueprint for our evolution.

This integrated heart consciousness in the West was repressed by both Church and State and lost to mainline culture, but it survived underground in the Hermetic arts, Alchemy, Gnosticism, Kabbalah, and Mystic Christianity. These powerful traditions emerged four times in European history in an effort to integrate the consciousness of the heart into mainline culture. Each attempt failed, but this tradition, on which our survival now depends, has once again emerged today — and it is changing the world.

Part I, the "Introduction," gives an overview of the material covered in this book. Since the time span is from 40,000 BCE to the present, this material is addressed again and developed in later chapters. The major themes appear as leitmotifs throughout the book.

Part II discusses the pervasive damage of the Western worldview, the repression of the blueprint for our conscious evolution, and the reemergence of this blueprint in our true soul stories and in quantum physics.

Part III relates part of my personal journey to discover the Gift of Soul.

Part IV explores the depth of the human psyche/soul, the symbolic nature of its language, and its evolutionary development in the ancient shaman-mystic-scientist cultures of our past.

Part V discusses the five major waves of awakening and remembering our past in Western culture, as well as the voices of indigenous peoples whose memory has been continuous. It also explores the present potential for a quantum leap.

Merchants of Light is structured as a labyrinthine journey that moves inward to soul and outward to history. The form and movement of a labyrinth is a spiral that takes us down into the depths of who we are and returns us to our daily lives with a new consciousness. With each circling of the spiral, we are able to view the discoveries of our journey from a different perspective. In fact, it often seems as though we are repeating the same experiences, yet, each time, we deepen our understanding of what we thought we already knew. As we spiral down and return, we are weaving the sustainable patterns of our becoming into a new tapestry of consciousness.

This book is dedicated to the indigenous cultures around the world that have protected and nurtured our legacy of knowledge; to the scholars who discovered the shaman-mystic-scientist cultures at the roots of Western civilization; to the quantum physicists whose discoveries are providing the intellectual scaffolding for a multidimensional world; and to all people whose longing for a life of love, justice, peace, and great meaning has drawn to our planet a highly organized energy field of light that carries the blueprint for a new consciousness.

Table of Contents

Foreword	xi
Acknowledgments	xv
A Note to the Reader	xvii

PART I INTRODUCTION/OVERVIEW — 1

The Gift of Our Ancestors: Fruit From the Cosmic Tree
Overview of Twentieth Century Discoveries of Our True Heritage: Cosmic Consciousness — 3

PART II DISCOVERING OUR TRUE STORIES — 55

Chapter One
Negative Stories of Our Past and the Return of Our True Stories — 57

Chapter Two
The Complementary Roles of the Scientist and the Shaman/Visionary — 63

Chapter Three
The Experience of the Quantum Field and the Intellectual Discovery of the Quantum Field — 69

Chapter Four
Evolution as "a single energy event" that is both Physical and Spiritual — 79

Chapter Five
Becoming Masters of a New Story — 87

Chapter Six
Giambattista Vico: The Symbol and the Idea — 103

Chapter Seven
The Struggle to Discover the Sacred Texts of Our Lives — 113

Chapter Eight
    Facing Our Addiction to a Story That is Destroying the World and Discovering the Visionary's Story in Dream and History   **129**

Chapter Nine
    The Hellenistic World, the Mysteries, Combining the Canonical and the Apocryphal Texts, and the Emerging Visionary's Story   **141**

Chapter Ten
    The Jewish Mysteries in the Greek-Speaking World, the Essenes, the Dead Sea Scrolls, the Therapeutae, the Kabbalists, and Their Roots in Israel's Ancient Shaman-Mystic Tradition   **149**

Chapter Eleven
    The Earlier Destruction of Israel's Ancient Shaman-Mystic Tradition by Josiah and the Deuteronomists in 621 BCE and Their Distortion of Our True Stories   **155**

Chapter Twelve
    Israel's Ancient Shaman-Mystic "Secret Tradition" in Christianity,* the Nag Hammadi Texts, Jesus as the Redemption of the Deuteronomists' Yahweh and Mary as the Return of Wisdom   **167**

Chapter Thirteen
    Mary as Visionary and Wisdom, the Organ of Soul, Jesus as Shaman-Mystic and the Great High Priest   **173**

Chapter Fourteen
    Other Forms of the Jewish Mysteries: the Allegorists, Philo Judaeus, the Moses Mysteries   **181**

---

* This "Secret Tradition" in Christianity found its continuity in Contemplative and Esoteric Christianity, both of which are mystical traditions. Throughout the text, I use the term *Mystic Christianity* to refer to the continuation of this early "Secret Tradition."

Chapter Fifteen
  The Blueprint for Our Evolution in All the Mysteries:
  Christ/Cosmic Consciousness — 185

Chapter Sixteen
  Wisdom (the Queen of Heaven) in Dream, Vision, History
  and Science — 195

Chapter Seventeen
  The Rise of the Church, the Reduction of Symbols and
  Images to History, the Destruction of the Ancient
  Intellectual and Spiritual World, the Loss of Our
  Evolutionary Blueprint: Christ/Cosmic Consciousness — 203

PART III THE GIFT — 217

Chapter Eighteen
  Facing the True Stories of Who We Are and Why We're Here — 221

Chapter Nineteen
  Peru, My Homage to Wisdom, and the Story She Must Tell — 225

Chapter Twenty
  Lake Titicaca and the Island of the Sun, Sillustani, Sacred
  Medicine, and Initiation into "the Strange, the Mysterious,
  the Inexplicable" — 231

Chapter Twenty-One
  The Gift — 239

Chapter Twenty-Two
  Our Children and the Shattering Myth of Violence, the Voice
  in the Desert, a Major Event for Our Future Evolution,
  Beinsa Douno, Integrating Experience, and the Pure Clay
  for All Our Children — 243

PART IV RETRIEVING SOUL   257

Chapter Twenty-Three
The Symbolic-Visionary Mind, its Intelligent, Organizing Blueprint for Our Evolution That is Deeply Rooted in Our Past   259

Chapter Twenty-Four
A Glimpse into the Development of the Symbolic-Visionary Mind, its Function as a Reflector and Bridge to Invisible Dimensions of Reality, the Cave Cultures in Western Europe (40,000–10,000 BCE)   267

Chapter Twenty-Five
The Flaring Forth of "Our Story" in the Cave Cultures   277

Chapter Twenty-Six
The Experience of Altered States of Consciousness and Our Quantum Leap into Becoming Fully Modern Human Beings, Integration of the Heart   283

Chapter Twenty-Seven
David Lewis-Williams' Insight into Cave/Rock Art as the Work of Shamans, Western Scholarship's Reduction of the Mind's Wholeness to an "Illusion," the Archetype as the Form Energy Takes at the Intersection Between the Quantum Field and Human Consciousness   293

Chapter Twenty-Eight
The San Culture in Africa (33,000 BCE–1800s CE): Stories, Rock Art, Love of Life, Joy, Laughter, Celebration, Wisdom, the Soul and the Invisible World   307

Chapter Twenty-Nine
The Shaman-Mystic-Scientist Tradition of the Megalithic Builders (12,000–3000 BCE)   325

The Shaman-Mystic Tradition of Old Europe (6500–2500 BCE; in Crete 1400 BCE)   327

The Shaman-Mystic-Scientist Tradition of Ancient Egypt (3000–1000 BCE)	327

Chapter Thirty

The Shaman-Mystic Jewish Tradition (832–621 BCE)	337
The Shaman-Mystic-Scientist Anatolian Greek/Presocratic Tradition (500 BCE to the Birth of Christ)	337
The Continuation of This Shaman-Mystic-Scientist Tradition After Christianity	342

PART V THE PROMISE OF THE PAST: FIVE WAVES OF REMEMBERING — 347

Chapter Thirty-One

The High Middle Ages: The First Wave of the Renaissance (1000–1300 CE)	349

Chapter Thirty-Two

The Italian Renaissance: The Second Wave of the Renaissance (1460–1527 CE)	369

Chapter Thirty-Three

The Northern/Rosicrucian Enlightenment: The Third Wave of the Renaissance (1600–1620 CE)	387

Chapter Thirty-Four

The German and English Reaction: The Fourth Wave of the Renaissance (1775–1850 CE)	393

Chapter Thirty-Five

The Twentieth and Twenty-First Centuries: The Fifth Wave of the Renaissance	403

Chapter Thirty-Six

The Reframing of Our Consciousness and the Voices of Indigenous Peoples	407

Chapter Thirty-Seven
  Our Evolutionary Future, Psychic Blueprints, the Western
  Aberration, and Strange Attractors   423

Conclusion
  Civilization as a Poetic and Scientific Endeavor, the Challenge
  of Working on What Has Decayed, the Dance of the Light
  and the Dark for Survival and Transformation   435

Appendix 1: Timelines   455

Appendix 2: Dreams/Visions   456

Appendix 3: The Complete Gospel of Mary Magdalene   457

Appendix 4: Kundalini   458

Endnotes   459

Selected Bibliography   485

Index   495

About the Author   511

PART I

INTRODUCTION/OVERVIEW

The Gift of Our Ancestors: Fruit From the Cosmic Tree

Sketch of Sumerian Cylinder Seal, The Goddess and God of the Tree of Life freely offering the sacred fruit of Enlightenment and Immortal Life; c. 2500 BCE British Museum.*

On the left is the Goddess with her rising serpent energy, which symbolizes the rising energy of consciousness, and on the right is the God wearing his *lunar* crown, which symbolizes life, death, and rebirth in the physical world. This Tree of Life stands in the Garden of Life where the fruit of higher consciousness is offered to all. In the original myths of the Garden, there is no danger, no divine vengeance, and no guilt. The fruit is freely given to anyone, male or female, who seeks it and is ready to receive its sacred wisdom.†

---

* From *The Masks of God: Occidental Mythology* by Joseph Campbell. Copyright © 1991, Digital Edition, Copyright © 2017, Joseph Campbell Foundation (jcf.org). Used with permission.

† Joseph Campbell, *The Masks of God, Vol. 3: Occidental Mythology* (London: Arkana, 1991), 14.

Introduction/Overview

Our ancestors have left us the most important gift of our lives: their knowledge and experience of who we are and why we are here. They understood that the outer laws of nature and the inner laws of the human being are the same and that nothing is more important than knowing these laws and living in harmony with them. Many thousands of years of observing and experiencing these laws opened them to an unseen, conscious dimension of reality, which they called the spirit dimension and scientists call the quantum field. They experienced this invisible world as the source of their own consciousness, and they realized that the fullness of their lives and indeed their very survival depended on their connection and relationship with that world.

It was their discovery of this dimension and their ability to communicate with it that catapulted us into what we now call modern consciousness around 40,000 BCE. This leap of consciousness occurred around the world once the human species had developed the ability to use symbolic language. And thus the stories began—the stories about our ancestors' experience with this *Other* dimension of reality and our role in the cosmic scheme of things. Their stories were painted on the walls of caves and engraved or painted on the faces of rocks; they were danced and sung; later they were expressed through number and geometric structures; they were written on the walls of pyramids or carved into the landscape in harmony with the moon, sun, and stars; they were written on papyrus and paper; and their stories were passed orally from one generation to the next and became the fairy tales and myths of cultures around the world while others became the core of the various religions of the world. *All* these forms are our sacred texts because they reveal the laws of nature and the laws of our inner life—the life of soul.

There are many levels and forms of experience within this spirit dimension, but the heart of all experience with spirit our ancestors called the fruit of the Cosmic Tree of Life. Those who ate this fruit— that is, all who went deep into the world of spirit—experienced a world of love and light, joy and ecstasy—what would later be called Cosmic Consciousness. They returned knowing who we are and why we're here. *Their message was clear: we are immortal, divine, and creative.*

Our ancestors understood that we could only know this message through our own inner experience—what would later be called *gnosis*. Their stories could open us and guide us, but we could only *know* by taking our own inner journey. We had to eat the fruit of the Cosmic Tree of Life. This is why our ancestors left artifact after artifact inviting us into the Great Garden of Life to show us the tree and the fruit and to offer us an opportunity to partake of it—just as is illustrated in the Sumerian seal that introduces Part I. Both the goddess and the god are offering us fruit from the Great Tree. For the fruit "is yielded willingly to any mortal, male or female, who reaches for it with the proper will and readiness to receive."[1]

Since *experience* was necessary for wisdom, our ancestors developed many techniques to open our hearts and minds to this other dimension. These techniques were structured to make the mind receptive to higher frequencies of consciousness. Such forms of receptivity or attunement would later be called *gnosis, mysticism, or altered states of awareness*. Interestingly, similar techniques, which I will discuss later in the book, were developed around the world at this time in what is now known as shamanism. The shaman, whether female or male, was a master of activating the visionary within us and of opening our consciousness to deeper orders of reality.

Scholars have been astounded to discover that the rituals our ancestors used to achieve altered states of consciousness create "a highly synchronized slow brain wave pattern" that enhances the integration of the various brain components.[2] Such rituals include the activation of the heart as a major component of the brain. We know the heart was integrated in experiences of altered states of consciousness since all the ancient spiritual traditions affirm the central role of the heart. Out of these experiences the great *myths of meaning* were formed—myths that shaped the worldview of our ancestors for tens of thousands of years.

During the last century, Western culture has become aware of some of these early ancestors who are still living sustainably on the land in harmony with the laws of nature—some for several thousand years, others for more than 40,000 years—since the time we call the Stone Age. There are many indigenous peoples here in the Americas who are trying desperately to help us *see* what we are doing to the earth and ourselves by ignoring the laws of nature and of our own soul. But the West has difficulty understanding their message because we have been split off from nature and soul for so long that their words mean very little to us. Since we are always on the go, we cannot understand this profound connection to the land. "Without the land," they tell us, "we have no life." And "We cannot separate our place on the Earth from our lives on the Earth, nor from our vision and meaning as a people."[3]

And yet, even as I write this, we are destroying their lands, their people, their traditions, and their ability to relate to the invisible realms. All our lives—as well as the life of our planet—depend on our ability to perceive this reality. We now have the evidence that our ancestors' love and respect for nature and its laws connected them to sources of knowledge that we do not have. Their connection to the land, to nature, to each other, and to the invisible dimension of reality is *a living gift* from them to us. However, we will not be able to receive this gift unless we can open our minds and hearts to a dimension of reality beyond the material world.

We will look at two groups of our Stone Age ancestors: the people who painted the great temple caves in southwestern Europe and the San Bushmen in the Kalahari Desert in Africa. The cave culture lasted more than twenty thousand years while the San culture lasted twenty-seven thousand years with remnants still existing today in Namibia and

Botswana. Amazingly, there is no evidence of war in either group. Anne Baring and Jules Cashford in *The Myth of the Goddess: Evolution of an Image* discuss what appear to be two great myths during the time of the temple caves: *the myth of meaning and the myth of survival*. We will see that these two myths also existed in the San culture in Africa. The myth of meaning is about the invisible dimension of life—its sacredness, wholeness, eternity, and its continual renewal. The myth of survival is about our need to rupture this wholeness—as in the great hunting cultures—in order to survive in the visible world of time and space. As long as the myth of survival can be contained within the myth of meaning a culture can thrive, but when the myth of survival breaks away from the myth of meaning and dominates life, as it does in our own culture, there is a loss of soul.[4]

Stability and unity were helpful in maintaining these sacred traditions, which in Europe stretched from Spain to Lake Baikal in southeastern Siberia. There was less stability in the lives of the hunters who became nomads in order to follow the hunt. However, the knowledge and experience of the great hunters from the more stable centers flowed into later periods and influenced the sacred art, shamanic traditions, and stories we know from the high civilizations that followed.[5]

For example, in Mal'ta near Lake Baikal, an image of the labyrinth engraved on a mammoth tooth was discovered and dated approximately 24,000 BCE.[6] The labyrinth was, and is today, a major image of the sacred journey from the visible world into the invisible realms of the spirit dimension. This image existed from the time of the cave temples with their labyrinthine journey through the caves into the world of spirit. It continued to exist all the way down to the Neolithic and Bronze Age (c. 6000–600 BCE) labyrinthine dances and the thousands of labyrinthine images engraved and painted on the body of the Great Goddess. It appeared on her life-containing vessels, the dancing floors, and the architecture—always as a *Way to the Light*.[7] The Light received at the center of the labyrinth was associated with the Great Goddess, "the mistress of the labyrinth," for it was she who symbolized the source and meaning of life, and thus the fruit of the Cosmic Tree.

Around the world, says historian of religion Mircea Eliade, the *tree* was the image of "the living cosmos, endlessly renewing itself." It was the Tree of Life, the center of the world, the source of life, and it was associated with the Great Goddess who symbolized "the inexhaustible source of creation, the ultimate basis of all reality." The tree was rooted in the waters of the invisible, unmanifest world out of which it emerged into the visible world of time and space. It reflected the sacred process of life, death, and renewal—the natural laws of all life. It was a cosmic tree because "what it expresses is a perfect reproduction of what the cosmos expresses."[8] Mystics throughout the ages have experienced the tree in similar ways: in the early seventeenth century, the German mystic Jakob Böhme experienced the tree as the *soul* whose seed is planted *in the heart* and grows from within to become the tree of knowledge: it is this fruit that can heal the world.[9] And the Irish poet, William Butler Yeats, writes, "Beloved, gaze in thine own heart, / The holy tree is growing there."[10]

Margaret Barker, Old Testament scholar, tells us that the ancient Hebrew tradition reveals a tree that is unlike any other tree in beauty and height. This tree is associated with *Wisdom*, the Queen of Heaven: "It is perfumed with the incense of the holy of holies and its fruit is for all to eat," and says the Queen of Heaven, **"those who work with my help will not sin."**[11] It is a tree with "a fragrance beyond all fragrance whose leaves and blossoms and wood never wither or rot."[12] Wisdom is the fiery tree, "gold looking and crimson, with the form of fire." Wisdom is "the Lady in the burning bush." She is the fiery, tree-shaped Menorah, and she is the Lady of the fiery tree who gives birth in the holy of holies.[13] The "color of the tree of life is like the sun, and its branches are beautiful. Its leaves are like those of the cypress. Its fruit is like the clusters of white grapes."[14] And the Queen of Heaven, the Great Tree of Life, was also the water of life flowing from the fountains of heaven, like "the four rivers flowing from Eden."[15] "She is the tree of life to those who lay hold of her / and those who hold her fast are called happy."[16] In the even more ancient Egyptian tradition the Goddess of the Celestial Tree, planted in the "waters of the depths," rises from the center of the tree to offer to those who seek it "the food and drink of immortality."[17]

What happened to this Gift—this sacred knowledge? Most of us know the story in Genesis in which God in the Garden of Life *denies* all human beings the gift of the Cosmic Tree of Life. This is an *inversion* of our true myth. Shamans and mystics always knew that this story was a *negation* of our true myth because they had already eaten the sacred fruit. They knew that the tree does not bring death but rather knowledge of our own immortality, divinity, and creativity. No *God* would deny us our birthright or punish us for seeking it. In other words, the cosmic laws of life would not negate themselves.

We now know that such a cruel story had nothing at all to do with God but rather with a political maneuver to gain power in 621 BCE on the part of the Deuteronomists at the time of Josiah, King of Judah. These radical reformists attempted to destroy the ancient shaman-mystic tradition of the Cosmic Tree of Life as well as Wisdom, the feminine dimension of the divine associated with the Tree. All objects associated with her were removed from the temple and the land so they could be destroyed. Her sacred groves of trees were cut down, her altars destroyed, her sacred images burned, her wisdom literature removed from the sacred writings, and her stories *re*written under the influence of the Deuteronomists.[18]

These reformers understood very well that their power *over* the people depended on the destruction of the *inner* power *of* the people. So the Deuteronomists told the people that the fruit from the Tree of Knowledge was forbidden; the feminine source of all life—symbolized as the Tree—was portrayed as a mortal woman who had sinned against God by eating and sharing the sacred fruit that she had always freely given to those who sought it; and both the male and the female were punished and exiled from the sacred Garden and the fullness of life. Since the inner life of soul is expressed in symbolic, artistic language, the Deuteronomists also forbade the making of any "image, or any likeness of anything that is in heaven above, or that is in the earth beneath, or that is in the water under the earth...."[19] They knew what they were doing, and their legacy of denial has continued to reverberate down through the centuries into our own time.

But this ancient shaman-mystic tradition would be remembered by Jews like Philo Judaeus, the Essenes at Qumran, the Therapeutae in

Egypt, the Gnostics and the writers of the Jewish Kabbalah. And, says Barker, all of the characteristics of this ancient spiritual tradition would reappear in Christianity.[20] But, unfortunately, this *secret tradition* of the early Christians would *also* be brutally suppressed by the Church of Rome. The Church, much like the earlier Deuteronomists, would distort their core myth in such a way that once again we would be denied our true birthright of eating from the sacred Tree of Life—and remembering who we are and why we're here.

This gift—the knowledge of our immortality, divinity, and creativity—has continued to exist in every generation—in spite of consistent efforts to repress it. Once our ancestors evolved into this consciousness, the greatest care was taken to preserve it. Most of the time, however, the politics of Church and State have forced this knowledge to remain underground until the need for it becomes so great that a large number of people become receptive to it and demand change. Each of us carries the memory of this gift deep within us so that it can emerge into consciousness through dreams, visions, intuitions, and actual physical events. This memory creates the stage, the receptivity, for its history to emerge in individuals and in culture.

Now is one of those times. During the last century—the most brutal and violent in the history of our species—we began to rediscover this lost Gift. After World War II and the invention of weapons of greater and greater destruction, culminating in the development and use of the atomic bomb and what now appears to be perpetual war, unnoticed by many, a deep and pervasive longing for an inclusive *myth of meaning* created an energy field for a very different kind of discovery. This might sound strange to us at first, yet we are beginning to be aware of how our minds and feelings affect not only our own bodies but the earth's energy field as well. The "influence of our minds and our basic state of consciousness," says John White, former Director of Education for the Institute of Noetic Sciences, "is there all the time inevitably affecting the total Earth-organism, for better or worse." It is called "bio-relativity, the interaction of people with their physical environment via psychic or mind energy."[21]

While two of the discoveries of this lost Gift—the Dead Sea Scrolls and the Nag Hammadi texts—came at the very peak of our despair and loss at the end of World War II, other discoveries of this knowledge took place throughout the twentieth century and are continuing into the twenty-first century. Some of these discoveries did not appear to be the result of the same energy field, but, as more pieces of the puzzle appeared, we could begin to see that each discovery revealed a larger reality that was initiating a radical transformation of our worldview.

This larger reality includes the discovery of our shaman-mystic past, quantum physics, and the twentieth and twenty-first century emergence of social and political movements, such as Women's Suffrage, the Labor Movement, the Civil Rights Movement, the Anti-nuclear/Anti-war Movement, the Feminist Movement, the Environmental Movement, the LGBTQ Movement, the Disability Rights Movement, the Animal Rights Movement, the Black Lives Matter Movement, the Indigenous Peoples Movement, and more recently, the Me Too Movement, the Never Again Movement, and the new Poor People's Campaign. Also beginning in the last century, but presently expanding at a rapid rate around the world, is the scientifically based, Natural Health Movement that is transforming the medical model for treating illness.

Similar movements for all forms of human rights and economic justice are erupting in many parts of the world today. This intense and widespread activity to bring about change is clear evidence that this energy field is affecting every aspect of our lives—as it must if an *inclusive myth of meaning* is to emerge. While all of these movements are necessary in imagining and creating a moral, healthy, and just society, they are beyond the scope of this book. *Below I will briefly discuss the major twentieth century discoveries of cultures that were shaped by a myth of meaning.* I will discuss these discoveries in greater detail in the book as well as those periods in Western history when these revolutionary ideas and experiences reemerged in Western culture—each time creating a renaissance that was ultimately rejected and repressed by those in power. I will also include in a very limited way the role quantum physics plays in our understanding of this emerging Gift from our ancestors.

But why, we might ask, was the century of such creative developments also the century that was the most violent in the history of our species? And why is this violence not only continuing but increasing? The unspeakable violence of the two world wars left the planet in shambles and millions of people dead—and it left the human psyche in unmitigated despair. Is there any wonder that a deep and pervasive longing for healing and peace should emerge in the human heart? What has been a surprise to those who were immersed in the Western worldview is that this longing in the material dimension of reality activated an energy field in the nonmaterial dimension of reality that is working with us to discover just how we can create a more humane, loving, and peaceful world.

The Jesus of the Nag Hammadi texts actually addressed this issue of human violence: "If you bring forth what is within you, what you bring forth will save you. If you do not bring forth what is within you, what you do not bring forth will destroy you."[22] When people begin to bring forth what is within them, they construct new, creative, and inclusive spiritual and social structures. These changes activate the old, limited beliefs in those who are not yet ready for change, and violence often erupts in an attempt to maintain the status quo.

Unfortunately, the power in Western culture has been predominantly held by those who have not brought forth what is within them. In fact, the Western worldview is that there is nothing to bring forth. Throughout the centuries those in power have denied, rejected, destroyed, and repressed the true stories of who we are and why we're here. We have been denied the fruit from the Cosmic Tree, and our world is the consequence of this denial. Tragically, many of us have become so addicted to the old story of denial that the transformation of our species may be a rough ride.

I will explain later in the book how the same power structures during the seventeenth century denied our scientists the right to explore reality beyond the physical world. This denial resulted in the most destructive worldview ever held by any known culture: there is nothing but matter, we are a fluke of nature, human consciousness has no effect on the world, and there is no meaning or purpose to life. Thankfully, twentieth century quantum physics has broken through this myth of matter and scientists are now free to explore the nonmaterial dimensions of reality.

These historical powers of repression have denied us the knowledge our ancestors attempted so fervently to give us. We have been locked into a belief that only what we designate as rational is worthy of investigation. Even when we consciously disagree with this view, most of us in Western culture, and now the world, have been programmed to live within a dangerously small frame of reality.

How can the consciousness of our world be reframed to include a greater reality? One thing is certain: a greater reality will have to include human experience—our ability to feel, to love, to imagine, to create, and to experience other dimensions of consciousness. No longer can we deny the reality of our own wholeness. Life is diverse, multi-leveled, and multidimensional. It cannot be reduced to our manageable concept of what is rational, *but* our understanding of what is rational can be expanded infinitely. What we have relegated to the *irrational* could simply be outside our *rational* framework.

One of the gifts our ancestors are bringing to us is a larger vision of life—one that includes the spiritual and the physical, the shaman-mystic and the scientist. Not only are these discoveries of our past reframing our consciousness to include experience of higher states of consciousness, but millions of people around the world are experiencing what the German poet Rainer Maria Rilke called "the strangest, the most mysterious, and the most inexplicable"[23] events that simply cannot be explained within the constraints of our old worldview. I will discuss this type of event below in "Two Phenomena of Our Time That Require the New Science."

Many people are also having big dreams, spontaneous visions, and Near-Death Experiences that are radically transforming consciousness. Shamanic techniques are being taught around the world and people are experiencing multidimensional realities. Also an ancient shamanic practice that uses sacred medicine emerged in Western culture during the twentieth century and exploded in the Counterculture Movement. Sacred medicine was, and still is, often dangerously misused and misunderstood in Western culture. Yet thousands of people around the world today are using it responsibly in a sacred context, and they too are experiencing multidimensional realities that reframe consciousness. And, with the discovery of quantum physics, the new science is shattering the limits of the old scientific worldview and transforming everything we thought we knew about reality.

We are experiencing a highly organized energy field that is bringing about a reframing of our consciousness. Through multiple discoveries of cultures that nurtured higher states of consciousness, the new science, anomalous events, and visionary experiences, something *miraculous* is happening on our planet.

We are not yet fully aware of these new, creative forms of consciousness because of the violence and despair that inundate the world. The focus of this book is on the new discoveries and experiences that are igniting, reframing, and transforming the consciousness of our time.

WHAT ARE SOME OF THESE MAJOR DISCOVERIES?

I. THE SHAMAN-MYSTIC TRADITION OF THE STONE AGE (UPPER PALEOLITHIC)

THE CAVE CULTURES IN WESTERN EUROPE (40,000–10,000 BCE)

THE SAN CULTURE IN AFRICA (33,000 BCE THROUGH THE 1800s CE)

THE REMAINING SAN SHAMAN ELDERS TODAY IN NAMIBIA AND BOTSWANA

While some discoveries were made earlier, it was the twentieth century that brought the breakthrough in our understanding of how the many thousands of years of observing and experiencing the laws of nature opened our **Stone Age** ancestors to an unseen, conscious dimension of reality. With the development of symbolic language around 40,000 BCE, our ancestors developed various shamanic techniques to trigger altered states of consciousness. Shamanism developed around the world, and the arts, spiritual practices, and culture were made possible. We will explore two of these Stone Age cultures: the western European shaman-mystic temple/cave culture which existed from approximately 40,000 to 10,000 BCE, and the African San shaman-mystic culture from 33,000 BCE through the 1800s CE and into the present.

In the late twentieth century, the few remaining San Shaman Elders in Namibia and Botswana released to the world their spiritual teachings and practices through Bradford and Hillary Keeney in *Way of the Bushman As Told by the Tribal Elders: Spiritual Teachings and Practices of the Kalahari Jul'hoansi*. Bradford Keeney has had extensive contact with the San Elders for twenty years, has participated in their sacred traditions, and is himself a "holder of their most important truths."[24]

The spiritual teachings of these Elders reveal that they are Masters of kundalini energy, the vital life force. They know how to ignite this energy in themselves and others, and they know how to use this powerful energy to heal. The Keeneys both witnessed and experienced the San Elders' ability to manipulate and transfer this vital life force in its cosmic dimensions of love, joy, light, and ecstasy. This is Cosmic Consciousness, and the rock art of the San along with the cave art of western Europe suggest that this ability has existed since the Stone Age.

II. THE SHAMAN-MYSTIC-SCIENTIST TRADITION OF THE MEGALITHIC BUILDERS (12,000–3000 BCE)

What happened around the world during the actual Stone Age as well as the transitional period into the **Neolithic** or farming era is not yet fully known. This transitional period is called the **Mesolithic** period and is usually considered to have taken place between 10,000 and 8000 BCE depending on the area. But structures characteristic of this period have been found around the world in both earlier and later periods. These structures are called **megalithic** because they consist of large, natural stones that interlock without the use of mortar or concrete, single standing stones or Menhirs, large multiple standing stones, dolmens, and stone circles. While there were significant discoveries in England as early as the seventeenth century, again, it was not until the twentieth century that scholars began to realize the magnitude and significance of these worldwide megalithic monuments. The lowest level of a megalithic structure presently being excavated in Indonesia, Gunung Padang (Mountain of Enlightenment), might prove to have been constructed as early as 20,000 BCE, and Göbekli Tepe in Turkey has been dated between 12,000 and 10,000 BCE. Some of the well-known structures, such as Stonehenge and Newgrange, were built around 3000 BCE and later.[25]

What is amazing about these more recent discoveries is that they place the earliest stone structures at the same time as the cave paintings. It was extremely difficult for specialists to accept that the cave paintings were made during the Upper Paleolithic, between 40,000 and 10,000 BCE. If the earliest construction of Gunung Padang proves to be 20,000 BCE, specialists will now have to accept that our ancestors were not only creating beautiful paintings on cave walls and engraving sacred images on rock canvases, but they were also master builders. The discovery of Göbekli Tepe is also a surprise as it may prove to be thirty times larger than Stonehenge, and it is at least 6,000 years older. Its monumental structure reflects the expertise of highly organized hunter-gatherer-builders, and there is evidence of the beginnings of agriculture at a date much earlier than anyone could have imagined. But Göbekli Tepe was remarkable in yet another way: it was a place where people came together and shared knowledge—"a prehistoric think-tank" whose shaman-mystic tradition was beyond simple shamanism and "more like an institution."[26]

The discoveries of these megalithic monuments pose questions that are still in the process of being answered—or ignored. For example, how do we explain the existence of these megalithic structures around the world? Why do the oldest layers of construction often display the greatest expertise? What are we to make of the similarity of some of the symbols found on these structures? What do the worldwide patterns in the landscape and the earthworks associated with these monuments mean? Who were these highly organized shaman-mystic builders? *Our focus will be limited to this last question.*

Twentieth century research on the later European megalithic monuments demonstrates that these ancient builders, in the words of Keith Critchlow, had "access to timeless scientific values"; they "placed their highest value on the objectivity of geometry"; and they employed

Pythagorean triangles a thousand years before Pythagoras. They had a highly developed and practical knowledge of the cosmos that enabled them to construct monuments that could "access and read" the rhythms of the cosmos so that people could live in harmony with those rhythms and experience the invisible dimensions of reality. Their structures were both temples *and* observatories since for them there was no separation between spiritual experience and logical thinking. They had achieved a "remarkable balance between the intuitive and the logical" that we do not have today.[27] In the words of one of the great scholars of this period, John Michell, these cultures possessed a truly "spiritual technology."

This *unity of vision* placed individual consciousness in the mediating role of integrating and harmonizing the world of spirit/cosmos with the world of matter, time, and space. The megalithic structures, says Critchlow, reflect a culture with "a full commitment to a spiritual reality which is invisible to the material or sensorial world,"[28] as well as an equal commitment to the integration of this reality into the life of the individual and the earth itself. We lost the *key* to this kind of "spiritual technology" when we separated the outer laws of nature from the inner laws of consciousness.

III. THE SHAMAN-MYSTIC TRADITION DURING THE NEOLITHIC PERIOD IN OLD EUROPE (6500–2500 BCE; IN CRETE 1400 BCE)

One of the great discoveries of the twentieth century was made by archaeologist Marija Gimbutas whose work revealed extensive prepatriarchal cultures that were peaceful, earth-centered, and predominantly feminine. The life-celebrating symbolic system of these cultures was so different from what was known from historical Western cultures that many scholars refused to accept her findings—in spite of overwhelming evidence.

Gimbutas began her work in her native Lithuania but eventually included prehistoric cultures stretching from northwest of the Black Sea southward through southeastern Europe (including southern Italy and Sicily) into the southern Mediterranean Sea (including Greece and Crete) and northward through western Anatolia (Turkey) all the way back to the western coast of the Black Sea. She would later call this area Old Europe.[29]

Why is her work important to us? It came as a great surprise to many people that these cultures were peaceful, egalitarian, sedentary, and artistic. Their art celebrated the feminine source of Life and its cycles of birth, death, and rebirth. No weapons of war were found, nor were there any depictions in their art of violence, war, or torture. Gimbutas emphasized that war is *not* endemic to the human species. "This material, when acknowledged," says Gimbutas, "may affect our vision of the past as well as our sense of potential for the present and future. We must refocus our collective memory. The necessity to refocus has never been greater as we discover that the path of 'progress' is extinguishing the very conditions for life on earth."[30]

This world was neither patriarchal nor matriarchal, but it was matrifocal: its focus was on the feminine characteristics of nourishing and protecting life. "The emphasis in these cultures," says Gimbutas, "was on technologies that nourished people's lives." This is in contrast to patriarchal cultures whose focus is on power and domination. Gimbutas insisted that the creative foundation of any *civilization* "lies in its degree of artistic creation, aesthetic achievements, nonmaterial values, and freedom." These are the qualities that nourish a respectful balance of power and "make life meaningful and enjoyable for all its citizens." This is the kind of civilization that Gimbutas discovered had flourished in Old Europe as "an unbroken continuity from Upper Paleolithic times." And it is the symbolism of these cultures, says Gimbutas, that has left "an indelible imprint on the Western psyche."[31]

The patriarchal West did not want to accept that a peaceful, non-patriarchal civilization had ever existed. And they simply did not know what to think about a culture whose central motif was the celebration of life. Since there was no written script and their symbolic system was much more inclusive than the symbolic systems of exclusive, patriarchal religious doctrines, Old Europe simply could not be understood within the framework of the Western worldview. Credit must be given to Gimbutas for decoding this symbolic language and allowing us to explore the life-giving worldview that nourished our ancestors for tens of thousands of years. We do not have to agree with her on every detail to credit her with this monumental breakthrough. Scholar Ashley Montagu expressed it well when he said, "Marija Gimbutas has given us a veritable Rosetta Stone of the greatest heuristic value for future work in the hermeneutics of archaeology and anthropology."[32]

Gimbutas understood the unified vision of prehistory, especially as it found its expression in the extensive art of Old Europe. "The Goddess in all her manifestations," she pointed out, "was a symbol of the unity of all life in Nature." Since Western culture has lost this sense of unity, it has also lost the fundamental relationship between death and birth. Gimbutas insisted that for Old Europe, "There was no simple death, only death *and* regeneration." Their celebration of life was rooted in their knowledge that birth and death are events in the cycle of life and that there is nothing but life. Their holistic perception was born out of living in harmony with the laws of nature, for it is this harmony that nurtures an awareness of "the sacredness and mystery of all there is on Earth." We have lost this perception, says Gimbutas, because we have severed ourselves from "the vital roots of earthly life."[33]

Once again, the core message from our ancestors is that living in harmony with the laws of nature changes us and opens us to a wisdom that brings us joy. In all the shaman-mystic traditions the Source of life is Nature, the Queen of Heaven, who brings us delight and joy. "She is the tree of life to those who lay hold of her / and those who hold her fast are called happy."[34] She is the water of life flowing from the fountains of heaven, and when we live in harmony with her laws, the fruit from the Tree of Life and the flowing waters of wisdom are available to us.

This sacred message is particularly prominent in Minoan art on the island of Crete, which was a later development of the Old European cultures. The Minoans' celebration of nature and their pure joy of life, not just human life but all life, permeate their art and create a sense of unity in all things. In fact, their art depicts no real distance between life in the material realm and the transcendent Otherworld.[35] Minoan culture was a visionary culture, deeply rooted in the ancient shaman-mystic tradition.

While Gimbutas did not use the words *shaman-mystic* to describe the civilization of Old Europe, there can be no question about these cultures' emphasis on the visionary life. In *Dionysos: Archetypal Image of Indestructible Life*, Carl Kerényi, a scholar in classical studies and the history of ancient religion, delineates the visionary foundation of Minoan life and art. From the abundant evidence of their visionary life, particularly prominent are the sacred gestures and the labyrinth. A major sacred gesture is the raising of both hands, which indicates epiphany: the experience of transcendence or a higher state of consciousness. This experience was achieved naturally as well as with the use of sacred plants. The wisdom, however achieved, was considered a miracle.[36]

The labyrinth also reflects the visionary life; this symbol existed in all the cultures of Old Europe. Gimbutas understood the rituals structured by this symbol as the celebration of Nature as the Great Mother, the Source of all Life, the Feminine Dimension of the Divine. This divinity was associated with the labyrinth as a mistress of the life-giving waters, and she was the crane whose dance led to the center of the labyrinth. She was the moisture that nurtures, the flowing waters of life, and the water bird, often with both feminine and masculine characteristics, who renews and regenerates all life.[37] The life-giving waters are both physical and spiritual.

Whether the labyrinth symbolized the life-giving waters of the material world or the life-transforming experience of a higher consciousness, it was always a way to the Source of Life. Kerényi's comparative study of the labyrinth reveals that our ultimate journey to the center of the labyrinth is a journey to the center of our deepest self, for it is there, says Kerényi, that we confront the divine, the cosmic Mind—not as Other, but as Self.[38]

This is the shaman-mystic-visionary's experience in the labyrinth, and this experience was the foundation of the spiritual tradition of Old Europe. The labyrinthine designs appear everywhere: they are etched on figurines of the female body as temple, the holy of holies. They are in the caves, on the dancing floors, in the structure of the dance itself, on coins and pottery, and within the architecture of their temples and monuments—always in honor of the "Mistress of the Labyrinth" and always as a *Way to the Light*.[39]

As mentioned above, Gimbutas has shown us that these labyrinthine designs reflect a long and unbroken tradition all the way back to the Stone Age. Similar labyrinthine designs have been found etched on objects from the Upper Paleolithic,[40] but it is in these Neolithic cultures that they reveal unmistakably their relationship to higher states of consciousness. The many sacred rituals and dances associated with the transformative experience of the labyrinth may also be inherited from a much earlier time. As in all of the shaman-mystic cultures, the emphasis is always on the *experience*.

These labyrinthine rituals were a part of the great Mystery Schools of Crete and of Eleusis in Greece. We know that they were related to the mysteries of the caves as well as the mysteries of Egypt and earlier surrounding shamanic traditions. And we also now know that these rituals were structured to trigger altered states of consciousness that would allow the initiate to receive the knowledge of immortality — the fruit of the Cosmic Tree of Life.

This way of life was rooted in the invisible dimension of reality, and this kind of experience formed the foundation of culture and consciousness from about 40,000 BCE to varying periods of time, depending on the geographical area. For Old Europe, this way of life existed until about 4500 BCE, when the first of three waves of warring tribes swept in from the Russian steppes and by 2500 BCE (in Crete 1400 BCE) destroyed or repressed this ancient tradition.[41]

The incoming culture was mobile, focused on war and conquest, and much less developed artistically and spiritually. Were these waves of invasions, as suggested by Baring and Cashford, made by the "nomadic warrior tribes from the old Palaeolithic hunting grounds of the steppes,"[42] who, in their return, destroyed the more settled worlds they had left behind? Or were they people whose ancestors had been displaced by a cataclysm and forced into constant migration and violence? We don't yet know. What we do know is that it was this mobile, warring culture that became dominant throughout Europe and the West, and with their dominance we lost both the knowledge and the memory of our earlier experience. With the work of Gimbutas we have been given the opportunity "to refocus our collective memory."

IV. THE SHAMAN-MYSTIC TRADITION IN ANCIENT EGYPT (3000–1000 BCE)

There was another breakthrough that took place during the twentieth century, but it did not begin to bear fruit until the end of that century and the beginning of this one. A few scholars began to understand the shamanic, mystical foundation of Egyptian culture. We can only realize how important this is when we know what these scholars were up against. In the early nineteenth century when the Egyptian hieroglyphs were deciphered and the discipline of Egyptology was born, the materialistic worldview blinded these scholars to the real achievements of Egyptian culture. In spite of being surrounded by the ruins of one of the most magnificent cultures of our human past, the Egyptologists' general conclusions were that the ancient Egyptians were not religious, philosophical, logical, or mathematical. They were practical people without spirituality, their imagery was crude, and their religious texts were jumbled, confused, and lacked the profound wisdom that the ancient world had attributed to them. They were simply a practical, materialistic people who "always remained semi-barbarians."[43]

Scholars who disagreed with the Egyptologists were either ignored or dismissed as not having the formal qualifications of the Egyptologist. One such scholar was R. A. Schwaller de Lubicz, mathematician, alchemist, and artist. His "detailed study of the theoretical principles and practical application of ancient Egyptian mathematics...and his studies of ancient Egyptian esotericism and symbolism"[44] made him a giant in the development of our understanding of ancient Egypt.

During the last century, his many books on ancient Egyptian culture revealed the depths of Egyptian mathematical, astronomical, architectural, artistic, medical, and spiritual development. His work made it exceedingly clear that not only was Egypt a major source of Western science and culture, but the entire civilization was grounded in a unified understanding of the scientific and spiritual principles of the cosmos. In fact, Schwaller de Lubicz concluded that **Egyptian civilization was based on the principles of Cosmic Consciousness and stands as the key to the evolutionary wisdom** of our ancestors.⁴⁵ Unfortunately, his work was completely ignored by the Egyptologists just as they had earlier ignored the ancient writers who held Egypt in the highest regard for its scientific and spiritual wisdom.⁴⁶

The extensive work of Schwaller de Lubicz is not easy reading but, thankfully, John Anthony West in *Serpent in the Sky: The High Wisdom of Ancient Egypt* provides a readable presentation and analysis of the conclusions of Schwaller de Lubicz along with the contrasting views of the Egyptologists. In West's words, "I set up the book to provide a simultaneous running contrast between the two schools," the work of Schwaller de Lubicz is developed in the main body of the text while the "opposing views and other relevant material is immediately accessible in parallel extensive margin notes." The opposing views, says West, "have been culled from a full spectrum of academic Egyptological sources in several languages. Taken together, they provide an accurate but unavoidably unflattering overview of contemporary Egyptology."⁴⁷

In spite of the fact that the Egyptologists ignored Schwaller de Lubicz, he did not ignore them. His work reflects the same meticulous methods of research and data that had been developed by the Egyptologists, but Schwaller de Lubicz used them to create a comprehensive synthesis of all aspects of Egyptian civilization.⁴⁸ His work offers mathematical, linguistic, mythic, and symbolic evidence of a highly developed and sophisticated civilization that was created by the shaman-mystic-scientist-builders of our past.⁴⁹ These Egyptian builders, like many of our earlier ancestors, but unlike the Greeks, did *not* differentiate and isolate the rational mind from the mind's ability to perceive, feel, intuit, and fully experience life. They developed the whole mind, a *unity of vision* that nurtured a sacred, *cosmic consciousness* centered in the heart. This synthesis or unified vision Schwaller de Lubicz called the *Sacred Science*.

This was a highly developed science that focused on the development of the individual. Just as Gimbutas discovered in Old Europe, Egyptian technologies were also structured to nourish people's lives. This *Sacred Science* was based on the knowledge that matter and spirit are one energy—a realization only achieved by quantum physicists during the twentieth century. This wisdom allowed the ancient Egyptians to construct a society that nurtured the development of innate human potentials. According to author Robert Masters, the work of Schwaller de Lubicz and West "confirm that it is possible to have a society in which the human potential is encouraged and enabled to flower." Since Egypt knew "how to awaken and use these potentials," Masters suggests that we today may be able to acquire this knowledge from what has survived of this ancient civilization.[50]

West explains how the ancient Egyptians integrated their knowledge of harmonic laws, that is, the complex vibratory systems, into their "architecture, art, music, paintings, rituals and incenses," all of which have an evolutionary effect on the human being.[51] Each temple is different: each has different astronomical orientations, different geometric structures, and a different theme. In the words of author Peter Tompkins in his discussion of the work of Schwaller de Lubicz, the "complex of Egyptian temples contain a global lesson of which each temple is a chapter where a particular theme of the Sacred Science is developed." For example, the Temple of Luxor, also called the Temple of Man, embodies in its proportions and harmonies "the story of the creation of man and his relation to the universe." **It is the temple of the human being who has achieved Cosmic Consciousness.**[52]

It is unfortunate that most Egyptologists are still blind to the heart and soul of Egyptian culture. This blindness is a result not only of a materialistic worldview in which only the rational mind is valued and developed, but it is also the result of a limited understanding of evolution, which perceives all history prior to the present as inevitably inferior. This blindness denies our human potential.

However, the more recent work of Alison Roberts and Jeremy Naydler lends further evidence of Egypt's powerful shaman-mystic-builder tradition. Roberts' scholarly and detailed study of Egyptian rituals delineates how the Egyptians sought, achieved, and attempted to maintain a cosmic, unified vision that is rooted in the heart. In *Hathor Rising: The Power of the Goddess in Ancient Egypt* and *My Heart My Mother: Death and Rebirth in Ancient Egypt* Roberts examines the Egyptian art of living, the art of death and rebirth, and **the powerful role of the fiery serpent**

goddess in achieving cosmic consciousness. This fiery kundalini energy is the feminine dimension of the divine who must be desired and loved and integrated into consciousness. The full realization of this creative, loving energy is symbolized by the serpent energy rising up the spine of the pharaoh and resting at his third eye. This is the symbol of the sacred marriage of love and harmony between the serpent goddess and the fiery solar god, and it is the symbol of cosmic consciousness.

And Naydler in *Shamanic Wisdom in the Pyramid Texts: The Mystical Tradition of Ancient Egypt* discusses the earlier limiting but changing attitudes of Egyptologists and presents extensive evidence of how the Pyramid Texts reveal the shaman-mystic-builder foundation of the ancient civilization of Egypt. These texts were written at the end of the Fifth Dynasty, about 4,350 years ago, and are "the earliest example of any piece of extended writing worldwide." However, it is "virtually certain," says Naydler, that they existed in oral form much earlier. They are "the prototype of a mystical tradition that is at the root not only of later ancient Egyptian religious life but also of subsequent Western mystical, esoteric traditions such as Platonism, Hermeticism, Gnosticism, and alchemy."[53] Both Roberts and Naydler show in detail how the sacred rituals of Egypt are structured to ignite altered states of consciousness and transformative experience in the spirit world. Their work reveals that *the Egyptian heart-centered experiential consciousness is rooted in the cosmic dimensions of reality that open the mind to the ecstasy and beauty of life in time and space.*

In spite of the limited views of many Egyptologists, the contributions of these and other courageous scholars continue to provide evidence of an Egyptian shaman-mystic-scientist tradition. The sacred fruit has now been made visible and we can see that our Egyptian ancestors have given us *abundant fruit* from the Cosmic Tree. "Egypt," says Naydler, "calls to us from deep within our own souls."[54]

V. THE SHAMAN-MYSTIC JEWISH TRADITION

THE DEAD SEA SCROLLS AND THE NAG HAMMADI TEXTS REVEAL THE CONTINUATION OF THE SHAMAN-MYSTIC TRADITION OF THE FIRST TEMPLE (832–621 BCE)

At the end of World War II, there were two important discoveries: in December of 1945, the Nag Hammadi texts, which the Church had earlier attempted to destroy, were found in the sands of Egypt, and in 1947 the first of what we now call the Dead Sea Scrolls was discovered in caves overlooking the Dead Sea. These texts were written or copied between 200 BCE and the fourth century CE.

But what could these old manuscripts have to do with our lives today? How could anything written that long ago about someone's religious notions have any relevance for Western culture today? First, they help us to rediscover what had been repressed by the Deuteronomists and later by the Church of Rome. These texts are some of the lost voices of our ancestors in their quest for mystical experience and communion with other dimensions of reality. Second, when both the Dead Sea Scrolls and the Nag Hammadi texts are read *along with* the previously known material, scholars can begin to reconstruct the early histories of Judaism and Christianity. Barker discovered evidence of the shaman-mystic tradition in the Jewish First Temple before the purges by Josiah in 621 BCE. The Dead Sea Scrolls reveal the continuation of this ancient shamanic tradition among the Jewish mystics at Qumran while the Nag Hammadi texts reveal its continuation in the *secret tradition* of early Christianity.[55]

These texts "possess the potential," says Stephan A. Hoeller, a modern Gnostic, "of aiding the West in the recovery of a substantial portion of its lost soul." This "long forgotten, or rather repressed, component of the soul of Judeo-Christian religiosity and of Western culture" emerged out of the earth in the hour of our greatest need. This "agonizing psychic need of the culture was thus met by a synchronistic response from the innermost center of reality." With this response, the West was able to retrieve a "hitherto missing ingredient of its collective soul."[56]

In many of the Nag Hammadi gospels the voice of Jesus is different from that of the New Testament gospels. According to Marvin Meyer, a scholar of Gnosticism and the Nag Hammadi texts, Jesus emerges *not* as a person who performs miracles, fulfills prophecy, or dies for our sins. No. *In these texts, the shamanic Jesus returns to teach us the way of an ancient mystical tradition.* This Jesus speaks of how our confusion and lack of knowledge have caused us *to forget who we are and why we're here.* This Jesus tells us we have *forgotten* that we are divine, that we are light, and that we have both the capacity and the responsibility to go within to experience the miracle of who we are. It is this knowledge, this *gnosis*, that is more important than *belief.* We are "not only to *follow* Christ but to *become* Christ."[57] And, of equal importance in the Nag Hammadi texts is the return of Wisdom in the form of Mary Magdalena, that part of God that had been exiled from God since the Deuteronomists, and now she returns as the beloved of God.[58]

The discovery of these texts has opened the way for a much larger picture of Judaism and Christianity to emerge. In fact, they have transformed our view of Israel's First Temple tradition as well as the early history of Christianity. And they have helped us to see the continuation of the shaman-mystic tradition of our species — in spite of tremendous setbacks and repression.

What these texts reveal goes far beyond any particular religion, in spite of the fact that they were part of Judaism and early Christianity. Ultimately, they are reminders to our materialistic culture that there are dimensions of reality beyond matter and that it is our evolutionary heritage to be able to communicate with these unseen worlds so that we can create our lives in a fuller and more meaningful way. In short, these texts give us information about a very different kind of consciousness from the singular rational mind that we so value today: they reflect our ancestors' journeys to the center of the labyrinth, to the visionary world — the Light — where they could eat the fruit from the Cosmic Tree.

VI. SHAMAN-MYSTIC PRESOCRATIC, ANATOLIAN GREEK TRADITION (500 BCE TO THE BIRTH OF CHRIST)

The Greek culture learned much from the Egyptians and maintained many rituals to awaken the mind to the spirit dimension and, in the Great Mysteries, to initiate the individual into the experience of death and rebirth. However, Greek culture centered in Athens was never able to achieve the depth of understanding that had existed in Egypt. Yet there were those Greeks who did maintain a shaman-mystic-scientist tradition, but we would not know about them today without the work of Peter Kingsley.

In 1958 there was an excavation at Velia in Italy, a city founded by Greeks from Phocaea (on the western coast of Anatolia) around 538 BCE. A two thousand-year-old sculpture of a man in a toga and two bases for statues were found. All three had inscriptions on their bases. The information in these inscriptions was not understood until Kingsley came across them. He realized that the inscriptions were a confirmation of a tradition that had existed for over 500 years, right up to the birth of Christ.[59]

This powerful—and lost—tradition was one of shaman-mystic-healers who were at the very roots of Western culture. We knew some of them as the Presocratic philosophers, which include Pythagoras and Parmenides, but we did not know that these philosophers were master shamans. Kingsley tells us that they were masters of entering altered states of consciousness, of experiencing other dimensions of reality for long periods of time, of initiating others and teaching techniques of ecstasy and healing. They were known for giving laws that could heal whole cities. They had access to the wisdom of Egypt, especially through Pythagoras who had studied there, but they themselves were part of a shaman-mystic-scientist tradition in Anatolia that stretched all the way to Central Asia. Through their wisdom and *visionary* abilities "they laid the foundation for disciplines that were to make the West what it now is: chemistry, physics, astronomy, biology, rhetoric, logic." Kingsley emphasizes the fact that their world was also "a feminine world of incredible beauty and depth and power and wisdom, a world so close to us that we've forgotten where to find it."[60]

But Kingsley discovered much more—so much more, in fact, that it challenges all we thought we knew about the origins of Western civilization. He discovered a continuity of shamanic traditions that stretched from southern Spain through Greece and Crete, northern Africa (including, of course, Egypt) to Lebanon and Syria, Babylonia, Anatolia, Persia, India and all the way into Central Asia, the Himalayas, Mongolia, Tibet, Nepal and India.[61] This surprising piece of the puzzle of our past reveals that Western culture emerged out of this ancient tradition of the shaman-mystic-scientist who, in the Greek/Anatolian form, was a practical technician, scientific thinker, lawgiver, political leader, and ambassador.[62]

Kingsley's work reveals not only the roots of the Presocratic tradition within this vast network of shamanic cultures but the beauty and power of the worlds they created. Wherever the Presocratics settled—whether it was in their place of origin along the western coast of Anatolia or in settlements on the northwest coast of the Black Sea or in Marseilles or in Velia in southern Italy—they created cultures that honored both the inner and outer worlds, the male and the female, the direct experience of Wisdom *and* the politics of governing these worlds. It was, says Kingsley, in the Presocratic culture that Plato "saw his own unrealized ideal of the philosopher who's also a lawgiver actually lived out and fulfilled."[63]

In Kingsley's work, *In the Dark Places of Wisdom*, he tells us about Parmenides, who, as mentioned above, was one of the powerful philosophers and healers in this tradition. He explains how profoundly Parmenides influenced Plato but, at the same time, how profoundly Plato *distorted* and *rationalized* the great tradition that Parmenides—and Pythagoras before him—represented. Plato, says Kingsley, was not the father of Western philosophy after all. The true father of Western philosophy was a shaman, and it was this shaman, not Plato, who invented logic.[64] It was also these same shamans who practiced samadhi, the various forms of divine or cosmic consciousness. But what India preserved and developed, "would soon be covered over and rationalized in Greece."[65]

Once again, as with the Stone Age, the Megalithic builders, the Old European cultures, the ancient shaman-mystic tradition of Egypt, the shaman-mystic tradition of Judaism, and later the *secret tradition* in Christianity, the very heart and soul of our heritage was distorted and lost.

It seems close to miraculous that during the twentieth century all of these shaman-mystic cultures emerged into consciousness. But this was not the first time the underground knowledge emerged into the consciousness of mainline culture. There have been four waves of the renaissance of this underground wisdom in Western history before the twentieth century.

The first wave was during the High Middle Ages (1000–1300 CE); the second was the Italian Renaissance (1460–1527 CE); the third was the Rosicrucian Enlightenment (1600–1620 CE); the fourth was the English and German Romantic Movement (1775–1850 CE); and the fifth is the present time. Each time this underground tradition emerges, it brings the sacred stories of our past—stories that return to us the power of the heart, the reality of the soul, and the unified vision of the shaman and the scientist.

TWO MAJOR REVOLUTIONS OF THE TWENTIETH CENTURY: THE SHAMAN-MYSTIC REVOLUTION AND THE NEW SCIENCE REVOLUTION

At this point we probably should not be surprised to realize that during the twentieth century there were two other major developments that have become so powerful that they can now be called revolutions: one is in the field of **consciousness studies and shaman-mystic-visionary experience**; the other is in **the new science of quantum physics**. Both revolutions are rediscovering the *unity of vision* that reveals the relationship between mind and matter.

The Shaman-Mystic Revolution

The revolution in our understanding of the mind and visionary-mystic experience began with the work of Sigmund Freud and Carl Gustav Jung. Their work opened the door to inner, symbolic experience through dreams, visions, and the cultural stories that emerged out of these experiences, such as fairy tales and myths. Jung recognized that much of our collective spiritual history continued to exist in the repressed underground traditions of Alchemy, Gnosticism, the Hermetic arts and the Kabbalah. Scholarship in these traditions as well as in shamanism, the ancient mystery schools, world religions, and symbolic systems around the world yielded evidence (1) of the "fundamental unity" of all spiritual traditions, and (2) that this unity finds its expression in "an inexhaustible newness" wherever it appears.[66] It is, in fact, the *Perennial Philosophy* that can only be apprehended by "direct perception."[67] Resistance to any form of spiritual experience in our materialistic culture was lessened by *the discovery that it was these underground spiritual traditions that had nurtured the mathematical approach to nature, which, in turn, had ignited Western culture's scientific revolution during the seventeenth century.*[68]

Since the laws of inner experience are expressed in symbolic language, scholars became aware of the limited, exclusive symbolic systems of Western religions. It became clear that a unity of vision required a complete, inclusive symbolic system. For almost two thousand years the West's symbols of the divine have been exclusively masculine and dangerously incomplete. The emergence of the rich and inclusive symbolic language of dreams, visions, fairy tales, myths, and the underground traditions shocked Western consciousness into an awareness of just how exclusive and repressive our concepts of the divine have been. In many of the underground forms, the feminine dimension of the divine reflected the *unity of vision* our culture needed for health and wholeness. Perhaps the greatest surprise to Western consciousness came, however, with the excavations in Old Europe of tens of thousands of images of the divine in the form of the female, her sacred body, and all the forms of Nature that so clearly shared her divinity.[69]

This new awareness of symbolic language awakened interest in theories of symbolic, mythic language—what our ancestors would have called the language of soul. This investigation led to the work of one of the early and most important theorists of symbolic language, Giambattista Vico (1700s). Vico understood that symbolic language is our first language and that it is equal to conceptual language. This equality permits no repression, censorship, or dominance of one mental function over the other. Symbolic language, says Vico, possesses a poetic logic that gives birth to the logic of conceptual consciousness. Both languages are necessary if the mind is to participate in its own wholeness. In fact, the mind's wholeness depends on an integral and dynamic continuum of movement between the symbol *and* the idea.[70]

Also important for the new shaman-mystic-visionary revolution is the scientific research on the brain. The HeartMath Institute has done extensive research on the heart-brain connection, the intelligence of the heart, and the heart's role in perception and healing. Other scientific research on the brain has revealed that the brain has the neurological mechanism for altered states of consciousness ranging from mild visionary experiences to a total mystic state of consciousness, the experience of the unity of all life. According to Andrew Newberg and Eugene D'Aquili, "There is nothing we have found in science or reason to refute the concept of a higher mystical reality.... The wisdom of the mystics...has predicted for centuries what neurology now shows to be true: In Absolute Unitary Being, self blends into other; mind and matter are one and the same."[71]

Millions of people have experienced just such visionary and mystic states of consciousness during Near (Actual)-Death Experiences. Scientists, scholars, artists, and many others around the world are having anomalous experiences, dreams, and visions that dissolve the border between spiritual and physical reality. While some of the visionary and mystical experiences are spontaneous, many have been made possible by the rediscovery of the role of sacred medicine, other ancient techniques, and newly developed techniques for experiencing altered states of consciousness.

The New Science Revolution

Early in the twentieth century scientists continued the line of experimentation that resulted in the development of quantum theory. During the rest of that century and continuing today, this new scientific understanding is radically changing our worldview. In fact, it is changing everything we thought we knew about the material world — as well as the nonmaterial, invisible dimensions of reality. This revolution is bringing back the relationship between the scientist and the shaman-mystic. While the visionary is experiencing the merging of inner and outer realities, the physicist is discovering that human consciousness not only affects matter but is central to its creative process.

The scientific description of the quantum field is very similar to the shaman-mystic's description of the spirit world: the quantum field is a vast, eternal sea of vibrating energy — "a quantum sea of light." All life exists and breathes within this infinite, indivisible, self-regenerating, interconnected, and inexhaustible sea of energy. It is "a state of pure potential, of infinite possibility." The Western worldview of nothing but a material reality is negated by the discovery that "there aren't two fundamental physical entities — something material and another immaterial — but only one: energy."[72] Physicist Fred Alan Wolf says that "Quantum physics shows us that matter is how spirit appears in the physical universe."[73] And, says physicist Amit Goswami, it is *this eternal sea of consciousness* that creates the universe. Modern science, he says, is creating a new paradigm that "validates an ancient idea — the idea that consciousness, not matter, is the ground of all being."[74]

For the first time, many of us submerged in the Western materialistic worldview can begin to realize that our ancestors were aware of and in communication with this quantum field. In *The Field: The Quest for the Secret Force of the Universe,* Lynne McTaggart states that this new science is, in fact, "a science of the miraculous."[75] Whether we are aware of it or not, *a scientific revolution is taking place* — one so powerful that the foundations of the old scientific worldview are being shattered.

Two Phenomena of Our Time That Require the New Science

The new science is able to tackle problems whose understanding requires the evaluation of both physical *and* spiritual evidence. Such a problem is the UFO phenomenon. While this phenomenon has probably existed for thousands of years, UFO activity increased significantly in the twentieth century, just after World War II and the development of the atomic bomb. Earlier I mentioned that thousands of people around the world are involved in anomalous events that are surely "the strangest, the most mysterious, and the most inexplicable"[76] experiences imaginable. The global experience of UFOs, whose "evidence is increasing daily," definitely falls into this category. There is a group of scientists who call themselves the Invisible College after the early seventeenth century visionary scientists who rejected the limitations of the Church and the State and committed themselves to working toward a unified vision of reality. These present-day scientists number about one hundred from five or six countries. Jacques Vallee, one of these scientists, writes about their revolutionary work in *The Invisible College: What a Group of Scientists Has Discovered About UFO Influence on the Human Race*, published in 1975 and again in 2014.[77]

The work of this group of scientists with UFOs relates to our study because these scientists realize that this phenomenon challenges an arbitrary split between physical reality and spiritual reality. They are aware that "It is not possible to study such data with the techniques of statistics or physics alone." While some scientists are ignoring, denying, or even destroying physical evidence of UFOs, these scientists are examining *all* aspects of the evidence. Using "every available piece of scientific equipment—from flying spot scanners to electronic microscopes," they have studied and carefully analyzed thousands of UFO cases. Applying his expertise in computer science, Vallee himself spent four years examining the 10,000 reports that were at that time in the files of the United States Air Force. Much of what was learned still is not public knowledge.[78]

Their extended, in-depth investigations indicated "it is only when one analyzes the thousands of similar occurrences in the last twenty-five years and in all countries that one achieves some degree of understanding." They realized they could not explain the phenomenon by hoax and illusion alone, and they could see that their investigation offered an opportunity for "genuinely new knowledge." Some of the aspects of the phenomenon they have examined include the concrete, material evidence and its ability to dematerialize; the self-contradictions; the apparent absurd or "meta-logical" aspects; the space-time distortions; paranormal events; spontaneous healings; its global manifestation; the influence on human consciousness and its impact on culture; and the similarities between the effects of close encounters and spiritual experiences. One conclusion that is especially important for our purpose is that **they see the phenomenon as some form of technology—perhaps consciousness itself—that is reframing the consciousness of our planet to include a much vaster reality.**[79]

How, we ask, might this reframing of our consciousness work? "We are faced," says Vallee, "with a *technology* that transcends the physical and is capable of manipulating our reality, generating a variety of altered states of consciousness and of emotional perceptions. The purpose of that technology may be to change our concepts of the universe." It appears to have no limitations in time and space, and "its pattern of manifestations" opens "the gates to a spiritual level," and points "a way to a different consciousness," which is making humanity more open to the reality of altered, spiritual, states of consciousness and other-dimensional realities. It is a technology that strikes deep into the collective consciousness, producing "irrational, absurd events," confusing us but, at the same time, molding us and changing our concepts of the universe. There is a transformation, says Vallee, in our collective attitude toward the possibility of civilizations throughout the cosmos as well as a belief in "a higher destiny" for humanity. The "human learning curve [is] bending toward a new cosmic behavior."[80]

Reframing also occurs through the pattern of responses that follows a phase of acute UFO activity: there will follow fakes, hoaxes, pictures of weather balloons, laughter and a wave of ridicule that "sweeps into oblivion hundreds of genuine sightings that deserved serious scrutiny." However, under this disguise of the "preposterous or absurd," *the public is able to dismiss the whole event but the images sink into the unconscious and influence our frame of reality.* "If," says Vallee, "the phenomenon is forcing us through a learning curve then it MUST mislead us." The UFO waves would have to be repeated periodically but with unpredictability since this is the pattern that changes consciousness slowly but irreversibly. Vallee suggests that this is precisely what is happening globally—and the phenomenon *is* bringing about a "shift in our world-view."[81]

If the UFO phenomenon is produced by a conscious technology, then such a technology, says Vallee, "can assume many more surprising forms than it has so far shown."[82] One thinks immediately of the worldwide phenomenon of crop circles that began in the 1980s. Genuine crop circles are also a mystery that appears highly conscious. In the words of one researcher, Freddy Silva, the designs "exhibit mathematical precision. They demonstrate principles of geometry. They portray ancient religious symbols." Silva tells us that "the science at the heart of the crop circle mystery....is so subtle, so wise, and so awe-inspiring that it has the power to humble you and wake you up to a greater reality." While crop circles have appeared in many countries, ninety percent of them have appeared in England, especially in the vicinity of the great megalithic monuments. During the first decade of their appearance in England alone, there were more than 10,000 crop circles.[83] Often UFOs are reported around crop circles, and just as with UFOs, fakes and hoaxes appear among the genuine crop circles. This allows the public to dismiss the entire phenomenon but, just as with UFOs, the exquisitely beautiful images, reflecting the principles of sacred geometry, sink into the unconscious and influence our frame of reality.

We will remember that the megalithic monuments were constructed by the great shaman-mystic-scientists thousands of years ago. These builders knew and used the principles of sacred geometry, just as the makers of the genuine crop circles. Nothing was more important to our ancestors than understanding the laws of the cosmos and living in harmony with those laws. Are these circles, like the UFOs, the result of a spiritual/conscious technology capable of reframing our consciousness and reconnecting us to the cosmos?

People who visit the crop circles consistently report "the strangest, the most mysterious, and the most inexplicable"[84] experiences within these circles. There are also reports of people privately meditating on a particular symbol that appears nearby as a crop circle in the next day or two. The mysterious appearance of these crop circles brings to England every season thousands of people from all around the world, many of whom bring their professional expertise to apply to the mystery and to exchange their research and experience. Numerous books have been published about the crop circles, and aerial photographs are made every year and sent around the world through email, calendars, and yearbooks.[85]

These sacred structures have been described as exquisitely beautiful labyrinthine temples that allow us to enter, to explore the paths, to feel the boundaries between the visible and invisible worlds dissolve—all the while their patterns and frequencies imprint themselves on our psyche.[86] We have seen how the labyrinth was a major structure during the Neolithic period— as were the megalithic monuments. The labyrinth was an image of a larger, multidimensional vision of life. It was symbolic of the Great Mystery whose center was the holy of holies. The very structure of the ancient labyrinth leads us to the center of our deepest selves where we confront the divine, the cosmic Mind, not as Other, but as Self. Silva suggests that these patterns and frequencies affect our brain waves and encode new systems of information. He asks, "Could these twenty-first century mandalas be effecting a subtle change in the consciousness of humanity?"[87]

It appears that what we think about the origins of the UFOs or crop circles may not be as important, at least initially, as the reframing effects these phenomena are having on our collective psyche worldwide. This reframing makes it possible for us to *ask* what could possibly be the source of this so-called "technology," or "conscious technology"? Vallee proposes "the hypothesis that there is a control system for human consciousness." He does not know if it is consciousness itself that spontaneously responds when human consciousness becomes dangerously out of balance, but one thing he suggests is that whatever it is, it "may be entirely determined by laws that we have not yet discovered."[88]

Or could it be that there *are* those on this planet who have discovered these laws? There are many answers to this question from hundreds of official witnesses, government documents from around the world, various types of whistleblowers, and several highly skilled UFO researchers. Much of the information being released is difficult to verify. There has been misinformation, disinformation, and propaganda surrounding this subject for almost seventy years.

It is not the intention of this book to discuss the UFO stories that are being revealed. To know and understand these stories, each of us must study the disclosures and step by step evaluate the material for ourselves and then integrate it into our own consciousness. *This evaluation requires both a physical and a spiritual approach.* When a culture has been denied information, just as Vallee suggests, it must go through a reframing and expansion of its own consciousness. When we are finally able to verify the truth of this phenomenon or phenomena, the reframing and expansion of what we have held to be reality may prove to be excruciatingly painful.

This is a major reason why it is essential that we know our own history—the sacred history that our ancestors have worked so hard to preserve for us and are now disclosing to us through the historical discoveries of the twentieth century. Our ancestors want us to remember that we are divine, immortal, and creative, and that we have the history *of* and the potential *for* Cosmic Consciousness.

A Shaman-Mystic-Scientist Understanding of Evolution

Twentieth century astrophysics and astronomy have revealed that we live in "a vast and evolving universe," and shaman-mystics have revealed that each of us is "one with the immensity of all that is and all that is in the process of becoming." This means that our own personal evolution is intimately related to cosmic evolution. And those of our ancestors who intuitively understood our deep relationship with the universe and our potential for Cosmic Consciousness are now releasing their knowledge to us through the discoveries of the twentieth century. It is becoming very clear indeed that, in the words of musician and author, Jessica Roemischer, "the spirituality of the twenty-first century has everything to do with the cosmic evolutionary process that we are part and parcel of."[89]

Mathematical cosmologist Brian Swimme explains every chance he gets why knowing this and acting on this knowledge *now* is vital for all life on our planet—and perhaps even for the Milky Way galaxy itself. He tells us that there was only one time in the evolution of the universe when galaxies could be formed. There are, he says, two types of galaxies: spiral galaxies that create new stars; and elliptical galaxies that do not. It appears that elliptical galaxies were once creative spiral galaxies that collided and destroyed their internal structure and thus their ability to create. Since these galaxies cannot create, says Swimme, their stars go out one by one. Swimme's point is that we can "actually move off from the mainline sequence of creativity in the universe…. So the challenge before us as humans is to see that what we think of as small is immense. **The very form of our consciousness has a cosmological significance…. It may have immense implications for the galaxy as a whole." Just as there was one time when galaxies could form, says Swimme, this is our moment to awaken to who we are and why we're here. This is our "moment for the planet to awaken to itself through the human."**[90]

We humans have often thought of ourselves as small and insignificant. But we are discovering that we cannot *live* with this meager view of ourselves. We become addicted to all sorts of substitutes for the immensity within us that we have not brought forth. The increasing violence of many of these substitutes is not only taking the lives of millions of people but it is eroding our senses and our ability to think. This is how we self-destruct. This is how our stars go out one by one.

The Western worldview has split us off from nature and our deepest self, and this split has robbed us of our true heritage and made it incredibly difficult for us to awaken to our responsibility to ourselves, the earth, and the cosmos. Scientist Candace Pert has taught us that every thought and feeling we have is immediately communicated to every system in our body.[91] Shaman-mystics—and now some scientists—say that our thoughts and feelings are also communicated to nature, our larger body. As stated above by John White from the Institute of Noetic Sciences, our minds and basic state of consciousness affect the total Earth organism. And, as also mentioned earlier, this could well account for the earth releasing the wisdom of our ancestors when we need it most.

It has been very difficult for us to accept that *what* we think can affect the material world. Yet our ancestors who built the megalithic monuments understood that human consciousness was the mediator between the consciousness of the earth and the consciousness of the cosmos. And the indigenous people of the high Sierras in Colombia, the Kogi, are also very well aware of these relationships, and they are doing everything they can to demonstrate to us what happens when we ignore and disrupt the intelligent laws and balance of nature. They insist that we understand how degraded thinking does, in fact, degrade matter. The Kogi say that **"thought is the scaffolding of matter; that without thought, nothing could exist."** They are deeply disturbed with our plundering and lack of relationship with the earth and the cosmos. They see our attitudes and thoughts as "dumbing the world down, destroying both the physical structure and the thought underpinning existence."[92] Shaman-mystics, and now some quantum physicists, know that consciousness creates the world, but the Kogi's message of the horrific consequences of Western thought is an urgent and sacred call for our attention.

It does appear that we are beginning to put the pieces of the puzzle together—but ever so slowly. Yet there is one more twentieth century breakthrough in our understanding, and it comes from both the West *and* the East. Swimme tells us how the French Jesuit paleontologist Pierre Teilhard de Chardin and the Indian poet, philosopher, and mystic Sri Aurobindo each independently realized that **the vast unfolding of the universe is at once a physical *and* spiritual evolution.** In the words of Swimme, the universe is "a single energy event." Everything is a manifestation of the same energy as the Big Bang. This energy has "its own deep aim" and we are part of that aim.[93] The "greatest discovery of the scientific enterprise," he says, is that hydrogen gas, left alone, "turns into rosebushes, giraffes, and humans." And it is human consciousness that will determine "the way this planet functions and looks for hundreds of millions of years in the future."[94]

This understanding of evolution reframes our consciousness and opens the door to a radically different worldview in which the physical and the spiritual are one. It appears that all the discoveries, breakthroughs, revolutions, anomalous phenomena, Near-Death Experiences, dreams and visions of multidimensional realities, and the calls from indigenous people, are preparing us for an awesome responsibility.

This is *our moment* at the crossroads when we can make a choice to align our own creativity with the "deep aim" of the energy that gave us birth. It is the moment for us to discover our role in the story of the universe.[95] And this requires *our transformation.* **It requires the Gift of our ancestors.** Will we now be able to claim our true birthright? Will we be able to *see* the Cosmic Tree and, without fear, reach for its fruit "with the proper will and readiness to receive"?

ON A PERSONAL NOTE

On a personal level our next question might well be "How do we *reach* for this fruit?" When our culture and our religions have lost the heart of our birthright, where do we find it? We have asked the **Question** and the question will lead each of us on our own individual journey. With the question the labyrinth opens, we enter, and our journey to the center begins. We have many adventures along the way, for it is a lifetime journey and the path is also the goal. But, as Kerényi understood so well, it is at the center of our deepest selves that we confront the divine, the cosmic Mind, the All — not as Other, but as Self. This is the fruit of the Cosmic Tree of Life. It is the essence of the Holy Grail. It is Cosmic Consciousness and the true meaning of Christ Consciousness. And it is the next step in the evolution of consciousness for our species.

This book is about my Question and my own journey toward the center of the labyrinth. The structure of the book follows the path that opened for me: inward to soul and outward to history. This winding path led me deep into my own soul through dreams, visions, and the outer events in my life, but it also led me spiraling back into the living history of our ancestors' discovery of the Cosmic Tree of Life and the artifacts they left to guide us on our way. I relate some of these dreams and visions that guided me as well as some of the significant artifacts of the past that confirmed the validity of my own experiences. I also relate some of the major events in my life that *opened the way* to the invisible dimension of reality.

The most significant lesson I learned in the journey was that there is no death. We truly are immortal. Within a three-year period, my mother, my son, and my husband were killed in separate automobile accidents. With the death of our son Pisti, my husband István and I entered a dimension of consciousness in which Pisti was very much alive, conscious, and present. In the powerful world of waking vision, Pisti reminded us of so much that we had forgotten.

Before Pisti's death I had thought that I was the only one in the family on this particular journey, but with his death, all three of us remembered that we were working on the same project for ourselves and the earth. We are all so much more than our Western worldview has allowed us to imagine. One of the joys of the journey is the discovery of who we really are and why we are here. I wrote about these experiences and the dreams, visions, and synchronistic events that surrounded the deaths in another book, *The Miracle of Death: There is Nothing But Life*.

Once we know there is no death of consciousness—what all the great Mystery Schools reveal to the initiate—we know another dimension of reality exists, and it is the source of all life. In no way am I suggesting that if you embark on your journey, you will have to go through something like this. No. This was my journey, but what we all do need to know is that "Birth and Death are events in time and space. There is Nothing but Life."[96]

As István and I continued to experience this larger dimension of consciousness, incredible things happened. One important experience relates to the writing of this book. After Pisti's death, István had a visionary experience in which Pisti talked with him about the symbolism of the Egyptian god, Anubis, who, Pisti indicated, is the kind of healer and guide we need in our time. In his jackal form, Anubis takes into his own body the dead, the spoiled, the decayed and transforms it into new life. Each of us has taken in the decayed worldview of our culture. If we become conscious of the decayed beliefs and ideas within us, and if we make a conscious decision to change, we attract the laws of transformation to us: we become Anubis. Pisti told István that the jackal is called "The Opener of the Way" because this process opens us to unlimited creativity.

Pisti then told István to look up a particular hexagram in *The I Ching* or *Book of Changes*. The code for the hexagram was ML or Merchants of Light. ML is contained within the hexagram itself. Placing the lines of the letters ML from the top of the hexagram to the bottom, the first line of M is a straight, vertical line; the next two lines are slanting or broken lines; and the last line is another straight, vertical line; the first line of L is a straight, vertical line; and the second line is a broken, horizontal line. Viewing the hexagram from the top to the bottom, the lines straight, broken, broken, straight, straight, broken form the Hexagram 18: "Ku/Work on What Has

Been Spoiled [Decay]." By reading from the top line of the hexagram to the bottom line, István was able to clearly see the letters ML within the structure of the hexagram.

Within the vision, István knew that while the ML structure was the same as the 18th Hexagram, ML entered the hexagram from the top, which indicated that it was the response of a higher energy frequency to the lower frequency of decay. Traditionally, a hexagram is read from the bottom line up to the top line. I would learn more about ML in time, but for now I was able to understand that **ML is a code for the transformative laws of an energy field that is activated when we work on what is decayed.** I cannot even begin to describe what we felt when we found this hexagram in *The I Ching* and realized that it contained the theme of István's vision. Pisti had told his Dad to **"Read this hexagram carefully. This is your work, and it is the work of the earth."**

István did not know much about *The I Ching*. And I did not know a great deal more. What I did know is that it is one of those artifacts from our ancestors that is rooted in thousands of years of observation and experience of both the inner and the outer laws of nature. This resulted in the knowledge that there is an **"immutable, eternal law at work in all change."**[97] And it is this law that gives shape and meaning to the changes in our lives. These ancient Chinese shaman-scientists were able to tap into the pervasive intelligence in the universe in both its physical and nonphysical expressions as they relate to each other in a non-causal, meaningful way.

It was clear to István and me that this hexagram and the Anubis/jackal symbolism were both calls for working on what has decayed. We both felt as though we had entered another dimension of reality whose energy was conscious, intense, and urgent. **We were beginning to understand that the earth was attempting to give birth to a new consciousness, but this birth would require our deep and committed participation.**

As we read this hexagram, I began to feel the presence of powerful Healers, and I knew they were the same spiral of souls that had come to me just after Pisti's death. As they spiraled down to the earth in that earlier experience, I heard them chanting, ***"Our brothers and sisters on the earth*** *are dreaming a terrible dream."* They were present at the reading of this hexagram because this was their work. Now we understood that it was our work and it was the work of the earth. We both knew very well what had decayed in our culture and throughout our planet. Our evolution had been thwarted and delayed because we had allowed the fruit on the Cosmic Tree of Life to spoil.

At the time, I must admit that I thought the name, Merchants of Light, was a little strange until István explained that they are called *Merchants of Light* because they describe the Jackal Healers: they are able to distill darkness into light, and like merchants, they "sell" the knowledge of this process for the "price" of consciousness, and the entire universe "profits." **This process of distillation releases archetypal energy patterns on the earth that ignite and nurture a new consciousness. This is the code or law of ML.**

These new dynamic forms of energy also bring about what we today think of as miracles, so they are also known as Miracle Lovers. But, István explained, ML stands for so many different energy patterns. Since their work is done in harmony with the deep Matrix of Life, the mother source, they are Mother Love. And since they work on multidimensional levels of life, they live Multi-Lives on Multi-Levels. They carry the Memory of the Light of creation; thus they are Masters of Light, Masters of Love and Masters of Life.

Then István turned to me and said, "This is your work. You are the one who always stays to write about ML." I can't remember now how István explained away my concern about this statement, but I certainly remembered the statement two years later when István was also killed in yet another automobile accident.

One afternoon about a year or so later, I was looking through a book I had read in the 1980s when I was working on my doctoral dissertation. It was Frances A. Yates' *The Rosicrucian Enlightenment.* Yates mentioned Francis Bacon's "merchants of light" from his book, *New Atlantis,* and how both Bacon and the Rosicrucians were committed to bringing about an enlightenment for the whole world.[98] I had not read Bacon's *New Atlantis* and had no memory whatsoever of Yates' mentioning the "merchants of light." And certainly István had never read either book.

This discovery made me want to know if the Merchants of Light had a *historical* existence beyond metaphor and myth. Given our experience with ML, I felt quite certain that Bacon's knowledge of them was not fictional, but I found nothing more about them until I read *Heaven's Mirror: Quest for the Lost Civilization* by Graham Hancock and Santha Faiia. Hancock *suggests* that the Merchants of Light from Bacon's *New Atlantis* might well be the great astronomer-priest-builders from an earlier civilization that Bacon may have known about but that we may be only presently discovering.[99]

In Hancock's latest book, *Magicians of the Gods*, he presents evidence for two global cataclysms that occurred around 10,800 BCE and 9600 BCE. Some scientists accept the reality of the first cataclysm, but there are still questions about the second. It is not within the scope of this work to explore the evidence for these cataclysms or the mounting evidence for a worldwide civilization that might have existed before such destructive events. However, it is important to mention Hancock's discussion of the sages and magicians who, according to myth and legend, sailed around the world after a worldwide destruction to reignite the wisdom of the civilization before the disaster.

These sages and magicians, says Hancock, may be more than myth and legend. Perhaps they actually were *survivors* of this earlier civilization. At any rate, Bacon, in his *New Atlantis*, depicts the survivors of an earlier civilization as the navigators and seafarers, the *Merchants of Light*, who traveled around the world after the great deluge to return the wisdom of the lost civilization. Bacon also describes the mission of these astronomer-priest-builders as nurturing and sustaining the creativity of the Light.[100]

Was it these *Merchants of Light*, asks Hancock, who have appeared throughout history to ignite and guide various cultures in the evolution of consciousness, such as "the Akhu Shemsu Hor of ancient Egypt, the 'plumed serpents' of Mexico, the Viracochas of the Andes, the god-kings of the Khmers." And, as Bacon suggests, were they "dedicated to the preservation of a mysterious legacy of knowledge from before the Flood."[101]

We now know that there was *a legacy of knowledge* that, at the very least, was in its formative stages during the Ice Age. By 40,000 BCE our ancestors all around the world had developed techniques that triggered altered states of consciousness and integrated the various brain components—what we would later call shamanism.[102] These techniques allowed them to experience an invisible dimension of reality and, as I mentioned earlier, to develop a new consciousness—what is today called *modern consciousness*. This new consciousness was rooted in a relationship with the invisible dimension of reality, and it marks the beginning of our ancestors' ability to create culture, spiritual traditions, and art. Equally important, it allowed them to live in harmony with the laws of a multidimensional universe. It now appears that at least some of these ancestors also experienced Cosmic Consciousness.

Those among our ancestors who achieved the highest level of understanding and wisdom were the astronomer-priest-builders. We now know that they were shamans, mystics, and scientists. We do not know the exact time they achieved this high development, but we do know that their megalithic structures have been discovered around the world. Two structures from the late Ice Age have recently been discovered. It could well be that a cataclysm or cataclysms destroyed much of what might have been achieved by 10,800 BCE and 9600 BCE. As mentioned earlier, the stories and myths of such a cataclysm or flood exist along with the stories and myths about those who sailed around the world to reignite the wisdom of the old civilization.[103]

An example of just such a story was discovered by E.A.E. Reymond during her study of the inscriptions on the walls of the Temple of Horus at Edfu in Upper Egypt. These inscriptions are called the Edfu Building Texts, which evidently were not composed at the time of inscription between 237 and 57 BCE but rather copied from a large library of ancient documents. In *Magicians of the Gods* Hancock quotes extensively from Reymond's work, *The Mythical Origin of the Egyptian Temple*. The Edfu texts, states Reymond, describe the "Early Primeval Age of the Gods," who were not originally Egyptian but who came to Egypt from their island home in a great ocean after a devastating cataclysm. The survivors, a seafaring people, wandered the world in search of places where they could recreate the essence of their lost homeland. The story etched on these walls, says Hancock, is "essentially the same story that Solon heard and passed on to Plato."[104]

The inscriptions from the Edfu texts deserve serious attention. Several scholars who have studied Egyptian civilization have been struck by the fact that Egyptian knowledge seems complete from the beginning. "The sciences, artistic and architectural techniques and the hieroglyphic system show virtually no signs of a period of 'development.'" It was this observation that convinced Schwaller de Lubicz that *Egyptian civilization was a legacy rather than a development.*[105]

The vast puzzle of our past is emerging piece by piece through the efforts of scholars around the world. Gradually, we will be able to know with some certainty *when* our ancestors achieved the high level of knowledge and wisdom attributed to the *Merchants of Light,* the *Magicians of the Gods*. **What is more important, however, is the fact that these astronomer-priest-builders attempted to preserve and perpetuate their knowledge for future generations through stories, myths, rituals, megalithic monuments, astronomy, geometry, dance, and other art forms. These are our true legacy, our true stories.**

As outlined above, my focus in this book is on the twentieth century discoveries of such cultures in areas that form the foundation of Western culture — *and* **the fact that these cultures carry "the mysterious legacy of knowledge" that our ancestors have worked so hard to preserve for us.**

The fact that these shaman-mystic-scientist cultures existed has been the great surprise of our time. And what is equally surprising is that their wisdom forms the very foundation of our culture and of each renaissance of thought in the West. Why haven't we known this? How was this knowledge lost? Sometimes it was simply through the vicissitudes of history, but much of the time we will discover that it was through the violent repression by those who held political and religious power.

We cannot study these cultures in the deepest sense of the word *study* without allowing them to direct us inward. For we must remember that these cultures developed out of the inclusive experience of the invisible dimension of reality. Western culture lost this "mysterious legacy of knowledge" that our ancestors worked so hard to achieve, to preserve, and to pass on to all future generations. It is this loss that has allowed our evolutionary potential to decay. We have forgotten how to activate and integrate the various components of the mind, *including the heart*. We have forgotten that the mind requires its own wholeness to participate in other-dimensional realities or to experience the unity of all life. And we have forgotten that we have the ability to experience a consciousness that is of cosmic proportions.

Out of this forgetting, we constructed a worldview that negates everything our ancestors discovered about who we are and why we are here. We have accepted the belief that there is nothing but matter, that the human being is a fluke of nature with no meaning or purpose, and that death is the end of everything we have ever loved. **However, we now have the opportunity to rediscover this legacy, this Gift, that holds the key to our evolutionary future.** But evidently there can be no evolutionary future without our deep understanding of what the loss of this Gift means for our culture and for the world. This negative view of life has brought us to the brink of disaster. **The decayed has surfaced. We have erupted in perpetual violence around the world. And our planet is dying.**

Life itself is calling us to become conscious of this death and to transform it within ourselves. It is a time for big discoveries and big dreams and visions. And this is exactly what is happening. We are rediscovering our ancient heritage painted in caves, carved on rocks, painted in pyramids and temples, and buried in the earth. **The modern astronomer-priests are rediscovering a quantum science that negates the old worldview.** And people are having dreams and visions that are guiding them to a deeper knowledge of who we are. Each of us has a role to play in the death of the old and the rebirth of this sacred legacy.

This book is part of my role. The Merchants of Light are our evolutionary potential. By working on what has decayed in us and in our culture, we can ignite and draw to ourselves the evolutionary power of ML. When István first indicated that it would be my work to write about ML, I thought it strange since I believed I had no real knowledge about them. But I was to discover that each time I acquired a new context for knowledge, I would understand something more about ML. I began to experience how the process of distilling the darkness into light releases an archetypal living energy on the earth that, as I said above, brings about what we call miracles, but which, in fact, are actually the effects of higher laws, the transformative laws of ML.

With each experience, I gained a deeper awareness that the Merchants of Light are a manifestation of the transformative energy field that we had drawn to the earth with our powerful longing for myths of meaning and our willingness to work on the decay in our culture that had destroyed these myths. I also realized that it was this energy, this resonance, that made it possible for the earth to release the lost knowledge of our past.

For years I had been aware of scientific discussions about energy fields that reflect nature's intelligence and capacity for "highly organized activity." These fields organize and structure matter but remain independent of it. During times of change, the field of organization that determined the old structure disappears and a new wave of organized activity appears.[106] The cells within this new wave are called *Imaginal cells*. These cells, says Saryon Michael White in *An Imaginal Journey of Peace*, "contain the imagining or blueprint of a whole new being." When these cells first appear, "they are attacked and resisted," but they continue to grow, connect, and finally create a completely new form. *"The old form literally dies, as a new being is born from within the old."*[107]

It would take time for me to realize the depth of what István's vision was communicating to us through the symbolism of the Jackal, *The I Ching's* 18th Hexagram of working on that which has decayed or spoiled, and the Merchants of Light—ML. The Jackal takes into his body the decayed food and transforms it into life; the 18th Hexagram was a literal message to work on the decayed; and the code for working on this hexagram was ML—the new wave of activity that transforms the decayed into a completely new form. **The Merchants of Light are the creative** energy—the Imaginal cells—that "contain the imagining or blueprint of a whole new being." This field supports individual transformation, and it also supports the birth of highly developed beings who are choosing to be born on our planet to intensify the energy field and help us to wake up from our terrible dream.

What does this mean for each of us? I thought again of Pisti's words: "Study this hexagram carefully. It is your work. It is the work of the earth." It seemed to be an answer to the Question, *How do we reach for the Fruit from the Cosmic Tree?* Symbolically, the Fruit and, literally, the Imaginal cells contain the blueprint for higher consciousness—Cosmic or Christ Consciousness. **Again and again our ancestors have assured us of our potential for this higher consciousness through the symbolism of the Fruit from the Cosmic Tree so freely offered by the Queen of Heaven, Wisdom. And the hexagram tells us that it will be our work as Imaginal cells that will transform the decayed worldview and allow the Fruit from the Cosmic Tree to be offered once again to all those "with the proper will and readiness to receive."**

But what does it mean to become an *Imaginal cell*? It means we become conscious of the "terrible dream" we are dreaming on the earth. As we begin our work on the decayed forms of this nightmare, we attract the new wave of "highly organized activity" that carries the blueprint for a new consciousness. Magical cell by magical cell we become "a whole new being." As we are transformed, so is the earth transformed. In this way we too become ML—the Merchants of Light.

This energy field has been available to our species since the development of modern consciousness. We know that our ancestors had techniques of attracting this energy field to themselves. In the Hebrew First Temple tradition, for example, this was the work of the High Priest in the Holy of Holies where he embraced his beloved Wisdom, the radiant High Priestess, the Queen of Heaven, "the One who gave birth in the holy of holies, in the glory of the holy ones."[108] Here the High Priest was transformed, for here he ate of the true Tree of Life—the Cosmic Tree—and received the gifts of wisdom, divinity, and immortality.

We know that Wisdom, the Queen of Heaven, was not only the Beloved who offered her Fruit from the sacred tree to all who desired it; she was also the energy field of Imaginal cells that entered the High Priest and transformed him as he embraced and merged with the High Priestess. In "The Wisdom of Solomon" we are told that when Wisdom, the Queen of Heaven, enters souls, she transforms them. "Though she is one, she can do all things, / And while remaining in herself, she makes everything new. / And passing into holy souls, generation after generation, She makes them friends of God, and prophets."[109]

It appears that individuals, the shaman-mystic-scientists among our ancestors, were able to eat of this fruit, that is, to attract this creative energy field to themselves and be transformed. During our time, however, there is visionary evidence, which I relate in the book, that this field has now connected itself to our planet. In other words, the consciousness on this planet has attracted this field to the entire planet, which makes its "highly organized activity" more accessible.

This is now our moment to become the High Priests and Priestesses of our culture, to begin the work of the 18th Hexagram, and to enter the Holy of Holies to align ourselves with the "deep aim" of the universe that gave us birth. In my own case, when I had finished writing *The Miracle of Death*, I decided to consult *The I Ching* about my next work—this book. The hexagram that emerged was once again "Number 18. Ku: Work on What Has Been Spoiled [Decay]." There was no way for me to ignore what I was to do.

As I continued on my journey, I could see that from the early breakthrough into modern consciousness some of our ancestors had eaten the sacred fruit and maintained their connection to the spirit dimension while others had not. Those who kept the connection continued to live in harmony with the laws of nature; those who lost the connection did not. With this loss came the loss of the great myths of meaning. We are the inheritors of this loss but, *in this moment*, we are rediscovering our true birthright and those ancestors who have guarded and protected this Gift for us.

If we reach for this fruit and follow our sacred, individual path, we will be able to cocreate—on an entirely new level—*myths of meaning* that can save our world. If we can do our work, we too will become the ancestors who will pass on the Gift of the Cosmic Tree of Life to all our future children.

PART II

DISCOVERING OUR TRUE STORIES

Chapter One

*"Stories have to be told or they die, and when they die,
we can't remember who we are or why we're here."*[1]
— **The Secret Life of Bees**

In Western culture, we have forgotten who we are and why we're here. So deep, in fact, has been our forgetting that we scoff at the notion that there is anything to remember. It isn't that we have not told ourselves stories. We have. But they have been stories about what we are not, about limits and negations and emptiness. These are the kinds of stories people tell themselves when, somehow, they lose their true stories.

Only recently have we begun to hear that Western culture emerged out of the repression and loss of the true stories of our origins and our becoming. But it isn't that we had lost our stories completely. We have had luminous fragments from these stories that have lifted us up and given us hope—even though over time many of these fragments have been forced into doctrines of limitation. And so much has been forced underground. This is why the dominant stories of our culture are about what we are not and what we cannot become. We have become the masters of negation.

We take great pride in this mastery, for we have come to believe that the story of our limitations is the only true story and that we, the great logicians of the West, are the only true guardians of what is real. Yet, as we all know, our reality is limited to the world of matter. Our story ends where matter ends. And this makes the end of matter—what we call death—both an absurdity and a sorrow that cannot be healed.

But there are other consequences of our story. We are often indifferent to things that ought to matter, we fall by the millions into pervasive depression, and we are addicted to power, violence, death, and legal and illegal drugs that promise to transform our experience of this Western story. *But the most serious addiction of all is our addiction to the story itself.*

And it is because of *this story* that we are dying—and our planet is dying with us.

We need to find our true story—a story about who we really are and why we're really here.

From the perspective of our Western story of negation, our first reaction to this statement is to reject even the possibility that the human species or life itself has *a story* of meaning and purpose. But if for a moment we suppose that we and our planet just might have such a story, how could we discover this story and how could we verify its truth? This is a question that haunted me for many years. I wanted a life that was larger than either the scientific or the religious stories that dominated my culture, but I didn't know how to find it. So, like Parsifal, I plunged into the quest not quite knowing what I was doing but always following a deep longing to find the Grail of truth—if indeed there was such a thing. This became the guiding force in my life, not because I *knew* anything but simply because I could not live with the emptiness. As I grew older I could see how deeply other people also suffered from this pervasive emptiness—and I could see how my culture exhausted itself in its efforts to fill this gaping wound with beliefs, power, sex, violence, drugs, fame, achievement, and entertainment—or even with the *intellectual* pride of accepting the emptiness of it all.

Since most of these substitutes were either beyond my grasp or not of interest to me, I had to look for something else. The only route open to me at the time was the way of the intellect. So I took this path and thought I was sailing free and clear of all the cultural substitutes so ready to snatch me from my goal. I had rejected the limited story of science—not the data but the interpretations that went beyond the data. And I had also rejected the religion story because it demanded belief without experience, failed to understand the evolutionary power of the Christ mystery, and, therefore, had a dangerously limited understanding of its own story. It would be many years later in my life that I would discover that while I had rejected the limited stories of science and religion, I had, on an unconscious level, been programmed to *believe* in their limits and negations.

I became conscious of this when my son Pisti was killed in an automobile accident. After Pisti's death, his father István and I experienced him — his consciousness — still alive and powerfully creative. This period in our lives was incredibly intense and transformative. We felt the energy of infinite possibilities within ourselves as we experienced dimensions of reality that were vast, loving, intelligent, creative — and filled with meaning and purpose. I grieved for all of us who had been or were still trapped in the meager worldview of the Western world. István was radically changed by these experiences, and he never wavered. I too was changed but not until I could deal with the doubt and fear that lingered from the old worldview. How could anything so magnificent be real? The unconscious addiction to a belief in limitation was activated and ready to do battle with a vast and loving universe.

I have since seen this addiction in other people when they were presented with astounding scientific facts or credible personal experiences that had the power to shatter their limited view of the universe: consciously they could accept the evidence and the experience, but often, without even realizing it, they would immediately slip back into the grip of their old worldview. Nothing had changed. Why should this have surprised me? We have all been programmed to believe in a meaningless universe, to think in terms of limits. And part of the addiction to the old story is its fiction of superiority: to believe in the Western story of limits and negation is held, consciously or unconsciously, to be a far superior position than to accept a story of meaning and purpose.

Given our addictions and the fact that evidence alone does not seem to break through this programming, what can? How can we learn to *perceive* the world in a different way? (1) *We need our own inner experience.*

For many this is enough, but for those of us who have been unconsciously programmed to believe in the old worldview, (2) we also need a scientific understanding of this experience. Some people, like my husband, are transformed after one powerful vision. After his first experience with our son in the world of spirit, he sat up on the side of the bed and said to me, "I had no idea. None. I will never look at the earth in the same way again." And he didn't. But it took longer for me. I discovered that after each profound inner experience, my rational mind would snatch it away and put it on trial. I wrote about this struggle earlier in *The Miracle of Death*:

> *my exploration had rooted itself all too long in the academic world where the rational mind had been conditioned to believe in the fiction of its superiority over all other mental functions. I had not consciously accepted this, but the programmed response of this fiction was present nonetheless. Any participation in the excluded realities brought me up against a response of denial and distrust. The deeper I stepped into "the infinite reaches of inner space," the greater the demand and pressure I placed on my rational mind. I was asking my rational mind to allow information that did not support its fiction to coexist with that very fiction whose trained response was to deny and destroy it. In short, the more I experienced that contradicted the rational mind's structure of reality, the more vigorously it denied the validity of the experience.*[2]

The visions opened my mind to another reality—a reality that was completely excluded from the Western materialistic worldview. While I was experiencing this vast other reality, I knew it was real—more real than anything I had ever experienced. But when I was not in the visionary, altered state of consciousness, *my rational mind denied what it could not understand*. As we will see, science is now able to explain to the rational mind how these experiences are possible and how they do in fact reflect the very source of all realities. I would not have known of these other-dimensional worlds without the visionary, inner experiences, but healing required wholeness—a loving, respectful relationship between the visionary and the scientist.

As this relationship developed—ever so gradually—it allowed my rational mind to trust its visionary experience and to understand that its own logic had developed out of the poetic logic of the dreaming, visionary mind. And further, it allowed me to understand rationally that the deep roots of the visionary, mystic mind were in an invisible dimension of reality that could only be accessed as real and living through our own *inner experience*.

However, as we will see, it is precisely this kind of experience that has been denied, rejected, and repressed again and again by the forces in power throughout Western history. We need to know *this* history. We need to know what happened to the stories that reflect our evolutionary potential. We need to know why these stories were denied, repressed, or lost while the stories of our limitations survived. Inner experience—soul experience—was the heart of these lost stories, and when they died, something died in us as well. We need these stories to awaken us, to inspire us, and to call forth our own inner experience—our own soul stories.

Amazingly, now, in our time, these soul stories are returning to us in (1) the discovery of the shaman-mystic origins of modern consciousness during the Stone Age; (2) the discovery of the continued development of this shaman-mystic tradition before, during, and after the Mesolithic era—that transition from the Stone Age into settlements and farming—which found its major expression in the sacred megalithic monuments and symbolic earth works that reveal the scientific knowledge of their builders; (3) the excavation of Old Europe and the discovery of a vast shaman-mystic symbolic system that guides the individual to the center of the labyrinth—the source of all life; (4) the discovery of the shaman-mystic consciousness of ancient Egypt; (5) the discovery of the shaman-mystic tradition of the Hebrew First Temple; (6) the discovery of the continuation of that shaman-mystic tradition in the Dead Sea Scrolls; (7) the discovery of the extensive roots of this shaman-mystic tradition and its direct influence on Western culture through the Anatolian Greek Presocratic philosophers, who were master shamans, scientists, healers, and law-givers; (8) the reemergence of this shaman-mystic tradition in early Christianity as discovered in the Nag Hammadi texts; (9) the Near-Death Experience of millions of people around the world; (10) the appearance of shaman-mystic dreams, visions, and anomalous experiences globally; (11) the appearance of UFO and crop circle phenomena; and (12) the discoveries of quantum physics, which are confirming the reality of shaman-mystic consciousness and the source of consciousness in the quantum field, what our ancestors called the Spirit World.

These twentieth century discoveries have developed into a renaissance or revolution of the shaman-mystic-consciousness in our time, and with the new discoveries of quantum physics, another revolution in science is taking place that is changing everything we thought we knew about reality. These two revolutions are returning to us our lost soul stories and helping us to discover our true evolutionary potential—Cosmic Consciousness.

This book is about the discovery of these stories in our time, how they were lost, how we are discovering them once again, and how they challenge us to remember who we are and why we're here. If we accept this challenge, we will find ourselves up against the Western beliefs in limits and negations, and—perhaps—our own addiction to these limits. This book is also about my own challenges in the journey to find these lost soul stories and my discovery that what I was looking for was guiding me.

Chapter Two

*Today the scientist and the shaman-visionary-mystic are beginning once again to recognize their complementary roles in **understanding** and **experiencing** our universe.*

In the beginning of my search I knew nothing about our history. I was a child who lived inside both of the dominant stories of my culture—the religious and the scientific. Since I was too young to respond rationally to either, I simply floated on the ocean of their beliefs. The profound contradiction that existed between them remained outside my awareness for a long time, but even during those unconscious years I experienced a kind of emptiness within myself. As a child I often felt a need for something I couldn't name. At first I thought it was water, but I quickly learned that it was not water that I needed. Since I was still in grade school, I just accepted this experience as part of the reality of life. Only later would I use the word *emptiness* to describe it.

When I became conscious enough to question the truth of these two stories, I looked for some kind of rational, verifiable evidence that life had meaning and purpose. But I immediately learned that the doctrines of both science and religion were not to be questioned. Science considered itself to be the sole arbiter of truth because it based its conclusions on observation and experimentation. This in itself is important, but there seemed to be two problems: (1) *limited data* could distort an understanding of the larger reality, and (2) the *interpretation* of any data could be distorted by the worldview of the interpreter. For instance, did Darwin—or those who followed him—really have enough data to conclude that the human being is an evolutionary accident isolated in a random universe without purpose or meaning? Religion, on the other hand, also considered its story to be the only true reality. And how were we to know the truth of this story? By simply *believing* it to be true. I felt I was in a maze with no clear orientation, and for years I bumped up against dead ends with the fear that, in fact, there was no larger truth.

In time I would learn that the rational, scientific method of investigation was an excellent method, but it could not be the sole arbiter of truth since it did not acknowledge the reality of feeling, intuition, dreams, visions, or conscious *experience* of deeper orders of reality. As a result, these very real and powerful human potentials were devalued, dismissed, and undeveloped. On the other hand, religion had no method at all because it simply demanded belief in an established doctrine. Dreams, intuition, and inner experience were considered reliable only if they followed doctrine. As a result of both the science and the religion stories, older techniques of achieving deeper states of consciousness were destroyed or forced underground.

Those of us who wanted more than belief were left with a scientific story that was deeply depressing. It was a violent and empty story with no place for the human heart. And it was the dominant story of Western culture. On the other hand, the religion story allowed a place for the human heart but imprisoned it within the limitations of doctrine. Neither story validated *individual experience*—science not at all and religion only if it confirmed doctrine.

True stories are living stories that are always maturing and expanding. Since both the spiritual and the physical universe are vast and dynamic, the conclusions of both religion and science have to be understood as incomplete and ongoing. This doesn't mean that we can't know certain spiritual truths, but it does mean that those truths are always vaster and more miraculous than we can imagine—so much so that they can never be fixed in doctrine. The same is true with science: the story science tells us about our reality is always incomplete and changing. When scientists forget this, they too can fall into doctrine. For example, the *belief* that there is no reality beyond matter is not a *scientific* conclusion because science has had no methods of exploring a potential spiritual dimension. Yet this *belief* has become part of the science story. And, unfortunately, the discoveries of science for the last few hundred years have not significantly changed this story: *we are an accident of nature without meaning or purpose.*

That is, until now.

But now—in this moment—science is in the process of radically changing its story. While most of us in the Western world today are still trapped in the old science story about reality, a scientific revolution is taking place—a revolution so radical that the very foundations of the old story are finally being shattered. The *beliefs*, the *interpretations*, the *dogma* surrounding the old data are no longer viable. In fact, this new science challenges everything we thought to be *real*. In her book, *The Field: The Quest for the Secret Force of the Universe*, Lynne McTaggart has called this new science "a science of the miraculous."[1]

But most people, including many scientists working in highly specialized fields, are not aware of the larger picture of reality that has been emerging since the discovery of quantum physics early in the last century. And many, even if they were aware, would not be able to accept this "new" reality. Yet, says McTaggart in her delineation of this larger, changing picture, the profound breakthrough of quantum physics has made it possible for a few scientists working independently from each other in top-ranking institutions around the world to make discoveries that are rewriting the story of who we are and why we're here.[2]

Of course, Western science is not the only test for truth. For tens of thousands of years our species throughout the world developed and used techniques for *experiencing* truth. Our ancestor-shamans, unlike most believers in Western religion, used these techniques to discover and explore the universe from *within*. They experienced the meaning of life and death and the role of our species in this beautiful and creative universe. When these ancestor-shamans returned from their experience in deeper orders of reality, they too were able to tell true stories of our origins and our becoming.

Both the scientist and the shaman pursue the truth: the scientist through experimentation and observation of the physical world and the shaman through exploration and experience of the inner world. As anthropologist and modern-day shaman Michael Harner explains:

> Both shamans and scientists personally pursue research into the mysteries of the universe, and both believe that the underlying causal processes of that universe are hidden from ordinary view. And neither master shamans nor master scientists allow the dogma of ecclesiastical and political authorities to interfere with their explorations.[3]

We need the shaman *and* the scientist. Had earlier scientists possessed techniques that enabled them to *experience* the worlds they studied, they would have drawn very different conclusions from the data of their research. For example, had Buddha studied the data of Darwin's research, he would not have concluded that the human being was an evolutionary accident isolated in a random universe without purpose or meaning. His own experiential research would have informed him otherwise.

Today the scientist and the shaman-visionary-mystic are beginning once again to recognize their complementary roles in *understanding* and *experiencing* our universe. McTaggart tells us that even the scientists who discovered quantum physics in the early twentieth century knew they had stepped out of the old scientific view of reality and into a world strangely similar to the descriptions of the shaman-mystic. Erwin Schrödinger, Werner Heisenberg, Niels Bohr and Wolfgang Pauli actually explored texts they thought might help them understand what they were observing in their laboratories. Collectively, their studies included the Kabbalah, archetypal psychology, Taoism and Chinese philosophy, Hindu philosophy and Platonism, but they were unable to form "a coherent theory of the spiritual implications of quantum physics."[4]

Later, in 1970, Fritjof Capra was sitting by the ocean one afternoon when he experienced what he had been studying as a theoretical physicist:

> *I suddenly became aware of my whole environment as being engaged in a gigantic cosmic dance. Being a physicist, I knew*

that the sand, rocks, water and air around me were made of vibrating molecules and atoms, and that these consisted of particles which interacted with one another by creating and destroying other particles. I knew also that the Earth's atmosphere was continually bombarded by showers of "cosmic rays", particles of high energy undergoing multiple collisions as they penetrated the air. All this was familiar to me from my research in high-energy physics, but until that moment I had only experienced it through graphs, diagrams and mathematical theories. As I sat on the beach my former experiences came to life; I "saw" cascades of energy coming down from outer space in which particles were created and destroyed in rhythmic pulses; I "saw" the atoms of the elements and those of my body participating in this cosmic dance of energy; I felt its rhythm and I "heard" its sound, and at that moment I knew that this was the Dance of Shiva, the Lord of Dancers worshipped by the Hindus.[5]

By 1975 Capra had brought together his studies in physics, his own inner experience, and his knowledge of Eastern mysticism in *The Tao of Physics: An Exploration of the Parallels Between Modern Physics and Eastern Mysticism*. This is considered the first comprehensive discussion of these parallels. The door was now wide open for the Western scientific mind and the shaman-mystic mind to come together in a respectful and complementary relationship—a relationship that could transform our world and make it possible for us to create together the true story of our role in this evolving universe.

The East did not force the shaman-mystic mind underground as we did in the West but allowed it to flourish. Unfortunately, the West denigrated and rejected this type of consciousness and forced it to remain dormant and forgotten. This repression was so successful that we are only now discovering that the West also had its own rich shaman-mystic tradition. In fact, we will see that it was shamanic-mystic consciousness that catapulted us into what we today call modern consciousness. We will also see how this visionary consciousness was consistently repressed in Western culture but did not die out entirely, for the great periods of awakening in Western history are due to a renaissance of this shaman-mystic experience and knowledge. But, unfortunately, each time this flowering occurred, it was destroyed by religion and politics.

Today we are witnessing the return of this shamanic-visionary-mystical consciousness. Whether we are aware of it or not, we are presently in the midst of the most pervasive and powerful renaissance of this consciousness that the West has yet known. *And it is certainly an event of synchronicity that the revolution in science and the revolution in shaman-mystic consciousness are taking place simultaneously.*

Chapter Three

>─┼─◄»─○─«►─┼─◄

> *To **experience** the quantum field — the eternal sea of consciousness — is to fall in love with the universe and to know that a consciousness that is cosmic pervades every living thing and every living being.[1]*
> — **Elisabeth Kübler-Ross**

> *To intellectually discover the reality of the quantum field is to step into a new science that challenges everything we thought to be real.*

Let's now walk through the door these two revolutions have opened for us and explore the core similarity between the shaman-mystic mind and the new Western scientific mind: *both have discovered an unlimited dimension of consciousness*. First, we will consider **the shaman-mystic experience of this dimension of reality**. Millions of people throughout the world are experiencing first-hand spiritual truths so profound and life-changing that, according to Near-Death scholar Kenneth Ring, they represent "a major catalyst for human evolution and planetary transformation."[2] Two important types of these spiritual experiences are occurring worldwide: (1) powerful dreams, visions or experiences of other types of phenomena that open consciousness to life in other dimensions, and (2) Near-Death Experiences. Today many doctors think the Near-Death Experience is more accurately described as an *actual-death experience*. As one person who had such an experience said, "there was nothing 'near' about it — it was there."[3]

Ring insists that it doesn't matter whether experiences are triggered by "meditation, childbirth, a personal crisis, a church service," or if they occur spontaneously, people "seem to have been touched by much the same thing that NDErs come to know during a near-death crisis." In other words, the experience some people have when pronounced dead by their doctors "has nothing inherently to do with death or with the transition into death.... It is just that coming close to death is one of the very reliable triggers that sets off this kind of experience."[4]

A well-known example of such an experience that was *not* triggered by death but by an evening spent with friends reading and discussing poetry is that of Dr. Richard Maurice Bucke during the second half of the 1800s. Writing in the third person, Bucke describes his experience:

> *He and two friends had spent the evening reading Wordsworth, Shelley, Keats, Browning, and especially Whitman. They parted at midnight,... His mind, deeply under the influence of the ideas, images and emotions called up by the reading and talk of the evening, was calm and peaceful. He was in a state of quiet, almost passive enjoyment. All at once, without warning of any kind he found himself wrapped around as it were by a flame-colored cloud. For an instant he thought of fire, some sudden conflagration in the great city; the next, he knew that the light was within himself. Directly afterwards came upon him a sense of exultation, of immense joyousness accompanied or immediately followed by an intellectual illumination quite impossible to describe....he saw and knew that the Cosmos is not dead matter but a living Presence, that the soul of man is immortal,...that the foundation principle of the world is what we call love and the happiness of every one is in the long run absolutely certain. He claims that he learned more within the few seconds during which the illumination lasted than in previous months or even years of study, and that he learned much that no study could ever have taught.*[5]

Even though his experience lasted only a few moments, it changed his life forever. He began to do extensive research on the subject to see if there were others presently living or throughout history who had experienced this type of consciousness. He discovered that it was precisely those people who had had such an experience—what he would later call *cosmic consciousness*—who not only had created the world's great religions but whose consciousness had seeded modern civilization. He realized that just as every normal human being today has achieved self-consciousness, so will each of us achieve cosmic consciousness in the future: it is the next stage in the evolution of our species. "The Saviour of man," says Bucke, "is Cosmic Consciousness—in Paul's language—the Christ."[6] Later, in our discussion of Christianity, we will see that this was, in fact, the teaching of the early Christian mystics. Unfortunately, the Church would distort these teachings.

When we all achieve cosmic consciousness, says Bucke, our world will be as different from the world we know today as this world is from the world before we achieved self-consciousness. There will be no belief or disbelief, no doctrines, no mission to save anyone, and no worry about death or the future, for each soul will be living in this radiant light of love and consciousness that is far greater than any religious teaching has ever been able to describe. "Churches, priests, forms, creeds, prayers, all agents, all intermediaries between the individual man and God will be permanently replaced by direct unmistakable intercourse."[7]

Bucke's findings were published in 1901 in *Cosmic Consciousness: A Study in the Evolution of the Human Mind*. At that time Bucke estimated that the better known experiencers of cosmic consciousness, both present and past, "could be accommodated all at one time in a modern drawing-room,..."[8] However, we are now learning that there were those among our ancestors even during the Stone Age who knew how to work with kundalini energy to achieve this state of consciousness. Today there are probably millions of people who have experienced some form of cosmic consciousness. Even glimpses of this quantum field of light, love, and consciousness are enough to permanently transform them.

When István and I began to experience altered states of consciousness after Pisti's death, we were not aware of the scope of other people's experiences. Yet our visions consistently reflected the emergence of a new planetary consciousness. In one experience István said that

> *Pisti told me that consciousness on the earth is going through a powerful transformation. He said that there is now enough energy on the earth, that is, love and longing for love, to hold the beam of light that is coming—whatever that means. I understood it in the dream. What I do remember is that light is energy that is conscious and loving, but it was more than that. Pisti also said that the new child of the human species will have another ring of DNA. Maybe that was a symbol, some way to tell me that the children of the future will be born knowing what we are struggling to understand. I felt that if we can heal ourselves, we can give them this gift.[9]*

Elisabeth Kübler-Ross, a psychiatrist who worked with many men, women, and children who had Near-Death Experiences, knew very well that such experiences were real and increasing during our time. She herself had such an experience that, like Bucke's, was *not* triggered by death. In her case it was triggered by a research project on out-of-body experiences. When she returned to her body, she had no memory of what had happened, but she did know that she had been healed of a bowel obstruction and a slipped disc. Those present described her as radiant and looking at least twenty years younger.[10]

But the next evening when she was alone in a guest-house in the Blue Ridge Mountains, she had an experience that changed her life. She felt she was literally experiencing the actual deaths of all her patients. While she desperately fought to endure the pain and agony of these deaths, she suddenly realized that all she needed to do was stop resisting and simply say *yes* to what was happening to her. The moment she did that, the pain disappeared and she stepped into another form of consciousness. She began to feel an intense vibration in her stomach that quickly spread throughout her body and then to the entire planet. The bud of a beautiful flower appeared and gradually opened to the light that her patients had so often talked about. As she approached and then entered this light, she became one with it. At that moment, everything stopped and she experienced a deep and pervasive silence. She felt a love so vast and so complete that she knew she would never be able to express it in words. She was in love with the universe, with everyone and every living thing. She later understood that she had experienced Cosmic Consciousness.[11]

Kübler-Ross was a true pioneer in challenging not only our cultural attitude about death and dying but the very nature of consciousness itself. She knew from her own experience that the kind of consciousness experienced by millions at death can be triggered by any number of situations. Or it can simply occur spontaneously. Like any pioneer researcher, she had to endure the criticism that comes with challenging a cultural worldview. But today there are medical doctors, psychiatrists, researchers, and experiencers around the world who are validating her conclusions and documenting the evidence.

Since there are so many documented cases of this kind of consciousness being triggered by death, it has been possible to establish the core experiences of the NDE, which are also the core experiences of the shamanic-visionary-mystic state or what Bucke and Kübler-Ross called cosmic consciousness. All of these experiences negate the old science story of a random universe without meaning or purpose. Most NDErs, like the other experiencers we have just observed, experience *a reality* of the most profound meaning and purpose for all existence. They perceive *a dazzling light*—a light that is totally conscious, loving, peaceful, and beautiful. There is no separation between the person and this light, which the individual realizes is the source of all life—of all that is. Many who experience this light as a state of being also experience it as a divine being who deeply loves and cares for them. One NDEr described a magnificent, formless Being of light and love whose very presence allowed her to experience "great waves of awareness." She understood life and death and experienced what she could only describe as bliss.[12]

Some call this light or being Jesus, God, Shekhinah, Allah, or whatever name they use for the divine. But this light is even more than a being; *it is the ground of all being*. One NDEr described his experience of realizing he was one with the light and that his existence on earth was only a brief moment. Some NDErs see brilliant, beautiful cities built of light, and they realize that the buildings are pure knowledge.[13] They are bathed in this radiant light that is love and consciousness, and they realize that they *are* this light—as is everything in the universe.

Most people experience powerful, supercharged emotions of joy, love, peace, oneness, reverence, awe, and ecstasy. There is an illumination of the deep meaning and purpose of the universe. And there is no longer a fear of death because they realize they are eternal. They can no longer see the world as empty material, for they now know that all matter is a manifestation of spirit. There is a deep sense of their own individual purpose when they return from these experiences, for many of them witnessed in their visions how we are destroying the earth out of our belief in the old story. They want everyone to know about this peaceful, loving consciousness. And after such an experience, they often appear radiant, and some develop extraordinary forms of psychic abilities.[14]

Those who have had such an experience stress that there is no way they can communicate what they have experienced. This is the case with all shamanic-mystic experience: *it must be experienced to be known.* Nevertheless, the experience is so profound and life-changing that there is almost always a sense of urgency to try to express their experiences the best they can. Such experience, says Ring, is "just the beginning of a long initiation into life's highest mysteries." It is *a legacy* that "can be traced back to the secret ceremonies of antiquity." We lost these secret initiations when the Church closed the ancient Mystery Schools, but now the Mysteries are returning to us in the most unexpected ways. "NDErs themselves, then," says Ring, "should probably be regarded as one distinct stream feeding into a larger river, with many tributaries, of spiritually transformative experience." When we look at these many ways people are now experiencing other-dimensional worlds, Ring suggests that they may "collectively represent an evolutionary thrust toward higher consciousness for humanity...."[15] Bucke would certainly agree.

Of course, there is the usual rejection of the possibility of Near-Death Experiences by some scientists. A rather recent study concluded that such experiences are "tricks of the mind triggered by an overload of carbon dioxide in the bloodstream." Even before this study, there were many people who dismissed such experiences as "tricks of the mind" that can occur at death. British neuropsychiatrist Peter Fenwick of the Institute of Psychiatry at King's College, London, disagrees: "The one difficulty in arguing that CO2 is the cause is that in cardiac arrests, everybody has high CO2 but only 10 percent have NDEs." The study, however, showed that the patients who had such experiences had significantly higher levels of CO2 than those who did not. But this is simply not an issue for Professor Fenwick since those persons who have a Near-Death Experience have "no coherent cerebral activity which could support consciousness, let alone an experience with the clarity of an NDE."[16] The brain is dead and yet there is a consciousness far superior to the waking brain.

To reduce phenomenal experiences to *nothing but* an overload of CO2 while ignoring brain death is another example of our addiction to limitations. This attitude reflects the typical disregard for *experience* of any kind but especially shamanic-mystic experience. It disregards the radical changes in the people who have had such experiences, as well as the verifiable events NDErs have experienced around them and in other parts of the world while brain dead. Of course, scientific studies should be done, but an effort should be made to acknowledge *all the facts* relating to such a phenomenon. Luckily, some scientists are developing new methods of acknowledging and understanding such *experience*. An open mind to all aspects of the event being studied allows many unexpected pieces of the puzzle to appear, such as the fact that similar experiences occur — and are occurring in thousands of people around the world — who are not dead and who are not experiencing high levels of CO2.

Now let's consider **the intellectual discovery of the reality of the quantum field** and return for a moment to McTaggart's statement that the present revolution in science is so radical that it is shattering everything we thought to be real. What we have just observed as the core experiences of the NDEr-shaman-mystic mind are certainly experiences of the "miraculous" realities of the universe. The scientist is *observing* the universe from without and the shaman-mystic is *experiencing* the same universe from within. Now let's look at descriptions of this reality from the scientist's *outer observational perspective*.

The quantum field is a vast, eternal sea of vibrating energy—"a quantum sea of light." All life exists and breathes within this infinite, indivisible, self-regenerating, interconnected, and inexhaustible sea of energy in which everything is related and in constant communication with everything else. It is "a state of pure potential, of infinite possibility." Within this field, which contains all fields, each person and all matter in the universe are connected to everything in the cosmos. This means that every aspect of the universe is capable of being immediately in touch with every other aspect. Even our own minds function according to the principles of the quantum field: every thought and feeling is a result of information from the quantum field flowing through our bodies. At its most basic level consciousness itself is "coherent light."[17]

The quantum field encodes and records everything that has ever happened in the universe, and its ability to encode and record is infinite. Thus, we have the *memory* of the universe. This field is "the ultimate holographic blueprint" of the universe throughout time.[18] Systems theorist, Ervin László, calls the quantum field and its memory system the Akashic-field, a term used for thousands of years in the East for just such a field.

As mentioned earlier, the belief in nothing but a material reality is negated by the discovery that "there aren't two fundamental physical entities—something material and another immaterial—but only one: energy."[19] "Quantum physics," says physicist Fred Alan Wolf, "shows us that matter is how spirit appears in the physical universe."[20] And, says physicist Amit Goswami, it is *this eternal sea of consciousness* that creates the universe. Modern science, he says, is creating a new paradigm that "validates an ancient idea—the idea that consciousness, not matter, is the ground of all being."[21]

Shaman-mystics also call this field the Ground of Being, as well as the Divine Matrix, Cosmic Consciousness, Universal Mind, Akashic Records, Spirit, the Source, the Web, or God. As mentioned earlier, shaman-mystics and NDErs have described this field as *dazzling light*—a light that is totally conscious, loving, peaceful, and beautiful—the source of all that is. And they experience themselves as this light. We are both the observer of this field and the field itself. No longer can we think of ourselves as isolated minds observing a universe we have no ability to influence. For we now know that even our act of observation affects the field.

I once had a visionary experience of this field as it imaged itself forth as an infinite, cosmic web of silvery light. Each time I breathed, it breathed. When I stopped breathing, it stopped. I could do nothing that wasn't simultaneously reflected in this beautiful web. In those moments, I experienced how intimately and completely we *are* the field, the web, the matrix. We are all a part of one vast, eternal, creative field of love and consciousness. *We can do nothing but create.* This is what the field teaches us.

The scientific *discovery* of this dimension of reality with all its implications is truly the beginning of "the science of the miraculous."[22] And the *experience* of this reality by shaman-mystics and scientists alike is always "a journey to the miraculous." Now, in our time, the rational, left-brain understanding of this dimension is merging with the mystical, right-brain and beyond-the-brain experience of this field, the ground of all being.

When I began my journey, I didn't really know how to go about discovering whether or not life actually had a story of meaning and purpose—and I had no idea if or how such a story could be verified. But what I discovered was that my *intention* activated the path to discovery and experience. And while experience is enough for some, for those of us addicted to the old story, the new science is giving us the ability to verify and rationally understand at least some of the miracles we are experiencing along the way.

Chapter Four

> *The evolution of the universe is "a single energy event" that is both physical and spiritual: everything in the universe is a manifestation of the same energy as in the Big Bang. This energy has "its own deep aim" and we are a part of that aim.*[1]
> — **Brian Swimme**

There is no way we can overestimate what these two revolutions in spiritual experience and scientific discovery mean for the earth and all life on our planet. Yet there are two major forces that inhibit our conscious participation in these complementary revolutions: (1) our addiction to the old story and (2) a lack of awareness of the existence of these two revolutions. The world we live in makes it difficult for people to become aware of them and their implications. Millions of men, women, and children around the world are experiencing the violent consequences of our old worldview and have little or no time to focus on such matters. And those living in peaceful and relatively prosperous areas also have difficulty becoming aware of this emerging new worldview because the media, education, religion and other institutions for the most part still reflect the old structures—the old interpretation of reality that has solidified into belief and doctrine. And, as mentioned earlier, even those scientists doing the breakthrough research often do not see—and do not have the time to try to see—the larger implications of their own work.[2]

Time always seems to play a role of *interference* in our desire to know anything about our world. We have to work to survive, shop for groceries, cook, clean, sleep — and we want to spend what little time remains with our children and others we love. Exploring inner and outer worlds begins to look like an unobtainable luxury. However, in spite of our lack of time and our cultural tendency to remain on the surface of life, we cannot avoid being aware of at least some of the violence in the world.

Unfortunately, there are people in relatively peaceful countries, such as the States, who tend to think of the source of this violence as being in *other* countries, in *other* groups of people, and they fail to *see* or *know* our own shadow side. Yet it is precisely through this knowledge of our own darkness that we can change and grow. Many people feel fear and helplessness in response to this violence while others cling rigidly to the old worldview that offers comfort in its familiarity and limits. This inability to release the old story results in many forms of fundamentalism. Whether in science or religion or politics, fundamentalism is perhaps best understood as one of the deepest forms of our addiction to the story. This frame of mind does not welcome evidence of a spiritual or scientific revolution.

Yet there are many others who do long for change and a deeper understanding of themselves and their world, for they know that at this moment in our history *time* is playing an even more powerful role in our urgent *need* to know. We are beginning to realize that our limited understanding of the world has let loose an avalanche of destruction and suffering that threatens everything we have ever valued. Our lives, the lives of our children, and the *quality* of life for everyone and everything on our planet depend on this sacred knowing.

The old worldview would have us believe that we are powerless to change ourselves or our world. But the new worldview, supported by scientists and shaman-mystics alike, reveals the creative power of our every thought and feeling. *We can do nothing but create.* This means that each one of us plays a role in creating the reality we are experiencing and that each one of us has an opportunity to play a role in transforming our worldview and shaping our future. In fact, during times of chaos such as our own when the very foundations of the dominant story about reality are being shattered, the potential power of each individual is greatly increased. László states it this way, "When a human society reaches the limits of its stability, it becomes supersensitive and is highly responsive to the smallest fluctuation. Then the system responds even to subtle changes in values, beliefs, worldviews, and aspirations."[3]

It is an astounding fact that, just when we are most pressed to change, we are discovering—through the complementary work of both the scientist and the shaman-mystic—so many things about ourselves that have the potential to change us radically. We are gradually awakening to the fact that we are involved in a story far larger than our own individual lives or even the combined lives of our species. This does not reduce our significance but vastly expands it, for we are an integral part of the story of our universe. Yes, our universe has a story, a vast and evolving story. And, as a part of this story, we are also evolving.

Historically, the human discovery of our physical evolution has gradually been merging with the shamanic-mystic knowledge of our spiritual evolution. Once again, it is the same story: scientists tell the evolution story from the outer, physical perspective and the shaman-mystics tell the story from the inner, spiritual perspective. Since quantum physics teaches us that matter and spirit are one, these two perspectives are now beginning to merge in human consciousness. Mathematical cosmologist Brian Swimme has made a significant contribution to our understanding of these merging perspectives through his own scientific work and by showing us how the Western thinker Pierre Teilhard de Chardin and the Eastern mystic Sri Aurobindo—even before the implications of quantum physics were known—had both arrived at the same comprehensive vision: *the vast unfolding of the universe is at once both a physical and a spiritual evolution.*[4]

Swimme relates how Teilhard saw the human discovery of the story of evolution as the most significant shift that has occurred in human consciousness.[5] In that moment the human species became aware that the universe was up to something—and that we were a part of that something. However, in the West our earlier understanding of this evolving story was limited to the physical in a way that "ripped the heart and soul out of the universe" and made the story completely unacceptable to some and tragically wounding to everyone.[6]

Thankfully, the discovery of quantum physics has resulted in an awareness of multiple dimensions of reality that are intimately interrelated to and accessible by human consciousness. This knowledge is bringing the heart and soul back into the universe and is allowing the vast new story of our spiritual evolution to emerge. And, as discussed earlier, "the universe," in Swimme's words, is "a single energy event" that is both physical and spiritual: everything in the universe is a manifestation of the *same energy* as in the Big Bang. This energy has "its own deep aim" and we are a part of that aim. In fact, we *are* the universe in the form of a human being. This discovery is so profound that Swimme thinks it will probably take the rest of the twenty-first century for us to really take it in. Yet, he says, "This is the greatest discovery of the scientific enterprise: you take hydrogen gas, and you leave it alone, and it turns into rosebushes, giraffes, and humans.... The point is that if humans are spiritual, then hydrogen's spiritual."[7]

Since the material universe, human consciousness, creativity, and feeling—including our ability to love—have their roots in the quantum field, it can no longer be said that the world or the human being is a *fluke* of nature. We are a completely natural expression of the Big Bang, or as Alan Watts used to love to say, we are a "symptom" of the earth. And because our consciousness is rooted in the quantum field or Universal Mind, the same organizing principles or laws that operate in nature also operate in human consciousness. The importance of this cannot be overemphasized. This was the perspective of Haridas Chaudhuri when he said that we need a worldview that can show us "how our deepest aspirations are related to the essential structure of the universe."[8] Once we realize the relationship between the individual mind and the universe, we can begin to understand that our deepest longings are also the deepest longings of the universe unfolding through us.

By the late 1700s the German poet Goethe had tapped into this shaman-mystic tradition in the form of Alchemy and was not only able to rationally understand but to experience the creative relationship between nature and human consciousness. He was well aware, before Darwin, of the dynamic tendency in nature to evolve—and he knew that this tendency manifested itself as "a single energy event" in all life forms. He understood that the laws of nature organize energy and manifest themselves in all the various forms of nature, including human consciousness, art, and our deepest aspirations.

His method of studying nature and consciousness was both scientific and shamanic: he studied everything in relationship to the particular form he chose to observe; then he *looked* at the form in a state of deep focus and contemplation. This for Goethe was the focusing of all one's forces, the intellect, feeling, intuition, and senses, to "a fine point of concentration"—a method that culminated in the meeting of nature and human consciousness. This meeting of mind and matter was the creative moment that released to the mind's focused view of outer structure the vision of inner form.[9]

Goethe knew that the outer shape or form of an object and its inner organizing principles were completely reciprocal: the outer shape was "an area of extreme sensitivity comprising the terminal points of some of the most inward-reaching systems of the organism, points at which they make contact with the environment."[10] What a different view of ourselves we could have if we understood this better: our human form is the outer shape—the sensitive terminal points—of the deep organizing principles of life emanating out of the quantum field—the field of light and love and consciousness. We are the field and the field lives in us and through us.

Goethe's method was what Wolf would call a "physics of spirit" since Goethe also understood that "matter is how spirit appears in the physical universe."[11] When Goethe observed the outer, material structure of form, he was able to *see* the inner, intelligent organizing forces of spirit. He also understood that when the individual mind *recognizes* this spiritual process in nature, there is a spontaneous awareness that *recognition* is possible only because the same spiritual process is at work in one's own mind. Individual human consciousness recognizes itself in the mirror of Universal Mind/the Quantum Field/the Light. This is an experience of the *sacred*.

Mircea Eliade, historian of religion, has defined the experience of the sacred as the recognition of that which is "irreducibly real." To experience the intelligent organizing forces of spirit as they shape themselves into an infinite diversity of material forms, including one's self, is definitely an experience that is "irreducibly real."[12] However, most of us would not describe our experience of the sacred in such a conceptual way because the sacred is experienced as *feeling*. It is the felt consciousness of the heart.

When we love deeply and unconditionally or when we intuit the presence of love, protection, or guidance from an unknown source, we know we are experiencing something we could call sacred. When the physical world responds to us in a way that we cannot explain within the framework of a materialistic worldview, or when someone we love telepathically communicates with us from around the world or even after death, we know these experiences are "irreducibly real." Even though our culture has denied and repressed their reality, these are the experiences, however large or small, that give our lives meaning and purpose. "Consciousness of a real and meaningful world," says Eliade, "is intimately connected with the discovery of the sacred."[13]

The study of human consciousness around the world reflects what Aldous Huxley calls the perennial philosophy and what Eliade calls "the profound and indivisible unity of the history of the human mind": throughout the world human consciousness has discovered the sacred and has created "inexhaustible" forms for its expression.[14] We might ask what these inexhaustible forms are all about. In the course of Bucke's research, he realized that as soon as the human species had achieved self-consciousness, there was a strong intuition or premonition, and we now know in some cases actual experience, of yet "another and higher consciousness...many millenniums in the future...."[15] This perspective helps us to understand that the sacred images and rituals around the world are evidence of this intuition, premonition, or experience: through these inexhaustible forms we are calling this higher/cosmic consciousness to ourselves.

The sole exception, of course, is modern Western culture, which has, says Eliade, completely camouflaged this experience of the sacred.[16] It isn't that people in the Western world have not experienced the sacred. They have, but without cultural understanding and acknowledgment, the sacred cannot sustain a vital cultural expression. The major religions of the West emerged out of profound experiences of the sacred—or as Bucke would say, *cosmic consciousness*—but their institutional forms have, for the most part, forced individual experience of the sacred into doctrines of limitation and obligation.

Now, however, as we have seen, things are changing. With so many people from different walks of life experiencing and daring to express the sacred, the old Western worldview is being shattered—and science is providing a conceptual framework for understanding this dimension of human experience. Eliade has said that the sacred "is an element in the structure of consciousness."[17] Perhaps it would now be clearer to say that to experience the "sacred" is to experience the very *nature* of consciousness itself.

We are self-conscious beings evolving toward cosmic consciousness. When we think how transformative even a few moments can be in this dimension of consciousness, we realize that we cannot even begin to fathom what it would be like to actually achieve that state permanently. Bucke is correct in saying that this consciousness will probably take thousands of years for our species to achieve, but once we *know* that we are part of a vast and creative purpose in the universe, everything changes. Our vision clears, our addictions dissolve, and we begin to discover and create true stories about who we are and why we're here. When this happens, the *path* is as sacred as the *goal*.

Swimme is surely one of the great storytellers of our time. He tells the story of our universe, of its physical and spiritual evolution, and of the crucial role we humans are now being called to play in this universe story. The human being, says Swimme, is the result of fourteen billion years of cosmological evolution—we really are born out of the stars. There was one time only, Swimme tells us, when galaxies could form. This, he says, is like the moment in which we humans now find ourselves. This is *our moment* at the crossroads when we can make a choice to align our own creativity with the deep creativity of our planet. This is the moment that our planet—*through us*—can awaken to "its own deep aim." Like the galaxies, it couldn't happen before and probably can't happen afterwards because, says Swimme, without *our* transformation, we and the planet would probably be in too degraded a state to pull it off.[18]

But in this moment, it is our call. We have a choice: we can choose to evolve or we can choose to self-destruct. We can choose to be a conscious and creative partner with the universe or we can choose to live our lives in such a way that we eventually self-destruct. Is it possible to grasp even for a moment the magnitude of our role at this time on this planet? Is it possible for us to really know that what we do matters and it matters to all life on earth? All of the great spiritual traditions of the world agree that we have the freedom, the "opportunity," in Gregg Braden's words, "to be imprisoned or free," and only we can make this choice.[19] Swimme emphasizes that the very evolution of our planet is unfolding through the consciousness of the human being: "it is the decisions of humans that are going to determine the way this planet functions and looks for hundreds of millions of years in the future."[20]

This is our opportunity—*our moment*—to release ourselves from the prison of our addictive belief in the Western story of negation, a story that we now know is tragically inaccurate and destructive. Scientists, shaman-mystics, and, if we will allow it, our own individual experiences will *open the way* for us to awaken to our true stories—stories that are worthy of the universe and our role in its vast creativity.

It is now our *sacred opportunity* to become masters of a new story.

Chapter Five

In the Gospel of Thomas found in the Nag Hammadi texts, Jesus teaches us to go within to develop what is within us. If we do not allow what is within us to develop, it will destroy us.[1]

To become masters of a new story—our story—we must go within. The wisdom of our ancestors is clear about this: if we do not take the journey inward to discover who we are, the creative potential within us will implode and we will destroy ourselves and the world. We can ignore this, deny this, repress this, but the organizing principles of the human psyche remain the same. Even when we are fortunate enough to have a brief experience of cosmic consciousness or to have profound dreams, visions, Near-Death Experiences or shamanic journeys, we still must integrate these experiences as we continue on our own unique path of growth and development.

Unfortunately, most people know very little about the human psyche or that it actually does organize its activities according to the principles of healing, growth, development—and evolution. Each of us has this creative energy within us, but at a given point it needs our awareness of its principles and our conscious cooperation for further development to occur. We all know that the physical body functions according to its own organizing principles and that if we ignore these principles, we become sick. It is to our great detriment that we do not have this awareness when it comes to our own inner development. The basic principles for the development of the psyche were lost in the West and we live every day with the results: *what we have not brought forth is destroying us.*

It is surprising for many people to learn that knowledge of these principles lies deep in the roots of Western culture. In fact, we will see that it was the knowledge of these principles that ignited the development of our culture in the first place. Just as Bucke discovered in his research, it was those persons who had experienced cosmic consciousness who not only had been at the heart of the world's great religions but who had seeded civilization itself. Through their knowledge of both the inner and the outer worlds they were able to blaze a path for all of us toward greater consciousness and creativity in time and space.

How could we lose this knowledge that is so vital to our survival? How was the major religion in the West able to shift the emphasis away from each person's sacred journey toward this greater consciousness and place that emphasis onto worshiping one person who had already achieved it?

As mentioned earlier, this book will attempt to answer these questions, for it is now clear that the present worldview was forged out of the denial and repression of this essential wisdom. Repeatedly, this knowledge rose to the surface of consciousness, but it was feared, rejected, denied, and repressed. Now, however, the wasteland of our denial has imperiled the entire world—a world that is urgently asking us to bring forth what is within *us.*

But just how do we do this? First, it is important for us to know that if nature requires that we bring forth what is within us, then nature has developed a way for us to do this. In spite of our own culture's conscious effort and unconscious compulsion to attract and hold our attention to the surface of life, each of us has an energy system that can and will respond to our *intention* to descend into the roots of our deepest nature to discover these principles. The response of the human psyche to this intention is *to release energy that structures our own personal path of descent and return.*

In the very moment of our choice we activate the laws of nature that support and guide our journey. Now it is up to us to stay focused on our intention and to be attentive and responsive to everything that appears on our path. *The structure of the path* is the oldest, most pervasive and inclusive structure known, yet it is a path that unfolds for each of us in our own individual and creative way.

This natural structure is *the labyrinth*: a circle that spirals inward toward a center and then outward to a return. It is both temporal and eternal, spatial and infinite since its movement circles around a central axis that exists on multiple planes of being. Once we choose to *know* who we are, the circle reveals an opening so we can *enter* with conscious *intention*.

We need to stop for a moment to review and simply ponder the miracle of this reality. Just as we have a *blueprint* for our physical growth and development, we also have a *blueprint* for our mental and spiritual development. We know that our physical blueprint contains the design for our complete physical development. This is equally true of our blueprint for spiritual development: it urges us to choose a path of completeness and wholeness. Our spiritual blueprint, however, requires our conscious creativity and participation.

When we do consciously choose this path, the blueprint rolls out before us as a unique and individual guide to this wholeness. Yet it is more. Since its central axis exists on multiple planes of being, its circular energy manifests in our time and space and simultaneously in eternal and infinite dimensions. As we move along our path, we discover that this blueprint is an energetic organizing system that is alive and loving and desirous of a relationship with us. This relationship requires consciousness and this is precisely what our labyrinthine journey is structured to bring about.

Its energy can take any form it needs to attract and beckon us into the next stage of our development. We have encountered this energy in the form of the animals, godmothers, wicked stepmothers and stepsisters, jealous brothers, daemons, trees and magical stones of fairy tales and dreams; the goddesses and gods of world mythologies; the fairy folk of Celtic cultures; the angelic light beings of religious lore; the circular images of flying objects peopled with otherworldly beings; and the beautiful circular designs in crops throughout the world. The particular form this energy takes has a direct relationship to our own psychic state as well as to our conscious ability or predisposition to perceive it.

Since we in the West lost the knowledge of this blueprint for wholeness, our ability to perceive its activity has atrophied. For centuries, we have seen very little of real value in these energy forms that were once powerful partners in our evolution. If and when we encounter them in dreams, waking visions, or even in outer events, we tend to deny them or dismiss them as meaningless.

Even when we acknowledge our dreams as significant, it is extremely difficult for us to understand them as the manifestation of intelligent principles of organization. We usually think of them as *just* images and symbols that could *perhaps* be used by the conceptual mind to help us understand a particular situation in our life. But seldom have we been able to fully realize that these images and symbols are actually the outer forms of our inner state. We forget that the laws of nature have organized our psychic energy into these forms to reflect back to us our particular situation and to engage us more deeply in our journey.

While this energy that manifests itself in images and symbols reflects our inner reality, it also has an outer reality. Sometimes our particular situation is reflected back to us in dreams or visions but sometimes it is reflected back to us in the outer world as events in time and space. And there is more. Since this energy is multidimensional, it organizes itself into images and symbols that are also the actual forms of other dimensions of reality. Because our worldview has limited our vision to the material world, we don't usually even perceive these forms, but if and when we do, we are usually pressured by our culture to deny their existence or to reduce them to *just* images and symbols. And thus, we are unable to realize that these Other worlds — or deeper orders of reality — actually exist.

In her book, *Songlines of the Soul*, Veronica Goodchild describes these other worlds as existing "both within the body spatially and outside it as a separate location in the cosmos." This is the subtle world: it is not exactly spirit or matter but rather it exists "somewhere in-between the purely intellectual world of angelic intelligences and the sensible world of material things and participates in both." In an interesting anecdote concerning the reality of these other worlds, Goodchild tells about an experience Edwin Bernbaum, who wrote *The Way to Shambhala*, had with the Dalai Lama. When Bernbaum "inadvertently suggested to the Dalai Lama that it [Shambhala] might be only an imaginary or immaterial paradise of the mind, he [the Dalai Lama] immediately replied, 'No, definitely not: Shambhala has a material existence in this world.'" The Dalai Lama did not go into detail about the exact nature of Shambhala, but he made it clear that it does exist.[2]

All of these images and symbolic realities can appear on our path as we journey to the center of our wholeness. If we can refrain from denying their reality and allow ourselves to be open to these powerful forms of energy, love, and consciousness, we will be transformed. However, most of us have difficulty accepting and relating to the reality of these symbolic energy forms, and this is resulting in serious consequences. Our failure to become conscious of the enormity of who we are is far more destructive than our culture has been able to acknowledge.

Fortunately, in Western culture this wisdom did not entirely disappear: it has always existed just below the level of consciousness and has thus been able to emerge into consciousness from time to time. These were the great periods in Western culture of remembering and creating — and we will explore these periods later. But for now one such period was at the end of the Hellenistic age and the beginning of the Christian era: Jesus himself was a part of this resurgence of the ancient wisdom and that is why in the Gospel of Thomas he could say, "If you bring forth what is within you, what you bring forth will save you. If you do not bring forth what is within you, what you do not bring forth will destroy you."[3]

But the knowledge of this Jesus was forced underground and was only rediscovered after World War II. The story of our discovery of these rejected truths precisely when we so desperately needed them is in itself a strange and miraculous tale that we will look at later. But, again, just for now, we need to look at the path we took when we lost this ancient wisdom.

As a culture, we no longer valued the path of direct inner experience. We forgot about the labyrinthine journey of the soul that beckoned to each of us. Its spiraling image became just another empty decorative form. As we devalued the symbolic, visionary mind, we focused exclusively on developing the conceptual, rational mind. We even began to believe that we had evolved beyond the symbolic and mystical modes of experience—and thus we lost the techniques, the paths, to direct inner experience. And then we even lost the memory that they had ever existed.

The development of conceptual, logical thinking cannot be overvalued, but neither should its dangers be underestimated when it is split off from its roots in the older brain components that allow us, in the words of Stanley Krippner, "to symbolize, mythologize and, eventually, to shamanize."[4] This split has been so severe that most of us were able to accept the view that we had evolved beyond those portions of our brain that released the blueprint for our growth and development through dreams, symbols, myths, feeling and intuition. Our focus on rational development became so specialized that we were no longer able to understand our ancestors for whom *nothing was more important than developing a sensitivity to nature and to the dreaming, mythic mind, so they could live in harmony with the "deep aim" of the universe.*

They understood that nature manifested its aim in the organizing principles of all life forms and that the human mind had the ability to experience these sacred principles. Until recently we have not been able—nor have most of us considered it very important—to understand the clues about ourselves that our ancestors left us in their stories, rituals, and art. And many of us still do not value our own dreams and visions.

Yet dreams, visions, fairy tales, rituals, myths, and sacred art reflect and *activate* the creative, organizing principles of our blueprint for spiritual growth and development. They are the *sacred texts* of the human psyche that speak to us, comfort us, and guide us on our labyrinthine journey. Think of the many fairy tales that take the young boy or girl through a dark forest journey with challenges to confront and problems to resolve. There are often extreme difficulties, but there are also helpers along the way.

This is beautifully reflected in Russian fairy tales when the person who is journeying through the dark labyrinthine forest periodically meets Baba Yaga, the wise old woman, the Great Mother, the shamaness of the soul. It is she who comforts and guides the initiate during each phase of the journey. And as the initiate leaves the comfort and guidance of Baba Yaga in order to continue the difficult journey, the old woman throws out a ball with the instructions to follow it wherever it goes. Sometimes it is a ball of thread that magically unwinds as it creates the path toward the desired destination. There could hardly be a more compelling symbol of the presence and willingness of the source of all life to roll out before us and guide us on our path.

When we do not take this journey to bring forth what is within us, we really do forget who we are and why we're here—and the world fills with darkness that no one claims. We find ourselves believing that this is simply the way life is. But it isn't. We *can* change the world by changing ourselves, and we change ourselves by distilling our own personal darkness into light. We do not have to claim the darkness of the world, but we do have to claim our own darkness. Several years ago, when I was thinking about the urgency of this work for myself and the world, I had the following vision:

> *My perspective is from outer space so that I can see the sphere of the earth. As I move closer, I see a huge cauldron at the North Pole. Gradually I realize that Pisti, my son who had died one year earlier, is there as a jackal man with other jackal men. Together they are stirring the contents of the cauldron and working feverishly to keep them in the cauldron so they will not spill out and cover the earth with disaster. Pisti looks at me and says, "The time is critical." I ask Pisti what was in the cauldron, and all the jackals answer at once, "Shit. Unclaimed shit." They are serious and yet jovial. I understand very well that the work of each of us is to claim our own "shit" from the cauldron. Had each of us acknowledged our own darkness on a daily basis, it would not have been forced into the collective cauldron that now threatens the life of the planet. We are being called to distill*

> *our own personal darkness into light. I feel the acute urgency of this work for myself and for our planet, but, at the same time, I also feel the powerful transformative potential for each of us if we can acknowledge our own darkness and begin the work of distilling it into light.*[5]

The journey that each of us chooses to take is a distillation of our own personal darkness, but this darkness is always connected to our cultural and planetary darkness. In fact, we usually begin our journey by trying to understand the darkness we see outside ourselves. Some see it first in the family; others see it first in the culture. When we look around the world today at the unbearable suffering and violence, we cannot avoid seeing a world that has lost its way in the depths of its own darkness. Each of us becomes conscious of this at different times and in our own way. For me it was World War II. I was almost five years old when my brother and I were listening to Gene Autry on the radio one Sunday afternoon. We heard a strange voice interrupt the show and announce the bombing of Pearl Harbor. I had no way of knowing what those words meant. There was no television then, and I don't think I had yet seen a movie, so I had no images of destruction to connect with bombing. We were promptly sent out to play and only later was it explained that the world was at war—whatever that could possibly mean. All I could even begin to understand was that it was the adults who were fighting. Over and over I questioned my mother about this, but of course no answer could take away the fact that it was the *adults* who were in trouble.

Since I was not in a country where the war was taking place, my initial questions sank below the level of consciousness. This changed when I was a little older and my brother and I were allowed to go to the movies on Saturday afternoons. It was there that I *saw* the news about the war. I didn't understand the reports, but the images of killing and destruction let loose a deep disturbance. This too sank just below the level of consciousness but would rise to the surface of my mind from time to time as a need for something I couldn't name. Later it would express itself as a feeling of emptiness and then the *fear* that death would take away the people I loved and leave me in an empty and lonely world like the images in the news.

During my college years I read extensively about the war, especially as it had been experienced by individuals caught up in its brutality and violence. Now the familiar disturbance surfaced in an overwhelming *fear* that life itself was random and without meaning or purpose. Everything in me resisted this possibility. I knew that there was always meaning and purpose in love, but this knowledge only intensified my fear of the deaths of those I loved.

I had now been initiated into the *story* of the Western world — and I would learn that this was the story of a spiritual *wasteland* that would either destroy us or force us to become masters of a new story. Of course, I was aware that the possibility of creating a new story depended on my rejection of life as random, without meaning or purpose. I would have to work from the premise that we are the result of an intelligent universe in which there are laws that organize and regulate our growth and development. When our species periodically negated these laws and fell into the brutal and unintelligent destruction of itself and other life forms, then such behavior could be considered an illness — and we would be justified in looking for a cure.

Yet I was haunted by the Western story of an empty, meaningless universe. If the universe really were a random accident without meaning or purpose, then a *wasteland* would be as natural as any other random event. And what I was calling illness would be nothing more than the random result of a nature that had no meaning or purpose.

This was the dilemma that landed me in the depths of the dark labyrinthine forest. I desperately needed Baba Yaga to throw out before me the magical ball of thread to guide me on my path. Of course, at that time I knew nothing of Baba Yaga, fairy tales, myths, spirals, or labyrinths — **and I knew nothing of the profound spiritual journey out of which Western culture had emerged and repeatedly repressed.** All of that would come later.

But the ball of thread did appear before me: in my senior year of college I dated a young man who had just completed his seminary training at Andover Newton. One evening he invited me, along with several of his classmates, to a party in his new parish home. They talked for hours about mathematics, physics, and the Swiss psychiatrist, Carl Jung. I listened. After everyone had left, I asked my friend about Jung. He took me into his library where I found Jung's *Modern Man in Search of a Soul* and *The Undiscovered Self*.

Well, I certainly was in search of my soul—if there was such a thing. Soul for me meant meaning and purpose not only in my life but also in the life of the universe. I could not bear to live in an empty, random world. And from what I was able to observe, neither could anyone else. Of course, we don't always realize what is missing, yet we all know that we are happier when we love and are loved and when we are able to fulfill ourselves by giving our unique gifts to others. And we are even more fulfilled and happy when we realize that our lives and work are an intimate and significant part of the larger meaning and purpose of the universe.

As a psychiatrist who had worked with thousands of patients, Jung was in a position to witness the illness that results from the loss of soul—or, in other words, the loss of meaning and purpose. During World War II he witnessed how this loss of soul had exploded into a collective darkness. We had failed to bring forth what was within us, and we were destroying ourselves and the world. Jung understood very well that nothing was more important for our health and survival than bringing forth what is within us by distilling our darkness into light. He also knew that this could not be done "by imagining figures of light, but by making the darkness conscious."[6]

As I read Jung, there were so many things I didn't know or understand, but what I did understand was that Jung was profoundly conscious of our spiritual and cultural wasteland. He asked the necessary questions and appeared to be willing to go anywhere for the answers. It would take a lifetime of study and experience for me to realize the magnitude of what Jung had discovered.

Only later would I know that he had spent his life attempting to understand our spiritual and cultural darkness through the dreams and visions of his patients and himself as well as the dream and visionary artifacts of our culture's past. He "opened the way" for us to acknowledge and understand those periods in Western culture when we re-membered and attempted to integrate our own ancient wisdom. By deciphering this ancient language of the soul as it spoke through dreams, visions, fairy tales, myths, and repressed underground traditions, such as Alchemy, Gnosticism, the Hermetic arts, and Kabbalah, he was able to reconstruct the lost, denied, and repressed blueprint for our mental and spiritual development.

And so it was in Jung that I found someone who had made the descent into his own personal and cultural darkness. By the time I discovered him, he was nearing the completion of his life and work. He had made his journey to the center of the labyrinth, and he had discovered a path to a new story for the Western world—*a story that was deeply rooted in our own history and in nature itself.* Not only did he become a master of this new story, but he also bequeathed to us a profound knowledge of Baba Yaga's guiding threads.

As I began to pick up these threads and plunge into these lost dimensions of soul, I had the following dream:

> *It is evening and I am in a dark forest. I am standing outside in the darkness of the night, and I am knocking on the door to Jung's study. As Jung opens the door, I see that he is dressed in a long, ruby-red silk gown; his hair is silver. The space is luminous around Jung and the books. The study is made of beautiful wood and the shelves are filled with very old books, many bound in leather. He invites me in, and as I attempt to enter, I trip, fly through the air and land on my belly on the floor of his study.*
>
> *In the next scene Jung and I are outside on his cement patio. The dark and light of the earlier part of the dream seem now to have merged into a kind of predawn gray. We are seated right on the edge of the cement as it gently curves out and back in to form a graceful patio that borders the wild growth of*

> the prehistoric world. There are gigantic prehistoric animals and vegetation living right at the edge of the cement of our modern world. Jung and I are discussing something, and we both seem to feel that the simultaneous existence of these two time zones is natural.

This dream certainly did reflect my reality at that time: I existed within my own darkness of unknowing, but I was seeking guidance. The door was opened and I was invited in. Jung made his appearance as the wise old Alchemist—something I knew nothing of at the time. I would later learn that the ruby-red color of his gown is called the rubedo in Alchemy, the color of the fire that intensifies the process of transformation. Finding Jung's work did intensify my own journey. This intensity was reflected by my loss of balance as I crossed the threshold from my world into the far more powerful energy field that Jung and his library symbolized. Of course, my arrival into this realm on my belly also reflected my own feeling of inadequacy. But I showed up, and I was determined to learn.

The next scene was more comfortable. The learning had begun. Jung and I sat together in mutual respect at the very edge of civilization. Jung knew that the answer to our loss of soul was connected to our severing ourselves from nature—in the outer world as well as the inner world. The shamans of old are said to live, both literally and symbolically, on the border between the village and nature, for they must be receptive to both worlds. Nature in this dream appeared in its pristine form, uncorrupted and uncontrolled by civilization. This was the nature to which I must be receptive.

The scene includes other pairs of opposites to which I must also be receptive: the male and the female, the past and the present, the mixture of dark and light in the gray color of the scene. The juxtaposition in this dream of opposite worlds is particularly important for us in the Western world because our materialistic worldview is based on our devaluing and excluding one half of each of these pairs of opposites. This means that we have paralyzed large parts of who we are: we have devalued and brutalized nature—our larger body, repressed both the female and the feminine dimension of reality, repressed our own spiritual history and the language of soul, and avoided darkness and death. My dream placed me at the border between these pairs of opposites. My own personal work as well as the work of my culture was clearly revealed in this dream. I lacked balance when I entered this world, but I was shown in a general way how I might achieve it. I had above all to be *receptive* and *open* to all that had been repressed in my life and in the life of my culture.

Jung, like Goethe before him, recognized the relationship between the human mind and nature. He understood that the laws of nature organize energy that manifests in all the various forms of nature. *And throughout his life Jung observed how these laws organize energy within the human psyche and communicate to our conscious minds through the language of metaphor, symbol, story/myth, feeling, intuition, and even outer events.* When consciousness devalues the language of these laws of growth and development, we lose our path and are unable to achieve our full mental development. We are unable to bring forth what is within us.

World War II revealed just how far our culture had fallen from the natural laws that guide and nurture our development—and just how far we had fallen from what we wanted to believe about ourselves. Who were we anyway? We had believed that the development of the rational mind would free us to create a peaceful and rational world. Germany was held in high esteem as a representative of the rational world, yet Germany had fallen into barbarism. We would come to realize, however, that Germany was just the first to fall and that this same barbarism existed as a potential in every individual who had lost the vital connection with the natural laws of our own growth and development. Unfortunately, the Western world was filled with such individuals. It was only a matter of time until this psychic barbarism would erupt again—and again. We had lost our true stories and could no longer remember who we are or why we're here.

When the full scope of the barbarism of the war was revealed, a deep and pervasive disturbance penetrated the world psyche. For many this disturbance would intensify an already existing depression, addiction, despair, violence and fanaticism that had developed, at least in part, as a result of the failure of The Great War, World War I, to end all wars. Long before World War I, there emerged in Europe a pathological belief that war was, as Karen Armstrong explains, "a Darwinian necessity in which only the fittest would survive." So deeply and pervasively had we forgotten the sacred principles of our own growth and development that we were able to believe that the horrible nightmare of destruction would give birth to a new world whose soul had been purified.[7]

It is difficult to understand how anyone could think of war as a purifying process. Yet both sides of the conflict in Europe entered what they called The Great War with enthusiasm.[8] But when the war ended with the nations of Europe in ashes, almost thirty-eight million casualties, a generation of men destroyed, women and children killed, homes obliterated, and the seeds already sown for the next war, enthusiasm as well as the fantasies of purification and the survival of the fittest had been translated into a nihilistic despair.

World War II so deepened this despair that many would never recover. Whether we understood it or not, the world had witnessed the collective loss of soul. No one has said it better nor supported it more thoroughly than the journalist Robert Fisk in his thousand-page tome, *The Great War for Civilisation: The Conquest of the Middle East*. War, he says, is "the total failure of the human spirit."[9]

Our experience and sensibilities shape the degree to which we can truly comprehend Fisk's meaning, but on some level, we must all know that war reflects the failure of the human experiment. The actual meaning of soul and spirit is far less clear to us. We sense that they have something to do with treating others as we would want to be treated; with having an inclusive respect for all life; and with having an inner mental and emotional coherence as a foundation for our behavior. And this is true, but these words also have a long history and a depth of meaning in Western culture.

Soul and spirit are not separate realities, but rather they are polarities that have an underlying unity. Soul is the unique, individual consciousness in the visible, material world while spirit is the eternal, invisible Ground of All Being out of which the soul emerges and to which it returns.[10] It is important to remember that we do not have to *believe* in any religious doctrine for soul to reunite with its larger self in spirit, which is the Divine Matrix, the Universal Mind, the Quantum Field. But we do need to be open to *experience* this divine energy within us and to become sensitive to its language. By going within to develop a conscious relationship with spirit—the mind of the universe—we will be able to bring forth what is within us. For it is out of this conscious relationship that our own creativity blossoms and branches out into the world: this is what saves us and our planet.

Religion *should* be a guide for going inward and developing this relationship. As mentioned earlier, all three of the major Western religions, Christianity, Judaism, and Islam, developed out of just such an experience of going inward and relating to the Divine Matrix. But, unfortunately, as each became organized into a religion, the focus shifted from guiding the individual to experience the divine within to a doctrine of belief and worship of the divine without. *This shift robs us of the experience of our own divinity and makes it difficult, if not impossible, for us to bring forth what is within us.*

Chapter Six

One of the first major theorists of symbolic, mythic language, Giambattista Vico, understood that symbolic language is equal to conceptual language. Symbolic, mythic language, says Vico, is our first language: it is not irrational but possesses a poetic logic that gives birth to the logic of conceptual consciousness. The symbol cannot be reduced to the idea, nor can the idea be reduced to the symbol. The mind's wholeness depends on an integral and dynamic continuum of movement between the symbol and the idea.[1]

As indicated earlier, the human psyche, that is, soul rooted in spirit, communicates to human consciousness through the language of metaphor, symbol, story/myth, feeling, intuition, and even outer events. We have also observed that this communication is regulated, but not determined, by the laws of nature. These laws or principles of organization guide us toward wholeness by supporting and directing our own individual creativity. This *soul* language is activated when we need its guidance. This is true on both an individual and a cultural level. If enough people are at a similar crossroads at the same time, the individual dream will become a cultural myth. When this happens, there can be an intensification of the developmental process for the whole culture.

For example, somewhere around 40,000 BCE, what we now call the Stone Age, there was an overflowing of the human psyche on a collective level. This appears to have been a worldwide phenomenon, but the main areas of evidence that have been discovered to date are the rock paintings, figurines, and engravings in more than 350 caves in Europe and the millions of images painted and engraved on thousands of rock canvases in Africa. What, we wonder, was the human experience that activated this symbolic response? We will explore this question later.

But for now, it is important for us to recognize that these early images and symbols are not simply an interesting historical discovery. They reflect back to us a lost knowledge of the principles of our own development. And the first major principle is that our development and well-being depend on our knowledge of these laws and how to maintain harmony with them. Our ancestors knew that it was through their dreams, visions, stories, rituals, art, and even outer events that they were able to align themselves with these principles and maintain harmony within their culture. These symbolic forms carry frequencies that are *felt* on deep levels. We in the West have tended to devalue feelings, but our ancestors knew that profound, transformative wisdom is communicated through *feeling*.

Since we as a culture have allowed the connection to our deepest selves to decay, it is more often than not a crisis that opens us to this living language of soul. For example, after our son's death, my husband István had a visionary experience of what it means both to be in—and out of—harmony with these life principles. He had been experiencing dreams and visions of his own death. He told me that he was no longer afraid to die; he just did not *want* to die. Then came the vision that he was in fact dying—and he proceeded to fight it with all his strength. I tell about this in *The Miracle of Death*:

> *In this experience his fear and his resistance were laid bare before him.... Suddenly he became aware that Pisti was present when Pisti handed him a sword. When István asked him what the sword was all about, Pisti smiled and István immediately understood the humor in his battle against the very process of life itself. Yet István's fear remained. As his fear increased, he was engulfed in darkness and chaos.... Then he felt Pisti's finger on his back. A loving warmth began to*

> *flow into him through that one small spot:...."I heard Pisti's voice, 'Flow with the force. Relax and let yourself flow with it.' Then somehow I started to loosen up a bit. I focused on the warm spot on my back. As I felt that warm energy flow through my body, I was able to relax. Then I realized that my energy and the flow were the same."*
>
> *"I knew that my own fear had hardened me and solidified me and thrown me out of the flow. That's when the darkness and chaos came. My fear had separated me from my own energy and from the energy of the life force. I was fighting against myself. It was wasted energy. This force did not need to be fought or tested or proven. It just needed to be experienced.... I started to experience the power that was in the flow. It wasn't the kind of power you can possess, but you can flow with it and create with it. Suddenly, I thought, 'My God, I'm experiencing the force of pure creativity.' I was totally relaxed. I knew that the 'essence' of the whole thing is forever, so there is no perishing of anything.... All I had to do was flow with it and create out of it."*[2]

Who wouldn't want to try to stay connected and in harmony with this force? If someone had told István in conceptual language the essence of what he experienced, it would not have changed him. Absolutely nothing can substitute for the actual experience—gnosis—but we also need conceptual language to give expression to our experiences, to communicate them to ourselves and others, and to rationally explore their depths. We can see that even while István was inside the experience, he was simultaneously delineating in conceptual language what he was experiencing in the vision. For example, he *felt* and *knew* that (1) his energy and the energy of the life force, *the flow*, were the same; (2) his fear and resistance threw him out of the flow and into darkness and chaos; (3) love and trust through Pisti's touch allowed him to relax and enter the flow; (4) this power cannot be possessed, does not need to be resisted, fought, tested or proven. We just need to flow with it and create out of it; (5) it is the force of pure creativity; and (6) it is eternal.

After this experience, István and I continued to use conceptual language to talk about the power of love and how all who love are working with this life force and helping others to trust and flow with this force. Nothing could be more creative. Through our visions, both István and I realized that *love* is the energy of the flow; it is the heart of all creativity. I now understood why shamans would say that one of the first principles is to *trust* the universe.

Our ancestors had techniques for triggering this kind of experience. We will explore some of the oldest known techniques during our discussion of the Stone Age, but much later, in Celtic cultures, it was the responsibility of the bards, the *storytellers*, to maintain harmony in their culture by aligning themselves with these principles. They told stories about people, about tribes, about the universe. They understood that these stories were reflections of the spontaneous principles of the mind's growth and development. These bards were visionaries, musicians, and poets who maintained their attunement with the deep ordering principles of life through their dreams, visions, music, and poetry. Because they were in harmony with the Divine Matrix, the ground of consciousness, they were able to ignite or transmit this attunement to their listeners. The Celts knew that without this attunement their world would lose its *ordered* structure and become a *wasteland*.[3]

This is the knowledge that Western culture lost—*and we have become a wasteland*. We have forgotten that symbolic, mythic language is a natural mirror of the inner structure of the mind's ground of consciousness. And we have forgotten that symbols and myths not only *mirror* the depths of soul but they also *activate* the deep ordering principles within us: *they are our tuning system*.

As early as 1725 Giambattista Vico, one of the first major theorists of symbolic, mythic language, understood this creative potential in symbol and myth. Vico acknowledged that our early growth and development is spontaneous and pre-reflective until we develop reflective, conceptual consciousness. Vico's use of the term *pre-reflective* could be misleading unless we understand that Vico is referring to symbolic/mythic consciousness whose language is a natural expression of the organizing principles of the mind. In no way is it inferior to conceptual language. For example, in István's vision, his experience was symbolic, but his effort to probe deeper into its meaning was conceptual.

Both languages are important, necessary, and equal. The use of conceptual language allows us to make the historical journey back into our symbolic/mythic past to discover these spontaneous organizing principles of our mind's own development. We can discover these principles in the symbolic artifacts, including the rituals, music, art, dance, monuments, and the poetic-mythic documents that mirror back to us the deep roots of our consciousness. Vico was convinced that such documents "derive from and perfectly reflect the inner structure of the spontaneous consciousness."[4]

Both Vico and Jung made this historical journey to discover the early chapters of the story of the human mind. Vico called this journey *ricorso* and he envisioned it as a labyrinthine journey that takes us spiraling down into the depths of the mind's origins as reflected in concrete history, and then allows us to return with our new knowledge into the light of conceptual consciousness.[5] Had the painted images, figurines, and engravings in the caves of Europe and the rock shelters and stories of Africa been available to him, this is where his work would have begun.

For both Vico and Jung the understanding we gain from studying these artifacts of the soul must be integrated into conceptual consciousness. But it is Jung who has been especially influential in helping us to be mindful not only of our historical past but also of the personal symbols and myths that arise out of our own pre-reflective/unconscious/symbolic mind. This attentiveness allows us to work, on a daily basis, to integrate their meaning and purpose into consciousness.

This historical work and the individual soul work complement each other. Together they keep us aware that human beings from all cultures are deeply interconnected—*but* that it is only the work of the individual that can heal us and nurture the evolution of our species. Jung called this the *individuation* process, for while we are indeed a part of our culture and the human species, it is only the individual who can bring about a synthesis of this past with our present. Both Vico and Jung place the individual at the very center of the historical process as a creating, participating subject, integrating the past and the present, the symbol and the idea, the unconscious and the conscious, individual wholeness and human evolution.

Part of Vico's genius was that he recognized that this earlier symbolic, mythic language is *not* irrational: it possesses a poetic logic that gives birth to the logic of conceptual consciousness. For Vico the symbol was not to be thought of as undeveloped or as something we had outgrown, for he clearly understood that the symbolic mind exists as a fully developed mode of the mind in and of itself, as does the conceptual mind. He recognized the *equal value of symbolic and conceptual language*, an equality that would permit no repression, no censorship, and no dominance of one mental function over the other. The symbol could not be reduced to the idea, nor could the idea be reduced to the symbol. For both Vico and Jung the life of the mind is an integral and dynamic continuum of movement between the past and the present, the symbol and the idea. Both thought of this movement between the major energy fields of the human mind as a *relationship* that is "the most intimate and self-generative process of the human subject."[6] And it is the only way that the mind can experience its own wholeness.

Vico understood that it takes tremendous effort to consciously return to and integrate into consciousness the historical artifacts that reflect the origins and principles of our mental development. Many of us do not realize that discoveries of these artifacts are vital for our own individual and cultural development. For Vico, the effort that could send a culture back into its own history "to grasp anew, in idea, the principles of its own spontaneous life and power is the greatest spiritual effort a nation [or a person] can make."[7] *Only now are we beginning to realize the profound truth of this statement, for it is this effort that reveals to us how the laws of nature organize energy within the human psyche to bring about growth and development. It is this historical work that confirms the individual soul work — and it is this complementary effort that releases to consciousness the blueprint for our own spiritual evolution.*

Vico's understanding of the mind was such a radical departure from the thinking of his time that it is not surprising that his groundbreaking work, *The New Science* (1725), failed to receive a serious response from contemporary European thinkers. For Europe—at the very time that Vico lived and wrote—was in the grip of the "Enlightenment" belief in the superiority of reason over all other mental functions. His contemporaries were captivated by the belief that the true life of the mind only began with the emergence of reflective, conceptual consciousness and that all which preceded this historical event was irrational and potentially destructive—thus the need for censorship and repression.[8] The notion that the logical brain could develop out of a component of the brain that was totally lacking in logic would be mind-boggling if it were not still held by so many people today. It is yet another example of how *irrational* the conceptual mind can be when it severs itself from an understanding of the laws of its own nature.

The Western achievement of the differentiation of conceptual thought from the symbolic, visionary mind was indeed a profound breakthrough in our understanding of the mind. We do need to understand the difference between their functions and languages. The mistake, however, is to value only the idea and devalue the symbolic/visionary mind. This *fiction* of the superiority of the conceptual mind over the dreaming, visionary mind has resulted in the censorship and dismissal of inner experience. It is this *fiction* and *censorship* that have produced the meaningless, purposeless, materialistic worldview of Western culture. Buddha's interpretation of Darwin's data would have been very different because Buddha was using his *whole mind*.

There are various types of censorship. In a later chapter, we will see how the early Church used Roman law, distortion of the truth, violence, murder, and the reduction of visionary experience to *evil forces* in order to censor any experience that was outside its doctrine. Given time, however, their power was so great that they no longer needed these methods. **It is ironic that it was the Church itself that prepared the ground for a materialistic worldview with its denial of authentic visionary experience.** Later we will see how early scientists did, in fact, explore both inner and outer reality but were forced by both Church and State to limit their research to the material world. Eventually, no force was needed to prevent research into something that was no longer believed to exist.

Such a world would, of course, dismiss or ignore István's visionary experience. In fact, István himself was unable to give any real attention to such experiences—until Pisti's death and István's own inner experience. During his first vision, however, he was opened to such vast and creative realities that he would never return to his old limited view of the world. But, as I said earlier, I had difficulty holding onto the reality of something that I had been unconsciously conditioned to reject. Time and more experience changed this, but I certainly know how our history has conditioned us to accept and support a very limited, materialistic worldview.

And this censorship and conditioning have resulted in the loss of soul. What does a world look like when the doors to soul are blocked, denied, and repressed? It looks like our world—a world in which the dominant story is that there is only matter and all action is random without meaning or purpose. It is a world that denies our deep interconnectedness to the ground of being just as it denies the central creative role of the individual. It is a world that makes it difficult—and for some impossible—to bring forth what is within us. And what we are not bringing forth *is* destroying us. We are depressed, and we are addicted to power, violence, death, legal and illegal drugs, and to the very story of emptiness itself.

Of course, we have achieved much in the field of technology and in the realm of human rights. But we often use this technology to destroy ourselves and others, and we are too often willing to forgo the rights of others for our own gain. If this seems too harsh, we must remember I am speaking of the most negative effects of a culture that honors only a part of itself. We are now being called by life to value the feminine equally with the masculine, the poet equally with the physicist, the musician equally with the mathematician, the dancer equally with the technician, the dreamer and visionary equally with the astrophysicist and neuroscientist.

When we are truly able to go beyond the limited view of "Enlightenment" prejudice and accept ourselves as powerful, creative beings, everything changes. Then we want to know the rules of the game—and then we will understand why the symbolic images from our past—and our present—are of such profound significance: *they reflect back to us the rules of the game.*

Now *we* must become the bards for our culture. We must rediscover the old stories of our culture, of other people, of the universe. We must create an attunement with the ground of being through our dreams, visions, music, poetry—and our science. And we must find and claim our own individual darkness so we can distill it into light. This is how we heal ourselves—and our culture. This is how we discover who we are and why we're here. This is how we create a new story.

Chapter Seven

>—⊷—○—⊶—<

Every person's life is a sacred text.

—Novalis

The journey to discover this text has been negated by the Church, the State, and the only science that could survive after the defeat of the shaman-scientists in the seventeenth century.

We don't usually think of our lives as sacred—in the deepest sense of this word—nor do we think of our lives as a *text*, let alone a sacred text. But the German poet Novalis was correct: each of us is writing our own unique chapter in the sacred text of our species. That is why the true history of our species, says Novalis, can only be known from a perspective that includes every person's life.[1] Our own individual development is our creative contribution to the living text of our species' physical and spiritual evolution.

But, we might ask, how can my life be sacred when it is filled with mistakes, failures, darkness? The answer to this is to remember that we can only distill light out of our darkness—and that failure itself is part of the process of healing. To bring forth what is within us, we must go deep into what we do not yet know or understand or even presently want to know. Darkness, just as light, is always a part of the sacred text.

An ancient Mayan oracle reflects this crucial understanding: "Polarity is the loom on which reality is strung." Only out of the power of these opposing principles can we create at all. They *are* the loom on which we weave our own unique form. We can be ripped apart by these polarities, but we can also develop the skill to balance them, to hold them in each hand and weave a tapestry of great beauty.

The tapestry of our species — *our collective sacred text* — includes the threads of all our attempts, failures, and successes. It reflects the whole of our physical and spiritual evolution. But what about those of us who die before we have been able to complete our process and contribute our own balance and wholeness? Again, an inclusive vision is needed: the great mystics tell us that they can see all their past lives. This helps us to know that our development is continuous and that nature's goal — and thus ours — is completeness and wholeness.

Every culture has its own sacred text or tradition, whether painted, engraved, danced, written or spoken. Such texts or traditions usually include the distillation of what has been experienced, learned, or believed by individuals in that culture as they made their own journey through the great labyrinth. At the core of each of these cultural traditions is the individual soul's encounter with spirit — that numinous experience with the Matrix of all Life. We absorb the stories of these encounters and are inspired. We are given hope and comfort. Often, they are like the ball of thread thrown out before us to guide us magically on our way.

It is to our advantage to be open to these traditions in all cultures, for there is much in all of them that can empower us. The danger comes when we allow such texts to take the place of our own soul's journey — our own encounter with the Matrix of Life. Each of us has the opportunity and the responsibility to go deep into our own soul, claim our own darkness, and bring forth what is within us. When our cultural sacred text does not guide us into our own unknown territory, it becomes doctrine, which then is often claimed to be the only truth. Such proclamations of "the only truth" reflect an abandonment of the role of religion to guide us inward on our own journey.

Each of us enters the labyrinth when our soul asks the question we most need to have answered. The question itself shapes our individual path, but all such questions can take us to the heart of the labyrinth. And all questions reflect not only ourselves but our culture. As I mentioned earlier, my journey began as my culture's journey. I was caught between its two opposing stories: the scientific story of a random, meaningless universe and the religious story of a universe with meaning and purpose. But neither story could even begin to shed light on the paralyzing darkness of World War II.

As is true with so many people in our culture, both of these stories lived in me. In my early years, I was nurtured by the Protestant Christian tradition. I experienced kindness, warmth, community, and wonderful stories that ignited my imagination. The model of Jesus as soul deeply connected to spirit was imprinted on my child's psyche. This model of love and peace had to have a profound effect on a still unconscious mind in which the early images of war and emptiness had brought about such an unresolved disturbance.

Later, when it came time to choose a college, I chose a small, liberal arts Christian college. It may seem surprising in today's atmosphere for me to say that in this college I experienced an honesty and openness in scholarship that I would later discover was not as pervasive in the academic world as this experience had led me to believe. Certainly, the school was rooted in doctrine, but it never made demands on me. On Sundays, almost everyone in my dormitory went to church, but after my first year, I no longer went. I enjoyed the time alone, and no one ever commented about it. These were wonderful years in a beautiful natural setting where I had scholarly mentors and the freedom to explore the world I had been born into. Students were encouraged to question everything—and many of us did.

I ended my studies there, however, as much my culture's child as when I entered. I still carried within me two possible worldviews, but now the story of meaning and purpose was becoming a remote possibility. I had not been able *to believe*. I had *to know* from my own inner experience. And the Christian tradition did not have the shamanic techniques to guide me inward on my own journey. This is because the Church had attempted to destroy all knowledge of such techniques. In 380 CE, Theodosius I declared Christianity the imperial religion; later there would be severe restrictions against the celebration of *gnosis*—direct individual experience—in the ancient Mystery Schools, and the possession of books that were earlier denounced as heretical by the Church became a criminal offense. Any belief, thought, or experience contrary to Church doctrine was to be destroyed. The main target, of course, was the direct experience recorded in the gnostic texts.[2] The Church feared *experience* and demanded *belief*. Thus, the European and early Christian gnostic-shamanic tradition of direct inner experience was forced underground—and there it would remain for the next seven hundred years.

This tradition would surface several times during the course of European history, and each time it did there was a renaissance of creativity, hope and transformation. In our own time this repressed tradition has surfaced more powerfully and pervasively than ever before. Texts the Church had thought destroyed have been discovered, and these texts are revolutionizing the way we perceive who we are and why we're here. Many of these texts reveal a Jesus who did not teach us to *believe* in him but rather to *experience our own inner divinity*. This Jesus was a shaman-mystic and he taught techniques for achieving gnosis. For at least two hundred years after his death such teachings were referred to as the *secret tradition*.[3]

In one of these discovered texts, the Gospel of Thomas, Jesus said,

> *I am not your master. Because you have drunk, you have become intoxicated from the bubbling spring which I have measured out.... He who will drink from My mouth will become like Me. I myself shall become he, and the things that are hidden will be revealed to him.*[4]

Since the Christian tradition I knew had no knowledge of these ancient teachings, I had to go my own way. My professors respected and supported my individual journey. That I would leave this tradition with no scars speaks well for the people who represented that tradition in my life.

Thankfully, it was around this time that I started reading the work of Carl Jung and was able to find at least some understanding of what I was going through. Eventually, Jung's work led me to Sigmund Freud. While I was impressed with Freud's work on the unconscious mind, I realized fairly soon that he was not asking the same questions that I was, nor did it appear—in spite of his pioneering spirit—that he was willing to explore certain aspects of mind and history that had been previously repressed.

Jung's work opened the floodgate to these other dimensions of human experience, but I could only take in and understand small portions at a time. My life in the outer world and my dreams seemed to set the pace. I became more attentive to my dreams from a new perspective, and I tried to respect and value my dreaming mind as much as my rational mind. This was not easy to do in a culture that still dismissed dreams, intuition, and visions as nonsense at best and symptoms of pathology at worst.

During my last year in college, 1960–61, I had a dream that flashed a beautiful and surprising light on my soul's activity. I had finished my B.A. in English and was working on an M.A. in American Studies. Since I was a graduate student, I was allowed to live alone in a lovely little apartment overlooking the wild growth of a ravine.

> *I am walking in a deep green forest lush with thick growth. It is evening and the colors of blue and green seem to blend into an essence that is alive and conscious. I come to a river that has a beautiful Japanese-style wooden bridge crossing over it. Standing in the middle of this bridge where it gracefully arches over the water is a beautiful woman dressed in blue. She is waiting for me. There is now a luminous glow to the entire scene. When I arrive before her, I look to my right at the water below: I see a great white spiral of mist rising out of the depths of the river. Each emerging circle of the spiral is larger than the last and it is moving toward me. I hear a voice ask, "And now do you believe in God?"*
>
> *Suddenly I am lying face down on the bridge before the woman in blue. The spiral continues to move toward me until*

> *it hovers just above me. Then it touches the base of my spine. The pressure is so intense that I immediately wake up.*

I sensed a presence so strong that I jumped out of bed and turned on the light to see if someone was in the room. There was no physical presence in the room, but I was so shaken that I sat up with the light on for the rest of the night. A beautiful fragrance filled the room and persisted most of the evening. I wondered if the fragrance could be coming from a plant or tree outside the open window that faced the ravine, but I never experienced it again. Only much later would I learn that a beautiful fragrance is often a part of experiences with the numinous. And I would also learn that the ancient Hebrews' Queen of Heaven was "perfumed with the incense of the holy of holies" and had "a fragrance beyond all fragrance."[5]

Whatever else I might say about the dream, it was first and foremost an experience with the divine, with soul, with spirit. At that time in my life I thought of divinity in exclusively masculine terms, so it wasn't surprising to me that the spiral and the voice seemed to suggest a masculine god, but the woman before me was also divine. I prostrated myself at her feet. It was clearly to her that I owed my homage.

Since I was no longer contained within the tradition of my youth, and since I had just begun to read about other religious traditions and the works of Jung and Freud, I still had no clear path. *But the amazing thing is that my psyche did.* Only later would I understand that the Western world and Western religion had severed the great loom of polarities on which reality is strung. When these magnetic poles are disengaged, we lose our balance and fall into a self-destructive spiral. I had certainly lost my balance, but I was desperately in search of a healing solution. The dream was a powerful response: it offered me a beautiful and loving image of the great loom of polarity.

Because the old pattern of divinity was no longer functional in my life, another pattern could emerge—one that was totally new to me. The new pattern reflected what had been missing in the old pattern: *the feminine dimension of the divine and the spiral/labyrinthine blueprint for evolving consciousness*. I would later discover that our ancestors had experienced soul in her feminine form for tens of thousands of years. During much of that time the spiral, spirit, and the labyrinth had also been experienced as feminine, but later the spiral became associated with spirit as masculine, the Holy Ghost, and the male God. Eventually, the female, the spiral and the labyrinth sank into the background of consciousness as Christian symbolism dominated the foreground.

Once the exclusive Christian images lost their power in my psyche, the ancient symbols emerged, but in no way did they negate the Christian symbols. What emerged was an experience of the potential fullness and wholeness of the human psyche: the Divine as both masculine and feminine lovingly working together to respond to my intention to know who I am and why I'm here. Out of the depths of the water, of nature, of my own psyche, the great mystical spiral of evolving energy arose and activated the spiral energy at the base of my own spine. Only much later would I discover that for thousands of years the base of the spine was thought of as the root of spiritual consciousness, which, in its dormant state, was symbolized as a spiral or coiled serpent. When activated, the serpent energy spiraled up to the brain to achieve full spiritual consciousness.

In Western culture this dormant energy was often symbolized as a coiled snake at the base of a tree that spiraled up the trunk when activated. The image of this rising serpent energy became known as the caduceus and would become the Western medical symbol for health. In ancient Egypt, full spiritual development was symbolized beautifully in the appearance of the serpent goddess at the third eye of the divine ruler. And in the East this energy is still symbolized as a spiral or serpent, well known today as kundalini energy.

It would only be after many years of working with the artifacts of our spiritual past and the almost daily encounter with the images of the spiral and the labyrinth that I would be capable of realizing how amazing it was that these same images had appeared in my dream when my conscious mind knew absolutely nothing about them. My dream had released the very *image of the journey* that my intention to know had activated. Here was an example of how the laws of nature organize energy in response to conscious intention and communicate this new organization of energy to consciousness through the metaphors, symbols, and feeling experiences of the dream.

At the time of the dream, however, I could not have spoken about polarities, old patterns or new patterns, the spiral, the labyrinth, or the feminine as divine. I knew nothing about these matters, and I had not yet read enough of Jung's work to know how these concerns formed the core of his own experience and research. While I was very much in search of soul, my outer focus at that time was historical and political. The year before, in 1959, I had studied in Vienna and had lived in a Studentenheim with students from all around the world, the majority of which were Hungarian refugees. That summer the Communist Youth Festival was held in Vienna, and my days were filled with participation in the meetings, fiery discussions of politics, communism, revolution, and democracy. Somehow, I had to find time for my own studies in European history and the literature of Thomas Mann.

When I returned to the States and began my graduate work in American Studies, I was especially interested in Jung's writings on individual freedom as opposed to the dogma of church or state. The individual had to be free to discover soul within; otherwise, we would more easily succumb to collective, mass thinking whether we lived in the Communist East or the Democratic West. Jung saw the political split that existed at that time between East and West as symbolic of the split in the human psyche: on both sides, the individual was split between the inner power and creativity of soul and the outward pull of collective thinking, whether that was religious, political, or scientific.

It was within the intense energy of this outer focus that soul made her appearance in my dream—standing before me, waiting for me. But even as I lay in reverence and awe before Her, the atmosphere in the dream reverberated with the question: "And now do you believe in God?" What a strange question to ask at the very moment that I was experiencing *God*. Yet this question was an accurate reflection of a problem that would persist for many years: in spite of powerful inner experiences, my rational mind would continue to question the reality of the divine.

It is interesting that the word *believe* and not *know* was used in the dream. I wanted to *know* the divine from actual experience, not from someone else's teaching. Yet in the dream *belief* is used precisely in this way. *The question was whether I could believe in something I was actually experiencing.* Even though I had not wanted to use the word *belief* in relation to the divine, the word seemed to resonate throughout my body, almost like a frequency moving through it. Belief was clearly the correct word within the context of the dream experience, not so much in the way we use it today but rather in its earlier meaning of *to like, to desire, to love, to have confidence in the truth and reality of a person or experience.*

Over the years I would come to realize just how difficult it would be for me to believe in the reality of my own experience when my culture denied the possibility of such realities. But it was this very difficulty that led me to search in the outer world for evidence of such inner experience in other times and in other cultures. So while I had embarked on my own inner labyrinthine journey, I was on another outer labyrinthine journey that took me spiraling back in time to the available concrete artifacts of our historical past—artifacts that just might help me to verify the reality of my own experience within the context of the inner experience of my species.

This was a true Vician ricorso before I had discovered Vico. And it would be on this path that I would meet him and many of the other giants who had traveled this way before me. We don't all need to travel this path, but we all do need to know what has been discovered on this path about who we are and why we're here. And this is why our stories and the stories of our ancestors have to be told. *When we do not tell them or listen to them, our stories die — the stories of our ancestors die — and we can no longer remember who we are or why we're here — or even believe our own experience.*

This is how we *fall* into someone else's story. This is how we get tangled up in a story of materialism and meaninglessness or we settle for a belief in someone else's divinity but do not take the journey to experience our own. And this is how we end up full of self-righteousness, fear, despair, addiction, anger, and violence—or just indifference.

Only we can write the sacred text of our own lives. Each of us has the sacred right to enter the labyrinth to discover and to create our own soul's story. We are not called to imitate the life of anyone else—divine or otherwise. While we do not want to live someone else's story, we do need to know the stories of others, for they can inspire us and guide us on our own way.

So my own journey to find my story and to discover the stories of my ancestors took the form of a double spiral. One spiral moved inward to find soul, the other moved outward to find history. As I continued to experience the language of soul within, I became better at recognizing this language in the artifacts of the past. It became clear that the rituals, metaphors and symbols in an ancient culture could not be reduced to that culture's social and political structure—as had so often been the practice of Western scholars. Rather, these artifacts must be recognized as reflections of that culture's experience of soul. Throughout the ancient world, spiritual experience is the major determining factor in the social and political structure rather than the other way around.

One of the unfortunate consequences of our Western story is that most scholars have not been able to see the significance of the spiritual artifacts in ancient cultures. We in the West speak about not projecting our own cultural structures onto the cultures we are studying; yet modern scholars often project their belief in a materialistic worldview onto cultures whose core organizing principles are rooted in the experience of the sacred. When we have not experienced the reality of shamanic-mystic consciousness, or what is also called altered states of consciousness, we tend not to recognize or to value the metaphors, symbols, or narratives that reflect such experiences. Far too often these spiritual artifacts have been reduced to trivia.

Therefore, my research was complicated by my own limited experience and by what appeared to be a lack of such experience in many anthropologists and archaeologists who showed very little ability or desire to recognize the artifacts of spiritual experience, that is, altered states of consciousness. Those few scholars who did recognize the artifacts of altered states of consciousness were usually ridiculed and relegated to the margins of credibility.

Yet these scholars have continued their research, and comparative studies of their work in culture after culture all around the world reveal that there exists, in Eliade's words, "a fundamental unity" in spiritual experience—a unity that is "inexhaustible" in its "newness."[6] This supports the view that there are principles or laws that organize energy within the human psyche and reflect these patterns of organization in metaphor, symbol, story, and myth. For many years scholars debated whether the similarity of these artifacts was a result of organizing principles within the human psyche or simply a result of cultural contact. We now know that there was far more cultural contact and exchange than was earlier thought possible. This does not mean, however, that the similarity of the artifacts is simply a result of cultural contact. We tend to respond to the stories that ignite the organizing principles of the psyche. There is also abundant evidence that the dreaming mind uses metaphors, symbols, and narratives that have appeared throughout history in cultures around the world even when the individual has no knowledge of them.

This knowledge of the inexhaustible creativity of the psyche within a unified pattern is a relatively recent discovery and, laments Eliade, "has not yet been sufficiently assimilated."[7] Even when scholars have recognized this unity, they have all too often continued to think of this spiritual/mystical experience as primitive superstition rather than to understand it as the record of real experience in altered states of consciousness—*and that such states of consciousness are necessary for our evolution.*

When I began my journey, I did not know that there was evidence of this unity/blueprint of spiritual experience around the world—and even if I had, I would not have been able to comprehend fully the significance of such evidence. For many years I simply did not have enough experience or knowledge to trust my own insights, and I also knew that my own comparative studies had to rely heavily on those scholars in the field who had access to the artifacts within their cultural context. It would take years of my own inner experience and the work of courageous scholars capable of recognizing and evaluating the artifacts of mystical consciousness for me to absorb what this actually means for each of us.

It is incredibly sad that in the West this evolutionary potential for mystical experience is denied by the very institutions that grew out of such individual experience. It took two to three hundred years for the Catholic Church to destroy the shamanic-mystic tradition that was such a powerful force in early Christianity and to replace it with belief in a set of doctrines. The teachings of Jesus now had to be about belief in Him and not about the direct inner experience of our own divinity.

This would be the decisive factor in Western culture: *individual experience was negated*. Our own inner experience had nothing to do with reality and could only be valued when it replicated doctrine and subordinated itself to power. As the power of the Church waned, individual experience was once again devalued and subordinated to another power—this time to the power of the rational, scientific mind.

We cannot blame the scientists for this, for we have seen how our early ancestors—the builders of the great megaliths—achieved a balance between inner spiritual experience and scientific values. They were shaman-mystics *and* scientists. We have discovered even more evidence of this in the great monuments of Egypt: these builders were powerful *visionary scientists*. And Kingsley confirms this balance in the Greek Presocratic shaman-mystics from Anatolia: not only were they masters of higher states of consciousness but they were scientific thinkers and technicians. This is part of the sacred knowledge that the West has lost but which is reemerging in our time: *science developed out of the shaman-mystic's experience*.

The true story of the development of Western science out of just such a relationship between inner experience and rational, conceptual thinking was so thoroughly destroyed by the Church and State that this powerful story fell out of history. It was not until the second half of the twentieth century that Frances A. Yates discovered this story beneath the known history of the early seventeenth century. Yates describes her experience in *The Rosicrucian Enlightenment* as being like that of an archaeologist, digging down through layer after layer of historical material until just before the Thirty Years War there emerged "a whole culture, a whole civilization," that had been "lost to view."[8] Yates realized that this culture was a continuation of the Hermetic tradition that had given such power to the Renaissance in Florence around 1460 when Cosimo de' Medici insisted that Marsilio Ficino translate the newly recovered *Corpus Hermeticum*. These texts embodied precisely the kind of teaching the Church had hoped to destroy. They were about gnosis — *individual experience*.

Ficino also translated the works of Plato and Plotinus but only after the Hermetic texts, and it was these texts that "coloured Ficino's entire conception of Platonism," which he viewed as a form of ancient Egyptian gnosis.[9] *This rediscovery of gnosis — direct inner experience — was at the very heart of the Italian Renaissance.* Here were texts about altered states of consciousness, the experience of the divine within—and the importance of valuing individual experience over external authority. And it was these very texts that initiated one of the great waves of the European attempt to reclaim part of her lost soul.

Yates had assumed that the impact of this discovery during the Italian Renaissance had begun to lose its power during the early seventeenth century until her research revealed that instead of losing its influence, there had been a rebirth and expansion of the tradition. During the hundred and fifty years since the Renaissance, this movement's open and inclusive atmosphere had made it possible to absorb the wisdom of the underground traditions, which included the Hermetic arts, Alchemy and the Jewish Kabbalah. This ignited creative and intellectual activity that spanned the distance between England and Prague. This movement, which Yates called the Rosicrucian Enlightenment, was "concerned with a striving for illumination, in the sense of vision, as well as for enlightenment in the sense of advancement in intellectual or scientific knowledge."[10] *Yates discovered that, in fact, it was this underground tradition that had nurtured a mathematical approach to nature and had given the impetus and direction to the scientific revolution.*[11]

This movement, says Yates, had held great expectations for the coming of a true Enlightenment — one rooted in both mystical experience and scientific exploration. Those who were part of the movement had a keen awareness of the dangers of scientific knowledge without inner experience. They realized that society, education, and religion would have to be reformed, and that such a reformation could take Europe beyond conflicting religious doctrines to a new sense of individual dignity and purpose.[12] They knew that freedom from the repressive tendencies of Church and State was absolutely necessary for such an Enlightenment to occur, and they made a remarkable attempt to gain political power over the dominant forces of the Hapsburg-Jesuit alliance.

They failed, and with that failure came the destruction of their world, successive waves of political propaganda against them, repression, witch-hunting, and the Thirty Years War between Protestants and Catholics. **It was in this "exquisite Renaissance culture," says Yates, that the potential existed for the culmination of the most creative and intelligent tendencies of the entire Renaissance.** But both the vision and the movement "slipped out of history."[13] *A whole world disappeared and with it the hopes of the shaman-scientists who had envisioned an evolutionary leap for the whole world.*

After the "convulsions of witch-hunting"[14] and the long, violent years of war, the Enlightenment would occur, but it would be a very different Enlightenment from the one envisioned by the shaman-scientists of the early seventeenth century. The visionary force that had given birth to the mathematical, scientific exploration of the world had been shattered and silenced. Abstract reasoning now dominated and inner experience once again was devalued and repressed.

When the Royal Society for the advancement of science was formed in 1660 in London, it had visible roots stretching back into this earlier movement but, as Yates explains, "in order to preserve its delicate existence great caution was required."[15] **Only the science of outer exploration could survive.** Political and religious power, misinformation, fear tactics, lack of adequate education, and years of repressing the human ability for visionary experience made this marriage of reason and vision impossible.

It would not be until the early twentieth century and the discovery of quantum physics that this vision would begin to return to the scientific world. When the pioneers of quantum physics realized they had stepped out of the old materialistic view of reality and into a world strangely similar to the descriptions of the shaman-mystic, they began to read the same kind of texts that had ignited the work of these early seventeenth century shaman-scientists. During the decades following the discovery of quantum physics, there were other remarkable scientists who were also visionaries working to reconcile inner and outer realities. Yet it would not be until Fritjof Capra experienced what he had been studying as a theoretical physicist and published his work about the parallels between modern physics and mysticism that the scientist and the mystic could openly begin once again to form a respectful and complementary relationship.

It is important for us to remember that even this dark history of failure is part of the sacred text of our ancestors. It reveals to us a remarkable attempt to become conscious of who we are and why we're here. *And it reveals how the ancient texts of our past emerged to lead us on our way.* Yet it also reveals how the darkness of our unconsciousness still overwhelmed us. Europe failed to bring forth what was within her, and what she did not bring forth was destroying her.

With soul shattered and science on her own, the world continued to destroy its own creativity in war after war until its alchemical retort exploded in atomic violence at the end of World War II. We had now achieved the ability to destroy ourselves utterly. Such a world would have to remain unconscious — or face the horror of its own darkness.

Chapter Eight

>-+-+>-+-O-+-+-+-<

The first darkness we have to face is the story we've been telling ourselves about ourselves. We have become addicted to a story that now has the power to negate the entire world.

Once we know the history of this story—the Western story of a material world without purpose or meaning—we realize that it could only come into being through violent censorship and repression of our true stories. We must know this history if we are to deal with our addiction to it. It is sad and difficult for us to realize that both the religion story and the science story have made zealots of us. But this always happens when a story comes into being through censorship because its continued existence depends on further repression. Once we realize that both stories contain only part of the truth, perhaps we can be more open to a larger, more inclusive truth. Yet this does not happen easily; without our knowing it, most of us have been conditioned *unconsciously* to either the science story or the religion story. This is part of our cultural heritage. **It is crucial for us to know that the natural development of both stories was thwarted through violence, fear, lack of understanding, and the desire for power and control. Both stories carry the wounds and limits of Western history.**

How do we go beyond the wounds and limits of our history? How do we find the missing pieces of our story within us? What is this *something* within us that Jesus asked us to bring forth? And what is this something that is so threatening that centuries have been devoted to denying it, repressing it, and destroying whole worlds to negate it?

This is *what* we have to know. This is the *hidden something* we must discover. Once we ask this question, our journey in the labyrinth begins. This journey cannot be determined by doctrines imposed on us from without. We are now in a sacred partnership with soul to bring forth what is within us. **This is a journey of pure creativity—and this is that *something* so feared and denied in Western history.**

The journey is our sacred path—even for those who have had glimpses of cosmic consciousness. This is the path of experience and discovery through dreams, visions, thoughts, relationships, and outer events. We become *mindful* of all aspects of our life—the darkness and the light. It is a path of cooperation, not competition. Pisti's girlfriend Jenny had a vision in which Pisti said, "Jenny, here there is nothing but cooperation." I also had a visionary experience with Pisti in which he talked about the dangers of our use of comparison. He wanted me to understand that since each of us is unique, our journeys will be unique, so comparison with anyone else cannot be helpful. The universe is creative, which means that it is infinitely diverse. When we enter the labyrinth, we activate the inner forces of a whole new being—and thus a whole new world.

In the late 1960s I had the following dream:

> *I am in a space that is not on the ground but somewhat in the air, and time is suspended between the Middle Ages and World War II. I am speaking with a man who is a news reporter just returned from covering the War. He is articulate and passionate as he discusses with me the horrors of World War II. He is both a modern war correspondent and a priest of the Middle Ages. I am a nun. We are both in a deep state of depression and grief because of the War and what it reveals about our civilization. We both feel the War also reflects a failure of our religion to prevent or to heal the pathology of the Western world. He tells me he is leaving the priesthood. I understand.*

Now we are no longer in the air, but solidly on the ground. As I watch the man leave, I realize that we are completely in the Middle Ages: he is a knight riding a horse down a dirt road that leads him away from the great Gothic cathedral that is now behind him. I slowly walk toward the cathedral, which is to my right. I stand in front of it and marvel at this vast, exquisite monument to "Our Lady." Then I look to my left and see a stone sarcophagus that is now an unnatural part of the cathedral. I know that within this sarcophagus is the dead body of "Our Lady."

Very slowly I turn completely around. I start walking down the long dirt road that leads away from the cathedral and into the woods. I see the knight on his horse in the distance ahead of me. I am barefoot as I walk slowly down the road and observe a miracle taking place in nature: on both sides of the road there is a continuous line of large silver wombs in the earth, each one opening to the road as I pass by and each one giving birth to the most exquisitely beautiful silver woman. She is "Our Lady" – the soul of the world. Her birth is like a graceful dance as her head and arms emerge out of the wombs and onto the road we are traveling. **I realize that I am experiencing the miracle that can heal our civilization.**

The emotional experience of the dream was powerful. Yet I knew that what I was experiencing was far beyond my capacity at the time to fully understand. I did know on some level of consciousness that Our Lady reflected my own soul and every other person's soul: She was the soul of the world. It was also clear that She could no longer live in the great cathedral that had been built in Her honor. But She was alive in nature, ever-present, fully mature, and continually coming into being with each step I took in space and time. She symbolized the central mystery, the *something* I was looking for at the center of the labyrinth. I knew that I had not fully experienced Her, but somehow I understood that this was an experience in process. I was given a vision of the center, but it was a goal that I had not yet achieved. I was a bit like Odysseus who *saw* Ithaca but was unable to actually arrive on its sandy shores until he had gone through many more experiences.

I had wanted to know what *this hidden something* was at *the center of the labyrinth* so my dream allowed me to experience *Our Lady/the soul of the world* to the degree that I was capable, but it also revealed the work I would need to do to get to that center. My problem was clearly depicted in the relationship between the World War II reporter/knight and the nun/visionary. We were friendly and had some kind of bond. We agreed about the War and the Church. He talked openly about how he thought and felt, but we made our choices independently. He did most of the talking while the woman did most of the listening.

If I look at this dream from the perspective that views all the characters in a dream as the dreamer, then the reporter would reflect my rational, more culturally-oriented side and the woman would reflect the side of me more connected to the earth, nature, and the dreaming mind. It is interesting that in the dream I identify with her, but once awake I could definitely recognize myself in him. While the man and I did communicate with each other, his discussion was more of an announcement to me of his decision to leave and, when he left, he didn't look back. He was unaware that I was on the road some distance behind him, and he certainly had not observed the miracle taking place in nature. If I look at these two people as aspects of myself, I would have to admit that a working relationship between the rational mind and the visionary mind is lacking. While he is clearly aware that I exist, he does not seem to feel that I have anything to offer him that could be helpful or healing. Yet I do. The visionary has experienced the miracle that could heal both of us — and thus our culture. But he has somewhere to go and has left me behind.

I was in my early thirties at the time of this dream and was still unaware of most of the history of soul in our culture. I had visited many Gothic cathedrals when I was a student in Europe, but I never had the opportunity to visit Chartres. Yet it was the cathedral at Chartres that had captured my imagination. I had read *Mont-Saint-Michel and Chartres* by Henry Adams and had been deeply impressed by his contrasting the masculine structure of Mont-Saint-Michel with the feminine structure of Chartres. So the cathedral in my dream was Chartres, which was certainly one of the most beautiful reflections of soul during this creative period of the Middle Ages. And, as I was to discover much later with great amazement, it appears that the very area of Chartres—even before Christianity—had been held sacred and was associated with "the Virgin about to give birth."[1]

It is significant that the dream takes place simultaneously during World War II and the High Middle Ages. World War II is a stark example of our loss of soul, and the High Middle Ages (from 1000 to 1300 CE) was the first wave of the emergence and exquisite flowering of soul in the Western world after its brutal repression by the Church in the fourth century. This repression had been so pervasive and restrictive that all opposition to the Church was forced underground—*and there it had remained for seven hundred years*. When this dam of repression broke, soul energy flooded society and found its expression in metaphors, symbols, stories, myths, architecture, strange new feelings and intuitions, and outer social structures—all in an attempt of soul to balance and heal itself.

Adams, in his *Mont-Saint-Michel and Chartres*, tells us that there was a shift in emphasis from the masculine to the feminine, from the military ideal to "Our Lady." Fashion became more feminine; the game of chess was changed to restrict the movement of the king and the knight while the Queen, who was called the Virgin, was given the greatest freedom and power on the board;[2] the Court of Love was established along with a code of conduct concerning manners, love, and service to woman; the music and poetry of the troubadours praised woman as soul that inspired men to great heights; the great Gothic cathedrals were built to "Our Lady"; for fifty years the Grail stories were written about the masculine entry into the great forest labyrinth to find the Feminine/the Grail/His Lady at the center; and later Dante wrote *The Divine Comedy* in which the love of Beatrice/soul guides Dante through the labyrinth of Hell, Purgatory, and finally to Paradise; and, of course, the various underground traditions that nurtured gnosis flourished in various spots in Europe, especially southern France. *All of these expressions reflect the reemergence of what Catholic Europe had repressed: soul, woman, and gnosis.*

Between 1175–1225 CE the powerful Grail stories that emerged "fired the imagination of the whole of Europe."[3] Those aspects of soul that had been repressed for centuries rose to the surface of consciousness: once again there was the inward journey symbolized by the labyrinthine forest, which the knights of King Arthur's Court entered independently in search of the Holy Grail at the center. The Round Table of the Court was a symbol of wholeness, equality, and loyalty to the masculine. And in story after story King Arthur's knights learn how to be sensitive to the feminine and to commit themselves to her service. The quest for the Grail itself was a quest for mystical experience and communion with the Otherworld through love, respect, and loyalty to the Queen of that world, the Sovereign of the Land, *Our Lady*, the soul of the world. Without this relationship, the world becomes a wasteland, for "The king rules the land by right of his true union with her and by his championship of her freedom."[4]

And if we now shift forward in time to my dream, it is painfully clear that my Knight, traumatized by the horrors of World War II and the Western worldview of a random, meaningless universe, desperately needs the wisdom of soul that had flowered during the High Middle Ages. He is now conscious of the wasteland of Western culture and his soul is calling him to join the knights of King Arthur's Round Table, for he too must learn how to be loyal to himself and yet sensitive to the visionary feminine. In fact, our entire culture is being called to enter into the quest for the Holy Grail, for we have yet to experience its mystery.

I was saddened by the fact that Western culture, once the Church had gained political power in Rome, had repressed the visionary component of our brains, the symbolic and physical feminine, as well as gnosis (direct experience) for seven hundred years. This same kind of repression occurred after each cultural attempt to integrate body, soul, and spirit. Because of the severity of this repression, none of these movements had time to fully develop. And now my dream, hundreds of years after the High Middle Ages, showed me in the same wasteland with the same need for a sensitivity to soul.

I had to be impressed with the visionary mind that could take me and my culture right back to the historical moment when the consciousness of the age had become aware of its own spiritual wasteland. This consciousness had ignited a quest for soul and a relationship with other-dimensional realities. The Grail stories show how their knights entered into a living mystery school—the labyrinth of soul—to discover how to bring forth what was within them. The knights incessantly found themselves in situations structured to teach them how *to see, to hear,* and *to respond* to their own visionary companion. This was the work of soul, the healing of the Western psyche.

My own dream had made it clear that my Knight did not know how to create a relationship with the visionary female who is with him. He is completely unaware that soul is being born all around him because *he cannot perceive this dimension of reality.* The visionary's world, on the other hand, is not a wasteland: it is a world in which soul is continually coming into being. "Our Lady," the "Virgin," is being born right onto the very road he is traveling. He is also unaware that the visionary female is walking that same road at some distance behind him *because* he is moving *away* from her and *away* from the miraculous events taking place in nature.

The reporter/knight in me had his intellectual focus on the outer world where he hoped to find answers. And this is exactly what I did: I wanted to understand *why* we had allowed our culture to become a wasteland. I also longed for a deep inner life with the visionary and whatever "Our Lady" or "the Virgin" or the births symbolized, but I simply did not know how to achieve this relationship. I only knew how to apply my intellect to the situation and to attend to my dreams. But did I really know how to "attend" to my dreams? Did I—or my culture—truly value the numinous *reality* of the dream or vision? My dream reveals that a part of me did not.

I would learn in time that no amount of intellectual understanding could be healing *unless* it had a direct, living relationship with the miraculous ground of its own being. And in my dream, this very ground—in the form of "Our Lady," the soul of the world, "the Virgin about to give birth"—was expressing its presence and its perpetual coming into being. I would later learn from my studies in prehistory that *Virgin* did not mean physical virginity but rather the divine feminine in her role of giving birth to the divine. She is sacred energy that is *"strong, free, and available."*[5] She is soul, and even in First Temple Judaism and early Christianity, she was the Soul of God, the feminine counterpart or spouse of God, often "embodied in the image of the dove." Only later was the dove masculinized. Mary was called the Virgin—and she was associated with the word *alma*, the "living soul of the world."[6] This feminine figure was the ground of being, and as *almah* she was also known as "the hidden one," the "secrets of wisdom," and the one about to give birth in the holy of holies.[7]

There is an extraordinary story about the disappearance of the "living soul of the world"[8] in "The Elucidations," which appears as a prologue in Chrétien de Troyes' *Perceval: The Story of the Grail*. We are told that in the Celtic worldview there are two aspects of the land or nature: the inner aspect was the soul of the outer physical world. These aspects were not separate but were simply the inner and outer dimensions of one world. As long as a loving, respectful relationship with the inner soul of reality was maintained, all the world was alive, fruitful, and peaceful. This relationship was made possible and nurtured by soul, in this case not in the form of Baba Yaga but in the form of beautiful Maidens who lived in caves, wells, and springs. When someone approached, the Maidens appeared and gave the traveler food and drink from golden bowls. Here the two worlds met and the traveler experienced the soul of the world in time and space. But one day King Amangon raped one of the Maidens, held her in captivity, and stole her sacred bowl. His men followed their king's example. And the beautiful, peaceful world disappeared. No longer were there Maidens to nurture the traveler, and all the wells and springs dried up. The Voices of the Wells were no longer to be heard. Soul sank back into the depths of the inner world and the outer world became a wasteland.[9]

This was probably a very old tale that reflects how we either forget or betray the Voices of the Wells over and over again. And when we do, we fall into a wasteland. The European wasteland would return again even after this exquisite flowering and remembrance during the High Middle Ages of Our Lady, the Virgin, and the Maidens at the Wells. The dark clouds of fear, intolerance, and violence would begin once again to form over Europe by the first quarter of the thirteenth century. The Grail stories that flooded Europe for about fifty years stopped abruptly by 1225;[10] a crusade was formed to destroy the Albigenses, the Gnostics in southern France; women's power began to steadily decline; the witch trials would come and continue for centuries; intolerance and hostility against Jews, Muslims, heretics, homosexuals, the poor, the infirm, and any other kind of difference would increase.[11] The creative, evolutionary forces of soul were once again forced underground. These forces would remain beneath the surface of the European wasteland until 1460 when Ficino would translate the *Corpus Hermeticum*. And we have already seen how this mystical tradition would slowly grow and flower into the Rosicrucian Enlightenment that would in its turn also be destroyed in 1620.

After World War II most of the world was acutely aware that we were in a vast and desolate wasteland. Many could not understand how the intellectual knights of the Western world could have destroyed all that they had so brilliantly constructed. People who had still believed in a world of meaning and purpose struggled to hold the faith — or they fell altogether into despair. And there were also those who were angry with a God who could allow this to happen. But such anger was rooted in our forgetting that it was we, not God, who had silenced the Voices of the Wells.

We had forgotten because we had created our culture through the worldview of our knights — our knights who had wanted meaning and purpose but could not find it in the great institutions of religion. Yet they rode right past the "living soul of the world."[12] From their perspective there was no soul, no Otherworld, no Voices of the Wells. They were on their own — and they were brilliant. They created the Western world and we all reveled in their accomplishments. But a darkness had been growing in us and it was destroying everything it touched. We did not know how to distill this darkness into light. We only knew we had lost something — something we could not even name, but we fiercely longed for that *something*.

This longing of people all over the planet was so deep and so pervasive that it ignited a response from the earth. Shamans have always known that our thoughts and feelings affect the physical world. Unfortunately, we lost this knowledge long ago, but now the modern shaman-scientists are rediscovering that human consciousness does, in fact, affect the earth.

And so it was this mind and heart energy that released from the earth some of the ancient Voices of the Wells—Voices that had been forced underground or hidden in caves for hundreds of years. In 1947 the first of what we now call the Dead Sea Scrolls was found in caves overlooking the Dead Sea. And in December of 1945, the very year that World War II ended, the Nag Hammadi texts were discovered in the sands of Egypt. These texts, written or copied between 200 BCE and the fourth century CE, are basically gnostic voices that reveal the struggles of our ancestors in their quest for mystical experience and communion with the Otherworld.

They "possess the potential," says Stephen A. Hoeller, a modern Gnostic, "of aiding the West in the recovery of a substantial portion of its lost soul." He reminds us that it was around the time that Jung was writing *Modern Man in Search of a Soul* that these texts were found: the "long forgotten, or rather repressed, component of the soul of Judeo-Christian religiosity and of Western culture" emerged out of the earth in the hour of our greatest need. This "agonizing psychic need of the culture was thus met by a synchronistic response from the innermost center of reality."[13]

Jung has said that when people need to find great meaning and value in life, the process always begins through a dream. I certainly had experienced this truth in my own life: when I was experiencing my own "agonizing psychic need," my soul responded with a dream of what was missing in my life—and in the life of my culture. The Loom of Polarity emerged: the divine feminine was restored to her rightful place with the divine masculine.

These texts from Egypt and the Dead Sea are some of the ancient dreams of our ancestors in their search for great meaning and value in life. Not only do they reflect the era of their writing or copying but they are the cultural assimilation and culmination of centuries of our ancestors' journeys to find soul and to write the sacred texts of their lives. Their stories reveal what they encountered in the labyrinth of the soul and how they responded to those experiences. We do not need to imitate their lives or come to the same conclusions about how to live life in the material world, but we do need to hear their stories. For they were cartographers of the soul, and when their stories were repressed, a part of us died.

Since World War II, we are becoming more aware each day that our darkness is overwhelming us—just as in my dream of the cauldron of *unclaimed shit* that was overwhelming the earth. We are now experiencing on a planetary scale what the Jesus in the Nag Hammadi texts had taught: "If you bring forth what is within you, what you bring forth will save you. If you do not bring forth what is within you, what you do not bring forth will destroy you."[14]

These ancient texts are one of the balls of thread that the great shamaness of the earth has thrown out on our path to lead us to that *something* that is within us. Will the reporter-knights in us see that ball and follow it to its destination? Will they be able to turn around into themselves to *see* the visionary walking the path with them? Will they be able to *hear* her Voice rather than proclaim their position and leave? Will they be able to love her, respect her, be loyal to her? Will they be able to allow her to reveal herself as soul perpetually coming into being?

For those who do, a whole new being and a whole new world will appear in the sacred texts of their lives.

Chapter Nine

"It is not our intention to set the canonical and the apocryphal gospels against each other or privilege one set over the other. Our aim is to read them together, to hold the manifest together with the hidden, the allowed with the forbidden, the conscious with the unconscious."[1]

—Jean-Yves Leloup

If we truly want to know who we are and why we're here, we must be open to all the crucial turns in the labyrinthine journey of our ancestors. For their experiences, interpretations, and decisions have shaped who we are. To know who we are, we have to know them. But we have not been able to know who they really are because we have been denied access to some of their most profound stories.

In the West, we think of our spiritual and cultural roots as reaching deep into the history of Israel and Greece. This is true, but we will see throughout this book that these roots penetrate much deeper into the past than we had previously known. **Since the discovery of the Dead Sea Scrolls, scholars have been able to piece together known texts with previously unknown texts to reveal an ancient shamanic-mystic tradition in Israel during the time of the First Temple.** From approximately 723 BCE efforts had been made to reform this ancient spiritual tradition, but it continued to endure until 621 BCE when Josiah, King of Judah, began the radical reforms once again. These reforms, including those after the Babylonian exile and the building of the Second Temple around 520 BCE, almost erased this ancient shamanic-mystic tradition along with the early sacred stories of Israel.

Yet the Dead Sea Scrolls reveal that the tradition and the stories did survive among various groups of Jews and later reemerged as a *secret tradition* in another form of Judaism that eventually became Christianity.[2] But once again, this tradition in Christianity would also be hidden, lost, or destroyed. For hundreds of years Jews and Christians have been denied access to their full spiritual heritage. However, the discoveries of the Dead Sea Scrolls and the Nag Hammadi texts have returned some of these lost stories to us—Jews, Christians, and the Western world. Now we are finally able to read the stories of our ancestors together, "to hold the manifest together with the hidden, the allowed with the forbidden, the conscious with the unconscious."[3]

So we will follow the ball of thread that was thrown out before us with the discovery of these ancient texts. This thread will take us back in time to the later part of the Hellenistic period, the rise of the Roman Empire, the Great Mysteries, the stories about the birth of a Messiah, and the destruction of Jerusalem and the second Jewish Temple—between 200 BCE and 70 CE. We will look briefly at the Hellenized world during this time since it was out of this multicultural complexity of experience, longing, despair, and hope that the major myth of the Western world emerged.

The Hellenistic period is usually considered to range from the death of Alexander the Great in 323 BCE to the rise of the Roman Empire under Augustus around 30 BCE. The end of the Greek city-states is usually given as 338 BCE when Philip of Macedon conquered Greece. In 333 BCE Philip was assassinated during his preparation for an invasion of Asia Minor. His son, Alexander the Great, succeeded him with an even larger ambition: his goal was to conquer and *Hellenize* the world. He defeated Persia, Syria, part of India, parts of Central Asia, Palestine, and Egypt, and for almost three hundred years Greek culture and language spread throughout much of the eastern Mediterranean and the Middle East.

Roadways connected people and allowed travel and trade to flourish. Along with people and goods came news of events in other lands as well as unfamiliar beliefs, ideas, and stories. People moved from one place to another to work, study, and live; new cities were built on the Greek model throughout the empire, as were schools, theaters, and markets; the famous library in Alexandria was built with the aim of collecting all the known books in the world; a museum was built as part of the library so that scholars could compile "encyclopedias of knowledge"; and there were significant advancements in science, the arts, and philosophy. This kind of contact among such diverse cultures brought about a new level of inspiration and development that affected people from Rome to India.[4]

However, it would be wrong to imagine that travel, trade, and exchange of ideas and customs had not taken place earlier. For thousands of years before Alexander the Great people had traveled great distances by both sea and land. Relatively late, Herodotus (c. 475 BCE) tells us about the ancient Persian Royal Road that stretched across what is now Turkey, from its western coast going southeast through the old Assyrian capital of Nineveh and on further south toward Babylon and the Persian Gulf. This Road linked into the famous Silk Road as well as many other routes that made contact possible between Central Asia, India, Mesopotamia and the Mediterranean. It is said that the first traveler on the Silk Road was around 959 BCE.[5] And Peter Kingsley tells us that during the seventh and sixth centuries BCE teachers came down to the Mediterranean from Central Asia and Tibet. One of their most famous students was Pythagoras, who, as we will see, is crucial to our understanding of Western civilization.[6]

However, it was with Alexander's expansion into Central Asia and India that the Silk Road and other routes became major connections between East and West. One of the great differences during the Hellenistic period was the extension of Greek power, culture and language throughout the conquered territories. As the Greeks built their new cities, large numbers of Greeks migrated from the Greek mainland "to assume lucrative positions in the military and administration."[7] While this certainly brought about the "exportation" of Greek culture, it also brought about a subtle merging of Greek ideas and experiences with some of the most profound aspects of the cultures Alexander had conquered. By the time of Alexander's conquest, the height of Greek culture was waning, yet the Classical period of Greek democracy, literature, architecture, and philosophy would influence Alexander's world, and in the process, it would undergo its own transformation.

But it is here that we must narrow our focus: if there is one thing that distinguishes the Hellenistic temperament from that of the rationalistic philosophers of Classical Greece, it is the longing to know, to understand, through actual inner *experience* what these philosophers had written and taught. There are many lenses through which we could view this period of our history, but our lens will be highly focused on this desire for *gnosis*, for inner experience, as it found its expression in the city of Alexandria and in the areas around Jerusalem. For it is here that some of the deepest and most ancient streams of mystical knowledge merged, rose to the surface of consciousness, and found expression in new ways of presenting a very old story: the sacred journey of the soul. It isn't that such experience wasn't taking place elsewhere. It was, but it was in this place and during this time that the flowering of mystical experience and its eventual suppression gave Western civilization its dominant myth.

As we will see in later chapters, these streams of mystical knowledge that began to merge and become more conscious during the Hellenistic period flowed in from ancient reservoirs of human experience—experience that reflected thousands of years of experience in altered states of consciousness through initiation, ritual, prayer, meditation, storytelling, and mythmaking. We will begin here with the Mystery Schools and their sacred myths, many of which flourished throughout the Hellenistic world. While there were variations on a central theme within the schools and their myths, the theme itself was basically the same: it was the soul's story of awakening to find itself in darkness and discovering the *Way to the Light*, the source of all reality. Through this process the initiates experienced their own divinity and immortality.

The Hellenistic world had become familiar with this theme through the Great Mysteries at Eleusis in Greece and through the ideas of Platonic philosophy since Plato's philosophy was rooted in Orphic-Pythagorean mystic experience. And now, because of the work of Kingsley, we know that Plato's philosophy was also rooted in Parmenides and the entire shaman-mystic-scientist tradition of which he, Pythagoras, and the Mysteries were a part. In Kingsley's work, *In the Dark Places of Wisdom*, he explains how profoundly Parmenides influenced Plato but, at the same time, how profoundly Plato distorted and rationalized the great tradition that Parmenides represented. For Parmenides and this shaman-mystic-scientist tradition, the idea was always rooted in actual mystical experience, but, once again, as with the ancient tradition of Judaism and later the *secret tradition* in Christianity, the very heart of our heritage was distorted and lost. Yet during the Hellenistic period this tradition continued to live in the Mystery Schools and people wanted "to experience emotionally the concepts…learned from Greek rationalism."[8]

The *experience* of the Mystery Schools was *a sacred text that was lived by the initiates*. And, as we will see, it was a text that was eventually repressed and forgotten. One of the most famous of the Mystery Schools was at Eleusis where the Mysteries were celebrated over a period of two thousand years—as long as the existence of Christianity—and they were rooted in rituals even more ancient. More than three thousand people were initiated every five years and there existed, says Kerényi, "a profound awareness that all Greek existence was inseparably bound up with the celebration of the Mysteries at Eleusis."[9]

The Mysteries continued to be celebrated throughout the entire Hellenistic period and into the Roman era. When Theodosius I closed the Mysteries in 392 CE, they had already undergone severe pressures from the changing times and the rise of Christianity. What remained of the Mysteries at Eleusis was destroyed by Alaric, king of the Goths, with the help of Christian monks, during Alaric's invasion of Greece in 396 CE.[10] It is difficult for us today to understand what the destruction of Eleusis meant for the Greeks. Whether we are a Jew or a Christian or neither, we have been imprinted with a particular version of the history of that period. The opinions and traditions of those whose beliefs survived have shaped our understanding of the past. In fact, Western consciousness has been so pervasively programmed with the "manifest," the "allowed" *truth* that it is extremely difficult for us to see the "hidden," the "forbidden" experiences of our ancestors. But for the Greeks, the destruction of Eleusis meant the end of Greek civilization.

There is a document that describes the Greek reaction to the Catholic Emperor Valentinian who in 364 CE sought to abolish the Mysteries of Eleusis: their reaction was that life would be "unlivable" for them if the Mysteries could no longer be celebrated. And thus, the office of proconsul in Greece permitted the celebrations to continue in spite of the edict. The Greeks understood that the visionary experience at Eleusis offered such joy and confidence to the individual and the community that participation in the Mysteries was not only "bound up inseparably" with the very existence of Greek life, but it was believed to "hold the entire human race together." Its vision, says Kerényi, "encompassed and concerned the whole world" because it was a response to that world's spiritual need: "Participation in the Mysteries offered a guarantee of life without fear of death, of confidence in the face of death."[11]

The gift of the Great Mysteries was an *initiation* into a larger vision of life—a vision so vast that all life became radiant. Such a vision, like Bucke's, offered confidence in the continuation of the life of the individual, and *it planted the seed of cosmic consciousness, a seed that was expected to flower from the depths of one's being.*[12] It was a longing for such a vision during the Hellenistic period that attracted so many people to the Mystery Schools and their sacred myths. These mysteries were, of course, rooted in ritual—in doing and becoming. Our ancestors understood very well that the great mysteries of life and death—and our role in these mysteries—could only be *known* through actual experience; they could not be conveyed through words or rational philosophy. In spite of all explanations, the experience itself remained, in Goethe's words, a holy open secret.

Kerényi tells us that the very word "Mysteria" comes from the verb "to initiate, to close the eyes or mouth." The initiates did not *read* about the mysteries nor did they *hear* a lecture or a sermon: the mysteries were not received through the *word* of a written or oral sacred text. They closed their eyes and entered into their own darkness. This tells us, says Kerényi, that the original sense of the word *Mysteries* was an entering into *darkness* in order to experience the particular goal of the initiation. The

Great Mysteries at Eleusis took place at night, for it was the night that had "the power to engender the light as it were, to help it come forth." It was out of the experience of utter darkness that the initiates experienced the culmination of "a sudden great radiance."[13]

This is the same truth that the Gnostic Jung discovered: we do not become enlightened by focusing on figures of light, but by working to make our own darkness conscious. And as we will see, the Gnostic Jesus also knew this well. The light is *hidden* within the darkness of our unknowing, he tells us, and it is this light that "lights up the whole universe."[14] Later we will see that the birth of light out of the depths of darkness was also at the heart of the earlier Egyptian Mysteries.

One of the most sacred of all the rituals that was a part of many of the ancient Mysteries was the circular, spiral dance. This dance was a symbol of the soul's labyrinthine journey to the light, to the memory of who we are and why we're here. The outer dance symbolizes and focuses the inner movement of consciousness as it spirals around and around and down into the depths of our own individual being. **At the center of our deepest selves** *we confront the divine, the cosmic Mind, the Christ—not as Other, but as Self.* In this great ecstasy of surprise, we remember who we are and why we're here. We know—we remember—that birth and death are events in time and space, that there is nothing but life, and that, in Kerényi's words, we are "the nucleus of the nucleus" of that life.[15] This is truly the heart of all the Great Mysteries—and, as we have seen—it is the core experience of the NDErs and all those who have had an experience of cosmic consciousness. It is the fruit from the Cosmic Tree. And this was the very essence of what was missing and so powerfully sought during the Hellenistic period.

Only when we *experience* this kind of consciousness are we able to understand how Kerényi could say that the core principle of ancient spirituality was the knowledge that the root aspect of all Being is in Nonbeing—that darkness gives birth to light just as death gives birth to life.[16] For those who had not yet been initiated, there were mythic stories that symbolically reflected the potential experience of the Mysteries—just as symbolic stories would later be associated with the Jesus Mysteries.

Such stories were not told to be *believed* literally but rather to *open* the mind and heart to the potential experience within the ritual.

For example, the myth of Demeter and her daughter Persephone was associated with Eleusis. The Homeric poem tells us that Persephone was playing in a sunlit meadow, dazzled by the beauty and fragrance of life when the earth opened and "the lord and All-receiver" sprang out of the gaping abyss and carried Persephone down into darkness and death. Demeter is filled with grief, sorrow, and rage. In this myth, we confront the great polarities of life: birth and death, light and darkness, joy and grief, presence and absence. And, says Kerényi, Demeter's story is *our* story: in life we all have felt robbed, we have failed to understand, and we have raged and grieved.[17] So this story tells us that the Mystery ritual embodies our darkest experiences.

But it also tells us something about this darkness: at the very moment that Persephone is touched by her husband of death, she conceives new life. Death impregnates Persephone. Nonbeing gives birth to being. And darkness is the source of light: Persephone returns to the world of light and with her she brings the child born out of death and darkness. The *story* cannot transform us but it can "open the way" *to experience* the potential within the ritual itself. Our ancestors who supported the Great Mysteries remained clear about the fact that it is the *experience – the gnosis* – that activates transformation. And it was the ability to engender this experience that gave the Mystery Schools their power.

Chapter Ten

In Egypt and most of the Greek-speaking world, Judaism was transformed into a Mystery.[1]

Jews also felt the impact of these ancient spiritual influences as well as the increasing pervasiveness of Greek culture. As with so much during this period, there are differences of opinion about the influence of the Mystery tradition on Hellenistic Judaism. However, Erwin R. Goodenough in *By Light, Light: The Mystic Gospel of Hellenistic Judaism* states that by the time of Philo Judaeus in Alexandria (20 BCE–40 CE), in fact, probably a hundred years before, "Judaism in the Greek-speaking world, especially in Egypt, had been transformed into a Mystery." The Jews, he says, were captivated by the Mysteries, but in order to remain a Jew they could not simply become an initiate of Isis or Orpheus, so they transformed Orpheus or Hermes-Tat into Moses and Isis into their Jewish Wisdom figure Sophia. In fact, says Goodenough, the entire *Torah* became an allegory of *the soul's journey to the Light with Moses as the God-Man, the Savior, the Great High Priest, who showed the way.* By Philo's time (which was also Jesus' time) Judaism, for Greek-speaking Jews, had become "the greatest, the only true, Mystery." In this way, they could remain Jews and at the same time participate in the Mysteries. "Indeed," says Goodenough, "they early claimed, not that they had borrowed it from the Greeks, but that the Greeks originally had taken it from them."[2]

Barker argues that indeed the Jews *did* have their own mystery tradition, for what we see in Philo, she says, is the resurgence of that shamanic, visionary, mystical tradition of the First Temple. This would make Philo's work a culmination of the efforts of many Jewish philosophers to understand this tradition in light of the Hellenistic Mysteries and to render their own ancient tradition in a Hellenistic style that could be understood by Jew and Gentile alike. It is known that the Jewish Greater Mysteries were open to Jews and Gentiles — just as the later Jesus Mysteries would be open to both. But it was, says Barker, from the earlier shamanic-mystic Jewish tradition that Philo "drew his theology... and not from an amalgam of Hellenized Judaism and contemporary Greek philosophy, as is so often suggested."[3]

During the Hellenistic period, there were evidently several groups of Jews who still continued to keep this ancient tradition alive. Some were in Egypt, others in or close to Jerusalem while still others were scattered throughout the surrounding area. These Jews not only rejected Greek influence on their way of life just as they would later reject Roman influence, but they rejected their own Jewish rule during the later Hasmonean Kingdom (c. 142–63 BCE), which they viewed as corrupt both in the spiritual practices of the Second Temple and in the political affairs of state. Some of these dissenters were the Essenes who left Jerusalem and some of them probably lived at Qumran where the Dead Sea Scrolls were found. Philo said that there were around 4,000 Essenes who lived in villages throughout Palestinian Syria, and Pliny locates one group near the Dead Sea.

Philo also mentions the Therapeutae in Egypt. While there were some differences between the Essenes and the Therapeutae, both were highly praised by Philo. He saw the Therapeutae as "men who realize the ideal life" of the true initiate.[4] While both the Therapeutae and the Essenes evidently did have their roots in their own Jewish shaman-mystic tradition, they had to be aware of this tradition's similarity with non-Jewish mysticism. The Jewish historian Josephus tells us that the Essenes were similar to the Pythagoreans, and Philo himself was known as "the Pythagorean."[5] Once individuals go inward and experience the organizing principles of the human psyche, they are able to recognize these same principles in the myths, allegories, stories, and practices of others.

The discovery of the Dead Sea Scrolls allows scholars to gain insight into the continuation, development, and transformations of this ancient Jewish mystical tradition. The Essenes were committed to what they believed to be the true Covenant between God and Israel. In their desert wilderness, they sought to renew this ancient Covenant through their own experience, just as they believed their forefathers had done before them.[6] The same can be said for the Therapeutae and the Jewish Kabbalists. In fact, all Gnostics — pagan, Jewish, and Christian — sought to know reality *through their own experience*.

What is amazing to me is the fact that there existed so many Jews who were dissatisfied with what they saw as corruption in the religious and social worlds. And, not only were they dissatisfied, they were willing to withdraw from those worlds and commit to the transformation of themselves and the social order. We are told that the Essenes developed a "revolutionary new form of social order," one that was democratic in religious and social relations. They are thought by many to be the first true monastic organization in the Mediterranean world, yet they must have learned much from the Pythagorean communities. They owned no property and shared everything — work, food, clothing, and shelter. They had a deep respect for freedom and were a pacifist community that allowed no weapons. Some say they were the first group to abolish slavery.[7]

The Essenes spoke of *right-teachers* or *teachers-of-righteousness* who were enlightened and who led them in *the way of the heart*. And they were aware that for others to receive the teachings of the heart, they too would have to become enlightened. These were mystics who sought to translate the darkness into light — or perhaps they thought more in terms of conquering the dark forces.[8] "The community considers itself, therefore, not only the remnant of Israel [the true and loyal Israelites] but also the specially 'enlightened.'" They knew that it was possible to experience in this life a higher dimension of consciousness, to "live even on earth in a dimension of eternity."[9] Or, in more modern terms, they knew that the human being is capable of experiencing cosmic consciousness.

Over 800 separate scrolls have been found in eleven caves near the Dead Sea. Fragments were found of every book in the Hebrew canon (Old

Testament), except the book of Esther, but this book is mentioned in some of the other texts found there. There were apocryphal [hidden] texts that relate to the Hebrew texts and which were widely read by Jews, and there were also the texts written by the Essenes.[10] The scrolls are the oldest Old Testament manuscripts yet discovered. For example, the Isaiah Scroll is 1,000 years older than all previously known copies of Isaiah. The Scrolls were written in Hebrew, Aramaic, and a few in Greek. According to Professor Lawrence H. Schiffman, a scholar in the history of Judaism and the Dead Sea Scrolls, the writing, collecting, and copying of the texts took place during the second and first centuries BCE, before the birth of Jesus. Neither the name of Jesus nor the names of any of the people associated with Jesus are mentioned in any of the Scrolls. But, this is no surprise, says Schiffman, because the Essenes were no longer writing texts during the time that Jesus would have been teaching.[11] There were, however, several practices such as baptism, communal meals, and vows of poverty that are clearly similar to what later appears in Christianity.

Both the Dead Sea Scrolls and the Nag Hammadi texts have not only given us valuable texts that had been lost to us, but they have leveled the scholarly playing field. The canonical texts are no longer "privileged" or considered more authoritative than the non-canonical texts. The importance of this cannot be overstated. As the mental framework constructed by the canonical texts dissolves, scholars are better able to read all texts together, "to hold the manifest together with the hidden, the allowed with the forbidden, the conscious with the unconscious."[12]

As a result of this new method of research, a larger and much more complex picture of both Judaism and Christianity is emerging. The Dead Sea Scrolls offer a clearer picture of what seems to have been the shaman-mystic tradition of the First Temple period as well as a fuller picture of the various forms of Judaism during the late Hellenistic and early Roman periods. They also help us place the figure of Jesus in the context of the history of his time. What had appeared to be unique to Jesus can now be seen as a natural—though extremely remarkable—resurgence and development of Jewish thinking and mystical experience.

I can still remember the great excitement I experienced when I first read about the Dead Sea Scrolls in Reverend Dr. Charles Francis Potter's *The Lost Years of Jesus Revealed: Newest Revelations of the Dead Sea Scrolls and the Nag-Hammadi Discoveries*. This was in the mid-sixties and I was about twenty-eight years old. Lost pieces of the great puzzle of the Christian era began to fall into place and open possibilities for new ways of telling the Jesus story. Potter sees Jesus as a great teacher and "a very great human being" who was "well-versed in the knowledge and culture of Rome, Persia, Athens and Alexandria,..." He had "an impressive personality of greater mental stature, deeper wisdom, and wider experience than has hitherto been claimed by his worshipers or suspected by his critics." Jesus, says Potter, was quoting from the Essene Scrolls when he spoke the beautiful sentences in the Sermon on the Mount and, he adds, this was something "he and his audience knew, though we may not." Many of the proverbs, prayers, beatitudes, and blessings familiar to Christians are of Essene origin. In fact, says Potter, there are hundreds of pieces of evidence that show us how the beauty and depth of Jesus' teachings reflect a long line of Jewish spiritual development.[13]

As mentioned earlier, the Essenes had rejected many of the Second Temple practices and had removed themselves from Jerusalem. Not only did Philo praise the spiritual and social achievements of the Essenes, but he actually requested that these men "who live naturally and reasonably, and are so free that they inspire their neighbors also with the spirit of freedom...come out to us and pacify our too turbulent and troubled lives, preaching to us to substitute for our wars and slavery and unspeakable evils their gospel of peace and freedom, and an abundance of their other rich blessings."[14]

Jesus was a young man when Philo wrote this. Given the interests of Jesus and his obvious knowledge of the texts found at Qumran, he must have known about the Essenes. Since the Essenes were usually older men who lived a monastic life, and since Jesus was a young man who did indeed associate with all sorts of people, we cannot assume that he was a member of the Essenes — although we cannot be certain. Potter suggests that he could certainly have studied in the Qumran library given that he often quoted from the Qumran texts, yet it is also possible that these texts were available to him from other sources. Potter goes a step further, however, and suggests that it could have been here with the Essenes that Jesus spent his "silent years," or the so-called "lost years." Could he have heard Philo's request, asks Potter, or out of his own compassion come out "into the marketplace to preach his own somewhat revised and improved version of the Essene gospel?"[15]

During the fifty years since Potter wrote about these texts and speculated about a different Jesus story, there has been an enormous amount of research on both the Dead Sea Scrolls and the Nag Hammadi texts. Barker's research is an excellent example of what can be *seen* when the canonical texts are read along with the non-canonical or forbidden texts. Her inclusive and exacting scholarship has added surprising and convincing pieces of information to the puzzle of our past. In Barker's view, some of "the most ancient traditions of Israel" are becoming clear and shedding light on Christianity. However, as Barker points out, the destruction brought about by the early waves of reforms and the Babylonian exile make absolute certainty impossible for anyone attempting to reconstruct these ancient traditions. Yet her work allows many of the contradictions and apparently stray pieces of canonical texts to fall into place and reveal a more coherent picture of Israel's past and the formative stages of Christianity.[16]

Chapter Eleven

>―•>―○―<•―<

> *In the most ancient tradition of Israel, Yahweh was both female
> and male, and it was they who co-created the world. The feminine
> side of Yahweh was called Wisdom, the consort of Yahweh, the
> Queen of Heaven, the bright and radiant one. But Wisdom was
> abandoned by her husband.*[1]
>
> — Margaret Barker

Earlier I mentioned that from around 723 BCE efforts had been made to reform the ancient shamanic, visionary, mystic tradition of Israel, but that this tradition had continued to endure until 621 BCE when Josiah began the radical reforms once again. It is usually acknowledged that Josiah destroyed all forms of foreign worship and practices that he deemed unworthy of the people of Judah. **But Barker suggests that Josiah destroyed much more: he destroyed the very heart of the ancient tradition—the feminine consort and co-creatress of God. She was Wisdom, the Queen of Heaven, the shamanic, visionary, mystical path to divinity and immortality.**[2]

How was he able to do this? The story is told that when Josiah ordered the First Temple to be renovated in 621 BCE, "the book of the Law" was *found* in the treasure room of the Temple. Josiah then made the massive reforms supposedly in accord with this book of the law. The details of the reforms are unclear, but what is clear, says Barker, is that "the Deuteronomists wrote themselves into history at this point, since in 2 Kings, they clearly identified the programme of reform with their own ideals."[3]

In 586 BCE, not long after these Deuteronomic reforms were in the process of being established, the massive destruction brought about by the Babylonian invasion took place. The reforms, the Babylonian invasion, and the exile shattered the most ancient traditions of Israel, and many would believe that this destruction was the result of the abandonment of the Queen of Heaven. When the exiled Hebrews, now called Jews, returned to Jerusalem in 538 BCE, the reforms were intensified. There appears to have been an effort on the part of the returning exiles to create a sacred *history* to bind the people together. Scholars are not in agreement about the age of the materials in the first five books of the Old Testament, the Pentateuch, but Barker asks, "Why is Moses not a part of the religion of the pre-exilic prophets?" And why do the authors of the Old Testament literature that is written before the exile "know virtually nothing of the patriarchal and Mosaic traditions...." that appear in the Pentateuch? In short, "much of the Old Testament has been edited and transmitted by the reforming Deuteronomists...."[4]

Yahweh, in the most ancient tradition of Israel, was both female and male, and it was they who co-created the world. The feminine side of Yahweh was called Wisdom, consort of Yahweh, the Queen of Heaven, the *bright and radiant* one whose "teaching was like the light of the dawn."[5] She was the Great Lady, Virgin, Lamp of the Gods, Holy Spirit, nursing mother and consort of the human king, the anointing oil for the high priests, winged sun, and *the great tree of Life* in the Garden of the Gods, called Eden. She was the water of life flowing from the fountains in heaven, like "the four rivers flowing from Eden." And it was she who brought all pairs of opposites into a harmonious balance. We are told that "The spirit of Yahweh *was* the spirit of Wisdom...."[6]

So here we have at the heart of the ancient Hebrew spiritual tradition *Our Lady, the soul of the world; the Cosmic Tree*; the sacred waters of life, flowing from fountains and rising up from wells and streams; the Sovereign of the land and protectress of Jerusalem, loved, honored, and in equal relationship with her male counterpart. For here too "The king rules the land by right of his true union with her and by his championship of her freedom."[7]

This relationship between Yahweh and Wisdom, the human king and Wisdom, reflects the psyche's blueprint for our growth and development. Unlike the knight who rode away from his feminine counterpart in my dream, Yahweh and Wisdom are together and *together* they create the world, guide Israel's history, and lead the initiate into knowledge of eternal life. *But this was not to last.* Wisdom was abandoned when the reformists attempted to destroy everything that related to her. All the objects associated with her worship and veneration were removed from the temple and the land so they could be destroyed. Her sacred groves were cut down, her altars destroyed, her sacred images burned, her wisdom literature removed from the sacred writings, and *her stories rewritten* under the influence of the Deuteronomists. *Wisdom had been abandoned by her husband.*[8]

Both Yahweh and Wisdom suffered. The stories after their separation reveal a Yahweh who proclaims that he is the only God, that there is none before him—when indeed the divine Queen of Heaven had been with him when they *co-created* the world. At one point, he even becomes "sorry that he had made [no longer *procreated*] man on the earth, and it grieved him to his heart. So the Lord said, 'I will blot out man whom I have created from the face of the ground, man and beast and creeping things and birds of the air, for I am sorry that I have made them.'" This is surely a dysfunctional response to what had once been a sacred co-creation. Evidently, his abandonment of Wisdom had caused him to lose the "happiness" that she gave, for we know that "She is the tree of life to those who lay hold of her/and those who hold her fast are called happy."[9]

But since Yahweh did not "hold her fast," he became a jealous God who demanded strict obedience, gave harsh punishment, denied the right to knowledge, denied the ancient birthright to immortality and divinity—and he even denied his people the right to create art. "You shall not make for yourself a graven image, or any likeness of anything that is in heaven above, or that is in the earth beneath, or that is in the water under the earth;..."[10] **Yahweh had become a master of negation.** The written Word—the Law—had replaced Wisdom—the visionary and the artist.

In this abandonment Wisdom also suffered. She saw how difficult the lives of her people had become. She called to them from outside the gates of the city. She offered them knowledge of life and death, of immortality and divinity. She longed to open their hearts to the secrets of the Otherworld through dreams and visions and mystic states of consciousness. She longed to give them happiness. But, as *The Book of Enoch* tells us, "All who lived in the temple *lost their vision*, and the hearts of all of them godlessly forsook Wisdom, and the house of the kingdom was burned and the whole chosen people was scattered."[11]

Evidently there were many people who believed that it was precisely this *loss of vision* on the part of the Deuteronomists that not only brought about the scattering of people during the exile but released a corrupted view of Yahweh and, as we will see, even of the Queen of Heaven. The people did not forget the real Yahweh, the Great High Priest, nor did they forget Wisdom. We are told that a large number of priests had even fought *with* the Babylonian forces against Jerusalem in 586 BCE because of Josiah's purge of the Queen of Heaven and the spiritual traditions of the First Temple. And Barker reminds us that the refugees who fled to Egypt after the Babylonian destruction of Jerusalem insisted that the disaster was a result of the abandonment of Wisdom. The prophet Jeremiah tells the refugees that Yahweh will destroy them if they continue to honor Wisdom, the Queen of Heaven, but they respond by saying:

> *As for the word which you have spoken to us in the name of the Lord, we will not listen to you. But we will do everything that we have vowed, burn incense to the queen of heaven and pour out libations to her, as we did, both we and our fathers, our kings and our princes, in the cities of Judah and in the streets of Jerusalem; for then we had plenty of food, and prospered, and saw no evil.*[12]

If the people and their fathers and their kings and their princes had indeed worshiped Wisdom, the Queen of Heaven, then it would appear that the Deuteronomists were "a vocal minority," but, even so, they were ultimately the minority in control. It was the First Temple, says Barker, that was remembered by many as the *true* temple—and Wisdom, the Queen of Heaven, was at the heart of that temple's tradition. Yet we are told that after the violent reforms, Wisdom could find no "dwelling place" on the earth and thus returned to take "her seat among the angels."[13]

Before we look at one of the best-known stories about the Queen of Heaven written under the influence of the Deuteronomists, we need to refocus our thoughts on how living, sacred stories come into being. They come to us, to individuals, through dreams, visions, mystical experience, and waking, altered states of consciousness. These stories are structured by the organizing principles of the human psyche—principles whose roots are deep in nature's cycle of birth, development, death, and rebirth.

In my own experience, I gradually came to honor the living text of my own soul as it unfolded and revealed itself throughout my life. This ongoing process taught me that the soul essence of this living text was *perpetually coming into being*. But, as I said earlier, I needed verification of this process from other cultures, so I plunged into the study of dreams, myths, rituals, and religions. At the same time, I studied the various theories of how myths and dreams emerge in the human mind and how symbol and story shape the evolution of our mental and spiritual life. I would spend my life studying and teaching what I would come to realize were the mythic patterns of the soul—the blueprint—for our human evolution. This was the *inexhaustible creativity* of the human psyche *within a unified pattern* that Eliade had discovered earlier in his much more extensive research. Once we know the patterns, we are able to recognize their distortions.

So now let's look at a soul story that was distorted and inverted. Most people in the Western world know the story in Genesis (Chapters 2–3) about the tree of knowledge of good and evil in the Garden of Eden in which four rivers flow. God told Adam and Eve that they could eat of every tree in the garden except of this tree, "for the day that you eat of it you shall die." But the serpent in the garden convinced Eve that she would not die and that the fruit would make her wise, so she ate of the fruit and gave some of it to Adam. When God discovered their disobedience, Adam blamed Eve and Eve blamed the serpent—and God punished all three.

God cursed the serpent and told Eve, "I will greatly multiply your pain in childbearing; in pain you shall bring forth children, yet your desire shall be for your husband, and he shall rule over you." And then God cursed the ground and told Adam that "in toil you shall eat of it all the days of your life; thorns and thistles it shall bring forth to you;...till you return to the ground, for out of it you were taken; you are dust, and to dust you shall return." God then exiled Adam and Eve from the garden because they had eaten from the tree of knowledge and because God did not want them to eat of the tree of life and become immortal.

This story is *not* in harmony with the growth and development of human consciousness. It is a distortion and inversion of the mythic pattern of the soul, the blueprint for our human evolution. How could we ever have accepted this story or told it to anyone? How could it ever have become part of religious doctrine? Its intention, conscious or unconscious, is to block the evolution of consciousness, disempower the people, and establish an outside, punitive authority. Unfortunately, Western culture inherited as part of its sacred text many of the distorted and dysfunctional stories that were told after the exile of Wisdom. *We lost our true stories.* Is it any wonder that we forgot who we are or why we're here?

Long before I knew anything about mythic patterns, this story in Genesis disturbed me. How could a God punish people who simply wanted to have knowledge? And how were so many people for so many centuries able to accept this story as a true reflection of God or humanity? It also seemed to me that even when we didn't believe that the story reflected any kind of actual relationship between the human being and the divine, the images still had an effect on us—especially since it was presented to us as part of a sacred text. I felt that there was something pathological about it, and I wondered why it would have been written at all. Once I understood the principles of mythic patterns, I could recognize their distortions, and once I had a better understanding of the historical context of the story, I was better able to explore the nature of its dysfunction.

The basic elements in the Genesis story are as follows: (1) God demands that human beings remain unconscious; (2) that they obey an outside power that is maintained by fear and punishment; (3) that the female be subjected to the male; (4) that nature be cursed; (5) that human beings should die—return to dust; and (6) that human beings *not* become like God.

Now let's look at the principles in the actual mythic pattern: (1) instead of remaining unconscious, life is a process of becoming conscious; (2) instead of obeying an outside power, we seek an inner knowledge so we are able to make our own choices; (3) instead of male dominance, male and female are equal partners in creating life—neither is subjected to the other; (4) instead of perceiving nature as cursed, nature is sacred and nothing is more important than understanding her sacred laws and maintaining harmony with them; (5) instead of perceiving ourselves as beings who die and are no more than dust, we are initiated into the knowledge that we are eternal; and (6) instead of perceiving ourselves as inferior beings, we are initiated into the knowledge that we are divine. This is the labyrinthine path to our own wholeness—our evolutionary goal.

The Genesis story uses and distorts several major images from world mythology: the mythic garden of life with its four rivers flowing with the sacred waters of life to the four corners of the world; the Cosmic Tree of knowledge/life (originally there was one tree) with the feminine kundalini serpent deity; and the woman and man who are either being shown the fruit with a welcoming gesture by the divine or they are being led in an initiation to partake of the fruit of the sacred tree and thus experience the mystical knowledge of their own divinity and immortality. In this soul pattern there is no restriction, hostility, or guilt associated with the quest. The fruit is available to any human being who is seeking knowledge of who we are and why we're here.[14]

But Barker's research shows us that we do not need to go to world mythologies to find the earlier myth whose distortion we read in Genesis. This story, written by or under the influence of the Deuteronomists, is clearly about the abandoned Queen of Heaven. For we now know that Wisdom, Our Lady, just as in other world mythologies, *was* the great tree of life in the Garden of the Gods, called Eden. Barker tells us that in several non-biblical texts, Wisdom, the Queen of Heaven, is described as the Tree of Life. For example, in *The Wisdom of Sirach* the tree is "planted in Jerusalem and unlike any other tree in beauty and height. *It is perfumed with the incense of the holy of holies and its fruit is for all to eat, 'and those who work with my help will not sin.'"*[15] Let's pause here for just a moment: this is *profoundly* different from the story in Genesis. **Here is the blueprint of the soul: Wisdom, in the image of the beautiful and fragrant tree, offers knowledge to all and she offers to work with all people to help them not to sin, that is, not to go against the laws of their own nature. Her fragrance, her wisdom, her guidance, her entire essence — all are the gifts of the holy of holies — and they are gifts freely given to all who seek them.**

Even in the canonical text of Proverbs (3:18) we are told that **The Tree of Life** makes one happy. In the non-canonical text of Enoch, during a mystical journey, Enoch "saw a huge fragrant tree whose fruit gave Wisdom...." and he further describes this tree of life as a fragrant tree with fruit like grapes — a tree with "a fragrance beyond all fragrance whose leaves and blossoms and wood never wither or rot."[16] Wisdom is, says Enoch (2 Enoch 8:4), the fiery tree, "gold looking and crimson, with the form of fire." Wisdom is "the Lady in the burning bush," in the fiery, tree-shaped Menorah, the Lady of the fiery tree who gives birth in the holy of holies.[17] A text from *The Nag Hammadi Library* states that "the color of the tree of life is like the sun, and its branches are beautiful. Its leaves are like those of the cypress. Its fruit is like the clusters of white grapes."[18] And **the Queen of Heaven, the Great Cosmic Tree of Life,** was also the water of life flowing from the fountains of heaven, like "the four rivers flowing from Eden." *These writers, says Barker, remembered the earlier Hebrew spiritual tradition.*[19]

What a difference! She is Baba Yaga who throws out the ball of thread to guide us on our way. She is the great Self — *the Light* — at the center of the labyrinth, the source of life, the axis mundi, the ground of being, universal mind, the quantum field. She is the spiraling serpent energy that rises as we near the center of the labyrinth. She is the soul of the world and the Spirit of the universe. Here she is never abandoned, for here "The spirit of Yahweh" *is* "the spirit of Wisdom."[20]

And here again we find that *hidden something* at the center of the labyrinth, that *missing something* that is so threatening that centuries have been devoted to denying it, repressing it, and destroying whole worlds to defeat it. **We certainly must wonder how our culture might have developed had it inherited its true soul myth.** But we did not — and Western culture is still working to heal the wounds of a Yahweh personality that continues to suffer from his abandonment of Wisdom, Our Lady, the Queen of Heaven. *The Jewish Kabbalists would later pick up this theme of how "a part of God had been exiled from God," and that our redemption would come only when God and Wisdom/Shekhinah were once again united.*[21]

But our question now is why such a powerful story would be distorted into the one that the Deuteronomists bequeathed to the Western world as part of our sacred text. The answer probably lies in Israel's history. Even before the exile, Israel was always in a precarious position and understandably fearful of being taken over and controlled by others — or even annihilated. Throughout the Old Testament this fear was deep and pervasive. When confronted with such fear, some of us respond with the need to control, others with the need to understand, while others simply recoil from it all in despair, indifference, addiction or self-destruction. But the response that won the day was the Deuteronomists' need to control, and the stories they told served their need to maintain that power. The methods used to achieve and maintain power are basically the same in every age: distortion, lies, fear, and violence. The value of the individual is negated and our development on all levels is thwarted. Such an *exclusive* dominator system confronts what it sees as the dark forces in the world with a belief in the necessity to control or destroy all opposition. Those who long to understand the world and to experience life as fully as possible are usually *inclusive*. They strive to create a system of equality for all people so that everyone can live life independently and creatively. They tend to confront what they see as the dark forces with perceptions and techniques to distill the dark into light, to transform self and other.

It would be easy to see oneself neatly on the side of those who seek to transform the darkness rather than to destroy it. In my own study of these two basic responses in our culture's history, I experienced myself as inclusive and on the victim's side. Yet my soul gently taught me otherwise. I had dreams and visions that allowed me to experience myself as both the victim *and* the perpetrator of the crimes in Western history. This was a painful period for me, but **I realized that my research—and my own development—could not be complete unless I could experience the responsibility for both sides. I had to experience how complicit we all are in the crimes of our culture when we do not take the responsibility to develop in ourselves** *the miracle that can heal our civilization.*

After all, had I not dreamed of my own knight riding away from—abandoning—Wisdom, my visionary, soul energy? It is true that I did not yet understand what this abandonment of soul would mean for me or for my culture. My earlier dream had revealed that I had within me both Yahweh and Our Lady, the Queen of Heaven. The deepest aspect of myself wanted a loving union between them, but I did not know how to bring this about. My culture offered me a path to develop the left-brain intellect, for which I am deeply grateful, but it had long ago lost the knowledge of how to nurture the right-brain visionary.

What is amazing is that on some level the Deuteronomists knew precisely what such abandonment of Our Lady would mean and they knew how to achieve it. They knew that by *exiling* the visionary, they would be able to gain power over the people and construct an orderly, *lawful*, more cohesive and predictable society. So they constructed a God who told the people not to create any image whatsoever—no visual art forms. Obviously, the visionary communicates through images and symbols, a function of the right brain. By denying images and glorifying the abstract *word*, the Deuteronomists were able to shift mental activity away from the right brain to the left brain.

Leonard Shlain in *The Alphabet Versus The Goddess: The Conflict Between Word and Image* explores how the invention of the abstract alphabet shifts our mental activity away from the right brain to the left brain—from images, symbols and holistic experience to words and linear, abstract, sequential thinking. The Deuteronomic reforms began in the seventh century BCE and, says Shlain, "The archaeological record suggests that by the seventh century BCE the Israelites, unlike their neighbors, were substantially alphabet literate."[22] If Shlain is correct, then alphabet literacy would have intensified the already existing fear and need to control.

It is this same fear that can challenge each of us at every turn in our labyrinthine journey. When our fear wins, we stumble and look outside ourselves for answers. This is when we are most likely to abandon the inner visionary path and to believe that the only solution to our fear is power. We believe that with this power we can build a just world. The Deuteronomic period was only one time in our history when fear won. Our knights are still riding away from their visionary companions and they are still unable to see soul perpetually coming into being. We *lose our vision again and again*, our hearts forsake Wisdom, our kingdoms are burned, and the people are scattered.

Yet there are those wonderful times of vision throughout our history. Such times are usually tolerated until they are perceived as a threat. Then they are brutally suppressed—just as Israel's ancient tradition of the visionary, mystical path to self-knowledge had been suppressed so many hundreds of years ago. But this tradition did not entirely die. The psyche of the Western world attempted many times to balance itself, to pull us back from fear and allow a creative and loving relationship to develop between Yahweh and Wisdom, between the intellect and the visionary.

We know that hundreds of years after Josiah's reforms, Wisdom and the ancient priestly tradition that offered "knowledge of the divine mysteries"[23] were still remembered by Jews like Philo, the Essenes at Qumran, the Therapeutae in Egypt, the Gnostics and the writers of the Jewish Kabbalah. And, says Barker, all of the characteristics of this spiritual tradition were to reappear in Christianity.[24] But this *secret tradition* of the early Christians would also be ruthlessly suppressed by the Church of Rome. **The Church, much like the earlier Deuteronomists, would distort their core myth in such a way that once again we would** be denied our true birthright of eating from the Cosmic Tree of Life—and remembering who we are and why we're here.

Chapter Twelve

>―•―O―•―<

The Gospel of Philip tells us that three women always walked with Jesus: his mother Mary; his sister; and Mary Magdalene, his companion: for Jesus, Mary is a mother, a sister, and a wife.[1]

The Jesus who walks with the feminine is the redemption of the Yahweh of the Deuteronomists who had abandoned Wisdom. For these mystics who were the early Christians, says Margaret Barker, redemption meant allowing Wisdom, the exiled part of God, to return as the beloved of God.[2]

We have already met the Jesus of the Nag Hammadi texts, for it is this Jesus who tells us to bring forth what is within us. What is within us, he tells us, will save us. But if we fail to bring forth what is within us, it will destroy us. And it is this Jesus who teaches us to become our own master, to remember that he is not our master: "He who will drink from My mouth will become like Me."[3]

Who wrote these texts? And why, we might ask, have these profound teachings been hidden from us?

The answer to the first question is that many of the writers were Christians. And the answer to the second question is that the Church rejected these teachings and attempted to destroy all knowledge of *this* Jesus. The Church would attempt to make the world believe that the writers of such texts were heretics, but now that the Nag Hammadi texts and the Dead Sea Scrolls have been discovered, a very different picture is emerging: **the movement that became Christianity began among those Jews who remembered Wisdom and the ancient priestly tradition that offered "knowledge of the divine mysteries."**[4] Christianity is a rebirth of the shaman-mystic tradition of ancient Israel, and the wisdom that is reflected in many of the Nag Hammadi texts is born out of this mystical tradition. The Jesus of these texts is a mystic who teaches a *secret tradition of the Way to the Light.*

The entire collection of the Nag Hammadi texts consists of a little more than twelve books within which are about fifty-two separate but brief essays. When duplicates within the library itself are subtracted as well as six texts that were already known, there are actually forty essays that exist only among the Nag Hammadi texts.[5] Not all the texts are Christian or Jewish; some reflect other religious traditions. Yet those who collected, copied, and translated the various texts were probably Christian Gnostics who saw in all the texts a similar concern and approach to life. The Nag Hammadi texts were written later than the Dead Sea Scrolls; in fact, from the historical perspective of Gnosticism, the Nag Hammadi texts pick up about where the Dead Sea Scrolls break off.[6]

The Nag Hammadi texts were found in Upper Egypt but were composed in Greek by Greek-writing authors who "may have been located anywhere in the ancient world where Greek was used,..."[7] But they were collected in Egypt, translated into Coptic during the fourth century CE, and buried around 400 CE when the Church made it clear that it would be dangerous to have such texts in their library.[8] Of course, there is disagreement about the dating of the original texts. Elaine Pagels tells us that some can be no later than 120–150 CE and that the Gospel of Thomas, written around 140 CE, probably includes traditions older than the New Testament gospels (c. 60–110 CE), perhaps as old as the second half of the first century (50–100 CE).[9]

In many of the Nag Hammadi gospels the Voice of Jesus is somewhat different from that of the New Testament gospels. According to Marvin Meyer, a scholar of Gnosticism and the Nag Hammadi texts,

Jesus emerges *not* as a person who performs miracles, fulfills prophecy, or dies for our sins. No. This Jesus speaks of how our confusion and lack of knowledge have caused us *to forget who we are and why we're here*. This is the Jesus who tells us to bring forth what is within us. This is the Jesus who tells us we have *forgotten* that we are divine, that we are light, and that we have both the capacity and the responsibility to go within to experience the miracle of who we are. It is this knowledge, this *gnosis*, that is more important than belief.[10]

Our problem as human beings, he tells us, is not sin but our own not knowing, our *forgetting*, and *the good news of these gospels is the wisdom of gnosis: the labyrinthine journey to experience who we are*. This is the Jesus who says in the Gospel of Thomas, "whoever drinks from my mouth will become as I am, and I myself will become that person, and the mysteries shall be revealed to him."[11] Pagels tells us that the name Thomas means *twin* and that "By encountering the 'living Jesus,' as Thomas suggests, one may come to recognize oneself and Jesus as, so to speak, identical twins." In several of these gospels Jesus emphasizes the inner journey toward the light that is hidden within each of us: "For whoever has not known himself knows nothing, but whoever has known himself has simultaneously come to know the depth of all things."[12] **Here in these texts the shamanic Jesus returns to teach us the way of an ancient mystical tradition.**

But there is more. This Jesus walks *with* the feminine. In the Gospel of Mary,[13] Mary Magdalene emerges as the visionary and the beloved of Jesus. She is not the prostitute and penitent the Church had made her out to be. She is Our Lady, the Virgin, the sacred feminine, "*strong, free, and available.*"[14] Here, in these gospels, Jesus and Mary together reflect the sacred wholeness of soul. Together they reflect the Holy Grail, the Sacred Marriage, the joy of what it means to be fully human. The Gospel of Philip tells us that Jesus loved Mary and kissed her often on the mouth. She "is a sister, a mother, and a wife."[15] He also tells us that "Three women always walked with the master: Mary his mother, <his> sister, and Mary of Magdala, who is called his companion. For 'Mary' is the name of his sister [sometimes translated *the sister of his mother*], his mother, and his companion."[16] The word translated as wife or companion is *koinonos*, which "in both Greek and Coptic, refers to coupling and could be translated as 'fiancée,' 'companion,' or 'spouse.'"[17]

The Jesus we know even from the canonical texts is radical in his acceptance and equal treatment of women, but he is denied an intimate relationship with a woman. This prohibits his ability to fully redeem the feminine, to allow Yahweh to embrace once again his beloved Wisdom, the Queen of Heaven. It is highly symbolic that in the Nag Hammadi texts we are told that three women always walked *with* Jesus. Here we see the masculine as intimately related to the feminine in her aspects as mother, sister, and companion/wife. How unlike my Knight who rode off on his horse and left his visionary companion behind. How unlike the Deuteronomists' Yahweh who had abandoned the Queen of Heaven and suffered the loss of his vision and joy. And how unlike all the "scattered" people who had also lost their vision and joy because it was this wounded Yahweh who lived in them.

In *The Sacred Embrace of Jesus and Mary: The Sexual Mystery at the Heart of the Christian Tradition,* Jean-Yves Leloup states that "The Gospel of Mary, like the Gospels of John and Philip, remind us that Yeshua was capable of intimacy with a woman." This intimacy between Jesus and Mary, he says, was "not merely of the flesh; it was also emotional, intellectual, and spiritual." We cannot even begin to be spiritual, he says, until we embrace *all* that we are, for it is only through our full humanity that we are able to imbue all the dimensions of our reality with "consciousness and love."[18]

It is an important discovery for most of us that, for the early Christians, Jesus was Yahweh. Barker gives us a deeper insight into the name of Yahweh in Israel's ancient religion. In this tradition, there was a High God, El Elyon, El, Elohim, and several sons of the High God, "one of whom was Yahweh, the Holy One of Israel. Yahweh, the Lord, could be manifested on earth in human form, as an angel or in the Davidic king. *It was as a manifestation of Yahweh, the Son of God, that Jesus was acknowledged as Son of God, Messiah and Lord.*"[19]

From this perspective, **the Jesus who walks *with* the feminine *is* the redemption of the Yahweh of the Deuteronomists who had abandoned**

Wisdom. The mystics who wrote the major gospels that found their way into the Nag Hammadi collection experienced a very different Yahweh and their experience is reflected in the mystic Jesus who *walks with his beloved* and who, with Mary, reflects the wholeness that the human psyche urges us to achieve. *For these mystics who were the early Christians, redemption meant allowing Wisdom, the exiled part of God, to return as the beloved of God.*[20]

Chapter Thirteen

Mary is a visionary. She is the personification of wisdom.[1]

In the Gospel of Mary, Jesus explains to Mary that there is an intermediate aspect of the mind that allows us to see visions.[2]

Henri Corbin tells us that in the Sufi mystic tradition there is also an intermediate aspect of the mind that allows us to see visions: it is the organ of the soul, which makes possible "a precise mode of perception" that allows us to see "a precise order of reality."[3]

We have no way of knowing what might have been lost or destroyed concerning the feminine dimension of Jesus/Yahweh, but in the other known gospels that tell us about her, Mary Magdalene reveals the depth of her partnership with Jesus and how this partnership is able to continue after his death. We learn that she is considered the "apostle of apostles": she is with Jesus when he dies and she is the first to witness his resurrection. In *Pistis Sophia*, Jesus says that Mary is a "pure spiritual woman," and elsewhere Mary is called "the spirit of wisdom."[4] Mary understands the teachings of Jesus in ways that the other apostles do not. In spite of the objections of some of the male apostles, Mary attempts to comfort them with this understanding after the death and resurrection of Jesus. She communicates to them secrets that are unknown to them but that she had received from Jesus in a vision.

Mary is a visionary, and she attempts to explain to the other disciples what Jesus has taught her about the visionary process. Mary had asked the Master how a person sees a vision, with the soul or with the spirit, and Jesus responded, "A person sees neither with the soul nor with the spirit. The mind [nous], which is between the two, sees the vision...." Unfortunately, it is at this point that the text breaks off.[5] It appears that Jesus is saying that there is an *intermediary* aspect of the mind that allows us to see the vision. This corresponds to what Henri Corbin translates from the Sufi mystic experience as "the imaginative consciousness, the *cognitive* Imagination," which Corbin, unlike Jesus, does call the soul. Perhaps the language or translation is misleading since both Jesus and the Sufis speak of an intermediary aspect of the mind that perceives the vision. Corbin states that it is actually *the organ of the soul* that perceives visionary reality. This organ makes possible "a precise mode of perception" that allows us to see "a precise order of reality." This order of reality Corbin calls the *mundus imaginalis*.[6]

The Sufi mystics of ancient Persia were excellent cartographers of the dimensions of otherworld realities. In their map of reality there are three categories of the universe that interpenetrate each other and that are supported by an underlying unity: there is the sense/material world, the subtle world, and pure spirit. These three realities have three corresponding organs of knowledge: the senses, the imagination, and the intellect, which correspond to body, soul, and spirit. The world of soul is the subtle, intermediate world that exists between the sensory/body and the supersensory/spirit worlds. As mentioned above, Corbin calls this in-between world the mundus imaginalis. It is, says Corbin, as "real as the world of the senses and the world of the intellect." And just as the body perceives through the senses and pure spirit is perceived through the intellect, the world of soul is perceived through its own cognitive organ, the organ of soul, which is "as fully real as the faculties of sensory perception or intellectual intuition."[7]

According to Corbin, everything that exists in the world of the senses has its counterpart in this subtle, intermediate world, even though we cannot perceive these forms with our physical senses. When physical forms cease to exist, their subtle forms continue to exist in the intermediate world. This includes everything we have accomplished in our lives, as well as our thoughts, feelings, and desires. All these forms, says Corbin, have an "immaterial materiality"—a subtle reality—whose nature is nevertheless precise and reliable.[8]

From the perspective of the material world, we would say that as we create in the physical world, we are simultaneously creating in the subtle world. However, since the roots of the physical world are in the subtle, invisible world, we could say that as we create in the subtle world, we are simultaneously manifesting that creativity in the physical world. This process is more easily understood in the mind-body connection. The research of Candace Pert as discussed in *Molecules of Emotion: The Science Behind Mind-Body Medicine* shows us that every thought, every feeling, every intention is simultaneously communicated to every system in our body. As she so clearly delineates, "Mind doesn't dominate body, it *becomes* body—body and mind are one. I see the process of communication we have demonstrated, the flow of information throughout the whole organism, as evidence that the body is the actual outward manifestation, in physical space, of the mind."[9] We can understand the relationship between our creativity in the subtle world and its manifestation in the physical world in the same way. Corbin adds to this, however, that the forms of our creativity in the subtle world continue to exist even after the physical forms no longer exist in the material world.

Research into the quantum field supports what Corbin says about the subtle world. Earlier I mentioned scientists' description of this field: the quantum field encodes and records everything that has ever happened in the universe, and its ability to encode and record is infinite. It is an eternal record of everything that has ever happened.[10]

Now that we know how the subtle, intermediate world relates to the physical world, we need to know how these two worlds relate to the world of pure spirit/intellect. The realm of pure spirit, pure intelligence, is the *ground* of all being. It is *formless* but it is *perpetually coming into being* in the subtle/intermediary world—the mundus imaginalis. As the formless energy of pure spirit/intelligence moves into the subtle/

intermediary world, it is shaped by the laws that organize energy: these laws are called the archetypes of light through which this energy manifests itself in *the essential structures of the universe* and in the autonomous forms and images of all things.

Since the three worlds of the material, the subtle, and the spirit interpenetrate each other and are supported by an underlying unity, we participate in the energy and creativity of each. The imagination, *the organ of the soul,* creates and receives the images and symbols through which we can perceive the intermediary world—a world of infinite potential with many levels of being. Perhaps this is what the Jesus of the canonical texts meant when he said that in his father's house there are many mansions. This realm is dynamic, creative, and ever-evolving.

And since the realm of pure spirit is ever present and continually coming into being, merging with all that is, we can experience pure spirit in two major ways: (1) the way of the visionary—through the subtle world of symbols and forms, or (2) the way of the mystic—as "an ultimate nonsensuous unity in all things, a oneness or a One to which neither the senses nor the reason can penetrate. In other words, it entirely transcends our sensory-intellectual consciousness."[11] It transcends the subtle world of forms. This is the definition of the mystical experience in its strictest form, but I have used the term *mystic* throughout this book for both types of experience. Pure spirit, then, is the ground of all being, the quantum field of fields, which can be experienced in these two important ways. We most often experience it through the symbols and forms of the subtle world or what we may also call the mundus imaginalis. We are able to perceive and feel these forms through *the organ of soul.*

While this world *appears* to exist in a place or space, it does not. The *place or space* where we find ourselves in this world is determined by *our state of being*. What appears to be a change of place is actually a change in our state of being. *Spaces* in this world "are simply the external conditions corresponding to the internal states."[12] This was understood by early Jewish and Christian mystics. In the Gospel of Philip we are told that *"People cannot see anything that really is without becoming like it.*

It is not so with people in the world, who see the sun without becoming the sun and see the sky and earth and everything else without becoming them. Rather, in the realm of truth, you have seen things there and have become those things,... in that realm you see yourself, and you will [become] what you see."[13] And in the Gospel of Mary, Jesus confirms this truth. When Mary tells Jesus that she saw him in a vision, he answers her by saying, "Blessings on you, since you did not waver when you saw me. For where the mind is, the treasure is."[14]

Since the text of the Gospel of Mary in which Jesus talks about the visionary is incomplete, we cannot be sure what Jesus meant when he said to Mary, "A person sees neither with the soul nor with the spirit. The mind, which is between the two, sees the vision...." But we do know that he was referring to an *intermediary* aspect of the mind that allows us to actually *see* the vision. We in the West lost the knowledge that there is an aspect of mind — by whatever name — that provides "a precise mode of perception" so that we can see a "precise order of reality." We lost this knowledge because these true stories were rejected and lost or destroyed.

Yet for thousands of years mystics and visionaries have experienced the precision and reliability of this intermediary/subtle world. That is how the Dalai Lama could say with total confidence that the subtle world of mystical cities, such as Shambhala, does indeed have a *real* existence. Corbin speaks of a world in which mystical cities of light are too numerous to count.[15] During the High Middle Ages the *mundus imaginalis* was known and experienced as the sacred ground of the Voices of the Wells where this world and the Otherworld intersect. It is the world of the shaman. And it is on this sacred ground of vision that Mary is able to see the *resurrected* Jesus. It is here that Jesus and Mary experience a love and consciousness that continue to exist beyond death.

Not only does Jesus refer to this intermediary world but, according to Barker, in the ancient tradition of Israel the design and major rituals of the First Temple reflect knowledge of these three worlds and their underlying unity. The Temple itself was divided into the invisible and visible worlds. The holy of holies within the temple was the *invisible* world, Day One of creation—"the intermediate state" between the material world and the world of pure formless spirit—understood not as *time* but as a *state of being*.[16] The sense-material or *visible* world was the great hall within the temple. In the temple, a veil of matter separated the invisible world from the visible world, and it was only the High Priest who could pass through this veil and enter into the holy of holies. When the High Priest entered the holy of holies, he wore a garment made of white linen—like the angels—and when he returned to the world of matter, his garment was made from the same linen fabric as the veil in the colors of blue, purple, and scarlet, interwoven with gold. This robe represented the visible, created world.[17]

In 1941 astronomer Gustaf Strömberg wrote a description of the quantum field that the High Priests of the First Temple, Jesus, and the Sufis would have understood:

> *Matter and life and consciousness have their "roots" in a world beyond space and time. They emerge into the physical world at certain well defined points or sources from which they expand in the form of guiding fields with space and time properties.... They are the roots of our consciousness and the sources of all our knowledge.... In this non-physical realm lies the ultimate origin of all things, of energy, matter, organization and life, and even consciousness itself.*[18]

Strömberg does not differentiate between the two dimensions of the invisible world—the formless world of pure spirit and the subtle world of forms. But he is very clear about the fact that all matter, life, and consciousness have their roots, their "ultimate origin," in the nonphysical world.

The scientist uses conceptual, rational language to express his or her findings while the shaman-mystic uses symbolic, mythic language—a language that we now have to acknowledge does indeed, as Vico told us, have a poetic logic. It was through symbol and ritual that the High Priests of ancient Israel mirrored their knowledge and experience of this timeless, spaceless, invisible world. They were the visionaries, the shaman-mystics of their culture, the mediators between the world of matter and the world of spirit.

These High Priests entered into the subtle world, the *mundus imaginalis*, and experienced the *presence* of the divine; the unity underlying all creation; eternity; and the past, present, and future. Here Yahweh embraced his beloved Wisdom, the radiant, divine archetypal High Priestess, the Queen of Heaven, "the One who gave birth in the holy of holies, in the glory of the holy ones."[19] **Such experience within the holy of holies transformed them, for here these shaman-mystics ate of the true Tree of Life—the Cosmic Tree—and they did indeed receive Our Lady's gifts of wisdom, divinity, and immortality.**

According to Barker, this creation story of Day One, along with its initiation ritual, is an older story than the creation story that is told in the Genesis we know. While absolute certainty is not possible, Barker thinks that this earlier story was remembered and written down by priests who had *not* accepted the so-called reforms of Josiah. Later traditions would remember that the holy of holies held the secrets of creation, for it was here that Yahweh embraced the Queen of Heaven in love and intimacy, here that the world and all life was held in delicate balance through this loving fusion of opposites. The Qumran texts would call these secrets "the mystery of being."[20] It certainly appears that the Jesus of the Gospel of Mary was a visionary rooted in this ancient tradition. **According to Barker, the structure of the First Temple and the rituals of passing through the veil, ascending into otherworlds and descending into matter were at the heart of the ancient Jewish Mysteries—just as they would become the heart of the later Jewish movement that became Christianity.**

The High Priests who entered this state of light and radiant knowledge, says Barker, became a part of it: "They had been raised up, that is, resurrected; they were sons of God, that is, angels; and they were anointed ones, that is, messiahs."[21] When the High Priest, who was now divine, passed back through the veil of matter from the holy of holies, he materialized, that is, *incarnated*, into a visible, human form. This is the *imagery*, says Barker, that the first Christians used to describe the incarnation of Jesus, "the great high priest." This was so well understood, she continues, that "The writer of Hebrews could say, without any explanation, that the curtain of the temple was the flesh of Jesus, the great high priest."[22] **This imagery helps us to see more clearly that the story of the birth of Jesus as well as his title** *Son of God*, **in Barker's words, "has a mystic not a literal meaning."**[23]

Chapter Fourteen

>―⊹⧫⊹―O―⧫⊹―<

Philo Judaeus considered the ancient Jewish Mysteries the true Judaism because its goal was to lead all souls to the Light,[1] in Bucke's words, to cosmic consciousness.

In these Mysteries it was Moses who was seen as the God-Man, the savior, the Great High Priest who showed the Way to the Light.[2]

The more we learn from Barker's research about the ancient shaman-mystic tradition of the First Temple and its reemergence in what became Christianity, the more convincing it becomes that it must surely be this same tradition that had reemerged a century or two *before* the time of Jesus in the work of the Allegorists and, as Barker has told us, in the continued allegorical work of Philo Judaeus (c. 20 BCE–c. 40 CE). Goodenough tells us that "Mystic Judaism" was the "ready made environment" of Philo's writing and that he drew constantly on the work of the earlier Allegorists. Who these earlier Allegorists were is not clear but, says Goodenough, one thing is absolutely certain: many of them "had gone to the logical end of the mystic position" and felt no obligation to live by the letter of the law. They lived by the mystic experience of Logos/Sophia/Love.[3] The Law and the Jewish Code remained for those who had not yet entered this state of light and radiant knowledge.

The Allegorists and Philo transformed the Torah from a book about Jewish mythic-symbolic history into a shamanic-mystic text about the

Great Mysteries. Every story was allegorized into a teaching story about the soul's journey to the Light. Moses' attempt to lead the people out of Egypt, through the desert, and into the Holy Land becomes the soul's long, labyrithine journey to achieve the Kingdom of God on earth. The desert wasteland can only become the land of milk and honey through love, respect, and loyalty to the Queen of Heaven, the Sovereign of the Land—the Soul. Philo considered these ancient Mysteries the true Judaism because its goal was to lead all souls to Sophia/the Light,[4] in Bucke's words, to *cosmic consciousness*.

In Philo's development of the ancient Jewish Mysteries it was Moses who was seen as the God-Man, the savior, the Great High Priest who showed the *Way to the Light*. Those who sought this Light prayed to Moses as the Savior to lead them to the subtle world, the Holy Land. Even in Philo's time the initiates did not pray, says Goodenough, as though Moses were "dead and gone." But rather they saw in Moses "an active and present power, and the prayer to Moses for guidance, light, and anointing, is precisely such a prayer as Christian mystics have for centuries been addressing to Christ."[5]

This transformative experience at the heart of the Mysteries, "the inflooding of the Light-Stream," was symbolized as the sacred marriage, the union within the soul of all opposing principles, *and* the entry into the *Holy Land*. The sacred marriage of Moses to Zipporah symbolizes Moses' experience of union with Sophia/the Light.[6] **It seems to me that this marriage, in spite of Philo's own views about the feminine, can also be seen as the redemption of Yahweh, the return of Wisdom as the beloved of God.**

Moses' entry into the *Holy Land* was through his visionary consciousness, that *organ of the soul* that perceives "a precise order of reality." Moses did not need to physically enter the Holy Land, for he "came to possess the Land in his vision more truly than those who later entered it." Thus, Moses experienced *The Kingdom of God* on earth through that intermediary aspect of the mind that opened his consciousness to *the subtle world*, the *Mundus Imaginalis, the Holy Land*. When Moses, now the Great High Priest, achieved this level of consciousness, he realized his own divinity and immortality and dedicated his life to bringing others to the Light. For he then understood that the Mysteries were not just for the Jews but for all people, "For in Moses the whole race has been accepted by God."[7]

Moses realized, however, that he would not be able to take all the people into the Mystical Holy Land. This was not, says Philo, because of any failure on his part, but because the people were not yet ready to enter into the Higher Mysteries. At this point in the allegory Philo shifts our attention from Canaan as the Holy Land to the Well, the waters of Life and the streams of Light flowing from Sophia, the Logos, the Soul. Now the focus is on the actual initiation into Sophia for those who *are* ready to experience the Higher Mysteries.[8]

For those who are not yet ready for such an experience, Moses leaves the Ark of the Covenant, which contains the Law—and *symbols* of the descending Light-Stream of the Higher Mysteries.[9] It is said that in rabbinic tradition, much later than Philo's stories of the Moses Mysteries, there is the statement that the Ark in the holy of holies in Solomon's Temple contained not only the Law but a "man and a woman locked in intimacy in the form of a hexagram." This holy hexagram symbolizes the merging or harmonious marriage of two triangles, the masculine fire facing upward, and the feminine water, facing downward and flowing into the earth. It is a very old symbol used in several spiritual and cultural traditions since the two equilateral triangles facing opposite directions and merging together harmoniously reflect the union of any two pairs of opposites.[10]

If rabbinic tradition does indeed place this symbol in the Ark in Solomon's Temple, it would be consistent with what we have learned about the First Temple tradition of the holy of holies where the secrets of creation were held, for it was here that Yahweh embraced the Queen of Heaven in love and intimacy and it was here that the world and all life were held in delicate balance through this loving fusion of opposites. We all recognize this symbol today as the Star of David, but it is not generally recognized as the symbol of the cosmic dance of opposing principles—the *Way to the Holy Land, the Holy of Holies*.

Chapter Fifteen

>―◦―<

Both the Moses Mysteries and the Jesus Mysteries are a continuation of the First Temple shaman-mystic tradition.

The true myth of the Western world is not just to follow the Christ but to become the Christ.

And it is this myth of becoming that is in harmony with the principles of our own evolutionary development. **This is the blueprint that is at the heart of all the world's great spiritual traditions, their Mysteries and their myths. And it is the blueprint in the heart of each person.**

Timothy Freke and Peter Gandy in *The Jesus Mysteries: Was the "Original Jesus" A Pagan God?* shift our attention from Philo's allegory about the Moses Mysteries back to the original story in the Torah/Old Testament. When the Moses of the Old Testament story realizes that he cannot take his people to the promised land, he appoints the prophet Joshua — the Hebrew form of the Greek name Jesus — to continue the journey "to the promised land of mystical rebirth." Freke and Gandy contend that Joshua/Jesus represents "the New Covenant of the Jewish Mysteries, which replaces the old laws and traditions represented by the Old Testament Moses."[1]

They also tell us that "The early Christians maintained that *Iesous*, the original Greek name we translate as 'Jesus,' was 'a name above all names.'"

In the ancient system of number symbolism, gematria, each letter in the alphabet has a number and the sum of each of the numbers of the letters in a word or name has a symbolic meaning. For example, the Greek name *Iesous (Jesus)* equals 888.[2] The single number eight symbolizes regeneration, the sunrise of a New Age, a new beginning, and a new creation. When numbers appear in a triple form, as in 888, they symbolize the *epitome* or *ultimate fulfillment* of the single number's original essence.[3]

If we view the Jesus Mysteries from the perspective of the Moses of the Torah/Old Testament, we do see a shift away from the *law* to the mystical experience of Logos/Love. *However, if we view the Jesus Mysteries from the perspective of Philo's Moses, we are able to see, thanks to Barker's work, that both the Moses Mysteries and the Jesus Mysteries are a continuation of the First Temple shaman-mystic tradition.* Since Barker's research on the First Temple traditions came after Goodenough's work, he was only able to see the roots of the Jewish Mysteries in the long line of thinkers and mystics whose work had shaped the Greek world during the Hellenistic period. Those influences are surely present, but according to Barker, the true roots of the Jewish Mysteries are in their own earlier traditions. It is clear, however, that Goodenough recognized the similarities between the Moses of the Mysteries and the Jesus of the later Mysteries.

We know that the Mysteries are always about an *initiation* into a larger vision of life—a vision so vast that all life becomes radiant. Such a vision plants the seed of cosmic consciousness, a seed that is expected to flower from the depths of one's own being. It is a vision of the divine, the cosmic Mind, not as Other, but as Self. We have seen how this experience of wholeness and creative unity is often symbolized by the sacred marriage between the masculine and feminine dimensions of the Divine. As mentioned earlier, in the *Moses Mysteries* the initiate experienced the union with the Logos/Sophia/the Light. In the *Jesus Mysteries* we also see this sacred union: Jesus *walked with* his mother, his sister, and Miriam of Magdala. The loving relationship between Mary Magdalene and Jesus formed the archetypal marriage that can bring the Kingdom of God into historical time and space.

We also know that since the destruction of the Wisdom tradition around 621 BCE, there were those groups of Jews who attempted to redeem what had been lost. They knew, as the Kabbalists (in fact, many of them were Kabbalists), that "there was a female element within God, Shekinah, and they dwelt much upon the theme of her exile.... a part of God had been exiled from God, and redemption would come when the two were reunited."[4] Since the feminine dimension reflects a wide range of characteristics, such as the visionary, the artist, the soul, and nature itself, it is difficult to know how many of these characteristics the various groups of mystics were able to integrate and manifest in the physical world. On a social level, these male groups might not have fared as well as we would hope.

We know that Philo had difficulty holding the actual female in equal value with the male. He viewed the female as material and passive while he viewed the male as rational and active. In fact, Philo rejected the femininity of *Wisdom*, for the feminine, says Philo, is always second to and less than the masculine.[5] This is disappointing, coming from one who writes about the union with Sophia and who is attempting to give new life to the ancient shaman-mystic Jewish tradition. We simply have to recognize that the prevailing male-oriented social structure could affect, consciously or unconsciously, the best of intentions. The shaman-mystic tradition often carries this deep wound even in its attempt to redeem everything within us that might be symbolized as the feminine dimension of reality.

Even the apostles in the Gospel of Mary have difficulty accepting insight from Mary Magdalene, and they resent her relationship with Jesus. It was a patriarchal world in spite of the fact that there were those who truly sought to redeem all that had been exiled within the human psyche. And yet it was within this very world that *the living myth* of a redeemed **Yahweh** emerged—a Yahweh who loved women, the rejected, and the poor. This was the Yahweh who lived the New Covenant—the sacred law of the heart. This was the New Covenant of the Jesus Mysteries. In all the stories about Jesus, whether in the manifest gospels we all know or in the hidden, forbidden texts, we see a man who is "radically egalitarian."[6] He personifies all that has been exiled, for this is the image of a man who has integrated into himself the Queen of Heaven. Such a personification reflects a spiritual and social revolution strong enough for some of the stories about him to live on for more than two thousand years and other stories about him to be rejected and forbidden by those who feared revolutionary change.

Part of that revolutionary change brought by Jesus meant that women could have significant positions of leadership. Karen Jo Torjesen in *When Women Were Priests* presents evidence that in early Christianity women were elders, priests, bishops, and prophets. Even slaves and artisans held leadership roles. We must remember that this "revolution" emerged within the Jewish community, so it should not come as a surprise that many of the women's leadership roles were modeled on similar roles of women in the synagogue, such as "ruler," elder, priest, and "mother of the synagogue." It was not until the Christians moved from the private homes of worship into institutionalized public places that the social and political patriarchy of the Greek and Roman worlds forced women back into private, subservient roles.[7]

All of these stories about Jesus, both the manifest and the forbidden, were written over a long period of time and we cannot be absolutely certain about their origin or origins. We know that there were many Jewish gnostic groups flourishing at the time of Jesus side by side with the Greek, Persian, and Egyptian Mysteries. And we know that the Pythagoreans were also very influential in Alexandria and that their views about women were balanced and mature. Some people have thought that the teachings of the Jewish Therapeutae in Egypt formed the foundation of what became the Jesus story. Interestingly, the great spiritual teacher from India, Vivekananda, tells in his autobiography that he had a dream in which a very old sage appeared to him and told him that the truths preached by the Therapeutae—to which the sage himself belonged—did indeed form the foundation of the later Jesus story.[8]

We can't be certain about all of the influences, but there is one thing about which we can be absolutely certain: there *were* those mystics who loved and honored the feminine and who always walked with the mother, the sister, and the beloved. This way of life is symbolized in the Jesus stories. **Only much later would the Church construct a view of Jesus that would exclude this "hidden tradition," that long and persistent effort within Jewish history to achieve this level of consciousness.**

As we have seen, this consciousness was also symbolized as the manifestation of the new Yahweh, the Holy One of Israel, the One who would once again embrace the feminine dimension of his own divinity and achieve the ultimate fulfillment of his divine essence. As mentioned above, in the number symbolism of gematria, this ultimate fulfillment would be 888, and this would make Jesus that fulfillment. Many people are unfamiliar with gematria and uncomfortable using it as any kind of evidence. And in this case, it isn't needed for further evidence. Yet it is actually quite interesting to look at the conclusions drawn from some of the more familiar symbolic numbers.

Not only does the gematric code conclude that Jesus is the ultimate fulfillment of the divine, but also that Mary Magdalene is the sacred feminine dimension of the divine. Margaret Starbird in *Magdalene's Lost Legacy: Symbolic Numbers and the Sacred Union in Christianity* shows us that nine is one of the significant numbers that relate to the feminine dimension of the divine. It reflects fulfillment, completion, and truth. "The spiritual connotations of the number three are extended to include nine—its square—and to the numbers...that can be reduced to nine by adding their digits." For example, Mary Magdalene's number is 153, which adds up to 9. The number for the feminine/yin/lunar power is 1080, which adds up to 9. The feminine principle is associated with the dove, whose number is 801, which adds up to 9. The Holy Spirit (originally feminine) and the Earth Goddess both have the same number of 1080, which adds up to 9. All numbers, says Starbird, were considered sacred but the number three was held to be "most holy." This is why, as we have already seen, the mystical meaning of any number is enhanced when it is tripled. When the sum of each letter in a name added together is 9, as with the feminine principle, there is "a trinity of threes," which is "the epitome of three." Through this system we can see that Mary Magdalene was considered *the epitome of the sacred feminine*.[9]

Starbird further explains that the archetypal masculine is associated with the solar principle while the archetypal feminine is associated with the lunar principle. The number 666 is the number for the masculine/yang/solar power—again, the epitome of a certain kind of energy. We all recognize this number as *the number of the beast*. But who or what is this beast symbolically? Here Starbird relies on the brilliant work of the British scholar John Michell. This number, says Michell, is the principle of positive, procreative energy in the cosmos — if it is united with the feminine principle. But if this energy becomes dissociated from the feminine principle, as it did when Yahweh abandoned the Queen of Heaven, it becomes brutal, tyrannical, violent. This is when the number 666 symbolizes *the beast*.[10]

But when the masculine/solar principle and the feminine/lunar principle enter into the sacred, equal, co-creative marriage, the union of all opposites, the Kingdom of God is manifested in time and space. Jesus says in Luke 17:21 that "the Kingdom of God is within you" and he tells us that this Kingdom is like a mustard seed. Once again, we are not surprised to learn that the numerical sum of the phrase, *grain of mustard seed*, is 1746 — the sum of the numbers of the masculine/solar principle 666 and the feminine/lunar principle 1080.[11]

Repeatedly, we are reminded that the depth of these ancient texts lies in their many levels of symbolic language and structure. The Gospel of Philip says that "Truth did not come into the world naked but in symbols and images."[12] In other words, the language of the subtle world is symbolic: its archetypal essence is made visible — that is, manifested — through symbol and image. Christians nurtured this language and the *secret tradition* that taught people how to pass through the veil to experience the subtle/Otherworld, Day One, the Kingdom, the holy of holies, the center of the labyrinth, and the fruit of the Cosmic Tree. "The earliest Christian writers," says Barker, "claimed that Jesus, as the great high priest, had revealed the secrets of the holy of holies: 'To Jesus alone as our high priest were the secret things of God committed.'" And Clement of Alexandria, a Christian who lived near the end of the second century, speaks of the *true* tradition of the early Church: in this tradition, he says, Christians entered into knowledge, *gnosis*, "by drawing aside the curtain."[13]

For these early Christians, the birth, divinity, incarnation and resurrection of Jesus took place in the bridal chamber — the holy of holies — where he had received the gifts of the Cosmic Tree of Life. When Jesus, the Great High Priest, experienced this Mystery in the holy of holies, he was born/resurrected as the Christ. "The resurrected one was anointed, spoke of God as his Father, and was given the status of the first-born. He became divine, and *his birth was described as his resurrection.*"[14] And it is this mystic Christ who teaches us that we too can enter the holy of holies hidden within each of us. For "whoever has known himself has simultaneously come to know the depth of all things." And it is in these depths of our own knowing that we encounter the "living Jesus" and become his "identical twin."[15] This is the goal of the *secret tradition* that Jesus taught — to become the Christ.

The Gospel of Philip tells us, says Meyer, "not only to *follow* Christ, but to *become* Christ." And, as mentioned above, the Gospel of Philip reminds us that what we experience "in the realm of truth," we become: "you have seen things there and have become those things, / you have seen the spirit and have become spirit, / you have seen Christ and have become Christ,..."[16] In the Gospel of Thomas, as we have seen, this Jesus does not even encourage *following* him but rather directs people to the light hidden within: "There is light within a person of light, and it lights up the whole universe." Not only does Jesus come from the light but all of us also come from the light. Jesus tells his disciples: "If they say to you, 'Where did you come from?' say to them, '*We came from the light, the place where the light came into being by itself,*...'"[17] Here in these gospels the emphasis is clearly not on *belief* in the Christ or even on becoming *like* the Christ, but very specifically on actually *becoming the Christ*.

This is the *true* myth of the Western world: *not to follow the Christ but to become the Christ*. And it is this myth of *becoming* that is in harmony with the principles of our own evolutionary development. **This is the blueprint that is at the heart of all the world's great spiritual traditions, their Mysteries and their myths. And it is the blueprint in the heart of each person.** Earlier we saw how the familiar Genesis story is an inversion of the principles of the mythic pattern worldwide. *In the Christ story of the Church there is once again an inversion of our evolutionary myth.*

The original Christ narrative reflects this dynamic potential in each of us to evolve: each of us is both divine and human; we are born in what seems a lowly birth in matter; but gradually we begin to become aware of our own divinity and immortality; we continue on the labyrinthine path of our own inner spiritual development until we are able to integrate and balance all the opposing principles at work within us—often symbolized as the sacred marriage between the masculine and the feminine modes of being; gradually we become masters of the laws of our own nature as well as the laws of the universe; such mastery can only be achieved through the deepest possible realization of love; this depth of love manifests itself in compassion, equality and justice for *all* life; when we achieve this unity and balance of a loving consciousness that is both vast and intimate, we become aware—as did Sri Aurobindo—that even this *nirvana or cosmic consciousness* is not our ultimate goal but rather it is the *foundation* that is needed for us to be able to align our own conscious creative evolution with "the evolutionary impulse" of the universe.[18]

The great challenge of this evolutionary journey in Western culture—and now in most of the world—is twofold: (1) the lingering power of the old scientific paradigm in so many people who still insist that neither the human being nor nature is divine, that all life is a fluke, that we are an accident of nature without meaning or purpose; and (2) the lingering power of the Church's inverted version of our evolutionary myth, which tells us to follow, to believe, rather than *to become* the Christ. Both the scientific and the religious paradigms devalue the individual and negate direct inner experience or gnosis. Had our scientists been allowed to continue to develop as shaman-scientists, they would have drawn very different conclusions from their data—as many of them now do. And had we not lost the ancient techniques of the journey—the *secret tradition* that Jesus is said to have taught—the West would have a very different story today.

Our creation of a new story is coming from what our culture has negated. We are *experiencing for ourselves* the laws—the archetypes—in the mundus imaginalis or subtle world. All around the globe scientists, shaman-mystics, and individuals from all walks of life are opening to the new scientific revolution and spiritual evolution that are shattering the old limiting stories of who we are. And as we are ready and open, the blueprint—Baba Yaga's ball of thread—rolls out before us. We begin to see that we are all perpetually coming into being, that "There is nothing but life," and that we are "the nucleus of the nucleus" of that life. The

Christ myth is our future calling us to remember who we are and why we're here.

For those Christians who believe in the *historical* Christ, it needs to be said that nothing is lost when we expand our consciousness of Christ beyond one individual in history. In fact, everything is to be gained. I know Christians who are profoundly sustained and nourished by the image of a Jesus who is loving, compassionate, and forgiving. Their relationship is deeply personal and creative. In no way is this relationship threatened by allowing the Jesus of the Nag Hammadi texts to expand our understanding of who this being named Jesus might actually have been. When we remember how Bucke discovered that the great shaman-mystics who had achieved cosmic consciousness were the ones who seeded civilizations and gave birth to the great religions, we are better able to understand the role of Jesus in helping us to achieve cosmic consciousness.

This Jesus would not want us to focus on the historical Christ but rather to find the Cosmic Christ within ourselves, to find the light within that "lights up the whole universe."[19] For this inward journey we need our first language, the symbolic language of the *mundus imaginalis*. This language is the key to understanding our own dreams, visions, and altered states of consciousness, as well as the deeper levels of visionary experiences in the ancient mystic texts. We all have and can reclaim what Jesus called the intermediary aspect of mind—*the organ of soul*—that provides us with "a precise mode of perception" so that we can see "a precise order of reality." What we have long forgotten is that we need symbolic language to perceive this order of reality.

When, for example, we read *symbolically* what appears to be the actual physical death and resurrection of Christ in the Gospel of Mary, we can understand that this story reflects a truth for all of us: we are born, we die, and each of us returns to the subtle world. The NDErs have experienced this return and, like Mary with the apostles, they try to communicate this sacred truth to all who will listen. Mary wants the apostles to understand that there is no death and that we all have that visionary aspect of the mind that allows us to communicate with the subtle world. The doubting apostles reflect our own inability to accept this truth, while Jesus and

Mary reflect our potential to evolve and live in the wisdom of this higher dimension.

Freke and Gandy remind us that this same symbolic story of death and rebirth was told and enacted in ritual throughout the ancient world, and, as we will see, it is a story whose roots reach deep into prehistory. These writers tell us, for example, that in Egypt, long before the birth of Christ, a great festival was held each year during which the dramatic representation of the death and resurrection of Osiris was enacted before "tens of thousands of men and women." When the Greek historian Herodotus (fifth century BCE) witnessed this ritual, he recognized it as the same ritual he had been initiated into at Eleusis.[20] And when people first heard the Jesus stories, they too recognized them as the core teachings of all the great mysteries and spiritual traditions. *They understood that the symbolic, Cosmic Christ is real and that there were shaman-mystics who brought this Christ into history by encountering him within.*

I celebrate our ancestors who saw that people had forgotten who they were and why they were here. Many of these ancestors lived lives separated from the world in ways most of us would not choose today. Perhaps this was the only way they were able to achieve the intensity and expansion of consciousness they sought. I am deeply grateful for all that they achieved. Yet Jesus was not a mystic who separated himself from the world, for he was in the world and among the people. He *walked with the feminine,* and the loving relationship between Mary Magdalene and Jesus formed the archetypal marriage that brought the Kingdom of God into present time and space. The existence of this sacred marriage reflects a long line of mystics who went within to bring forth that which was within them—and what they brought forth saved them. These mystics encountered the *"living Jesus" who always walked with Wisdom,* and they brought forth this "living Jesus" to the world to teach us to become our own masters.

Chapter Sixteen

> *In The Wisdom of Solomon, we are told that Wisdom has the power to transform the world. When She enters into souls, She renews life and brings us love and joy.*[1]
>
> *Imaginal cells "contain the imagining or blueprint of a whole new being." When these cells first appear, "they are attacked and resisted," but they continue to grow, connect, and finally create a completely new form. "The old form literally dies as a new being is born from within the old."*[2]
>
> **— Saryon Michael White**

I had seen in my own experience that a truly "living" energy had emerged within me once I was no longer able to sustain a belief in the outer, *historical* Jesus. Unwittingly, I had made room in myself for the living images of soul to emerge within my own psyche. Certainly, Jesus is a soul image, whether he is discovered without or within, but the *living Jesus* — the living sacred text — is found within. This sacred text is both universal and personal. Its organization follows the natural principles of growth and development — and it reflects where we are on the path and what is needed for our further development. *But it is even more than this: the images themselves resonate at the higher frequency needed for our growth and transformation.* This is why it is called a *living text*.

Both Jesus and Mary—the Queen of Heaven, Our Lady, Wisdom—are names for the archetypes of the soul. There are many names and no names. The images of soul in my dreams never had names, but when they appeared, I always felt a heightened energy in my thoughts, feelings, and inspiration. Decades after the dream at Chartres I can still feel the sacred resonance that the images created in me. This dream focused my attention on what would be the work of a lifetime, but it also provided me with the healing solution. I experienced the condition of my left-brain, rational knight: he was deeply concerned about the suffering of the world as revealed in World War II; he could no longer see religion as a healing solution; he went out into the world to understand it and hopefully to help it; but he had a great wound: he could not see soul perpetually coming into being. Yet there was an aspect of him—the right-brain, visionary—who could see and experience soul, but the knight left her behind.

The knight's wound was my wound—and it was my culture's wound as well. I could not have hoped for a clearer revelation about the condition of myself and my culture. And I understood that my culture could only be healed through the inner work of the individual. I desperately needed to know how the wound had occurred in my culture. **How had it happened that we continually lost the threads to our own living text? How had so many of these living stories about who we are and why we're here been destroyed over and over again and replaced with stories that demean us, depress us, and ultimately destroy us?** My own journey into our history for the answers to these questions was made possible by the work of many scholars and mystics who were seeking answers to the same questions. And it was also made possible by a certain quality of the time in which we were born, for even the earth was working with us and leading us to the ancient buried—or misunderstood—texts that reveal our ancestors' attempts to find and follow the threads to their own inner *living* texts.

As my own historical journey to understand the spiritual experiences of my ancestors progressed, I was better able to understand my own personal journey. Sometimes, however, it would be years after a dream that I would discover in mythology a much larger context for what was so urgently trying to take place within me. Had I not known—or at least in time come to know—these mythic patterns of my ancestors, I would not have recognized those patterns within myself. I discovered that knowledge of their past expressions always created a larger dimension for their present reality. It was these two spiraling paths—the outer, historical and the inner, personal—that saved me from the nihilism of the rational, materialistic, and dogmatic world I had been born into.

So I continued to follow Baba Yaga's thread. Almost a decade after my dream of the dead body of Our Lady in the stone sarcophagus at the Cathedral of Chartres, the miracle of her perpetually coming into being in nature, and my rational knight leaving it all behind, I had other powerful dreams with Our Lady. This was in the 1970s and I was now in my late thirties. By this time, I was married, had a young son, was teaching in college, and working on my Ph.D. in Comparative Literature and Theory of Symbolic/Mythic Language.

The university had welcomed my Knight but not Our Lady. Fortunately, my husband István welcomed them both, however developed or undeveloped they were. I had met him in Europe where I returned to work after I completed my Master's degree. He had fought in the Hungarian Revolution, come to the States as a refugee, and later returned to Europe. We lived in Europe, New York City, and finally settled in southern California. Nine years after our marriage, our son Pisti was born. István and Pisti had such an optimistic and joyful love for life that I began to feel much more rooted in the earth. Yet my doctoral work at the university was often a challenge to this more balanced state of being. One evening when I was particularly worried about the university's resistance to some of the recent archaeological work on prehistoric images and my use of them in my dissertation, I had the following dream:

> *It is evening. I am sitting in my kitchen wondering how I should handle the situation at the university when I feel a powerful presence in my study. The energy is so strong that I feel compelled to move toward it. I enter the study to find it filled with exquisitely beautiful elderly women with silver hair. They are all dressed in a blue mist that also fills the room and creates an Otherworldly atmosphere. They are*

> *seated comfortably and quietly as they wait for me to enter, but there is an urgency about them. They have a message for me: I must continue the work I am doing. They will take care of any resistance at the university. In their presence, my worries dissolve. I feel grounded and joyful. I have a profound sense of confidence in my work and an inspiration that I had not felt for a very long time.*

I did continue my work, and the resistance at the university resolved itself without any effort on my part. I felt that the dream had created a higher frequency in me and, evidently, in others as well.

During this time, in spite of the intense left-brain atmosphere at the university, I knew I was changing. This change had been painfully slow, and often in spite of myself, but gradually the old programming was beginning to dissolve and something new was coming into being. The following dream reflects this shifting of perspectives and the return of the Knight to Our Lady.

> *Once again, I am in a vast forest that is green and lush. There is a waterfall that is flowing from the Upper World. The water is clearly sacred and other-dimensional. There are three levels of the waterfall. At the first level, there is a large circle — a living womb. Within this circle a male and a female are in a yang/yin position: their backs softly curve against the inside of the circle. They are moving toward the bottom or mouth of the circle, the woman first. Their movement is beautifully choreographed. As the female's head touches the opening of the circle, the male, who is still inside the circle, holds her shoulders to assist her birth out of the circle/womb. He seems to emerge from the womb after her, but the emphasis of the dream is on her birth. A blue cord connects them. As the woman emerges, her left arm is stretched above her head and in her hand she is holding a smaller circle that contains two fish swimming toward the left.*

> *I am aware that there are two more levels of the waterfall below, but I do not see them. To the left of the waterfall a beautiful woman dressed in blue is standing by observing the birth of the feminine. In her hands, she is lovingly holding a large book, out of which a river of water is flowing. The woman is clearly presiding over the sacred ritual that is taking place.*

At the time of the dream I knew that something profound and sacred was taking place within me. Here the masculine was intimately connected to the feminine within the yin/yang circle of wholeness—and he was gently and lovingly assisting in her birth. I felt that the smaller circle containing the two fish swimming toward the left symbolized my Knight's movement into deeper levels of consciousness. Or I could say that he was allowing the feminine dimension of his own being to lead him into greater depths of experience.

This great forest of nature was indeed the bridal chamber, the womb, the holy of holies, where the male and the female were coming together in a harmonious way to bring about the birth of the feminine principle and ultimately their sacred marriage. The two people (male and female), the two fish, and the remaining two levels of the waterfall suggest the theme of the *two* born out of the *one*—the pairs of opposites that work together to bring into being, in Goethe's words, "a new, a third, a completely *unanticipated* other." Even though our creativity is guided by the organizing principles of nature within the human psyche, it remains a mystery—we cannot anticipate its uniqueness. It is born in the holy of holies, and it unfolds throughout our lives in time and space.

In the earlier dream at Chartres I had grieved the death of the feminine in the Cathedral, but I had observed her in nature alive and perpetually coming into being. In this later dream, I was once again an observer of her birth, but I also knew that I was the one being born. And in the earlier dream I had observed the separation of the Knight from his Lady and his inability to even know that a birth was taking place. *In this dream, he was assisting her birth.* As I look back at this dream so many years later with the historical knowledge of Our Lady, the Queen of Heaven, I am able to experience a much deeper connection to my ancestors and to the subtle world and its language. Such dreams reflect our experience in that world, the holy of holies, just as the visions of the First Temple mystics reflect their experience in this very real subtle world. How clear it now is that this beautiful Lady dressed in blue is Our Lady, Wisdom, the radiant, divine, archetypal High Priestess of the subtle world, the Garden of Eden, the Kingdom. How much more the words, "Thy Kingdom come," mean to me now, for how much more I understand that it is our work to bring into material existence what we experience in the subtle world, the Kingdom, the holy of holies.

Knowing more about the historical expressions of the masculine and feminine archetypes also allowed me to experience more deeply the power of the two of them working together in the earlier dream I had while I was still in college. That evening I had experienced as masculine energy the great spiraling mist that arose out of the sacred water while the feminine energy was symbolized in the beautiful woman who, again dressed in blue, was waiting for me at the arch of the bridge. It felt as though the energies of the masculine and the feminine were not only working together but that they could each merge into the other. At that time, I had no knowledge of their history in the lives of our ancestors. Now I was able to *feel* such gratitude for their presence and for their gift of awakening me to the journey ahead by touching the base of my spine with the frequency of the cosmic spiral that arose out of the mists of the sacred water. In my dream they were nameless, but every culture gives them names, sometimes very different names. Yet it is not the names that are important but rather their essence, their presence, and their creative resonance in us and in the universe.

As mentioned earlier, the topography of the subtle world is complex and multi-leveled. In this realm of the *archetypes of light,* Wisdom and Yahweh are always one, lovingly creating together in harmony with the universe. As Barker has said, the "spirit of Yahweh" *is* "the spirit of Wisdom."[3] When they are split within us—as they are and have been for many hundreds of years in Western culture—we project our split onto the subtle world. But that world—the realm of light—is not split. We are. I experienced them in the dream as the unity they are in the subtle world, but in my life — and in the life of my culture and its dominant religion — I experienced the abandonment of Wisdom and the dominance of Yahweh.

Since I and my culture had abandoned Wisdom, she was seeking birth in me — and in countless others for the many hundreds of years since her exile. Before her exile, it was only the High Priests who entered the holy of holies *in the First Temple* to experience Wisdom, yet the ancients knew very well that Wisdom could enter individual souls anywhere, anytime. It was clear to them that the Kingdom — the holy of holies — is *within* us. In "The Wisdom of Solomon" we are told that "Though she is one, she can do all things, / And while remaining in herself, she makes everything new. / And passing into holy souls, generation after generation, / She makes them friends of God, and prophets."[4]

Today science is giving us a new way to understand the work of *Wisdom* in what is called *Imaginal cells*. As mentioned earlier, such cells "contain the imagining or blueprint of a whole new being." The caterpillar is an example of how these Imaginal cells work. When these cells first appear, they are "attacked and resisted," but gradually the Imaginal cells continue to grow, connect, and finally create a completely new form — the butterfly. The old form dies as the new form is born.[5] Our ancestors understood that *Wisdom* enters souls and "makes everything new." She is that "wave of organization"[6] that can move through us and transform us, as Goethe would say, to such a degree that we are different in kind.

Once again it is clear that we need both the scientist and the mystic: the scientist is able to explain to us how this field of organization transforms matter while the mystic poet or bard is able to reflect our *experience* of that transformation. The *symbol* of Wisdom carries a dimension of meaning and inspiration beyond the scientific description: she is not only a vast field of organization but she is also intimate, beautiful, conscious and loving. When she enters into our souls, the poet tells us, we become friends with the divine. It is the mystic poet who has given the organizing fields images and names that reflect their essence: these images or archetypes are all Imaginal cells that can create waves of re-organization within the human body, mind, and heart.[7]

I felt a deep connection to the ancient Jewish mystic-poets who had experienced and written about Wisdom as the water of life that flows from the source of all being and as the four rivers flowing in the divine garden of Eden. And I felt the same closeness to the later Christian mystic poets who had experienced Wisdom as Jesus and Mary Magdala, his beloved mother, sister, and wife. I felt a deep bond with the bards, poets, and musicians of the High Middle Ages who sought the Holy Grail of Wisdom at the heart of the great forest and experienced her as the Voices at the sacred wells and fountains of the Otherworld.

I felt honored to experience her birth in the garden of Eden while the waters of life flowed down from the Otherworld. I knew I was connected to these ancestors in the holy of holies where Wisdom was holding the great book from which her sacred water flowed. *There were no words in the dream: it was a silent, sacred ritual to bring back to me that exiled part of myself, to redeem what had been lost, to allow Wisdom, that exiled part of God, to return as the beloved of God.* And Wisdom herself was present as the Queen of Heaven directing and overseeing this ritual of her birth in the holy of holies. This was certainly a turning point in my life, a beginning of the long work toward the sacred marriage of Wisdom and Yahweh within my own psyche.

I deeply valued these dreams, their numinous quality, and their guiding support. There were many other dreams of different kinds throughout the years. Some I simply did not understand, but I tried to allow their images and the feelings they ignited to live in me and speak to me on whatever level was possible at the time. Of course, there were some dreams that, in the rush of life, I forgot before I could write them down. But the big dreams I never forgot. These dreams really were living threads in the tapestry of my life, and it was becoming clear that *Wisdom*, the feminine dimension of the divine, the Queen of Heaven, was emerging in this tapestry as a central figure in search of her beloved Yahweh.

Chapter Seventeen

>―┼◆>―○―<◆┼<

The Gospel of Philip tells us that truth is expressed in symbols and images.[1]

"But the misreading of myths and allegories....threw a possible great civilization under the pall and handicap of the most fantastic conception that ever misdirected the moral genius of man.... It killed the psychological efficacy of the whole religious enterprise, diverting zeal from the one pivot point where zeal alone counts, — the life of the inner consciousness and seat of character, the soul."[2]

— **Alvin Boyd Kuhn**

As I continued to explore the mythic images of history, I could see that the feminine image had been a central figure in cultures for tens of thousands of years before the Deuteronomists exiled her in Jewish culture. But what does her figure really mean? She was the living water — and I would later discover that she had been a symbol of the sacred waters for tens of thousands of years. She was the tree, the serpent, the earth, the sky, the stars, the moon, the sun, the hills and mountains, the caves, the animals, the seasons: she was nature, she was life — both genders — and all life was divine. She was the natural cycles of life: she was birth; she was the force that maintained life; she was death; and she was the force that brought the rebirth of all that had died. She, both as a woman and as the earth, was the great mother who carried life within her and nurtured that life with her own body. She loved and protected all life through all its cycles.

Today we could say that she symbolizes the right-brain functions of connecting us to other dimensions of reality through the symbolic/mythic language of dreams, visions, feeling, senses, intuition and instincts. She is our *experience* of life and love in the material dimension as well as in the subtle world. *She symbolizes living from the heart center, which gives us joy, happiness, and relatedness to all life.* And she is all this within every living human being, both male and female. She is the unity of the invisible Kingdom and she is the essence of its diversity as it manifests in the visible, material world. In the Kingdom, she is spirit, and in the individual, she is soul.

What then, we might ask, are the specific characteristics of the masculine dimension of the divine? For thousands of years it appears that the masculine was symbolic of each of us in time and space. We come into being, live, die, and are reborn. The erect penis was a major symbol of the amazing creative force of our masculine nature, its very visible manifestation, and its timely disappearance or death. The mushroom was another symbol of masculine energy — that magical emergence of an energetic force and its quick disappearance or death. I often think, not of the mythical Zeus, but of the marvelous statue of Zeus (some think Poseidon) in the Archaeological Museum in Athens as an excellent symbol of what the ancients experienced as masculine energy. His exquisite body is tall and straight, his left foot steps forward, his left arm stretches out in the same direction while his right arm is stretched back and up, presumably ready to throw his great thunderbolt. He is pure balance, energy, and a thrusting out into life to explore and accomplish. He is the risk taker, and historically he has been the great hunter, warrior, builder of cities, scientist, shaman, artist, and protector of life.

Today we could say that he symbolizes the left-brain functions of logical, reflective, conceptual language. He is our ability to analyze and evaluate all the material that comes to us from the outer and inner worlds that we explore and experience. He is the unique individual who creates in the material world of time and space. And he is all this in every living human being, both male and female.

However, if he, we, lose our connection to *nature*—to all that the feminine dimension of the divine symbolizes—our energy becomes random, unbalanced and violent. Without a relationship with her, the world becomes a wasteland. Those who experienced Wisdom and "held her fast" understood that our *redemption* is possible only when the exiled part of us returns to us as our beloved creative partner. And Wisdom did return again and again in her attempt to heal our blindness and open our hearts. There were both Jewish and Christian mystics who responded to her and embraced her, for they "fell in love with her beauty" and knew that "in kinship with wisdom there is immortality, / And in her friendship there is pure delight, / And unfailing wealth in the labors of her hands, / And understanding in the experience of her company, / And glory in sharing her words,..." And they knew that "the Lord of all loves her."[3]

When our ancestors experienced this kind of response to Wisdom, our evolutionary myth could emerge once more. **And so, Jesus, the Great High Priest, became the model of the return of Wisdom to Yahweh. Jesus embraced Mary and redeemed Yahweh. Once again "The spirit of Yahweh *was* the spirit of Wisdom."** Out of the balance achieved by this sacred marriage in the holy of holies, **the Cosmic Christ—a true manifestation of the masculine—could emerge as cosmos, nature, and human consciousness evolving and perpetually coming into being.**

The crucial question then is just how did we lose this evolutionary myth once again? We have already seen that the Deuteronomists destroyed the wisdom/mystic tradition of the First Temple and replaced it with the Law. The Church did the same: gnosis was replaced with dogma and belief. Laws and dogma demand obedience from the many and allow for control by the few. It is clear-cut, efficient, and predictable. When the Roman Emperor Constantine the Great legalized Christianity in 313 CE, he cleared the path for Christianity to become the dominant religion in the Empire. And it also allowed those who had *not* experienced gnosis, and who therefore had little or no understanding of such experiences, to take control of shaping the new dogma of the Church and establishing which of the many texts used by Christians would be included in the canon. All other spiritual texts—and there were many—would be excluded, discredited, or destroyed. It isn't that the Jesus in the gospels chosen by the Church isn't a beautiful, loving, inclusive being worthy of deep and profound admiration. He is, for the Jesus of the New Testament reflects a long line of Jewish mystical development—a development that had itself been nurtured from even more ancient reservoirs of human experience. But the canonical Jesus is incomplete.

Eusebius, a Church historian writing during the fourth century, appeared to be aware to some degree of the long line of spiritual development that emerged in the early Christian movement. He thought that the Essenes or the Therapeutae were the early Christians and that they had written the canonical gospels and epistles. Actually, as we have seen, the Essenes and the Therapeutae were of the same era. They were mystics, and they or mystics like them did write the mystical literature of their time. We will remember Vivekananda who had a dream that an old sage appeared to him and told him that the teachings of the Therapeutae, to which the sage himself belonged, formed the foundation of the later Jesus stories. Certainly, they—and the Christian mystics who followed—taught the *Way to the Light*. Alvin Boyd Kuhn, a twentieth century scholar of Christian origins and early Church history, states that "Eusebius was merely testifying to what nearly all men of intelligence in his age knew to be the truth, that the Gospels, Epistles and Apocrypha were just portions of the mass of arcane esoteric wisdom transmitted, for centuries orally in the Mysteries, and later in written form, from remote antiquity to their age."[4]

Kuhn adds that the problem is that the Church, from lack of understanding or desire for power, or both, distorted in various ways much of this ancient evolutionary heritage. But the decisive factor in the loss of this heritage was the loss of an understanding of symbol, myth, allegory, image—the language of the subtle world. This loss of the *mundus imaginalis* has been so complete and pervasive in the Western world that we are not yet able to assess the magnitude of what we have lost. Knowledge of the mundus imaginalis and its language persisted underground in small groups of mystics and visionaries, rose to the surface of culture for short, creative periods of time, but was always misunderstood, feared, and quickly repressed. Not until the twentieth century and the development of depth psychology would we begin—gradually—to rediscover as a culture the power of this language, the right brain, and the potential of this language for human consciousness.

It appears that the Deuteronomists really did understand the actual power of this language when they forbade its artistic expression. They certainly knew that by controlling this language they could destroy the power and influence of the visionaries. It is not so clear, however, just what was understood by those in the Church who nullified the power of the myths, allegories, rituals, and dramas about Jesus when they presented them as actual history. It certainly seems to me that a misunderstanding could easily occur from the language used by the mystics of the First Temple tradition. They spoke of a God who could incarnate in a son, such as Yahweh, in the Davidic Kings, and in the High Priests/shaman-mystics who were transformed in the holy of holies. Jesus, as such a High Priest, would have been spoken of as *the Son of God, the Messiah, the Anointed One, and the Resurrected One.* For those who did not know the language of this tradition, misunderstanding was bound to occur.

Another problem is that it was not unusual in the ancient world for myth to merge into history. It appears that the Deuteronomists consciously used such myths as the Exodus story as sacred history in order to unite the Jewish people after the exile. It is sometimes difficult to distinguish between myth and history, but in this case it is telling, says Barker, that Moses is "not a part of the religion of the pre-exilic prophets."[5] Yet this myth functions meaningfully as symbol and ritual within the lives of the Jews as a people. The Exodus story uses the universal story of the hero who leaves the known world, enters into a world of supernatural forces, often called the underworld, endures many tests, and finally returns to the known world with a gift of greater consciousness for his culture.

The hero is often thought of as a God who enters the material world, lives and teaches a higher knowledge, dies, and is resurrected. The Exodus story differs from this model in one important way: rather than the single hero or God, it is the Jewish Patriarchs who descend down into Egypt—the Underworld—and it is the Jewish people who ascend up out of Egypt. *As a people* they have suffered death, exile, and a rebirth into a promised land worthy of their spiritual development. Joseph Campbell reminds us that in "the Hagadah of Passover, in the course of the family ceremonial, the following meditation is read aloud by the father of the household: 'In every generation, one ought to regard himself as though he had personally come out of Egypt.'"[6] The symbolic structure of this myth reflects the inner life of a people, but it can be destructive when it is reduced to actual history in time and space.

When the Christians allowed our evolutionary myth of the Cosmic Christ to merge into history—that is, when they reduced *the language of the mundus imaginalis to history—for whatever reason—it had cataclysmic effects on the evolutionary development of Western consciousness.* In the words of Kuhn, "It threw a possible great civilization under the pall and handicap of the most fantastic conception that ever misdirected the moral genius of man.... It killed the psychological efficacy of the whole religious enterprise, diverting zeal from the one pivot point where zeal alone counts, —the life of the inner consciousness and seat of character, the soul."[7] *The labyrinthine journey of the soul to the center of the Self, the Christ within, was destroyed.* And slowly the image of the labyrinth itself disappeared. Chairs were and still are often placed on the great labyrinth in the cathedral at Chartres as if no memory of its ancient symbolic power survived.

When Kuhn speaks of "the most fantastic conception that ever misdirected the moral genius of man," he is obviously referring to the reduction of symbol to history. **The mystic/visionary has always known that the divine could never be limited to one Christ in one historical time and place.** *This defies the entire evolution of human consciousness.* It defies the awakening of the soul as it journeys toward its own great center to confront the divine, the cosmic Mind—not as Other, but as Self. It defies the mystic's knowledge that "There is nothing but life" and we are all "the nucleus of the nucleus" of that life. And it defies the very heart of the original Christ story. The divine—all life—is *perpetually coming into being*. All of nature reflects this reality, and that is why the Christ myth— and all similar myths—are always told within the story of the universe.

Our ancestors understood that the laws of nature organize energy and manifest themselves in all the various forms of nature, including human life and consciousness, and the deepest aspirations of the human psyche. Nature was indeed a sacred text that reflected these sacred laws equally in the birth, death, and rebirth of vegetation, the seasons, the dying and resurrecting gods, and the great astronomical cycles of the cosmos. Whether the god was Osiris/Horus, Attis, Tammuz, Orpheus, Dionysos, Adonis, Mithras, or Christ, his birth, death, and resurrection coincided with those of nature. For example, Kuhn tells us that there was a difference of opinion in the early Church as to whether Christ was born in the winter solstice, December 25, or in the vernal equinox, March 25. But Rome maintained that March 25 was the day of "the miraculous conception in the womb of the virgin, who gave birth to the divine child at Christmas, nine months afterwards." Just as the sun is born again each year in the winter solstice, Christ, as well as each of the other *dying and resurrecting* gods, is the "Ever Coming One."[8]

At the very core of the myth was its eternality, its ever-returning, ever-existing nature, *not its single appearance in one historical moment*. For thousands of years before Christianity, this myth—enacted in ritual—had reflected back to the human psyche the sacred laws of its own nature: the soul was "the divine seed that had been, like the grain, buried in the earth of flesh and sense." This seed was the sun, the light, "the central divine fire in the human heart." And this light within us would lead us to the place where the light comes into being by itself. Christ is a symbol of that divine fire that is incarnated in flesh, lives, dies, and is ever resurrected. All of nature sings the hymn of our becoming and eternality.[9]

As mentioned earlier, this myth was a part of all the great Mysteries of the ancient world. In *The Jesus Mysteries* Freke and Gandy make it very clear that the so-called *pagan* Mysteries "inspired the greatest minds of the ancient world"; these great minds were the so-called pagan philosophers who were, in fact, "the enlightened masters of the Mysteries;" the Mysteries were practiced in almost every culture in the Mediterranean; they consisted of the Outer or Lesser Mysteries that were open to all people and the Inner or Greater Mysteries that were "known only to those who had undergone a powerful process of mystical initiation"; the core myth in both the Outer and the Inner Mysteries was the myth of the incarnation of the soul, its death and resurrection—symbolized in the birth of the god in human form, and his or her death and resurrection.

Only the initiate in the Inner/Greater Mysteries *experienced* the spiritual reality of the symbolic myth. As Jesus says to his disciples in the Gospel of Luke, "To you it is given to know the Mysteries of the kingdom of God, but to the rest of them it is only given in allegories."[10]

Since this myth was known throughout the ancient world, the similarities between the Christian Mysteries and all the ancient Mysteries were obvious. **The ancients understood that the myth was the blueprint for the soul's evolution and thus belonged to the world.** Criticism only began when non-gnostic Christians, those who were not initiated into the Inner, Greater Mysteries, began to say that the myth was not rooted in initiation, but was actually historical, revolutionary, and unique to Christians. For this they were severely criticized not only by the philosophers and initiates into other Mysteries but also by those Christians who knew otherwise because they themselves had been initiated into the *secret tradition* that was at the heart of the early Christian movement.

Celsus, a famous philosopher and Roman encyclopedist of the first century, made it clear that there was "nothing new" in Christianity.[11] Behind the Christian views, he insisted, there is "an ancient doctrine that has existed from the beginning." Celsus goes further in his criticism of what he saw as the Christians' "systematic corruption of the truth, their misunderstanding of some fairly simple philosophical principles—which of course they completely botch."[12] Those who understood Greek philosophy and the Inner, Greater Mysteries had no difficulty seeing that those who insisted on the historical originality of the Christian Mysteries were simply lacking this understanding. Ammonius Saccas (c. 175-240 CE), teacher of Plotinus, one of the founders of Neoplatonism, and one who certainly understood both Greek philosophy and the Mysteries, strongly asserted that there was no difference between Christianity and the ancient Mysteries.[13]

Even St. Augustine himself said that "The very thing which is now called the Christian religion existed among the ancients also, nor was it wanting from the inception of the human race until the coming of Christ in the flesh, at which point the true religion which was already in existence began to be called Christian."[14] And the Church historian Eusebius wrote that "our manner of life and the principles of our religion have not been lately devised by us, but were instituted and observed...from the beginning of the world, by good men, accepted by God; *from those natural notions which are implanted in men's minds.*"[15] This last statement seems to reflect his realization that the Jesus story is structured by the organizing principles of the human psyche, that it is part of the blueprint of our becoming.

Yet this was not the understanding that prevailed. Those who had little or no understanding of the evolutionary myth of our species won the day. Thousands of years of spiritual experience were misunderstood, misinterpreted, inverted, and lost. How could this happen when so many knew otherwise? How could the Church actually succeed in convincing people that the Jesus story was a one-time historical occurrence and that the Christ did not reflect the individual soul in its journey to the light, but was God who came to save us—*not by our own becoming but by our own believing?*

The answer to this question opens the door to another dark and tragic turn in the history of Western culture. During the first centuries of Christianity the discord intensified between those who had been initiated into the Greater Mysteries and those who had only participated in the Lesser Mysteries. The initiates or Gnostics who had been initiated into the Greater Mysteries spoke of Jesus as their Great High Priest who imparted a *secret tradition* of higher knowledge to his inner circle of disciples after his resurrection, that is, after his own transformation in the holy of holies. Whatever else this Jesus was, he was symbolic of the High Priest—or initiate—who is transformed, realizes his divinity, and returns to teach and lead others into the experience of the holy of holies.

While it was said that such experiences were open to *loving souls* and to the *pure in heart*, just how available the Inner Mysteries appeared to those in the Outer Mysteries is not clear. What is painfully clear is that over time many in the Outer Mysteries developed a strong hostility against all those who claimed to be initiated into this *secret tradition*.[16] And since there were many within the Church who did not really know or understand this tradition, it is highly possible that they actually believed that the initiates (Gnostics) were fabricating knowledge of a *secret tradition*.

The battle lines were clear-cut: the Gnostics/initiates were the ones who understood symbolic language and experience in the mundus imaginalis/the subtle world. They rejected the vengeful God of the Deuteronomists in the Torah/Old Testament. After all, they were the continuation *and* revival of the shamanic/mystic/Wisdom tradition that had been ousted by the Deuteronomists under Josiah. They had existed for hundreds of years, and they had been writing for hundreds of years. Their major concern was to nurture the mystic path. We cannot know how much they wrote because the Church excluded most of their work, fraudulently mangled much of what was kept, and attempted to destroy the rest. The Church labeled their work *Pseudepigrapha* in yet another attempt to discredit it. The gnostic writings discovered among the Dead Sea Scrolls and the later Nag Hammadi texts have helped scholars to piece together a clearer picture of the Christian Gnostics and their conflict with those who shaped the religion of the Church.

The Church Christians who interpreted the Jesus story as history presented themselves as the original and only true Christians. This claim is extremely ironic since no initiate into the Christian Mysteries or any other Mystery would ever claim *originality* or *exclusivity*. **The myth belongs to life in that it reflects the laws of nature working throughout the cosmos and within the human psyche.** Little did the Church Fathers know just how much they revealed about themselves with such a claim.

Yet the early Church historians set out to support this claim to unique authority through any means that might achieve their goals. Kuhn points out that they filled the first centuries with books against "heresy." These books contained so many false stories about the Gnostics that archaeologist and historian of religions, Godfrey Higgins, concluded that *nothing* the Church Fathers said against the so-called heretics was credible. These Church historians held the belief that "fraud and deception" were acceptable if applied toward a worthy cause. Such "pious frauds" were thought not only "justifiable" but "laudable." Even St. Augustine admitted that "There are many things that are true which it is not useful for the vulgar crowd to know; and certain things which although they are false it is expedient for the people to believe otherwise." And Church historian Eusebius inadvertently revealed that he told only what might glorify the

Church and suppressed all that might disgrace it. Such findings have caused some scholars to conclude that the very foundation of the Church was built on falsehood.[17]

"Pious fraud" was practiced not only in relation to the Gnostics and their works, but also with the canonical texts, and it is now generally agreed that statements about Christ were even inserted by the Church into the writings of Josephus, a historian who wrote during the time Jesus was said to have lived. As far as the canonical texts are concerned, they were edited, cut, and rewritten to such an extent that Kuhn laments the possibility of most people ever being "awakened to the enormity of the corruption of old texts."[18] And G.R.S. Mead in *Fragments of a Faith Forgotten*, concludes that the Biblical texts have suffered "so many misfortunes at the hands of ignorant scribes and dogmatic editors that the human reason stands amazed at the spectacle." Mead's amazement is extended to the "general ignorance" most of us have about the history and origins of the Church. A student of this period, he says, "gradually works his way to a point whence he can obtain an unimpeded view of the remains of the first two centuries, and gazes round on a world that he has never heard of at school, and of which no word is breathed from the pulpit."[19]

Since the roots of the Church were deep in the Great Mysteries, Greek philosophy, natural science, and the great sophistication of the so-called *pagan* world, the Church chose to obliterate that world, to destroy all evidence of its connection to it. They were so successful that most people today still think of the pre-Christian world as ignorant and undeveloped when, in fact, it was the other way around. In Charles B. Waite's lengthy review of the early years of the Church in *History of the Christian Religion to the Year 200*, he concludes that what "strikes the attention, in a comprehensive review of the period, is the ignorance and superstition, even of the most enlightened and best educated of the fathers. Their bigotry has been noticed — their ignorance and superstition were no less." In almost all cases, says Waite, they hated learning, especially pagan knowledge of natural science, and, in fact, anything that concerned the laws of the material universe.[20]

It is, of course, well known that for centuries the Church continued to censor all the sciences, including the study of the mind and human consciousness. Waite concluded that the Church Fathers had "a sublime disregard for truth; not so much from perversity, as from carelessness, and indifference to its sacred character. Their unscrupulousness when seeking for arguments to enforce their positions is notorious; as well as the prevalence among them of what are known as pious frauds."[21] Not only were they often unscrupulous in their arguments, but they were often irrational as well. One of their responses to the overwhelming evidence of the preexistence of the Christ myth was that the Devil knew that Christ was to come so he plagiarized Christ's life in the ancient pre-Christian myths and rituals. This position was known as plagiarism by anticipation or "diabolical mimicry."[22] What better evidence is there that intellectual discipline and rational argument were either not known or not respected among the Church Fathers?

In 380 CE, when Theodosius I made Christianity the sole official state religion of the Roman Empire, the Church was empowered to go beyond the use of fraud and forgery. It now had the power of the Roman Empire to physically destroy the ancient world. And so, says Kuhn, "the orgy of destruction set in."[23] For centuries continuous violence ensued against any and all who opposed the Church. Whole cultures were destroyed — men, women, and children murdered. Even the lowest estimated number of people who were tortured and murdered during these early centuries paralyzes the mind. All intellectual pursuits and spiritual disciplines outside the Church were made illegal and eventually destroyed. So much was destroyed that it is not possible to be absolutely certain about the details of the destruction. Major sources do not always agree on the details, but they do agree in general that people were tortured and murdered; libraries were destroyed; Gospels burned; collections of gnostic writings burned; Jewish texts burned; Arabic manuscripts burned; temples, monasteries, and sanctuaries destroyed; Mystery Schools and academies of higher learning closed.

The intellectual and spiritual genius of the so-called pagan world was ravaged. Greek philosophy and rationalism were lost for centuries. The Great Mysteries were discredited and their knowledge forced underground. An understanding of mythic/symbolic language was lost. The mystic and visionary life was discredited and lost. Knowledge of the subtle world—the mundus imaginalis—was lost. The Gnostic Jesus was destroyed and his beloved Mary Magdalene pronounced a whore. Yahweh had once again abandoned his spouse and once again the people had *lost their vision*. The Church had succeeded in silencing all that had preceded it. While there were many reasons, both external and internal, for the decline of the Roman Empire, one wonders if any other reason was needed to plunge us into the Dark Ages—the residues from which we have yet to fully recover.

PART III

THE GIFT

The Gift

The Great Goddess, in her form as the Maiden Trinity, with Hermes, the guide of souls, and a reluctant Paris. This image appears on a black-figured vase from the later Greek Archaic Period (c. 800–480 BCE).*

The earlier Greek artistic tradition does not depict the later story we know as *The Judgment of Paris* in which Paris is to choose the most beautiful goddess. The later reduction of the story to a beauty contest, says classical scholar Jane Ellen Harrison, is a vulgar debasement of the original spiritual tradition. The ancient depiction of the goddesses as the feminine trinity or Charities reflects the One Great Goddess, Soul, the *Bringer of Gifts*. Each Goddess is a variation of *the Gift*. Hermes, says Harrison, had traditionally led this trinity of sacred Gifts in her many forms before the eyes of all humanity. It appears that Paris is reluctant to face the Great Gift, but the guide of souls is attempting to help him confront his larger destiny.†

---

* Jane Ellen Harrison, *Prolegomena to the Study of Greek Religion* (Princeton: Princeton University Press, 1991), 295.

† Harrison, 289-298.

Chapter Eighteen

"We only move into the future when we turn to face our past and become what we are."[1]

— Peter Kingsley

When Kingsley wrote these words, he was not talking about the past that has shaped our worldview of limits and negation and despair. He was not talking about belief systems that focus our energy outside ourselves. No. He was talking about that past which has been repeatedly denied, rejected, and repressed. He was talking about that past which has been buried for centuries in the ruins of misunderstanding, distortion, and violence.

Most of us, says Kingsley, are aware of the terrible extinction of species that our Western worldview brings about each year. Yet how many of us, he asks, are aware of **"the most extraordinary threat of all: the extinction of our knowledge of what we are."**[2] We have seen over and over again how this knowledge of "what we are" has emerged in Western consciousness and has, in fact, been the inspiration of each of its creative periods. But we have also seen how this knowledge was forced underground again and again and how the Church itself so thoroughly obliterated this knowledge that to speak of the Christ as our own inner potential to achieve Cosmic Consciousness would be considered blasphemous.

Yet the Christ of the Nag Hammadi texts has told us that if we will learn from Him, we will become like Him: "He who will drink from My mouth will become like Me. I myself shall become he, and the things that are hidden will be revealed to him."[3] He does not ask us to worship Him, but *to bring forth what is within us.*

If we embark on this journey to bring forth what is within us, we will be guided by the organizing principles of the psyche/the soul of the world, Baba Yaga's ball of thread, the inner Christ. *It is this journey that becomes our sacred text.* That is why Novalis could say that every person's life is a sacred text or every person's life will become a Bible. Of course, we can honor all other sacred texts to the degree that they honor the sacred journey of each person and to the degree that they are guides to help us along the way to our own spiritual becoming. Not all these texts will be what we think of as *religious,* for the sacred knowledge of our ancestors can come to us in the form of cave paintings and engravings, ritual and mystic/shamanic practices, oral traditions, myths, and fairy tales. But whatever guides we may have, it is our responsibility to work toward the achievement of the Christ Consciousness *within.*

It is this knowledge that is on the brink of extinction.

And it is the lack of this knowledge that leaves what Kingsley calls "that vast missingness deep inside us."[4] It was that missing something that even as a child I tried to fill with water only to realize that I didn't know how to fill whatever it was that was empty. It comes as no surprise that the stories we construct out of our emptiness are stories of limits and insignificance. We have seen how even the religious stories are about the divinity and creativity that are outside of us. Our experience of this emptiness reinforces our belief in the stories of negation despite significant evidence to the contrary. Consciously or unconsciously, we are *addicted* to such stories because our own inner emptiness seems to confirm their truth.

The only way we can heal our addiction and find our true stories is by *turning inward.* This truly is where our future lies, not only for us as individuals but for our planet as well. Swimme is correct in saying that the very evolution of our planet is unfolding through the consciousness of the human being. What we believe, the stories we create, the decisions we make "are going to determine the way this planet functions and looks for hundreds of millions of years in the future." The universe definitely is *up to something,* but it is up to that something through us. This is the moment, says Swimme, that our planet—*through us*—can awaken to "its own deep aim."⁵

I now realize that during my college years, once I could no longer believe in the Christian story, it was that *missingness* deep inside me that erupted in the old fear that the Western stories of emptiness might be true. But, at the same time, there was now room in myself for the presence and guidance of soul through my dreams. It would take years for me to dissolve this addictive fear and be able to live in the knowledge of soul. But through those years I gave respectful attention to my dreams and I studied the sacred experiences of my ancestors.

I was deeply grateful for that first numinous dream of soul presence. In this dream soul had presented herself in the image of the woman in blue who was waiting for me on the bridge crossing the sacred water. Her divine counterpart appeared in the energy of the great misty spiral that emerged out of the depths of the water and touched the base of my spine. And she had filled my bedroom with a beautiful fragrance, for she was the Queen of Heaven who was "perfumed with the incense of the holy of holies" and had "a fragrance beyond all fragrance."⁶

Somehow, even then, I knew that it was to her that I owed my homage. For it was she who had been forgotten, devalued, and exiled. In this dream, the divine appeared in its natural polarity: the masculine and feminine dimensions of the divine were One and lovingly working together. But in the outer world, in myself and in my culture, the masculine dimension of the divine had abandoned the Queen of Heaven. I had seen in a later dream how my own Knight had ridden away from the birth of soul without even knowing such a miracle was taking place. And we saw how Yahweh had abandoned his Queen and, as a result, had become exclusive, arrogant, jealous, forgetful, and violent. He had forgotten their love, their partnership, and the great joy she had brought him. Because of

His unconsciousness, the stories about their love and partnership were lost and we could no longer remember who or what we are.

It was clearly the aim of the woman in blue to renew their relationship in me. It was she who would be my guide, for she was the visionary partner that my Knight was now trying to acknowledge and understand. But even though I had witnessed in a later dream how my Knight had actually assisted in the birth of Our Lady within his own being, I discovered that it would take him many more years before he would be capable of being a true partner with his Queen. He was prone to periodic forgetfulness and a dreadful *unconscious* belief in the superiority of reason alone. His training in the academic world had conditioned him to work *exclusively* with concepts and what he thought of as logic. This consistently blinded him to the intelligence of feeling, intuition, and the poetic logic of soul. Just at a critical moment of perception, he would *turn away* from her and miss the magic and the miracle of her presence. Each time he fell into this *single vision*, he felt unhappy and could find no joy.

She, on the other hand, could be relied upon to relate to my Knight. She knew how to retain her own unique individuality even as she included her Knight's very different perspective. She was *inclusive* and never distorted or negated his scholarly process. And she always provided a larger context in which the material could be understood. It was clearly my Knight who had yet to learn how to become a reliable and respectful partner with soul.

Chapter Nineteen

>——◆——O——◆——<

I was beginning to experience what it really means to owe homage to Our Lady, the Queen of Heaven, for it was only She who could lead me into the Holy of Holies. But first, she had a story to tell.

As soon as I finished my doctoral work, I made a real effort to find ways to experience "Our Lady" and to allow her to teach me how to relate to her. I had spent all too much time in a world of noble knights who appeared to know even less than I about their visionary partner. So I went to Peru on a journey to meditate in some of the ancient sacred sites with indigenous shamans.

The land itself had a powerful effect on me. I began to realize that my focused attention was relaxing and my senses were becoming more active. I was actually beginning to perceive the environment through my body rather than through my rational mind. This felt like a new form of perception, but, I thought, I must have experienced this mode of perception as a child when my brother and I played all day in the meadows and fields around our house. I remembered feeling such joy during those childhood days. Gradually, I began to realize that *the senses* were actually sacred gateways to the Queen of Heaven. The vastness of the mountains, the sky, the river below, the greenness of the earth, and the sounds of nature penetrated my body and allowed both my mind and my body to become porous.

But when we arrived at Machu Picchu, I began to feel a profound sadness. We did the death ceremony the night before we entered Machu Picchu the next day. This was the ancient tradition of the Incas: we must die to our old selves before we can enter this sacred space. Consciously, I participated in the ritual out of respect for my ancestors, but unconsciously something in me *really* was in the process of dying. As we climbed the mountain the next morning, the unexplainable sadness was intensifying. I found myself thinking about all that I had learned from men throughout my life, both in content and in the very structuring of that content. And I was grateful now to the male shamans who were working with us during this journey. But I knew that these shamans could not guide me where I needed to go. There was something moving through my body that had its own intention. I was beginning to experience what it really means to owe homage to Our Lady, the Queen of Heaven, for it was only She who could lead me into the Holy of Holies. But first, she had a story to tell.

Finally, we arrived at the Intihuatana, called the Hitching Post of the Sun, where we would have our first ceremony on the mountain. Inti is the name for Father Sun, and the hitching post of the Sun is where the Sun connects to the Mother Earth through his love and deep devotion to Her. The Incas thought of themselves as Children of the Sun who reflect the love of the Father for the Mother in every aspect of their lives. All of their rituals and ceremonies were structured to maintain the love, the balance, and the harmony between these two great forces in the universe. They expressed this love through their devotion and care for the earth and all living things. They understood that their love for Her brought them happiness and joy.

I was later told by Incan shamans that they have been able to keep their Incan tradition alive for the last 500 years since the Spanish Conquest by discreetly passing this ancient knowledge on from one shaman to the next. They did not have to reject Christianity, for they could accept many of the ancient truths within it and, at the same time, keep alive their own gnostic tradition of inner experience. Earlier, when I was in the Catholic Cathedral in Cusco, I had been amazed to be immediately greeted by a large painting of both Jesus and Mary standing as equals. I was told that the indigenous people would not allow only one aspect of this great polarity to appear.

As we circled around the Intihuatana that fateful morning, one of the shamans began the sacred chant in Quechua. The vibration of the chant sank deep into my bones and flesh. The sadness in me was becoming unbearable. Then each of us in turn stepped up to the sacred structure and placed our foreheads on the stone. When it was my turn, I moved forward, kneeled, and felt the hard coldness. Something in me collapsed and an ocean broke loose.

I cried, and history cried through me.

We had abandoned our deepest self and we had forgotten who and what we really are. We had even denied that there had ever been anything to abandon. For us, there was no Queen of Heaven, no soul of the world, no Pachamama, no meaning or purpose. And we, like Yahweh, had become arrogant and violent. *We had mutilated ourselves and we were destroying the world. We had released a sorrow so vast that it could no longer be contained.*

I shuddered at the thought of my own complicity.

I can't remember how I got from the Intihuatana to the famous Pachamama Stone where our next ritual was to take place. After we arrived there, I do remember one of the shamans asking people to move a little away from me because he said there were spirits of women around me. That was *his* vision. All I could feel was the overwhelming sorrow from my experience at the Intihuatana.

The Pachamama Stone is a large stone altar dedicated to Pachamama, the eternal Great Goddess of the earth, the cosmos, time and eternity. She is the Earth Mother and the Cosmic Mother, the Feminine Dimension of the Divine, the co-creatress of all that is. She is an indigenous version of Our Lady, the Queen of Heaven. The ritual began with the shamans in turn standing before the great Stone with arms raised in reverence to her. One of the shamans placed the serpent staff along the spine of the other as he himself chanted, once again in Quechua. After their renewed dedication to her, one of the shamans came to me and said that the Great Mother had asked him to bring her daughter to her. So he took me to the Stone for the dedication to Her. Then I led each one of our group to the Stone for dedication.

My own experience at the Intihuatana had so consumed my attention that I was not really aware of all that was taking place around me. But later my friend from Ecuador told me that she and the others had observed the most unusual event while the ceremony at the Pachamama Stone was taking place. There was a beautiful woman who walked into the sacred space of the Stone and smiled as she walked by and observed the ceremony. That in itself, she thought, was not unusual, but the reaction of the shamans was: they both immediately sank to their knees in homage to her as she walked by. Later each had separately told my friend the same thing: she was the physical manifestation of Pachamama, the Great Mother. Sometimes she appeared as a beautiful young woman and, at other times, she appeared as the Old Woman of the sacred Mountain, Huayna Picchu. My friend wanted to know how they both immediately knew who she was, and each, once again separately, had answered that the chakra above her head was fully illuminated.

When I heard this, I could not really relate to it because I myself had not seen it and, given my unconscious belief system, I would not have been able to see what the shamans saw. For them, her appearance was sacred but not unusual, for the material world was not experienced as separate from the subtle world. Each was always flowing into the other. But it would only be much later, after more of my own experiences with her, that this event would become meaningful to me.

But for now, Pachamama, the Queen of Heaven, was leading me deep into the *history* of her abandonment and exile. It was becoming painfully clear to me that my intention to honor the historical past equally with my own personal present was opening me to an energy field of experience that I had not quite anticipated. To know with the conceptual mind that our culture had abandoned soul is one thing, but to experience even for a few moments a fraction of what this means in human and planetary suffering is quite another.

Not only had this spiritual dimension of ourselves been abandoned, it had been ignored and silenced. I thought of what Rilke had said about our inability to perceive spirit: "through our daily defensiveness" we have "so completely eliminated from life" the strange, the mysterious, the inexplicable, "that the senses with which we could have grasped them have atrophied."[1] Had my senses been awakened on this trip just enough for me to perceive — at least to some degree — the effects of this continuing historical act?

I realized that it is not only the strange, the mysterious, the inexplicable that we have difficulty perceiving. **For once our senses begin to atrophy, we also have difficulty perceiving the very reality of history itself. This allows us to be in denial of the horrible violence our worldview has let loose on the world.** As I lay in bed that evening thinking about my experience that day, I grieved for the mutilation that had taken place within my own body — and I grieved for the world. I was aware that for my culture the word *mutilation* would seem exaggerated. But I *knew* it was not.

Later, when I returned home, I was asked to write a chapter about my experiences in Peru for *Earthwalking Sky Dancers: Women's Pilgrimages to Sacred Places*. The following is a description of the pervasive sense of horror and sadness I felt that evening:

> *I lay awake thinking of how Lavinia in Shakespeare's* Titus Andronicus *could be seen as a symbol of our intuitive, feeling, visionary self, of all those modes of the mind that we reject as insignificant or deceptive. As daughter and woman she is potential mother, the very source of life. Yet her tragic fate is a chilling reflection of the consequences of our culture's [rejection of her]. She was gang-raped by the sons of a man her father had captured in war. So that she could not tell her story, they cut out her tongue. So that she could not write her story, they cut off her arms. But she was not defeated. She took a stick by her teeth and tried to scratch her story in the earth.*[2] *Yet even those scratchings have been ridiculed, ignored, or denied. Could it be, I wondered, that Lavinia might eventually forget she had a story to tell?*
>
> *Since the historical denial of her story shapes the foundation of our model of reality, to remember Lavinia's story as symbolic of excluded reality is to break through centuries*

> *of addictive, abusive behavior. If we do not ridicule, ignore or deny her altogether, we may seek her out only to do her further harm by demanding her to be what she uniquely is not. In our addiction to the rational mind, we say she must prove herself with the same "rigor" we demand of reason. We do not recognize that reason's way must demand rigor of itself, but it must allow Lavinia to present herself to us in her own way. To demand of her how she should do this is to rape her, to dominate her, to insist she be her opposite rather than herself. We fail to realize that we have so devalued and mutilated her that she cannot reveal herself to us in her full power — and this we take as proof that she has nothing to reveal. Our finest university cackle is reserved for anyone who would throw her a sop. In our attempt to uphold reason, we betray the very open, exploratory nature of reason itself.[3]*

As appalling as the story of Lavinia might be, she *is* an appropriate symbol for what we in Western culture have done to our abilities to perceive "the strangest, the most mysterious, and the most inexplicable experiences that can meet us."[4] Our continual denial of and violence against this deepest part of ourselves has "done infinite harm to life." We have betrayed and silenced our visionary partner until we — *not she* — actually did forget that she had a story to tell us. Later, when I would read the line, "Stories have to be told or they die, and when they die, we can't remember who we are or why we're here,"[5] I thought of this story of denial and abandonment. *It was becoming evident that I could not learn how to relate to soul unless I could walk the path of her exile, denial, and abandonment.* My soul and the soul of the world wanted me to know this story to the degree that I could carry it. It would not be the last time I would have to experience her story, for now that I was listening, she had so much to tell me.

Chapter Twenty

>-+◄)►-○-◄(►+-◄

The ultimate fruit of this Cosmic Tree is the knowledge that we are all part of Universal Mind, that we are immortal, that we are divine, and that we are all creators.

A few days later we took a small motorboat from Copacabana across Lake Titicaca to the sacred Island of the Sun. The Islands of the Sun and the Moon were two of the most sacred places for the Incas as well as the people who were there long before the Incas arrived. The Island of the Sun was thought of as the birthplace of the sun, the masculine dimension of the divine, and the Island of the Moon was thought of as the feminine dimension of the divine. Both islands were thought of as emerging out of the womb of the Great Mother, which is Lake Titicaca itself. I don't know why there was no plan for us to visit the Island of the Moon. In fact, at the time, I didn't even know of its existence. We spent most of the day on the Island of the Sun. We meditated as we sat in a circle: then we waited for the appearance of the sacred bird, which I assumed was the condor. The appearance of the bird would be the signal that we had been accepted as pilgrims to the rock from which the sun first emerged.

We waited for some time, but finally the bird actually did appear, and we were able to proceed with the next stage of the ceremony. Each of us in turn was allowed to enter alone the small rock cave, make the traditional offerings, and meditate for a few moments. The womb-like structure was only large enough to crawl into and curl up like a fetus. *It was there, in that moment, that I made it very clear to myself that I did not want a teacher or shaman or any other guide from the outer world. I had ended my apprenticeship with the masculine, with Father Sun and the visible world. The only guide that I could accept now was Our Lady, the Queen of Heaven, Pachamama, the Woman in Blue who had waited for me so long ago on the bridge crossing the great water.*

The last day of my journey in Peru was spent at Sillustani, near Puno by Lake Umayo, which was probably once a part of Lake Titicaca. Sillustani is a pre-Incan burial ground built on the shores of the Lake and on the tops of the surrounding hills and mountains. The burial structures are circular, megalithic towers called chullpas. The indigenous people say that these chullpas were far more than places of burial. They believe that they were also used as places for initiations and sacred ceremonies. And Sillustani itself, they say, was a place of many temples. As one modern-day Aymara-Incan writer, Jorge Luis Delgado, expresses it, its "main purpose in pre-Incan and Incan times was as a temple, an oracle, a place to understand this life and other lives." It is, he says, "an important Power Place" where the vibrations are so different that "The 'veils' between worlds are very thin, and it feels like you are looking at different realities,..."[1]

But I would not read this description until twenty years later. When I was there, the only thing I knew about Sillustani was that it was an ancient burial ground. We were the only people there except for one man who watched over the chullpas. So each of us could spend the day in a quiet place alone where we could meditate and prepare for the fire ceremony that evening. This was to take place in an ancient stone circle at the foot of one of the burial mountains that bordered the lake on one side and the valley and stone circle on the other. Near the end of the day each of us privately wrote on a piece of paper our renewed commitment to life. During the ceremony, each of us would kneel before the fire with this intention in our hearts as we placed our paper in the fire. The ceremony began just as it became dark; the fire was strong, and the moon was full. We chanted the water chant for what seemed like hours. During the chant, the shamans came to each of us with the sacred cactus drink, San Pedro.

Here we need to pause and reflect for a moment on the indigenous use of sacred plants. In the West there exists among a growing number of people a profound understanding of and participation in this practice. Yet, at the same time, there are still many people who have little or no understanding about the nature of the plants or the tradition. Given the pervasiveness of addiction in our culture and our experience of the discovery and often misuse of mind-altering substances during the 1960s, there have been good reasons for concern. Since I was a mythologist, I knew that many early cultures throughout the world had used sacred plants as a part of their initiation ceremonies as well as part of their meditative practices. I had been particularly interested in this practice in the Minoan and Greek cultures and later in the indigenous cultures of the Americas. Very early on it became clear to me that I could not be a scholar of the symbolic and mythic structures of these spiritual traditions without an *experiential knowledge* of this sacred practice. But I was cautious and waited many years before I participated in the experience itself.

I actually began my research of such experiences by reading Aldous Huxley's *The Doors of Perception* when I was in my late twenties. I was particularly impressed with Huxley's reference to Henri Bergson's suggestion that the function of the brain was mainly to limit our access to Universal Mind so that we could function on a daily basis and not be overwhelmed and confused. This limited focus was necessary for our biological survival. In other words, we are all "potentially Mind at Large," but this Mind "has to be funneled through the reducing valve of the brain and nervous system. What comes out at the other end is a measly trickle of the kind of consciousness which will help us to stay alive on the surface of this particular planet."[2]

Our ancestors understood this and developed various techniques of relaxing the efficiency of the "reducing valve." There must have been those people then, as now, who experienced the releasing of this valve spontaneously or through a crisis or through a Near-Death episode. Such experiences would have nurtured the development of meditative techniques to achieve such states of consciousness at will. And we now know that all around the planet our ancestors discovered the plants that release this valve.

Such plants do not reduce the ability to think clearly. Huxley stated that his use of mescaline (which occurs naturally in the San Pedro cactus and other plants) did not hinder his ability to remember or to "think straight."[3] Later, in my own work with sacred medicine, I felt that I was experiencing an intensification of reason. Not only did this seem to be a result of the relaxing of the "reducing valve" but it seemed that *this enhanced ability to think was also a result of both hemispheres of the brain working in a loving relationship – the creation of a true harmony.* We usually think with the conceptual left brain severed from its deep roots in the symbolic, mythic, feeling, intuitive older brain. When the two work in harmony, ideas are *thought, seen* and *felt* in their larger context. It truly is a marriage of Yahweh and the Queen of Heaven.

But, of course, such experiences can take us far beyond both reason and symbol. There can occur a knowing, *a wisdom*, that transcends all the polarities of our life in time and space and we experience *the unity of all life*. Or, sometimes, there is a *remembering* of origins and meaning and purpose and love that, as so many people have said, can never be expressed in either conceptual or symbolic language. But perhaps more often a particular problem is resolved, an illness cured, or a harmful attitude revealed for what it is. Plant medicine will often reveal our limitations in such a loving and sometimes humorous manner that we end up being deeply grateful for the knowledge of our own darkness. However, this is not to discount the experiences of some of the plant medicines that can open us up so powerfully to unfamiliar worlds that we do experience fear and uncertainty. This is one of the reasons for caution in their use; for these plants we need spiritual grounding and the presence of a person or persons who know how to work with this kind of energy.

From what we know about the earliest use of these plants, it appears that they were used in much the same way as indigenous peoples use them today. The plants are considered sacred. They are prepared in a prayerful and meditative manner and given during ceremony by the elders or shamans of the tribe or community. They are not addictive, and used within the sacred tradition, they are not available for habitual, casual use. It is important to repeat that many of these sacred plants require considerable courage and respect to be able to participate in the consciousness they release.

Of course, not all ancient cultures used plants. Sometimes the plants were not available or, for other reasons, they were not used. In their absence, other techniques were often developed to trigger the release of this valve and allow Universal Mind to flow through individual consciousness. From the outset, it is important to know that the plants, the techniques, the spontaneous occurrences, and the Near-Death Experiences *all* allow us to participate in various ways and to various degrees *in the same reality*: *Universal Mind, Mind at Large, or Cosmic Consciousness*. But, of course, since this reality is vast, the potential for experience is infinite. Sometimes our experience is limited, but it is what we can perceive at the time. Shamans often say that our experience will be exactly what we need in that moment. For example, as I will explain below, my experience that evening at Sillustani was the perception and observation of another reality. That was precisely what I needed. *While every experience is important, the ultimate fruit of this Cosmic Tree is the knowledge that we are all part of Universal Mind, that we are immortal, that we are divine, and that we are all creators.*

San Pedro has been used in Andean culture for several thousand years but acquired the name of the Christian Saint Peter after the Conquest. People have wondered if this name was given to the plant in an attempt to save it from the Inquisition or if it was because Saint Peter holds the keys to the Kingdom of God in the Christian tradition just as San Pedro opens the doors of perception to a higher consciousness in the Andean tradition.

And now to return to my own experience with San Pedro that evening at Sillustani. After we drank the San Pedro, we continued chanting and remained in a meditative state. Our eyes were open. I was highly focused on the fire and the chant for what seemed like hours, although it probably was not that long. Then, suddenly, my attention was drawn to the top of the mountain, and to my complete astonishment, I saw that the mountaintop was filled with people. Most of them were facing us and observing our ceremony, but others seemed to be engaged in their own activities. I knew there was no one else in this place other than the one guard and ourselves. I could not take my eyes off of them long enough to look at my friend who was sitting next to me, but I was able to reach over, grab her arm and ask her if she saw what I was seeing. She emphatically replied, "Yes!" Neither of us said *what* we were seeing. We were both too engaged to speak further.

But suddenly my Western mind asserted itself and suggested that the shamans must have arranged to have a busload of people brought from Puno to the site to stage this scene for us. I was rather shocked that I had such a thought, but what was even more surprising was that the moment I had the thought, it was as though the beings on the mountain were aware of it and responded by showing me that they were not full-bodied people but fluid, spirit forms. For a few moments, they appeared more like images in water. Then they returned to more substantial forms.

My attention was then drawn to my left just a short distance away. I saw one very tall being step off the mountain into the air, turn, and begin to walk through the air directly toward our fire circle. There was a white misty essence within the figure. He — or she — spread out his arms and it looked as though he had sleeves like wings. So much for the people from Puno idea. But, strangely, the very moment I knew he was approaching us, I looked away. Later, I wondered why I did this. My only answer to myself was that I just was not ready to see this being at close range. Then to my right I saw a young boy racing across and down the mountain in a playful way. As I continued to observe the spirit beings, I saw what looked like a staff in one man's hand and a tall headdress on another. Then I saw a dog running around among these beings. I observed from the corner of my eyes that our shamans were aware of their presence and were acknowledging them in a ritualistic manner. The more I relaxed and opened myself to this strange reality, the more I was able to feel its power.

Then it was my turn to walk to the fire. I approached the fire, kneeled before it and allowed my hands and arms to slowly move through it. The fire was now what the shamans called a *friendly fire* that would not burn us. I gently and reverently placed into the fire the paper on which I had earlier written my commitment to Pachamama, Our Lady, the soul of the world. I wanted to live in a world that allowed and nurtured our full development, that honored the whole mind, that made room in itself for the immensities and mysteries of the universe.[4] In that moment of total commitment, I felt I was surrounded by another dimension of consciousness.

Later that evening when we returned to the small hotel, my friend and I had a chance to talk. I did not tell her anything I had seen until she told me. She too had seen the boy running to the right, the dog, the staff, the headdress — and the tall being walking in the air with sleeves like wings. I was grateful she had spoken first, for now I knew that we had seen the same things.

A couple of years later I met one of the shamans again and told him what I had seen that evening. When I described the tall being with sleeves like wings, he said, "Oh, those were not sleeves. They *were* wings. This spirit always takes the form of a winged being. Did you not see him enter the fire circle and participate in our ceremony? He is always present at our rituals at Sillustani." I remembered so well how I had *turned away* from him and missed the mystery and miracle of seeing the winged being in the circle with us.

It would be years later that I would read Delgado's description of Sillustani as an important power place, a place where the vibrations are different and the veil between the worlds is thin, and that, because of this, Sillustani probably had been used as a place for initiations and sacred ceremonies. When I was there, all I could say with certainty was that I felt the power of the place and I saw a very different reality. *I was initiated into the reality of the strange, the mysterious, the inexplicable.* This was a significant breakthrough for me, for I knew that I had experienced something that my Western mind could neither dismiss nor explain.

The next morning, I returned to Los Angeles. István and Pisti met me at the airport and we spent the day with relatives. It was Easter Sunday and in my heart I celebrated what this season had meant long before Christianity: *the perpetual birth of the soul of the world and the renewal of all life*. I could feel an ancient wisdom rising in me, something yet to come but somehow making its presence known.

Then it came.

Chapter Twenty-One

*She took me to the Cosmic Tree of Life and offered me the sacred fruit
in the Holy of Holies — my own soul.*

I was lying on the bed listening to shamanic music when I began to laugh uncontrollably. Some long-forgotten memory began to flow through my body. Before it reached rational consciousness, I already knew it, knew it in my body, and the cells were laughing with memory.

Suddenly a rather unclear figure appeared and moved quickly toward me with definite purpose. I knew she was Pachamama, the Young/Old Woman of the Mountain, the soul of the world. In seconds she was no longer visible, but I felt her presence. Then I was back at Machu Picchu.

I became aware that I was a tall blue being with wings walking through the air and looking down at my dead body wrapped in canvas and tied with rope. The death of my body was no more than the shedding of an old skin. From the perspective of the blue being, I knew I was eternal. Yet I carefully observed how the body below had been placed on a hospital gurney and was now being pushed quietly and quickly across the mountain by four spirit-like beings. Suddenly my consciousness shifted back into the body below. I saw that I was being pushed toward Huayna Picchu. I was elated. I was to be allowed to enter the Holy of Holies. The ancient ones would speak to me, mysteries would be revealed to me.

But just as the beings arrived at the entry into the sacred mountain, they stopped.

Within seconds the ancient memory flooded my consciousness. What my body had known from the beginning had finally reached the rational mind. While my body laughed, the images had moved in linear fashion to communicate with the brain. Now all of me remembered.

What a joke I had played on myself!

I was the Sacred Mountain, the Ancient Ones, the Old Woman, the Mystery, the Source.

I laughed uproariously. Never had I laughed like this before. It was a molecular laugh, a laugh that vibrated in the cells and shot straight through the toenails, skin, and hair. **This was** *gnosis,* that knowing for which no proof is asked because the experience is the knowing. To question it would bring forth more uncontrollable laughter.

Then I saw myself sitting in a forest and I was surrounded by deer. I struggled to translate this gnosis into my practical life. I heard myself say, "But I can't create a world!"

And a voice answered: *"You just did create a world in which you cannot create! We can do nothing but create."*

These words exploded into the realization of what I had just done — but also into what I could do. I knew this now. I remembered this fully and completely. And with this memory — this wisdom — I began to fly through the air. I passed Huayna Picchu and as I did, I began to speak my new creation: "Then I will create better games, games where all our children will be healed, where all our children will live in a world of ecstasy, joy, love, and peace." As I spoke, I myself was in a state of ecstasy. I was in love with the universe and I was filled with joy. I saw so clearly that our world did not have to be as it is. *I knew it is what we have created.* In the moment, this did not make me sad. I was experiencing what we can do, not what we have done. There would be time for sadness later.

There was no egotism in this experience, for egotism is only a substitute for gnosis. It was simply that sacred memory of who I am, who we all are. Pachamama, the Queen of Heaven, had responded to my deepest aspiration to know her, to know how to relate to her. I had experienced her absence—and now her presence. She had always known—of course—what I did not know: that I would not be able to relate to her until I could know *who I am and why I'm here*.

So she took me to the Cosmic Tree of Life and offered me the sacred fruit in the Holy of Holies—my own soul.

Chapter Twenty-Two

>—•>—O—<•—<

Our work is to bring the gift of pure clay to our children: the knowledge that we are immortal, we are divine, and we are creators.

Our Lady—the Lady in Blue who, so long ago, had waited for me on the bridge crossing the sacred water—had led me into the Holy of Holies. But I was soon to realize that she had not yet finished telling me her story. I needed a much deeper knowledge of the consequences of her abandonment and exile. She was the soul of the world, the fragrance, wisdom, beauty, and joy of Life. She was the fruit of the Cosmic Tree and we had allowed that fruit to decay. *Gradually, I would realize that her story was the heart of my work and the work of the earth.*

A few months before Pisti's accident, I went with a small group of people to meditate in Chaco Canyon and Canyon de Chelly, and it was in Chaco Canyon that I had a chilling dream of darkness and violence with a young man I came to call the World Child. **I experienced how the soul of this Child had been shattered by the horrible myth of violence we have let loose on our planet.** When he proposed a violent solution to a problem and saw my disapproval, he asked in an adult voice, "How long will it take you to understand what we must become to survive in this world?"

There was such terrible power in his voice. I told Pisti this dream when I returned home, and it reminded him of a dream he had about a year earlier:

> *He dreamed he was in his room painting on a large canvas. A great spirit appeared behind him, and Pisti asked the spirit what we can do to heal the earth. Suddenly, the spirit was in Pisti's right hand and was painting a woman holding a child in her left arm and looking back over her right shoulder at the coming storm. Pisti remarked that the dream was pretty straightforward since it was evident that the child needed to be protected from a very present danger. "But," Pisti added, "just in case I missed the point, the spirit said, 'Protect everything that is coming into being.'"*[1]

The World Child was the child who had not been protected, and he was not through with me. After Pisti's death he appeared in dreams and visions and even in everyday experiences so often and with a message so powerful that I wondered if I could be losing my mind. I could not bear to tell anyone, not even István, because I was afraid that the telling of it might actually shift me into that Child's dimension of reality. **This Child carried within him the horror of our worldview, and he was determined that I follow him into the darkness we have bequeathed our children on this planet.**

I wrote in *The Miracle of Death*:

> *When I opened the newspaper or turned on the television, I received news of his death, torture, suicide, murder, abandonment. He appeared in the addict, the zealot, the indifferent. I saw his eyes in the murderer, hardened, detached, no longer lovable. I was seeing, hearing, and knowing with an intensity I had never experienced. Whenever this wounded child appeared, I felt as though I were that child's mother. Sometimes, in dreams, the World Child looked at me with Pisti's face, and I woke up grateful that Pisti was already dead. I realized that Pisti's death had dissolved the filter that had regulated the degree of empathy I could endure without my balance being threatened.*[2]

I was so affected by these experiences that it would take months for me to realize that if the Queen of Heaven had a story to tell about the consequences of her abandonment, this was it. Yet, there were times that I could only cry and beg her to release me from this unbearable knowledge.

About a year after Pisti's death, István, a shaman, and I planned a trip to Death Valley for an all-night ritual. I secretly thought this might be healing for me, but, in actuality, it became a horrifying culmination of what I had been experiencing. Throughout the meditation I felt paralyzed in an underworld of darkness. During the last hours of the night I began to experience a sorrow that was so vast, so deep, and so intense that I began to feel a painful energy, almost like "an electrical current" pass through my vocal cords and explode in a lament of shattered words. I must have fallen into unconsciousness for a few seconds. The shaman splashed water in my face and responded to this voice with love, "What, Great Mother, can we do to heal your pain? We are here. What can we do?" All three of us were shocked and silent as we heard the voice screech through my throat and scream out across the desert dunes: *"It can never be healed!"*

I had felt the voice coming. It seemed to have swept across the desert sands and into my body. I knew what the voice was going to say, and I longed for it *not* to be said, not to be true. But I had no power to stop it. This was a sorrow far beyond any that I could ever experience in a lifetime. It was a collective scream of loss and grief.[3]

Later that week István had a vision in which he was able to see my journey in the underworld. He told me that he realized that I had felt completely alone during the vision, but he saw many female spirits working with me. "You went," he said, "very deep—almost too deep to return—but you—and the spirits—made this journey *to bring back the pure clay for our children.*"

I didn't really know what this meant, but it touched my heart that István had experienced a constructive effort in my vision beyond the collective grief. I had learned to take István's visions seriously. But for a long time, I simply could not move beyond what we have done and are continuing to do to "everything that is coming into being" throughout the world. I knew that we had all been deeply wounded by the same violent and empty worldview of our culture. And it was my focus on this that released the meaning of the *pure clay*.

Clay is a substance we can use to mold the forms of our imagination — the worlds we choose to create. But the clay we have bequeathed our children is *toxic* with the belief that nothing they create could possibly have meaning or purpose since our very lives are a fluke of a meaningless, material world. **But the *pure clay* would be the knowledge of a loving, creative universe with infinite possibilities. It would be the knowledge of who they are and why they are here.** *It would be the Fruit from the Cosmic Tree: the knowledge that we are immortal, we are divine, and we are creators.*

It was several months after Pisti's death that István had the vision of how the Jackal Healers work: they are individuals who come to the earth, take on the toxic worldview and heal it within themselves — just as the jackal takes in decayed food and transforms it into nourishment within his own body. This was when Pisti talked with István about *The I Ching;* he told István to look up the hexagram whose lines from the top to the bottom were straight, broken, broken, straight, straight, broken. I mentioned this in the "Introduction." As I said there, neither István nor I knew much about *The I Ching*, but I did have the book. I ran into my study, found the book, and showed the hexagram to István. We could hardly believe what we read: Hexagram 18. Ku / Work on What Has Been Spoiled [Decay].

As I mentioned earlier, Pisti told István that we should read this hexagram carefully. It was our work and it was the work of the earth. I then asked István how he remembered the lines for this hexagram and he said the code was ML, Merchants of Light. Then he said that there are so many words that ML stands for, such as Mother Love, Miracle Lovers, Matrix of Life, Multi-Lives on Multi-Levels, Memory of Light, Masters of Light, Masters of Love, and Masters of Life. They are called the Merchants of Light, said István, because they know how to distill the darkness and decay into light and life. Like merchants, they "sell" the knowledge of this process for the "price" of consciousness, and the entire universe "profits."

I must admit that I did not put all the pieces of these experiences together for a long time, but finally the pieces started falling into place. I came to realize that while the Merchants of Light can be individuals, they are also an intelligent and highly organized energy field. Earlier I had read Gustaf Strömberg's discussion of such fields of organization as nature's intelligent, "highly organized activity" that, like "a wave of organization" moves into an organism, such as a caterpillar, and cell by cell creates a butterfly, a completely new entity. As mentioned earlier, scientists today call these cells Imaginal cells — cells that contain the blueprint of a new being.[4]

ML, then, is a wave of organization that is moving through the present consciousness of the human species and, cell by cell — person by person — it is creating a completely new form of consciousness. Its energy resonates at a higher frequency than the energy field that maintains our present consciousness. We are like the caterpillar that is in the process of becoming a butterfly.

As I said in the "Introduction," at the time of this experience I had thought of the Merchants of Light as a strange name, but later when I was rereading Frances A. Yates' *The Rosicrucian Enlightenment*, I was surprised to see that she mentioned the "merchants of light" from Francis Bacon's *New Atlantis*. It appears that the Merchants of Light and the Rosicrucian Brothers of the early seventeenth century were men who held a vision for a global enlightenment. They were also referred to as the Invisible College. Many of the scientists of this group were later part of the newly formed Royal Society of scientists in England.[5] So I had heard of the name before but had completely forgotten it. But István did not know this, and I didn't rediscover it until after his death.

When István spoke to me that day just following his vision, he said that the Merchants of Light are universal. They are born into a world that is ready for a major transformation. It is interesting that they are truly an "invisible college" *and* a visible, material college working together. The 18th Hexagram is a symbol of their work: they create light out of the decay and, in this way, they are also creating the *pure clay* for our children. And all of us who do this work are creating *pure clay* out of the transformation of our own lives. In this way, we too are becoming Merchants of Light.

I also explained earlier that at a later time I would realize that I had experienced the Merchants of Light in a vision the day after Pisti's Memorial. I saw a great circle of beings emerge out of the universe and spiral down toward our planet. They were chanting as they spiraled down and intuitively I heard them say: "Our brothers and sisters on the earth are dreaming a terrible dream." I knew that this terrible dream is the story we have been telling ourselves for centuries: there is nothing but matter and we are a fluke of nature with no meaning or purpose. I could see that these great beings were being born all around the world to help us awaken to this story for what it is: *a terrible dream.*

It was years later when I read in an article by the author Patricia Cota-Robles that her son had had a similar vision. When he was a little boy, he told his Mother, "Mom this is a very special time and there are thousands of Light Beings being born on Earth who are going to help all of us." She asked him how he knew this, and he answered, "Because I saw them. They are descending from the Higher Realms and when they reach the Earth they are being born as babies all over the world."[6] I have since heard of others who have had this same vision.

It was clear that in such "a terrible dream" we all suffer. We divide up as victims and as perpetrators, but we are all suffering inside this nightmare of not knowing who we are or why we're here. We are a world that is destroying itself because it does not know how to bring forth what is within it. In fact, we suffer from the belief that there is nothing to bring forth. We need our true stories — the stories of our evolutionary destiny — *the heart wisdom of a higher consciousness.*

I thought so often about the haunting Voice in the desert. She felt like the Great Mother screaming out in rage and grief for her children, for the World Child. She was the Voice of our Wasteland. *Deep inside this grief, there was no belief in healing. She was the Queen of Heaven in her abandonment and exile.*

But the Queen of Heaven also existed outside of time and space in the fullness of her being. About a year earlier I had had a vision of her in the wholeness of her light and joy and love. Two friends and I planned a ritual for the healing of all children. As we meditated and entered into the inner world of consciousness:

> *a very large circular object appeared out of the southern sky and moved through the closed sliding glass doors of the room where I was sitting. This disk of radiant conscious light hovered directly above my head. Its powerful energy gently pulled my body into an upright position. Suddenly, a spiral of light flowed very quickly out of the bottom center of the disk and simultaneously shaped itself into the form of a woman who spiraled into my body through the center of my head. The movement was so quick that I could catch only a glimpse of her from her head to her breast. She wore a fitted white satin dress and a white satin four-cornered hat. I was aware that the four corners of her hat and the circle of the disk formed a beautiful mandala, an ancient symbol of wholeness.*

This disk of consciousness was cosmic, multidimensional, and far too powerful for me to hold, but I knew that the beautiful feminine being, I will call her the Queen of Heaven, was like a transformer as she created herself into a frequency I could experience.

She sang through me but addressed all three of us:

> *You have called us*
> *And we are here*
> *To be with you all three.*
>
> *Can you feel us?*
> *You have called us*
> *And we are here.*
>
> *We are the Light.*
> *We are the Light*
> *Circling around your planet.*

Can you feel us?
Your planet has called us
And we are here.

As she spoke, a knowledge far beyond her words flowed through me. I knew that this energy field had been around our planet for a very long time and that every person who had ever longed for love and a myth of meaning had drawn this highly organized energy field around the earth. It would be a long time after István's vision of ML that I would realize that I had also experienced ML in this vision even before Pisti's death. This Light had appeared in one of the many forms of ML. I also knew that our human longing for this Light had now reached the critical mass necessary to pull this hovering energy field directly to the earth itself. The Voice had actually said, "**Your planet has called us / And we are here.**"

When I realized that **this energy was descending and connecting to the planet through us**, she sang again:

You have drawn to yourselves this day
All those on your planet
Who are creating worlds
Of Love and Peace.

Then the female form spiraled back up and into the disk of light, which moved out through the glass doors and toward the mountains to the North.... this vision was a jewel that reminded me again and again of the power of every single person's love, grief, and longing to create a better world....[7]

I had experienced this energy field as the archetype of the Queen of Heaven in her wholeness. This conscious and loving light was the highly organized wave of Imaginal cells as they penetrated our planet. This was certainly confirmation that the human call for a myth of meaning is being responded to in the most loving and conscious way. I still feel the vastness of her presence when I read the words, "**You have called us / And we are here.**" **I knew a major event had taken place on the earth—one that would be decisive for our future evolution.**

Many years later I read William Irwin Thompson's *Beyond Religion: The Cultural Evolution of the Sense of the Sacred from Shamanism to Religion to Post-religious Spirituality*. He discusses the Integral Yoga of Sri Aurobindo and the Mother. This is a yoga, says Thompson, that is post-religious. There are no techniques or gurus to follow. When consciousness is deeply rooted in the *heart*, the individual is opened to and united with a "Supramental" energy that guides each person on her or his own unique evolutionary path. This is the next stage in our human evolution, a stage beyond all religions, and it is now more accessible through "the Descent of the Supramental." Mystics at the Aurobindo Ashram say this "Supramental Manifestation began its process of emergence and envelopment of the Earth in 1956."[8]

I knew that what I had experienced was a **Supramental Manifestation**: it was a vast consciousness of love and light—and it was here for all of us. Once our way is opened to experience this Light, our paths are unique and individual. **That is why it is beyond religion, that is, beyond doctrine. We each become the unique co-creator we were born to be in a universe of infinite diversity.** I was interested in the mystics' knowledge of the Descent of this consciousness in 1956 although Thompson uses the phrase "began its process." I experienced it as happening Now. I know there is only Now in the universe, so we sometimes experience events in the present tense that have a different historical time. When the event is a cosmic process that will span a long period of historical time, the dates often differ to some degree.

For example, the great sage and Spiritual Master, Beinsa Douno (Peter Deunov), spoke of this process as beginning in 1914. **He thought of this event as giving the direction for the evolution of a new consciousness.** At this time, he says, our solar system "moved in to a purer and more spiritual region of space" in which a new consciousness will be manifested. The transformation, he says, will take time, but this new energy field will direct its course.[9]

Beinsa Douno was born in Bulgaria in 1864 and died in 1944. He was a contemporary Master who, like Christ, Buddha and others, gives us a glimpse into the possibilities of our evolutionary future. Thanks to the work of David Lorimer, who learned Bulgarian so that he could study the life and translate the teachings of this Master, English readers are able to know about this extraordinary person.

The Master said that he had "arrived in this decaying world at a very important moment." He knew he had come to "sow the seeds of a new culture of love." He understood that when he left this physical dimension, he would continue his work from the other side. Douno was a Master of Light, for he lived consistently in "Divine Consciousness" — "the white and diamond rays" of Christ Consciousness. Douno was a man of the twentieth century who not only had experienced Cosmic Consciousness for a few moments as did Bucke, but he lived consistently in this consciousness. He knew that this consciousness was the next step in our evolutionary future. **"If Christ is to be born again,"** he taught, **"it is in your souls that He must be born.... When He is born in your soul, that is the resurrection, that is the awakening of the human soul."**[10]

This great being had also come *to work on what has decayed* by sowing the seeds of *love*. His teaching was subtle but powerful; he likened it to the perfume of violets:

> *you must have breathed this marvelous perfume without seeing the violets. You might then have discovered the little flowers which were sending you their perfume hidden under some shrub. That is how we work, like violets. Our radiant thoughts, our noble feelings, as well as our useful and unselfish actions are like the perfume of the violets.*[11]

The stories of healing the sick and lovingly teaching people are like many of the stories told about Jesus. Lorimer met people who knew the Master and had actually experienced not only his ability to heal but also his ability to work with the laws of nature in what we would call a miraculous way. Much of his work was in the high mountains where he taught with song, music, and dance. His aim was to help people achieve "a harmony between the heart and mind" as well as a relationship between themselves and the intelligent beings of nature.[12] He taught three key principles: Love, Wisdom, and Truth. The whole of existence is based on Love; Wisdom "brings knowledge and light to the mind"; and Truth "frees the human soul from bondage."[13] In these ways this Master worked to transform the decaying world into Love, Light, and Cosmic/Christ Consciousness.

After one of István's visions, he said that Pisti had told him that it is now possible that the earth will be caught in a beam of light. István wasn't exactly sure what this meant, but he did know that the light was a new consciousness of love. This image of a beam of light reminded me of the time when Pisti, as a little boy, painted the same picture over and over: it was an image of the earth in the center of dark space with a small margin of light around its surface. From above was a large beam of light coming toward the earth. It was clear that it would penetrate the earth. Strangely, I didn't remember these paintings until I found them when I was going through some of Pisti's things after István's death. I don't know whether István had ever seen them. If he had, he evidently did not make the connection between them and his vision.

There was yet another piece of the puzzle to appear:

> *One evening I was meditating on all that had transpired when my consciousness moved into another dimension of reality. The room seemed to be filled with a deep blue light, and I became aware of a river that was flowing gently in front of me. Then I felt a sacred energy enter from the East. I knew it was the Queen of Heaven. She was a beautiful Native American dressed in white deerskin. As she walked along the shore of the river on the other side from where I stood, I saw her tilt her head back and I heard the vowels of my first name slowly sung out, and I realized that this is what had given me birth. The deep resonance of the vowels seemed to reverberate in me. Then I saw a canoe moving along the shore by her. It stopped, and she gracefully stepped into it as it turned toward me to cross the sacred water. She continued to stand as the canoe magically and smoothly moved to my side of the river. When she reached the shore, she stepped out and merged into me. As she did, I saw her wounded, exiled*

> *self – the Great Desert Mother of rage and grief – waiting for her in the alembic of my heart. They embraced.*

This is *The Great Mystery*.

The Jewish Kabbalists knew that when "a part of God had been exiled from God," *there could be no healing* until the exiled part of God is able to return as the Beloved of God.[14]

We have seen how the Divine Feminine in Judaism, the Queen of Heaven who symbolized the wisdom tradition of the heart, was exiled and abandoned by Josiah and the Deuteronomists in 621 BCE. Her wisdom literature was removed from the sacred writings, her sacred groves were cut down, and all objects associated with her, including her altars, were destroyed. The shamanic, visionary, mystical path was no longer a part of official Judaism. We have also seen how her tradition was reborn in the early movement of Christianity and then lost again with the establishment of the Church of Rome. We also know that this wisdom tradition went underground and was maintained in the various forms of Alchemy, Gnosticism, Mystic Christianity, the Hermetic arts and the Kabbalah, which emerged multiple times in European consciousness but was repeatedly repressed.

The heart and soul of Yahweh were lost when he abandoned Wisdom, and he became a jealous, violent, arrogant, and vengeful God. But now we must bring the symbolism home. God, the divine intelligence of the universe, did *not* abandon his Queen. *We did.* **The great rational Knights of the Western world abandoned her again and again, and there can be no healing until we know this and finally allow her to tell us her story – the planetary consequences of her abandonment.**

Then *The Great Mystery* in the alembic of our hearts can occur.

The heart wisdom of a higher consciousness will then flow through us, and cell by cell we will become a whole new being. The spirit of God will truly be the spirit of Wisdom when the Queen of Heaven is able to return as the beloved of God.[15] We do not know how long our transformation will take, but we must remember that the path is also the goal. Whatever is healed in us affects the collective consciousness of the planet, and it will be imprinted on the human psyche. This will be our gift to future generations—just as our ancestors have bequeathed their gifts of experience to us.

In Part IV we will spiral down into the depths of the human psyche to explore the symbolic artifacts, rituals, and poetic-mythic documents that mirror back to us some of these gifts from our ancestors—gifts "from which our present consciousness has evolved."[16]

PART IV

RETRIEVING SOUL

Chapter Twenty-Three

"The psyche is not of today; its ancestry goes back many millions of years. Individual consciousness is only the flower and the fruit of a season, sprung from the perennial rhizome beneath the earth; and it [individual consciousness] would find itself in better accord with the truth if it took the existence of the rhizome into its calculations. For the root matter is the mother of all things."[1]
—C. G. Jung

"To live fully, we have to reach down and bring back to life the deepest levels of the psyche from which our present consciousness has evolved."[2]
—C. G. Jung

The Symbolic/Visionary Mind

My initiation into the depth of the human psyche began with that first numinous dream of the feminine and masculine dimensions of the divine creatively working together. This dream had occurred during the early 1960s while I was still in college. The feminine dimension of the divine—soul—had beckoned me to follow her into a deeper order of reality. While it was clearly to her that I owed my homage, there was a unity of intention working within the feminine and masculine images. The symbolism of the feminine as soul or divine or as an equal partner with the masculine divine did not exist in my culture or in my own consciousness. At the time, I wondered if this more inclusive image had been able to make its way into my consciousness because it was no longer blocked by the Christian, less inclusive, belief system.

But I also wondered what could possibly be the source of such imagery. As I have related in previous chapters, it was *the question* itself that called forth Baba Yaga—that organizing, guiding principle—within my own psyche. She threw out her magical ball of thread, and this has guided me for a lifetime through the inner labyrinth of my psyche as well as the outer labyrinth of history. Over and over again I was astounded to discover the historical material within my own psyche long before I discovered it in history.

Gradually, I could see that *the guidance from this source was never random:* whether in the form of Baba Yaga, the Queen of Heaven, or a multitude of other forms, *the guidance revealed a structure—an intention.* Jung's use of the acorn as a symbol for the psyche seemed appropriate to me. The acorn contains the blueprint for the full development of the oak tree just as the psyche contains the blueprint for the full development of the individual. In the case of the human being, of course, the individual co-creates with nature to achieve her or his own unique development of this blueprint. *Our questions, longings, and choices activate the blueprint and it guides us on our way.* It has taken me a lifetime to know this from my own inner and outer work, but I have to admit that I would not have had the confidence in my own findings without the extensive evidence from Jung's experience and discoveries.

It was amazing to me that Jung had become aware of this truth relatively early in his career, and his confidence appeared unshakable. Yet he spent the rest of his life in exhaustive research that did, in fact, confirm his earlier conclusions. This confirmation was drawn from extensive comparative material, such as his own personal dreams, visions, and synchronistic experiences as well as those of thousands of his patients. It also included the dream and visionary artifacts of our culture's past, such as recorded dreams and visions, fairy tales, myths, the early symbolic structure of Christianity, and the culturally repressed underground symbolic traditions, such as Alchemy, Gnosticism, the Hermetic arts, and Kabbalah. This knowledge allowed him to recognize the same symbols or symbolic structures in the dreams of his patients as those that had appeared, for example, in alchemical texts completely unknown to the dreamer.

This massive evidence made it clear to Jung that the forgotten images of the archaic mind were not lost. In fact, nothing that has been a part of the psyche is ever lost. Jung called the source of all these images the rhizome or the collective unconscious, but today we can call it the mundus imaginalis—all within the quantum field. As we have discussed earlier, all life and consciousness are rooted in the quantum field since it is the field that contains all fields. This means that it is potentially present in each of us.

And, more specifically, Jung states that the sum of all the images of our species' past may be drawn upon by all individuals and all cultures, and they do, in fact, exist in the mythologies of all peoples and all ages. "The sum of these images constitutes the collective unconscious, a heritage which is potentially present in every individual." This is why, Jung explains, "mythological images are able to arise spontaneously over and over again, and to agree with one another not only in all the corners of the wide earth, but at all times." Since these symbols and symbolic structures are always present and exist everywhere, "it is an entirely natural proceeding to relate mythologems, which may be very far apart both temporally and ethnically," to each other as well as to the symbolic experience of an individual. "The creative substratum is everywhere this same human psyche and this same human brain, which, with relatively minor variations, functions everywhere in the same way."[3]

This would mean, of course, that if we want to understand our own individual psyche, we would need to have at least some understanding of its larger dimensions. As Jung expressed it, "To live fully, we have to reach down and bring back to life the deepest levels of the psyche from which our present consciousness has evolved."[4] When we do this, a much vaster picture of ourselves emerges, both as an individual and as a creative member of our species. We join our ancestors and, with them, we are able to consciously participate in the deep creativity of our planet.

Each time I discovered my own personal dream patterns in the historical material, not only was I able to understand a deeper intention within the images themselves, but I actually was able to feel a living connection with my ancestors. I knew that I was continuing their work—

with them—as well as the work of my culture, and ultimately the work of our species. But there was something else: I always felt a loving personal quality in the dream experiences. I was always amazed at how these images organized themselves in order to communicate to me exactly where I was in my own personal development and what it was that I especially needed to tend to for my own growth. It became clear to me that this deep organizing principle within the human psyche was uniquely personal as well as profoundly universal.

Jung is correct in saying that the ancestry of the psyche, the totality of the human mind, goes back many millions of years since this is, in fact, the vast span of time that we have been involved in the process of becoming human. And now, with the knowledge of the quantum field, it is easier for us to understand and to accept the fact that the human mind, the psyche, is rooted in what Jung calls "the perennial rhizome beneath the earth." But I had to wonder, if my individual psyche is a flower, a fruit, of this vast source, *why this particular flower, this particular fruit?* I understood that this flower, this fruit, was *the myth* I was living in this particular life, but it took many years for me to understand the depth of the myth and why it was emerging in me—and in my culture.

During those years my dreams revealed that it was *Wisdom*, the feminine dimension of the divine, the Queen of Heaven, who was the central figure in my myth. She was the very heart of nature, of life, and she was radiant with love and creativity. She was everything our culture had ignored, denied, and forgotten. She reflected what we had lost.

She was soul—and she was in search of her beloved Yahweh. It had been painful for me to realize how the Yahweh in me had so often turned away from her at a crucial moment or unconsciously blocked her way. It was even more painful for me to see how my culture had not only blocked her way but was, in the main, still unconscious of her and the potential creative force that she reflected in the individual as well as in the cultural psyche. She was soul, but what was soul in our culture? She was our connection to the quantum field, the subtle world, but what did that mean to most of us in this culture? She was the loving, organizing, integrating principle within us, but most of us were not aware that there *is* an organizing principle within the human psyche or even that there is what some call a *psyche* within us.

Western culture had long ago forgotten her *ordering intelligence*. And in such utter forgetting, we had constructed a world in which all life is random and each of us is a fluke of nature without meaning or purpose. Over the years we have had to observe the fragmentation of the Western cultural psyche that this forgetting has brought about. Like Yahweh after he had abandoned his partner in creation, the Queen of Heaven, we have become violent, jealous, brutal, vengeful, and unconscious. In such a world, many among us have become extremely ill and mentally pathological. The fragmented psyche, in its lonely distress, can rip apart its meaningless world—and this we see on a daily basis. We are witnessing what the Jesus in the Gospel of Thomas had warned us about so long ago: we have not brought forth what is within us and what we have not brought forth is destroying us.

Is there any wonder that this infinite source, this rhizome, this living, evolving blueprint for the growth and development of the human species, would send out powerful forces to counteract this pervasive fragmentation?

Thus, in time, I came to realize that the myth of my life was a result of these forces attempting to heal the individual and collective psyche. It was a healing, balancing myth that was emerging in the lives of thousands, perhaps millions, of people. And I gradually understood that *the myth of soul is all-inclusive: it flows through and embraces all myths—all life.* When we lose or forget this myth, all our stories suffer, and the joy of life dissipates. Our stories lose their meaning, their purpose, and their inner sense of connectedness. So when the myth of soul returns, it does not express itself in a singular way: it permeates, expands, and gives life and inspiration to all our myths—in all their unique particularity. And this is why we can say that it is the myth of soul that is at the root of the revolution in science. This is the science that McTaggart calls "a science of the miraculous."[5] The myth of soul is also at the root of the revolution in spiritual and mystical experiences. These two revolutions are transforming the lives of people around the world. They both reflect the power of soul to shatter the old limited stories of science and religion and to awaken us to the *heart* of the universe and the vastness of who we really are.

While it is true that the myth of soul—as the manifestation of spirit in time and space— *flows* through and embraces all myths, there is a traditional image that reflects soul itself as the *origin of all forms*—and in Western culture that image is predominantly the female body. She is the symbol of the myth that contains the seeds of all myths. For many thousands of years, the female body has been the icon for nature, wholeness, and eternality. There is, of course, a poetic logic to this symbol: the female conceives new life, gives birth, and feeds the child from her own body. The earth conceives the seed, allows the seed to grow in her great womb, and thus she feeds and nurtures all life. And just as the dead are buried in the earth—the great womb—symbolically, the dead are given back to the Great Mother from whose womb they are eternally reborn. Thus, in the poetic imagination, the female is the earth; she is nature—and she is divine. *In her function as nature, she contains the masculine and the feminine, for she is all forms, all life.* But she is also the young maiden, the individual mother, and the crone. In these forms, she and the masculine are equal partners: she is his lover, companion, and co-creator.

When individuals—or an entire culture such as our own—lose their experience of the reality of soul to embrace all that is, eventually, this very image—the feminine dimension of the divine—will reemerge into the consciousness of individuals in that culture. In Western culture, we recognize her as Our Lady, the Queen of Heaven, Wisdom, Shekhinah, and Mary. In these forms, she reflects the unity of all life, the love at the heart of the universe, joy, ecstasy, inspiration, relationship, nature, the cosmos, creativity—and the source of all forms.

When such an image recurs in dreams or visions throughout our lives, we know that She is the myth of our individual life. Gradually, I came to realize that She was the myth of my own life, but only in time would I know what She had in store for me.

Once we become aware of the particular myth we are living, we are confronted with another crucial question: **are we unique individuals**

who chose this myth or are we simply the conscious flower and fruit of the rhizome? The strange, the beautiful, the inexplicable answer is that *we are both*. On the soul level, we made our choices to live the myth we are living. Unfortunately, given the culture we are born into, it can be very difficult to become conscious of that choice and live in alignment with our myth. It has to be said, however, that many people do live their myth but would not think of it in these terms: they simply live the life of their deepest interests. Even so, we still need to know and experience how our individual life fits into a much larger and purposeful universe.

And this is what the myth of soul brings us, and this is why She is returning to our culture. For "Though she is one, she can do all things,... she makes everything new." And she contains within herself the "imagining or blueprint of a whole new being."[6]

Gradually, I realized that it was this myth of soul that entered my consciousness in that early dream of the woman in blue waiting for me on the arched bridge between two worlds. She is the Queen of Heaven, Our Lady/the Soul of the World/the Sovereign of the Land, the Voices at the Wells, and "the Virgin about to give birth." In my dream of the Middle Ages at Chartres Cathedral, I had seen her giving birth to herself all along the sides of the road as I followed my Knight—*who saw nothing*. Over the years she taught me that my Knight could accomplish nothing enduring until he learned how *to see* and to enter into a true relationship with her.

Our Lady had entered into my life to unite with her knight, both within me and within my culture. Certainly, I was not alone. **The myth of soul is becoming—once again—the core myth of our culture—the very mystery we had forgotten.** This mystery had emerged in Western culture several times, but it was never allowed to develop. *Without a true relationship with her—with soul—none of our myths can thrive.* But now the Voices at the Wells are returning. **The Sovereign of the Land is being born in us, and our very survival depends on the sacred vision of our knights and their ability to** *relate* **to her once again.**

We have seen how She is transforming the stories of science and religion. But now—with the greatest urgency—we need to return to the past to find the earliest expressions of soul in the history of our evolution—"to reach down and bring back to life the deepest levels of the psyche from which our present consciousness has evolved."[7]

Chapter Twenty-Four

Through symbolic language we translate the invisible world into sensuous form.

This tendency in nature to express itself symbolically had been developing for millions of years before it came to full bloom in our species in the sacred art of the temple caves.

The Development of the Symbolic/Visionary Mind

Shaman-Mystic Tradition of the Stone Age: The Cave Cultures in Western Europe (40,000–10,000 BCE)

As we spiral back in time, we will stop at the *first extensive expression* of the archaic human psyche that has, as yet, been discovered — the magnificent cave art of our ancestors who lived in what we call the Upper Paleolithic, Stone Age, or Ice Age, which is usually dated from approximately 40,000 to 10,000 BCE. This Stone Age art reflects a world that was so unimaginable to Western culture that its very existence was denied for decades. Once again it was the Western sense of superiority over all that had preceded it that blinded many of the archaeologists and anthropologists to the exquisite reality of the magnificent cave paintings of our ancient ancestors. The incredible intelligence, beauty, and innovative skill of the paintings were considered to be far *too modern* to have been painted 30,000 to 40,000 years ago. Artistic techniques believed discovered during the Renaissance were already well known by these artists. This realization found expression in a story about Picasso who was said to have visited the caves and remarked that artistically "we have invented nothing." To accept this world for what it was would take time.

It is difficult for us today to realize that the very concept of *prehistory* did not exist until the nineteenth century. At first there were the discoveries of small, portable pieces of art that were finally recognized to be from a time between 40,000 and 10,000 BCE. Then in the 1870s, a remarkable thing happened: Don Marcelino Sanz de Sautuola discovered paintings on the walls of a cave in Altamira, Spain, and was able to recognize the similarity in style between the paintings on the walls of the cave and the portable art from the Ice Age. But when his work was presented at the International Congress of Anthropology and Prehistoric Archaeology in Lisbon in 1880, it was rejected as fraudulent and a "vulgar joke." The paintings were thought to be too good to be that old, yet none of the prehistorians who held these objections would even visit the cave to see the paintings for themselves.[1]

In spite of the rejection by the establishment, there were those who persisted until the proof was so overwhelming that this strange and incredible reality could no longer be ignored or denied. So, finally, twenty years after the discovery of the cave in Altamira, Paleolithic cave art was officially recognized, and to date approximately 350 such caves have been found in Spain and France alone. Cave paintings and rock art have since been found throughout the world, some very old cave paintings in Australia, and the most extensive rock art in the Sahara and southern Africa. By the late Paleolithic period, around 10,000 BCE, our species was creating art all around the world.

Since the discovery—and finally the acceptance—of this magnificent art, it was generally assumed that this was the first symbolic expression of our species. While cave art is the earliest *known* art that is pervasive, highly organized, and masterfully rendered, it is not the first symbolic expression of our species or of other branches of the hominid family. In fact, *this tendency in nature to express itself symbolically had been developing for millions of years before it came to full bloom in our species in the sacred art of the temple caves.*

Richard Rudgley in *Secrets of the Stone Age* tells the story of a pebble found in South Africa that is dated two to three million years old, the time of Australopithecus. The pebble has indentations on it that make it look like a face. These indentations were not artificially made, but what is important about this pebble for our purposes is that it was valued enough to be carried about 20 miles from the natural source of such stone to the site of Australopithecus. Rudgley says that this is the earliest known artifact that gives us some indication about our use of symbols or the origins of art. The pebble could not have been used for any practical purpose, so this, he says, leads one "to the conclusion that its peculiar natural form was what attracted the individual who collected it." Rudgley thinks that such stones may well have inspired our ancestors to artificially modify or accentuate their naturally suggestive forms.[2]

There is something very touching about this gesture from such a remote ancestor. Two dots and a straight line on a roundish stone definitely require a symbolic imagination to see in it a face, something valued enough to keep. Such a story helps us to understand how important nature deems the symbolic function. It is a surprise to most of us that nature worked for millions of years to achieve it.

Rudgley also tells us that about one and one-half million years ago the hand-axe was the characteristic stone tool that was made for almost one million years. It has been found in Africa, Asia, the Middle East and what is now Europe. It is quite clear, says Rudgley, that those who made these hand-axes took great pride in their work, for the axes are artistic as well as practical. Sometimes a hand-axe was made by working around a fossil that was embedded in the stone, such as the one found at West Tofts, Norfolk, England. What is astounding about this particular stone tool is that the maker had worked around the embedded shell so that it was precisely in the center of the tool. Such work, says Rudgley, "can only have grown out of aesthetic awareness—the desire for precision, symmetry, and beauty."[3]

Other archaeological evidence of very early symbolism—between 110,000 and 90,000 years ago—has been found at several sites in southern Africa. These are also beautifully made stone tools, but they were far too fragile to be useful. Graham Hancock in *Supernatural: Meeting with the Ancient Teachers of Mankind* says that these tools "seem to have been hoarded and exchanged rather than used. The obvious implication is that these objects must have had important symbolic value to their owners."[4] It is important to remember that the human species had achieved its modern anatomical structure approximately 200,000 years ago.

Rudgley also mentions a volcanic pebble that has *a natural form* similar to the female body, but it also has *artificially made grooves*, especially around the neck, to accentuate its natural shape. It was found in Israel and has been dated between 800,000 and 233,000 years ago.[5] We have no way of knowing what this female figure meant to this artist, but we do know that the image of the female body will later abound throughout the Middle East and across Europe, from Spain to Lake Baikal in Siberia. These figures have similarities and differences, but one thing is certain—they are all expressions of the symbolic function.

Then there is the symbolic use of ocher, the red and yellow pigment used by the cave painters, but also used in Africa, Europe, and India over 250,000 years ago, perhaps for practical uses at first and then for symbolic purposes, such as painting the body to identify oneself as a member of a particular hunting group or for some other form of self-expression or communication. Of course, it could be that the practical uses were discovered later as a result of its symbolic use. Rudgley points out that we can't be sure about its very early practical uses, but in more recent times it has been used with fat as an insect repellent and as a sunscreen. It also disguises odor so animals are not alerted to the hunter's presence and it can be used to preserve animal hides. Rudgley suggests that using ocher to paint the human body may have been "one of the earliest forms of symbolism practiced by our remote ancestors."[6] Ocher was also extensively used in graves, on the bodies, and scattered around the graves.

It appears that our ancestors in southern Africa were *mining* ocher thousands of years ago. A 100,000-year-old ocher toolkit and workshop have been discovered at Blombos Cave in South Africa.[7] Around 45,000 to 35,000 years ago ocher was still being mined, as well as the sparkling, shimmering specularite, both of which were used symbolically. There are reports that at these mines—and some were very large indeed—the "excavations had been painstakingly refilled when the site was abandoned." Some of the mines were in what is now Swaziland and the modern Swazi still work the mines. We are told that they do their work mostly in secret and then they too refill the mines when they are finished. This is required, they explain, by the Earth spirits.[8]

We know that the Neanderthals not only used ocher in their burial practices, but they used other items as well. In Shanidar, Iraq, a 60,000-year-old grave was covered with seven different kinds of flowers, six of which have healing properties that are still known and used in the folk medicine of Iraq today.[9] There is also evidence that the Neanderthals looked after their own who were disabled, and that they were capable of surgical operations, such as amputations. Rudgley suggests that they may have used the herbal flower medicines with their surgical knowledge. They also buried flint tools with their dead.[10] Every single one of these practices is evidence of the existence of symbolic thinking—the ability to imagine solutions, possibilities, and realities within and beyond their physical, everyday world.

In 2013 a 100,000-year-old ocher pebble with over twenty engraved lines was found in Klasies River Cave in South Africa. The meaning is unclear, but the pattern appears to have had some kind of symbolic significance. Another piece of ocher with geometrical patterns dated around 77,000 BCE was found earlier at Blombos Cave in South Africa. The patterns on both pieces appear to be similar but the 100,000-year-old piece is too badly worn for a real comparison to be made. Interestingly, thousands of pieces of ocher had been hauled into Blombos and used for various purposes. Also found in the Blombos Cave is an example of personal adornment: a set of small shell beads with pierced holes.[11]

And now just a few examples from the behavior of present-day chimpanzees. In *The Mentality of Apes* Wolfgang Köhler describes how the chimpanzees he worked with would become attached to objects that were of no practical use to them whatsoever. One adult female became attached to a round stone that was beautifully polished by the ocean. There was no way anyone could get the stone away from her and in the evening she carried it with her to the place where she slept.[12] What, we may wonder, was it about the object that attracted her? We have to admit that it is the sort of object that any of us might also pick up, admire, and take home with us.

Köhler also describes the sense of play that could easily erupt between two of the chimpanzees, a kind of spinning round and round "like dervishes." This activity was like a dance that seemed to be friendly and joyful. Sometimes a whole group of chimpanzees would begin to join together in patterns of motion that would result in "a rough approximate rhythm" in which they would tend to keep time with each other. Some of the characteristics of the group's "motion-patterns," such as a circular movement around a post as the center and a trance-like pleasure, are suggestive of what later occurs in the rituals of early human societies. Joseph Campbell reminds us that in later mythologies the central pole becomes "the world-uniting and supporting Cosmic Tree, World Mountain, *axis mundi*, or sacred sanctuary, to which both the social order and the meditations of the individual are to be directed."[13]

And, of course, there is the more recent research of Jane Goodall. I especially like the marvelous picture she gives us of an older chimpanzee tickling the bottom of a younger chimp with a flower. But she also tells us that the chimpanzees hug, kiss, and pat each other on the back. Such gestures would probably not be initiated without an imagination of the kind of response one might receive. All of these examples of chimpanzee behavior clearly reflect "that wonderful sense of play, without which no mythological or ritual game of 'make believe' whatsoever could ever have come into being."[14]

Even more surprising, perhaps, is what prehistorians John Clottes and David Lewis-Williams tell us in *The Shamans of Prehistory: Trance and Magic in the Painted Caves*. The ability to see images in the mind is "probably a feature not just of the human but of the mammalian nervous system."[15] This would mean that chimpanzees, baboons, monkeys, rats, cats, dogs, and dolphins are apparently capable of seeing mental images. And, strangely, the research of Matthew Wilson and Kenway Louie at MIT suggests that, in fact, rats do dream.[16]

We have looked briefly at some of the major, officially acknowledged examples of symbolic activity from the last two to three million years, and **we have considered the possibility that it was within the entire mammalian nervous system itself that nature was working to achieve imaginative, symbolic consciousness.** It is deeply humbling to realize that not only did our remote ancestors participate in the evolution of symbolic consciousness but our entire mammalian family as well — **and it appears that we are the flower and the fruit of this immense adventure.**

In our ancestors we are able to discern the slow development of *the imagination*, that wonderful ability to *see* images and *feel* sensations that are not directly perceived by the physical senses. To be *attracted* to an object such as a round stone is to imagine something in it other than what meets the physical eye. To *imagine* beauty or meaning, to play, to feel joy, to laugh, to be inspired — none of this could happen without some development of the imagination. And we know now that our ancestors did perceive something *other* in the round, highly-polished stone, the living blood-color of ocher, the sparkling quality of specularite, the rhythm of the dance, and the make-believe of play.

We modern humans stand on the shoulders of all those who helped to build this great bridge between the visible and the invisible worlds. I am overwhelmed when I think of the hundreds of thousands of years of creativity — the endless efforts to shape the ocher, the stone, the bone, the clay, the wood into forms that allowed them to *see* and *experience* more meaningful realities than the ones in which they found themselves. It would be difficult to deny that all of this is evidence of a *tendency* — or perhaps now we can say an *intelligent force* in nature — **to develop a consciousness capable of perceiving realities beyond the visible world.**

Yet even these last few million years do not tell the whole story. During this time, we have seen evidence of the budding imagination in our ancestors. However, these early sparks of the imaginative mind are themselves deeply rooted in additional millions of years of behavior regulated by *intelligent organizing principles* that we so easily call *instincts*. I had said earlier that some quantum physicists and all mystics agree that consciousness creates matter. *Instincts or laws of nature are simply names for that creative consciousness that intelligently organizes and regulates the structure and development of life.* There could be no life without them. When the shaman-mystic experiences the *source* of these laws, he or she experiences consciousness, light, and love. This is what they call spirit and the scientists call the quantum field.

From this perspective, we are better able to understand what physicist Fred Alan Wolf meant when he said "matter is how spirit appears in the physical universe."[17] So the *whole story*, so to speak, is that consciousness is rooted in this invisible source of all intelligence. **And one of its great achievements is the evolution—in matter—of a creative, symbolic imagination that is capable of conscious communication with itself, that is, with spirit. This is what Corbin means when he speaks about our** *faculty of perception, the organ of soul.*

Why is this knowledge of symbolic consciousness so important to us? Why is it important for us to know that nature has been working for millions of years to achieve this particular mode of consciousness? To answer this question, we need to focus a little longer on what the symbol allows consciousness to do. Perhaps the most important is that the symbol, the image, allows us to see and experience realities that are not physically present. Since our faculty of perception is rooted in the source of consciousness, what we perceive to be beautiful or meaningful reflects that source. We can discover this anywhere, in nature or natural objects or in objects that we ourselves create.

So the symbol frees us from the limits of the literal world of everyday life and allows us to experience or create meaning and beauty within that world. It allows us to use the materials of the physical world to create forms that reflect our *response* to being in and of that world. The artist might begin, as Rudgley suggests, by simply enhancing a meaningful natural form seen in a rock. Or we, ourselves, might be the work of art by painting ourselves with ocher or rubbing specularite in our hair to enhance our appearance. All cosmetics and clothing designs are reflections of a symbolic consciousness that allows us to play with that very real urge in nature to enhance itself or to go beyond itself. We are able to create an image of ourselves that is more than we perceive in our natural selves.

But, of course, it is more than that: the artist in us can create a world that reflects and recreates the depth of our feeling, the power of our thought, and the complexities of our understanding. In their symbolic forms, we can re-live our experiences in ways that are more focused, intense, inclusive, and meaningful. We can play with matter to give shape to the wonder, the awe, the mystery, and the sacredness of the great adventure of life and death. We can use story, music, dance, ritual, sculpture, paint, architecture, and any natural form to express and *experience the miracle that nature has achieved in us*. In all of this we are playing with nature, enhancing nature, and going beyond nature. We are translating *the invisible world* into sensuous form. We are—at last—co-creators *with* nature—and now we can understand how this was nature's desire all along—to be conscious of itself and co-creative with the universe.

Symbolic language is not only our first language, but it is a sacred language; it is the key to our deepest selves—our bridge to the invisible world. It is this faculty or organ of soul that over the millennia has evolved so that we can perceive spirit. Once we are able to experience this world, we remember who we are. This is the core of the shamanic/mystic experience. We remember—we know— that we are the creative spirit that manifests itself in us as soul. We are the great rhizome *and* "the flower and the fruit of a season." To live life fully, we need to know this, for this is *our* story.

Chapter Twenty-Five

>—◆—O—◆—<

Our ancestors had two fundamental kinds of vision: the myth of the goddess, which is the image of wholeness and eternity, and the myth of the hunter, which is the myth of survival. Both of these myths are essential to human experience. When the myth of survival is contained within the myth of meaning, all life is experienced as sacred. But when the myth of survival gets split off from the myth of wholeness and eternality, we suffer the loss of soul and lose our sense of the sacred.[1]
— **Anne Baring and Jules Cashford**

The Flaring Forth of Our Story in the Cave Cultures

It is the discovery of *our story* that blazes forth around 40,000 BCE in the magnificent cave art of our ancestors. The faculty of perception, the organ of soul, was now fully developed and able to perceive our story. This crucial perception takes place at different times in different cultures all around the world. But the caves in France and Spain reflect the *first extensive expression* of this story that has yet been discovered. Since this story is multileveled, multifaceted, and always evolving, each person and each culture experiences different aspects of the story in their own way. We don't know with certainty how much of the story was understood by our hunter-gatherer ancestors at this particular time, but we do know that their faculty of perception, the organ of soul, was highly functional. **We can safely say that the heart of the activity in the caves was our ancestors' experience of the invisible world of spirit.**

The caves themselves are the key to the mysteries that were celebrated within them. It was here that the visible and the invisible, the physical and the spiritual worlds touched and experienced their Oneness and co-creativity. Here the Great Mystery of birth and death was acknowledged, enacted, and celebrated. These were the great spiritual wombs of nature that formed the delicate membrane between worlds—a membrane so thin that it could be penetrated through the sacred rituals of art, music, dance, touch, darkness, light and shadow—and, of course, the arduous labyrinthine journey into the realms of initiation.

And She, of course, was always present—whether in the form of the great cave wombs or in the form of the female body, such as the female figure that is carved in stone over a rock shelter in Laussel, which is now thought to have been a ceremonial center. In her right hand she holds a bison's horn that is shaped like the crescent moon. There are thirteen notches on the horn, which probably relate to the thirteen days of the waxing moon and the thirteen months of the lunar year. Her head is tilted toward the crescent moon while her left hand is placed on her growing womb. Her relationship with nature is clear: all life participates in the same great mystery.[2]

Baring and Cashford in *The Myth of the Goddess: Evolution of an Image* point out that the image of her body was always carved or etched in stone, bone, or ivory while the animals were painted and not sculpted. They suggest that this might reflect "two fundamental kinds of vision" that were experienced by our Stone Age ancestors:

> *One is expressed in stone, bone and mammoth-ivory, the enduring substances in which the sculptures of the mother goddess were carved, either chiseled out of the structure of the cave rock or modeled into small statues in burial sites. The other is expressed through painting, on the inside walls of the caves, where the animals come alive, where the ritual of the hunt is dramatized and reflected upon, and where human and animal shamans offer the rites of initiation.*[3]

Baring and Cashford call these two fundamental kinds of vision the myth of the goddess and the myth of the hunter. The myth of the goddess is "the eternal image of the whole." She reflects the abundance, the unity, the sacredness, and the transformative power that permeates all life. She includes all myths, for she is life itself. The myth of the hunter is the myth of survival. Both of these myths are essential to human experience. When the myth of survival is contained within the myth of meaning, all life is experienced as sacred. But when the myth of survival gets split off from "the eternal image of the whole," we suffer the loss of soul and lose our sense of the sacred.[4]

Everything we know about the culture of the caves reflects the intention to nurture soul, to be in communication with the spirit world, to co-create with it, and to experience the unity of both myths. Later, we will see that the San Bushmen also celebrated these two major myths of human existence. One was called the dance of the little hunger and the other the dance of the great hunger — the first was a dance for the food necessary for survival and the second was a dance for great meaning and the unity of all life.[5]

Since such sacred knowledge is experienced during altered states of consciousness, achieving such states would be the core of their spiritual tradition. The famous scene in the most secret part of the cave at Lascaux — the Holy of Holies — depicts the shaman's entry into just such a state of consciousness. The scene is a detailed depiction of a story that includes, among other details, a shaman with an erect penis, a dying bison, and a bird on a staff. There have been different interpretations of the scene, but from the perspective of another group of Stone Age people, the San Bushmen of Africa, it becomes quite clear. As the bison dies, the man/shaman enters a higher dimension of reality. The bird has been a symbol of such realities in almost all shamanic cultures, and for the San it is the dying animal who releases its potency to the shaman so he can enter an altered state or trance.[6]

There were probably many different kinds of initiations and rituals within the great cave wombs, but the major initiation would have to be the initiation of the hunter into an awareness of the relationship of his need to survive *and* the unity and sacredness of all life. Let's consider what the initiation of the hunter might have been like.

Imagine for a moment that you are a young man on your way to be initiated, for you will soon join the hunt for the first time. You will participate in killing an animal for food, clothing, and so many other things that your community needs. You know that all life is sacred and divine, that all animals have souls, and yet you and your community must eat and be clothed. You know that your elders nurture a profound relationship with the animals, who themselves have an intimate relationship with the spirit world. You also know that the shamans in your community can go into trance, merge into animal consciousness, and return with answers to many of the mysteries of life. And yet you must become a hunter of these animals—you must kill to survive. Knowing all this, you are afraid of the potential wrath of the animal soul whose body you will kill, but you are equally afraid of not becoming a hunter, a man who can provide for his community.

This is the conflict that the initiation must resolve. How can the young be prepared to become killers who will not fear the animals' wrath and who, at the same time, will maintain respect and honor for the life they are taking for their own needs? This conflict had to exist in the human soul from the time man became a hunter. We don't know exactly when it was resolved, but it was probably thousands of years before the culture of the caves because it is rooted in an even larger conflict: *the fundamental question of death itself.*

Let's return now to you as a young man on your way to be initiated into the life of a hunter. As you walk toward the great cave with the shaman, the elders, and a few other young men from your small tribe, your mind reflects back on the ones who have gone before you. Your brother had been different after his initiation. You especially remember the calm and knowing look in his eyes and how, as was expected, he had remained silent about that day. Your mind returns to the path. You know that even this part of the journey is important preparation for what is to come.

You arrive at the opening of the cave. You enter and leave the world of common day behind. You are in utter darkness. All orientation is lost and the "normal habits of mind" are obliterated.[7] You immediately realize that you have to be extremely careful not to slip on the wet and slimy ground beneath your feet. You soon come to a very narrow passage where you have to crawl on all fours for about ten yards. Then you pass through several great chambers, but always through another narrow passage. Finally, you arrive in a large gallery where you can hear the dripping of water from the ceiling. But soon this gallery also merges into another small tunnel. Now you have to lie on your stomach and slither like a snake along its floor. The tunnel is so low that your face is on the earth and you have great difficulty breathing. But you have to keep moving. The tunnel seems unending. It crosses your mind that you won't make it through. But you notice that you are still moving, still struggling to breathe.[8]

Finally, you come to the end and you push yourself out of the tunnel as from the birth canal. You are still in total darkness, but you can stand upright—and you can breathe. But you are standing and breathing in another world: the spirit womb of the Great Mother. An energy flows through you, an energy far larger than you, but it is also you. You breathe as you've never breathed before. The power of the energy increases, and you begin to remember. The memories at the heart of life flow through you and you flow with them through the great living web of all creation. You see yourself, your tribe, the animals—all life—as the sacred threads of this great web. You breathe and the web breathes. The whole universe is breathing—in and out—eternally. It is you and you are it. It is everything that ever was or ever will be. You laugh and you cry with joy and pure delight. How could you ever have forgotten this?

You begin to sense light on your closed eyelids. You open your eyes and before you is the Great Hunt. You see the wild horse, the mammoth, rhinoceros, bison, bear, reindeer, and so many more. As the light moves, you can see some of the great animals stampeding while others seem almost still. You are amazed by their strength, their movement, their beauty. Then, suddenly, you become aware of darts flying everywhere, all flying at the animals. You see the bears with blood gushing from their mouths. Suddenly, right in the midst of the animals, you see the transformed shaman: he is part bison, part man. He is playing the musical bow and dancing. You hear the music and you too begin to dance and, as you dance, the animals speak to you:

We give you our bodies.
We give you this gift.
We give our life for you to live.

We will return
If you remember the gift.
Honor the gift.
Honor the balance.
Honor the Great Web!

You cry. Never have you felt such *gratitude*.

As you continue to dance, you are the bison, the bear, the reindeer. You are the darts flying through the air, the gaping wound, the blood. You are the hunted—and the hunter. *Respect* for all of life flows through you. *But respect has a completely new meaning for you now. You respect yourself and everyone and everything to such a degree that the whole world is sacred.*

Suddenly, your body stops dancing and for some reason you look up. There, several feet above you, is the Master Shaman, the Master of the Animal World. He too is animal and man, and you are looking directly into his eyes—eyes that have been watching you all along.

You know—and he knows—that now you have "the Heart of the Hunter."

Chapter Twenty-Six

What is astounding for us to realize is that this spiritual tradition lasted for more than 25,000 years. And it is this sacred tradition that is at the heart of our own origins – our quantum leap into becoming fully modern human beings.

A Matter of Heart

The cave I have used for the description of the initiation is the Cave of the Three Brothers (Trois Freres), engraved and painted around 13,000 BCE. Such an initiation would have taken place in some form long before this particular sanctuary was in use. But this sanctuary—as well as a knowledge of shamanism—gives us a few clues to the initiation. The description of the difficult path the young man had to take to arrive in the great hall of the cave is taken from Herbert Kühn's description of his visit to the cave in the summer of 1926. One of the walls of this hall is completely covered with engravings of the mammoth, rhinoceros, wild ass, reindeer, wolverine, ox, musk, wild horse, and bear. There are darts flying toward the animals and some of the bears have blood spouting from their mouths. In the center is a creature that is half man, half animal, looking as though he is playing a musical bow. At the opposite end of the sanctuary above the teeming life of the hunt is what is called the Sorcerer, the Animal Master, who presides over the animals and the hunt. He himself is at once both human and animal, he is dancing, and his antlered head is turned to face, not the hunt, but the hall. The vision of the hunter-to-be is based on the basic principles of shamanic/mystical experience.[1]

Of course, we can't know with absolute confidence what happened in any of the caves, but from the perspective of shamanic practices around the world, as well as continuing mystical experience, we can imagine with some degree of authenticity. There were many cave sanctuaries that were probably used for various types of initiation and experience, such as puberty rituals and vision quests. As mentioned earlier, around 350 caves have been discovered, some only recently. The dates now stretch back a little more than 40,000 years. What is astounding for us to realize is that this spiritual tradition lasted for more than 25,000 years. And it is *this* sacred tradition that is at the heart of our own origins – our quantum leap into becoming fully modern human beings.

However, it has only been since the 1980s that anthropologists and archaeologists have even seriously considered the possibility of cave art reflecting shamanic practices. Various theories about the paintings and the use of the caves were put forth earlier. None of them is broadly accepted today – and certainly none of them would have been accepted wholeheartedly by shamans or mystics. In any case, their voices would not have been considered relevant. Once the old theories no longer inspired confidence, a general consensus developed among the specialists who have access to the caves that *any* attempt at *interpretation* is simply a waste of time and effort. The work of these specialists now consists mainly of preserving the caves and collecting and filing data. There has been a "moratorium on explanation" since 1986 when the scholarship on cave art entered what a major anthropologist has called "an interpretive void."[2]

This "moratorium on explanation" was broken in 1988 by David Lewis-Williams, the highly respected anthropologist, cognitive archaeologist and specialist on the San rock art in southern Africa and the Upper Paleolithic cave art in western Europe. In fact, it was Lewis-Williams who spoke of the "interpretive void" and the "moratorium on explanation" in his criticism of scholars who seem to believe that we need more data before any theory about the meaning or function of the art can be attempted. "What is now needed," he says, "is not yet more data (though more data are always welcome), but rather a radical re-thinking of what we already know."[3]

Lewis-Williams' method of approaching cave art does in fact reflect a "radical re-thinking" of what was already known. He does not attempt to answer all the questions that arise in the study of cave art since, as he explains, "we do not have to explain everything in order to explain something."[4] His extensive knowledge of the prehistoric rock art of the San people, the Bushmen, in southern Africa allowed him to see similarities between this art and the art in the caves of western Europe. But the real breakthrough into the *meaning* of San rock art, and ultimately European cave art, came—ironically—from the voices of shamans and San Elders. Lewis-Williams became aware of ethnographic records in the form of notebooks containing extensive interviews with San Elders. These interviews had been conducted in the nineteenth century by two scholars, Wilhelm Bleek and Lucy Lloyd. There was other ethnographic material from this same century: two French missionaries left descriptions of some of the San rituals; an English magistrate traveled in the Drakensberg mountains with a San Elder whom he was able to interview extensively; and explanations of many drawings of San rock paintings were given by San Elders and recorded by Bleek.[5]

In *Supernatural: Meetings with the Ancient Teachers of Mankind,* Hancock speaks of the San people as "a murdered culture" whose "declining remnant" during the nineteenth century was still struggling "to preserve their Stone Age culture." It was during that century that "the very last rock paintings at the end of a 27,000-year tradition were still being made."[6] It is estimated that there are ten to twenty million images of rock art spread throughout Africa, with the main concentrations in the Sahara in the north of Africa and in the Kalahari Desert in southern Africa. Some scholars have pointed out that the *earliest* art of the San, between 33,000 and 15,000 BCE, much of which has now vanished, would have been contemporary with the cave art in Europe.[7] And it has even been suggested that the painters of the caves in Europe and the San rock artists may have shared a common ancestor.

So here then were two Stone Age cultures—the culture of the painted caves in western Europe, which had lasted more than 25,000 years and ended around 10,000 BCE and the San culture of the Kalahari Desert whose "declining remnant" was still alive and able to explain the intention behind and within their art until the 1800s CE. Lewis-Williams' knowledge of the art of both cultures and the explanatory material from those who were thought to be the last of the San Elders provided the *key* to a "radical re-thinking" of the cave art in western Europe.*

The material from the San Elders makes it clear that San rock art was the work of what we today call shamans. In the translated words of the San Elders, the artists were those among them who were "filled with supernatural potency." The shamans activated this potency by causing it "to 'boil' up their spines until it explodes in their heads" so they could enter the spirit world; that is, so they could enter an *altered state of consciousness*. They achieved this by strenuous dancing for hours and hours with rhythmic stamping, clapping, singing, and the swishing sound of the dance rattles they had placed around their calves. This exhausting dance leads to dehydration, hyperventilation, the spurting of blood from their nostrils, cramps and bending, and the pricking and needling sensations of the skin. Once in trance, the shamans experience leaving their bodies through the tops of their heads,[8] traveling throughout the spirit world, merging with a power animal, receiving the power to heal, to control the weather, to know the movements of animals, and to experience realities that not only aid the survival and well-being of their community but give depth to their worldview. Lewis-Williams tells us that in any one San camp about half of the men and a third of the women were shamans.[9]

As mentioned above, this practice of entering altered states of consciousness to experience the invisible dimensions of reality has existed around the world for thousands of years and continues to exist in many indigenous cultures today. Several techniques were developed to achieve this state. The most common was probably the use of psychoactive plants, which may well have been the major technique used by the shamans in western Europe, although sensory deprivation was surely a part of the cave experience. The use of psychoactive plants during the Stone Age has been questioned by some scholars, but the recent discovery in 2010 of a

---

* Later in the book I will discuss information from the few still remaining San Elders in Namibia and Botswana.

woman buried around 18,700 BCE in the El Miron Cave in Cantabria, Spain, confirms the use of these plants. Embedded in the woman's teeth were spores from various species of mushrooms, including the Fly agaric mushroom, which is a psychoactive plant.[10]

In addition to the use of various psychoactive plants and total sensory deprivation to achieve an altered state of consciousness, our ancestors also made use of music and ritual, of repetitive sounds, such as drumming, chanting, and clapping; strenuous dancing; painful physical stimulation that overwhelms the senses; an isolated condition with intention and focus as in the vision quests of many Native American groups; and, of course, various breathing techniques. We have already discussed the fact that the mind can spontaneously shift into such a state unexpectedly.

We now know that our ancestors nurtured and cultivated this state of consciousness: it was the heart of their existence and the determining force in the structuring of their societies. It is this practice that we have labeled shamanic, a practice that began developing around the world by 40,000 BCE. **It was precisely this ability that launched our species into what we now call modern human consciousness—a fully developed symbolic consciousness capable of experiencing invisible dimensions of reality and of creating spiritual traditions, mythologies, religions, art, and culture.**[11]

We need to pause for a moment to remember that while there are many levels of altered states of consciousness, what we are talking about here are the altered states that are of the intensity to allow consciousness to enter deeper orders of reality (the quantum field), to experience unseen worlds, to communicate with *spirits* or beings from another dimension, and to receive knowledge, information, and wisdom necessary for our evolution. Anthropologists Michael Winkelman and John R. Baker in *Supernatural as Natural: A Biocultural Approach to Religion* tell us that *altered states of consciousness do, in fact, trigger a frequency of energy that flows through and integrates the various brain components.*[12]

The work at the Institute of HeartMath has demonstrated how focusing on the heart through *breathing and positive emotions* activates a flow of frequencies that integrates the various brain components with the heart and radically shifts our perspective. This allows information from the unconscious mind, the higher brain centers, and the *wisdom of the heart* to be available to us. Since the heart's electromagnetic field extends into space and interacts with other fields, it is now possible to speak of the heart's relationship with the quantum field.

If, in fact, our species achieved what we call fully modern behavior once they had developed the capacity for symbolic language and learned how to enter into such altered states of consciousness, there is still the question among many scholars concerning what they call "the great time gap." Since we were anatomically modern around 200,000 years ago, why did it take us until 40,000 years ago to achieve the capacity for symbolic language, altered states of consciousness, spiritual traditions, and art? Why was there such a delay and what happened that brought about the radical change in our behavior?

Certainly, from the archaeological material that we have briefly observed, it appears that this great leap into modern behavior is *a manifestation of the long evolutionary journey* to develop our imaginative abilities and our capacity for symbolic language. But the intensity of the symbolic manifestation around 40,000 BCE suggests that something more was happening. **And that *more* appears to be our ancestors' development of various techniques for entering altered states of consciousness.** Of course, there would be no need for such techniques until there was a fully developed symbolic, imaginative capability, and we do not know with certainty how much time existed between the achievement of full symbolic consciousness and the development of the shamanic techniques for altered states of experience.

It seems quite possible that our species could have completed the development of our imaginative abilities and capacity for symbolic language long before 40,000 BCE, but did not develop techniques to enter altered states until much later. There could have been those few individuals who did enter altered states, but they were too few to effect noticeable change in the short run. Certainly, Hancock is correct when he says that "some sort of 'critical mass' was reached" around this time.[13]

It now seems very clear that the "critical mass" not only included our capacity for symbolic language but also our ability to enter altered states of consciousness.

It's important to remember that today we all have imaginative abilities and the capacity for symbolic language, yet our culture has reduced its understanding of the imagination to *fantasy* or *illusion*. **We have lost and forgotten the very capabilities that activated our leap into modern consciousness.** This cultural amnesia makes it difficult for most people to understand what the Sufis mean when they speak of the *mundus imaginalis*. We all have the anatomical capacity to experience the *mundus imaginalis* through various modes of altered states of consciousness, but the majority of our species never activates this evolutionary capability—or even knows of its existence. This suggests that our ancestors could have had the capacity for modern behavior long before they learned how to activate it.

There is yet something else to consider in our attempt to explain the time gap. This concerns the prefrontal lobes, which are, as Joseph Chilton Pearce states in *The Biology of Transcendence: A Blueprint of the Human Spirit*, evolution's latest and most advanced brain component. Pearce explains that these lobes have an elaborate connecting network with all other parts of the brain. Even though they develop in utero, they continue to develop after all the other brain components have developed and achieved stability. There is significant growth in their neural network at age fifteen, eighteen, and twenty-one.[14]

> Logically we could expect that on the completion and maturation of nature's latest, largest, and highest brain at age twenty-one, we would possess capacities more dramatically different from and more powerful than anything previously experienced. But, in fact, nothing much happens at all.[15]

So now we have another question: Since we are anatomically complete by the age of twenty-one, why is there no behavioral change commensurate with the full development of the neural network of the prefrontal lobes? As Pearce says, "the development of these new prefrontal additions should ideally result in a mind that is so remarkably different from the one we operated with before that it would present to us in full the biological possibility of transcendence."[16]

Pearce believes that our prefrontal lobes *in their present size* only appeared in our ancestors around 40,000 BCE. Not everyone agrees, but if this is true, then perhaps we have an answer to our question about the time gap since the prefrontal lobes would be necessary for the explosion of symbolic activity that occurred at that time. However, if the prefrontal lobes were complete thousands of years earlier, then the time gap question remains. If this is the case, then our question is twofold: (1) why did it take our ancestors so long to know how to enter altered states of consciousness and experience other dimensions of reality, and (2) why does this potential lie dormant in most of us today?

It could be a matter of Heart.

The research at HeartMath and the documents from ancient spiritual traditions indicate that the awakening of the mind to higher orders of intelligence and emotion require the heart. The HeartMath research tells us that the heart is the fifth brain component: it gives more information to the brain than the brain gives to the heart; it starts beating before the development of the brain; its electromagnetic field is 40-60 times stronger than that of the brain and extends several feet away from the body; its magnetic field is 100 times stronger; its rhythm pulls into entrainment the brain and all of the other systems of the body; and positive emotions increase order and balance in the heart's rhythm. The scientific research of HeartMath has validated the beliefs about the heart that have been held by people for thousands of years. All our ancestors' sacred documents emphasize the central position of the heart, the depths of its emotions, and its connection to spirit—or, in our present language—the quantum field. So it may well have been the discovery of the heart connection that led our ancestors to develop techniques that would activate the wisdom of the heart. **Wherever this heart connection has been established and maintained, the myth of survival is always contained within the myth of meaning.**[17]

Once the heart is entrained, it not only releases a flow of frequencies throughout the brain as mentioned above, but it also triggers the prefrontal lobes to release a cascade of frequencies that flow from the prefrontal lobes to the heart. Before this can happen, however, the prefrontal lobes, as the latest and most highly developed brain component, will have to have incorporated the lower brain components into its service, to have transformed the nature of the lower components into the nature of the higher.[18] This would mean reversing the flow of mental energy backward to the reptilian *survival* brain so that it could flow forward into the prefrontal lobes and the heart. Any activation of the survival brain would be temporary and contained within the forward flow of energy through the heart: **in other words, the survival myth would be contained within the larger myth of meaning.** This, according to Pearce and others, requires nurturing and modeling from those around us. This kind of nurturing and modeling appears to have been the intention of our Stone Age ancestors. Such activity would result in a relatively peaceful, nonviolent environment, and, interestingly, there is no evidence of violence in the culture of the caves or among the San Bushmen.

This is no small accomplishment and I can imagine that it could have taken several thousand years for our ancestors to achieve this—even after the full development of the prefrontal lobes. Once even a few of our ancestors could achieve this, they would know how to nurture and model this achievement for others until a critical mass was reached, which appears to have occurred around 40,000 BCE. Then they developed a culture around this achievement and initiated others into the experience of this vast evolutionary accomplishment—which they were able to maintain for more than 25,000 years.

Unfortunately, this quantum leap forward would be lost repeatedly, rediscovered, destroyed, disbelieved and finally forgotten—especially in the West—until now.

Chapter Twenty-Seven

One of the tragedies of mainstream Western scholarship is its reduction of the mind's wholeness to an illusion or a neurochemical activity within the brain.

If we could think of matter and spirit as different frequencies of energy flowing in a continuum between our brains and the quantum sea, we would no longer feel the need to dismiss our most creative experiences.

We could then begin to understand the symbol/the archetype as the **form** *that energy takes as it flows from the quantum sea into matter. In the words of anthropologist Charles D. Laughlin, the archetype "exists as the intersection of spirit [quantum sea] and matter." It is "the local embodiment of the structure of the sea, and at the same time the structures mediating consciousness." This perspective does not invite or allow the reduction of spiritual experience to its neurophysiological foundations.*[1]

Archetype: The Meeting of the Quantum Sea and Human Consciousness

When a part of who we are has been lost for so long, our perception becomes displaced and distorted and we are often unable to evaluate new discoveries. We have already seen how the academic world—for two decades—resoundingly rejected even the suggestion that the art in the caves could possibly be from a culture as old as the Upper Paleolithic. Now we see that it took many more decades for an anthropologist to put forth the idea that this art is, in fact, the work of shamans. However, the understanding of shamanic activity is still severely distorted by the Western worldview.

Let's pause for a moment to recall my dream of the intelligent knight riding away from the great cathedral and the worldview it represented. As I stand before the cathedral dedicated to "Our Lady," I see a stone sarcophagus that has now become an integral part of the cathedral. I know that within this sarcophagus is the dead body of "Our Lady," and I realize that the *heart* of this spiritual tradition is dead. I understand why the knight has left it and is riding out into the world to find a larger truth. As I too leave the cathedral and walk along the same road, I observe a miracle taking place in nature: on both sides of the road there is a continuous line of large silver wombs in the earth, each one opening to the road as I pass by and each one giving birth to the most exquisitely beautiful silver woman. I know she is "Our Lady" — the soul of the world. In the dream, I know I am experiencing the miracle that can heal our civilization.

My Knight sees nothing. He doesn't even know I am with him on the journey. Unfortunately, so much of Western scholarship is the work of these brilliant knights who have long ago forgotten about the Voices of the Wells or the Maidens in the forest who could offer them food and drink from their golden bowls. For many of these knights, shamanism and all other experiences of the soul are viewed either as an illusion or simply as a neurobiological activity within the brain itself.

Now let's return to David Lewis-Williams and his discovery that Stone Age art, both in Africa and in western Europe, is the work of shamans. This means that the core of their experience is the entering into altered states of consciousness and *traveling* or *communicating* with the spirit world — another dimension of consciousness. The San shamans depict the process of going into trance and the experiences they have during the trance state in the rock art itself. Without the ethnographic material, it was impossible for a Westerner to understand the activities depicted in their art. In the case of the cave art of western Europe there was, of course, no ethnographic material. But there are similarities between this art and that of the San, and one of the important similarities is the existence of several types of geometric forms. Lewis-Williams was to discover that these images are indicative of entering an altered state of consciousness or shamanic trance state. As he continued his research he discovered that these images are, in fact, common to the art of many shamanic cultures.

Gradually, he developed a view of shamanic experience that rests on the foundation of a neuropsychological theory: the mind of all human beings is hard-wired in such a way that in its movement into an altered state of consciousness induced by shamanic techniques, there are three discernable stages of visions. In Stage One "people 'see' geometric forms, such as dots, zigzags, grids, sets of parallel lines, nested curves, and meandering lines." Some cultures give meaning to these images while others do not. In Stage Two people in trance, says Lewis-Williams, will attempt to make some sense out of the Stage One images by "seeing" them as objects that are meaningful to them. In Stage Three the person in trance travels through a vortex or tunnel that has a light at the end. The sides of the tunnel may have a lattice that has images of various types. At the end of the tunnel, one enters the full trance state.[2]

Lewis-Williams emphasizes that all "three stages are universal and wired into the human nervous system," though the meanings that are given to the images in each stage reflect the culture of the shaman or person in trance. However, according to Lewis-Williams, these three stages "provide a framework for an understanding of shamanic experiences."[3] It would be incorrect to adhere strictly to the sequence of the stages since they do not always appear in the same order. But, says Lewis-Williams, this does not affect the usefulness of the neuropsychological model. The fact that the geometric forms appear very often in shamanic art and even in laboratory studies of subjects who experienced induced altered states of consciousness is strong support for the model.[4]

Given the similarities of the Stage One geometric forms in the shamanic San rock art, in other shamanic art around the world, in laboratory subjects in trance, and in the western European cave art, Lewis-Williams became convinced that the European cave art was indeed made by shamans who had experienced altered states of consciousness. But there are *other important similarities between the San shamanic art and the art in the European caves*: (1) the rock is *not* seen as a blank canvas but as *a membrane* between the physical and spirit worlds. It is the shaman's work to help give birth to the spirit forms just behind or within the rock; (2) there are many paintings made over other paintings, which makes sense when the emphasis is on the dynamic movement between the dimensions; (3) horizons and grounding surfaces do not exist, which gives the appearance of the figures floating; (4) scale is ignored; (5) there are hybrid animals and strange monster-like creatures; (6) there are images of wounded men who often appear to have instruments of potency, such as needles, arrows, or darts sticking into their bodies; (7) there are images of a composite of animal and human forms; (8) the death of an animal and the shaman is used as a metaphor for entering the trance state, that is, of going into the spirit dimension. When the shaman leaves the physical world and enters the spirit world, he often takes on the power of the dying animal; (9) *touching* the paintings of animals and making handprints with the sacred paint on the walls of the rock membrane were ways of receiving potency and making contact with the spirit world. It seems, says Lewis-Williams, "that this was not done to make 'pictures' of hands. Rather, the potency-filled paint created some sort of bond between the person, the rock veil, and the spirit world that seethed behind it."[5]

Lewis-Williams' new way of perceiving and understanding cave art through his neuropsychological model was first published with his co-researcher Thomas Dowson in *Current Anthropology* in 1988; then with Jean Clottes, world-famous expert on European cave art, in *The Shamans of Prehistory: Trance and Magic in the Painted Caves* in 1996; and in his own larger work, *The Mind in the Cave: Consciousness and the Origins of Art* in 2002. This has become the predominant theory of cave art today in spite of its rejection by some anthropologists and archaeologists. Lewis-Williams is a highly respected scholar; Professor Emeritus of cognitive archaeology at the University of the Witwatersrand, Johannesburg in South Africa; Director for twenty-one years of the Rock Art Research Center, which today, because of his work, is one of the major rock art institutions in the world; and famous throughout the world for his research on the art and beliefs of the San Bushmen. He is a Western scholar in the truest sense of the word, and I am grateful that he has convincingly shown that the painting we see in the caves is the work of shamans.

But the *heart* of the shamanic world is absent. Lewis-Williams has repeatedly made it clear that while the brain is wired to experience "hallucinations" which may make people feel there are gods or spirit entities that will help them control their environment, these images are, in fact, more like a "'spillover' between neural circuits in the brain,...."[6] In the last chapter of *The Mind in the Cave* Lewis-Williams cites the work of Andrew Newberg and Eugene D'Aquili, scientists who have spent years studying the neurobiology of the brain. Yet Lewis-Williams' conclusions about the brain are in complete opposition to their scientific evidence. His references to them make it appear as though they support his position while, in fact, they do not. Their conclusions go far beyond the reductionism of a "'spillover' between neural circuits in the brain." It is extremely important that we know what this research actually does tell us about shamanic/mystical experiences.

In *Why God Won't Go Away: Brain Science and the Biology of Belief,* Newberg and D'Aquili present their findings about how the brain works. They used a high-tech imaging device called the SPECT camera, which gives accurate pictures of blood flow patterns in the brain during activities that range from mystical states to eating a piece of apple pie. *Everything* we experience is "tracked in the brain." They admit that they started out as typical scientists who believed that there was nothing but material reality and that the brain was simply "a biological machine, composed of matter and created by evolution to perceive and interact with the physical world." *But their research taught them otherwise.*[7]

It became very clear to them that the brain has the neurological mechanism for altered states of consciousness ranging from mild visionary experiences to a total mystic state of consciousness, which they call Absolute Unitary Being. They knew, of course, that one *could* reduce this entire range of experience "to a neurochemical commotion in the brain." But, they say, their understanding of the brain would not allow them to draw such a conclusion.[8]

They give two major reasons: (1) If we dismiss such experiences as only "neurological activities," we would have to distrust all our brain's perceptions of the physical world. When we eat a piece of pie, for example, the neurological activity can be tracked in the brain, but we would not, therefore, be willing to believe that the pie existed only in the brain. In other words, since everything has a neurological base, it is not *rational* to dismiss the reality of any activity for that reason. (2) The brain tells us what is real through *feeling*. Contrary to what we have been led to believe, "emotions are critical to human reasoning and rational thinking." We know through feeling that "true reality possesses an unmistakable quality." When the brain needs to communicate to us that something is real, we *feel* it to be real. Those who have experienced mystical states of consciousness say that these experiences feel more real than any other kind of experience. In fact, this is what the ancient philosophers and mystics called *gnosis*: a knowing for which no proof is asked because the *experience* is the knowing.[9]

In the visionary experience I described earlier, the moment I arrived at the foot of Huayna Picchu, I entered a state of consciousness far vaster than anything I had ever known before. I not only *knew* I was experiencing something that was "realer than real," I knew that it was the source of *all* reality. It felt as though I was remembering something I had always known but had forgotten, and I was filled with uncontrollable laughter that I could forget such a thing. The thought of questioning its reality or wanting some kind of proof made me laugh even more uncontrollably. No proof was needed.

Of course, there are many levels of intensity in visionary and mystical experience. The fully developed mystical experience, in the words of the late Walter T. Stace of Princeton University, is the experience of "an ultimate nonsensuous unity in all things, a oneness or a One to which neither the senses nor the reason can penetrate. In other words, it entirely transcends our sensory-intellectual consciousness."[10] As mentioned above, Newberg and D'Aquili call this state of mind "the ultimate unitary state," or "Absolute Unitary Being." After years of research, they conclude that "There is nothing that we have found in science or reason to refute the concept of a higher mystical reality.... The wisdom of the mystics, it seems, has predicted for centuries what neurology now shows to be true:

In Absolute Unitary Being, self blends into other; mind and matter are one and the same."[11]

Now we need to return to Lewis-Williams' view of shamanic, mystic experiences. Hancock relates that he was surprised to learn from Lewis-Williams that he himself had never experienced an altered state of consciousness and was certainly not interested in using any of the shamanic techniques in an attempt to do so. Hancock was surprised that "the leading exponent of the visionary theory of Upper Paleolithic art" had no interest in having a visionary experience himself. Lewis-Williams thought it was better for him to be "objective" in his study of patterns in cave art and in what the scientists studying the brain have to say about the visionary experiences, which he calls "hallucinations."[12]

His expertise on cave art and San rock art cannot be denied. Lewis-Williams certainly had the courage to put forth his knowledge that both are the work of shamans. He broke the "moratorium on interpretation," and he has continued to support and clarify his research. But we have just seen that he did *not* accurately represent Newberg and D'Aquili's research on shamanic, mystic states of consciousness. And, unfortunately, he is not qualified to evaluate experiences he has never had. What could the word *objective* possibly mean in this case? When he speaks about such experiences, he seems to have in mind some form of religious literalism rather than an altered state of consciousness. In a conversation with Hancock, Lewis-Williams expressed his view of such experience as "just a silly illusion," which our ancestors, unlike us, did not realize.[13]

He does make it clear, however, that we do not need to deny the value of the art that expresses such experiences. "If," he asks, "we dismiss such things as merely the functioning of the brain, are we in danger of losing something supremely valuable?" He thinks not, as long as we remain clear that "What is in our heads is in our heads, not located beyond us." Also important to remember, he adds, is that "the exaltation that those great creators excite in us does not justify mystical atavism."[14]

Professor David Lewis-Williams personifies *the tragedy* of mainstream Western scholarship. He is brilliant in his knowledge of the physical dimensions of his field but has no *experiential* knowledge of the phenomenon he is studying. The brain cannot communicate what is *real* until it experiences it. Without such experience, no *reasonable* judgment can be made. Yet scholars continually do make that judgment in spite of their lack of experience.

There is yet another aspect to this Western tragedy. For decades most of the dominant voices in anthropology dismissed spirituality in very much the same way as Lewis-Williams—as "just a silly illusion." Recently, however, there have been brilliant and courageous scholars who have challenged this view. In *Supernatural as Natural: A Biocultural Approach to Religion*, Michael Winkelman and John R. Baker, for example, have shown how human ritual is deeply rooted in the behavior of our animal ancestors, all the way from reptiles to mammals to primates, especially the ones closest to us—the chimpanzees. Their lengthy comparison of chimpanzee ritual behavior with human ritual behavior offers a broad view of the evolution of our capacity to imagine, to imitate, to play, and ultimately, through ritual, to produce altered states of consciousness.

Such states, they say, are not supernatural: they are "natural products of our mental hardware." And, they add, "Ritual techniques for altering consciousness are found in more than 90% of world cultures." These types of experiences have "a biological basis in the overall dynamics of our nervous system and consciousness." And they can be adaptive by enhancing our ability to access information that is generally unconscious and by increasing individual and group bonding, loyalty, and cooperation—all of which are necessary for surviving crises.[15]

> *These spiritual experiences manifest an "integrative" mode of consciousness in which the enhanced activities of the lower brain structures create a highly synchronized slow brain wave pattern. By making information that is normally stored in the unconscious mind accessible to consciousness, spiritual experiences can offer significant adaptive advantages to both the individual accessing that information and the group to which they belong.*[16]

Winkelman and Baker show how human rituals evolved beyond the basically "instinctual patterns of ritualized animal behavior" to the "full flowering" of worldwide shamanic/spiritual activity around 40,000 BCE. This takes us to the time of western European cave art. The emergence of shamanism in foraging societies around the world suggests, according to our authors, that there is a biological basis for its major characteristics. Winkelman's work with Baker and his own individual work on the biological, neurological, psychological, and cultural aspects of shamanic/spiritual consciousness shed a bright light on our evolution into fully modern human consciousness.

Unlike Lewis-Williams, Winkelman does not think of the experiences during altered states of consciousness as "just a silly illusion." The experiences themselves are real, adaptive, and integrative. However—and here is the tragedy—his work is brilliantly reductive in its own way: according to Winkelman, we do have Out-of-Body and Near-Death Experiences, but it is *all* in the brain. Let's look at some of his statements: "Like religion, NDEs can be seen as a personal engagement with a fantasy world that protects one from the emotional shock of reality—imminent death—a form of dissociation that provides for emotional tranquility." OBEs also provide "an antidote for anxiety regarding the physical trauma to self and body, an assurance of continuity in the face of potentially mortal crisis." Such experiences with an alternate reality are described as *fantasy proneness, absorption, hypnotic susceptibility and dissociation.* Winkelman sees these experiences as "the natural response of the organism to threats to its well-being."[17]

For decades, shamanic-mystic consciousness has been dismissed as silly nonsense. Now with work such as Winkelman's we have an exceptional presentation of how these states of consciousness function for adaptation, survival, the integration of the various brain components, as well as for our future development. Yet, while Winkelman does not see altered states of consciousness as "just a silly illusion," he does reduce such states to highly complex, *functional illusions.*

So this brings us once again to the core problem of modern Western academic thought. The dominant academic worldview has not yet absorbed the implications of quantum physics—and they have not yet taken seriously the implications of mystical experience—until recently and, as we have seen in the brilliant work of Lewis-Williams, Winkelman, and Baker, these experiences are perceived as existing only *in* the brain. While Winkelman and Baker acknowledge the evolutionary advantages of altered states of consciousness, its reductiveness leaves us with a brain that deceives us so that it can survive and thrive in a world that is still without meaning or purpose beyond the scientific materialism of the past.

Yet it is important that we recognize this work as a step forward in anthropology. As Winkelman himself points out, "the dominant voices in biology and anthropology" have described religion and spiritual experience "as quaint cultural traditions, misguided attempts to explain the world, and even 'parasites' that exploit human nature." Winkelman's work counters this dominant "scientific ethos by asking questions about what is adaptive about religion and spirituality."[18]

But our understanding of religion, spirituality, and the human ability to experience altered states of consciousness must go beyond the limited perspectives of Darwinian evolutionary theory. Scholars around the world are doing research in quantum physics and human experience that support the existence of realities *beyond the brain*. These scholars have moved far beyond the view that only the material dimension exists. For them, "matter is how spirit appears in the physical universe."[19] Perhaps what is now seen as *illusion* in our experience is actually our *delusion* about matter. If we could think of matter and spirit as different frequencies of energy flowing in a continuum between our brains and the quantum sea, we would no longer feel the need to explain our most creative experiences as illusions. We could then allow ourselves to be inspired by the numinous reality of what our ancestors called the gods, the spirits, the Baba Yagas, or the archetypes: the *great mediators between spirit and matter,* the quantum sea and individual consciousness. And we could then begin to understand what the Sufi mystics experienced as the *mundus imaginalis*.

This is precisely the view of anthropologist Charles D. Laughlin in his article, "Archetypes, Neurognosis and the Quantum Sea." The archetype, he says, runs "deep into the instincts and beyond, outward into the universal ground of existence." It "exists as the intersection of spirit [quantum sea] and matter." The experience of the archetype is "the local embodiment of the structure of the sea, and at the same time the structures mediating consciousness." **This perspective does not invite or allow the reduction of spiritual experience to its neurophysiological foundations.**[20]

Laughlin is also an anthropologist who, with Eugene D'Aquili, developed the theory of biogenetic structuralism, which brings together the structuralism of Claude Levi-Strauss and neuroscience. Laughlin has extensive knowledge of Jung's concept of the archetype and explains in this article that biogenetic structural theory uses the term neurognosis or neurognostic structures to mean archetypes conceived as structures within the nervous system. "Jung's genius," he says, "was in steering a course between the Scylla and Charybdis of mind-body dualism.... It was clear to Jung that an individual's experience is both structured by processes universal to the human psyche, and the manifestation of individuation."[21]

Jung never fell into the belief that our spiritual experience is either a "silly illusion" or a functional illusion. He understood very well that our spiritual experience is structured both by universal processes beyond the brain *and* the choices we make in our own individual journey. And he would agree with Laughlin that these structures or archetypes exist "as the intersection of spirit [quantum sea] and matter" and that they are "the local embodiment" of the quantum sea. It is the work of the individual to come to know these archetypes "by experiencing their myriad activities in the arena of our own consciousness and then reflecting upon them."[22]

Such archetypal experiences and reflections—my own and those of my ancestors—form the core of this book. In the course of a lifetime we encounter the archetypes in many ways—in relationships, in physical occurrences, dreams, waking visions, and intense altered states of consciousness. **Our culture has forgotten that we can gain a deep knowledge of the quantum sea through its "local embodiment" in the archetypes that manifest in our individual lives. No individual will experience *all* the archetypes, but the archetypes that do manifest in** our individual lives will reflect our particular myth—the flower and fruit that our soul has chosen to bring forth during this lifetime.

Through these powerful and numinous mediators between our consciousness and the consciousness of the quantum sea, we can come to know the laws or the organizing principles of this field of fields. We have seen how the scientists who discover this field with the rational mind will speak of these laws in rational, mathematical language. But even they approach a poetic language with such words as a vast, eternal sea of vibrating energy—"a quantum sea of light."[23] The shaman-mystic who experiences this ground of being speaks of this same light as a *dazzling light* of love, consciousness, and peace—the source of all that is.

The scientists and shaman-mystics who have intellectual knowledge or mystical experience of this field of fields are clearly a part of the revolution in science and spirituality that is transforming our worldview. They see our physical evolution *and* our spiritual evolution as "a single energy event": everything in the universe is a manifestation of the *same energy* as the Big Bang. This energy has "its own deep aim" and we are a part of that aim. Just as the mathematical cosmologist Swimme says, "This is the greatest discovery of the scientific enterprise: you take hydrogen gas, and you leave it alone, and it turns into rosebushes, giraffes, and humans.... The point is that if humans are spiritual, then hydrogen's spiritual."[24]

This is the view that I have taken in following the development of the human ability to imagine, to perceive the invisible world, to use symbolic language, and to experience altered states of consciousness. I view this evolution as the deep aim of nature, the quantum field—Spirit. It is nature's effort to be conscious of itself and co-creative with the universe. From this position, it is not possible to accept the Darwinian perspective that reduces our spiritual evolution to *a silly illusion or the biology of the brain.*

When we shift our perspective away from this old worldview that has "ripped the heart and soul out of the universe"[25] to this new/old story, we realize that we *are* the universe in the form of a human being, that our consciousness is rooted in the quantum sea/spirit, that the same laws or organizing principles that operate in nature also operate in human consciousness. And that is "how our deepest aspirations *are* related to the essential structure of the universe."[26]

So now we can understand the promise of our past from a much vaster perspective: not only does soul exist at the deepest levels of our psyche, but soul is a manifestation of the same energy as the Big Bang.

Chapter Twenty-Eight

>―·‹›·―O―·‹›·―<

The early people of Africa, says Laurens van der Post, regarded the loss of soul as the greatest misfortune a human being could experience.[1]

The San Culture in Africa (33,000 BCE through the 1800s CE)

Since the psyche is not of today but has an ancestry that goes back many millions of years, Stone Age consciousness continues to exist within all of us. While we cannot know the details of the lives of the Stone Age people who painted the caves, we can know much more about the lives of the Stone Age Bushmen. Once we become aware of the power and wisdom of the Bushmen, it becomes easier to imagine that the painters of the caves must have had similar power and wisdom, albeit reflected in different images and stories. As mentioned earlier, during the nineteenth century there were still elders among the Bushmen who were able to impart the meaning of their stories and their art. And, as I mentioned in the "Introduction" and will also address in a later chapter, the San Elders in Namibia and Botswana have more recently released their sacred teachings through Bradford and Hillary Keeney in *Way of the Bushman As Told by the Tribal Elders: Spiritual Teachings and Practices of the Kalahari Jul'hoansi.*

During the twentieth century, a deep appreciation for the San people found a sensitive expression in the works of Laurens van der Post, a man whose family came to South Africa three hundred years ago. He grew up surrounded by a mix of many of the African races whose lives and stories shaped his imagination. He was the thirteenth child of fifteen, and since his father was a statesman who, with his wife, had to travel often, his nurse, who was part Bushman, brought him up. He says her face was the first human face he remembered, and her stories were among the ones that had a profound effect on his life.

Van der Post describes the men's extraordinary skill as hunters and the women's ability to gather food in the desert; their profound knowledge of nature; their capacity of being aware of events before they took place; their ability to communicate at a distance; to see the infinite in the very small; their natural inclination to share everything and their lack of interest in possessions; their mobility; their peacefulness; their sense of the equality of everyone when it came to living fully and being all that one is; their respect for all forms of life; their deep, authentic, joy-of-life laughter; their ability to feel kinship with all life; their complete trust in nature and their sense of oneness with the universe; their ability to dance, to tell stories, to imitate anything and anyone, not judgmentally but just for the pure joy of its reality; and their ability to experience spirit and express their experiences artistically.[2]

They had a dance for everything. Van der Post tells us about two of their greatest dances: the dance of the little hunger and the dance of the great hunger. The first is the dance of the physical hunger that must be addressed throughout one's entire life, but the second dance expresses the hunger for spirit, which no food can satisfy. The dance of the great hunger for meaning contains the dance of the little hunger for survival.[3] As mentioned earlier, this appears to be the case in the cave culture as well: the myth of great meaning, symbolized in the cave-wombs and the female body, contains the myth of the hunter for survival. Unfortunately, for most people in our culture, our present-day myths of survival have no living myth of great meaning to contain them. We have lost the myth of soul that contains all myths.

Among the San Bushmen, however, the myth of great meaning—of soul—contained all their dances and all their artistic expressions of life. There were the dances for grief at death, and there were the dances for gratitude at the birth of a child, the return of the moon, the fire, the animal that allowed itself to be killed so they could live. There was nothing, says van der Post, for which they did not have a dance.[4] We already know of their paintings and engravings—the millions of images that appear on the great African canvases of nature. But they also had a profoundly rich mythology that complements and enhances the spiritual experiences that they had recorded in stone.

These people are our Stone Age ancestors, among the first modern human beings. What they embodied—in spite of all they suffered—is what we have lost and what we desperately need now for our own healing. But how can we find what we have lost? *How* do we reach down and bring this consciousness back to life within ourselves? I think the *how* is within us and we discover it as we follow our intention to *see, hear,* and *experience* soul. It is this *intention* that can change everything.

Strangely and beautifully, great changes often appear in small and what we consider insignificant things. One of the most important symbols of the San Bushmen is the praying mantis. For them it is the image of the divine—and the hunter, not so much of "big game but of great meaning." In *A Mantis Carol* van der Post tells a heartfelt story of how mantis enters Western culture through a recurring dream in the life of a woman in the States, Martha Jaeger, who was an analytical psychologist with considerable knowledge and influence in the matter of dreams. But this dream pattern baffled her as she had never seen a mantis and she simply could not understand the appearance in her dreams of an insect she had never encountered. For five years the dream recurred, after which it began to recur almost nightly.[5]

She consulted everyone who might shed some light on this puzzling situation, which was a challenge to her conviction that the psyche does not present random and meaningless images in its communications with the conscious mind. Finally, someone sent her a book on Africa by van der Post. She began a correspondence with him since he was the only person she could find who knew anything about the significance of the praying mantis among people living today. His knowledge and experience changed what had seemed meaningless into a source of transformation.

It restored her faith in her profession and changed "the whole course of her being."[6]

Interestingly, the woman's last name, Jaeger, is *hunter* in German. Certainly, says van der Post, this woman had spent her life in the hunt for great meaning. **The intention to live fully was alive in her, and it was this intention that allowed mantis to emerge from the unconscious mind of one of the most sophisticated persons in the Western world today,** "seeking apparently to inform it of an unknown and profoundly rejected self."[7] In dream after dream with mantis, this rejected self gently and subtly began to reveal its living presence within the psyche of the dreamer.

As I read this story, I kept thinking about Jung's statement that if we choose to "live fully, we have to reach down and bring back to life the deepest levels of the psyche from which our present consciousness has evolved."[8] The question of just *how* we "reach down" is confirmed in the story of this dreamer, for **it actually was her *intention* to live fully that activated this deepest level of her psyche to reveal itself through mantis. And why mantis? Because mantis was the messenger from the San Bushmen in whom this deepest level of the psyche is still active and creative.** Mantis activated the archetypal web of connectedness to and communion with all life in the dreamer. It was this web of soulful being and becoming within the continuity of life that gave birth in the dreamer to *the myth of great meaning*. Not only did the dreamer know she had been "restored to her natural self" but mantis had awakened in her "the voice of the infinite in the small."[9]

This woman's experience confirmed for van der Post that this "particular pattern of the imagination" that had been nourished for thousands of years by the San Bushmen was not only important to the Bushmen but was vitally important for modern consciousness everywhere.[10] Although it is dormant in most of us, it is the foundation, the creative ground of consciousness. It is the ground of *soul*—the ground that reflects itself in eternal images of wholeness and in the myth that contains all myths. It is this *pattern* that regulates the flow of energy from the depths of the brain *through the heart* and allows us to experience our own wholeness with the very source of life. And it is that mode of imagination that allows us to participate in life with the intensity and joy that van der Post observed in the San Bushmen.

The image of this joyful wholeness would rise and fall in Western consciousness throughout the many centuries of its existence. We have seen how it was symbolized in such images as the Queen of Heaven, the living Christ and Mary Magdalene, the Voices at the Wells, the Sovereign of the Land, and later we will see it emerge again in the images of Parsifal and his quest for the Holy Grail. Each time such images emerged in dreams, visions, and art, they initiated a powerful creative period of activity. But such activity was never allowed to flourish: it was always repressed by the dominant forces of our culture. I found it extremely interesting that this pattern of wholeness emerged in the mind of an American woman in the form of a praying mantis—and that this dream of the mantis continued until she was able to discover—and experience—the depths of its meaning.

Now I have to pause to tell a story that reflects how my own interest in the San Bushmen, their imagination, and the image of the divine in the form of the praying mantis entered my life in a living way. I had been impressed with the appearance of the mantis in the American woman's dream—and its living appearance on the door of the hostess of van der Post when he arrived in this country to talk about the Bushmen. To my knowledge, I had never seen a praying mantis, but as I was writing this section about mantis, a friend came to visit and brought a card for my dear friend Kim, who had not been well. Kim and I have worked together for years and, when her son left home to marry, we decided to live together and have our offices in our home. The card was a beautiful photograph of a praying mantis! Later Kim said to me, "Mantis has come to visit." She gave the card to me to place on my desk where I do my writing. We knew that it was not a matter of mantis *belonging* to either of us, but that its appearance, its presence, was what was of utmost importance.

Its presence was a confirmation for me that our energy frequencies were in harmony. I felt the spirit of my Bushmen ancestors had come to guide me and be present in my life and work. Three weeks passed. The appearance of mantis in the form of a picture touched me deeply and I remember thinking that it had taken this form because it would be too difficult to appear in actual physical form. Wrong! One morning Kim and I went outside on the patio to have breakfast. Suddenly, Kim said, "Look at that grasshopper on the chair next to you!" I turned to my left and there it was, gracefully perched on the chair by me. I immediately said, "That's not a grasshopper!" Kim laughed and said, "I guess you're going to tell me it's a praying mantis." And I said, "It is. It is." We watched it for a long time. Kim took photos and even made a short video of mantis.

I could not overlook the fact that even though I was the one writing about the San, mantis had come to both Kim and me. We were in the same energy field, and now we were both responsible for mantis' story. And my first lesson was to acknowledge my own limited imagination in not being able to believe that mantis could easily appear physically right outside my study door. I can now add that mantis stayed with us in the jasmine bush for a month, mated, and left her small womb-cocoon of eggs on one of the twigs of the jasmine bush—all while I was writing about the mantis stories of the San Bushmen. We haven't seen her since but her woven container of incredibly small eggs is a beautiful symbol of her future.

This type of occurrence is what Jung called a meaningful coincidence or synchronistic event. It is the simultaneous occurrence of two meaningful events that are not causally related but rather are symbolic of the meeting of the inner and outer dimensions of reality, of spirit and matter. They are associated with the archetypes and are an excellent example of the *local embodiment* of spirit in time and space. Van der Post called such events manifestations of a cosmic law that reflect the relationship of the outer world to the inner world.

Just in case it appears that I am making much about very little, there is a Bushman story that can help us here. It is a story about the loss of *soul* that was told to van der Post when he was a child, not by a Bushman, but by one of the indigenous servants in his household. The story is about a young man who had wonderful, numinous cattle. Each day he found the best grazing places for them and each evening he brought them home and put them into their protected stalls by his hut. During the night, he dreamed of the milk they would give the next morning. But one morning he was surprised to find that they gave no milk at all. When the same thing happened the very next morning, he decided to stay awake during the night to watch over his cattle. He was amazed to see a cord descending from the stars, and he saw beautiful, young women of the sky people descending the rope, one after the other, and playfully laughing and whispering among themselves as they milked his cattle. He angrily jumped out to catch them, but they scattered so quickly that he managed to catch only one. Yet he was no longer angry because she was the most beautiful of them all, and he was able to make her his bride.

They lived happily for many years, but then one day the man began thinking about the promise he had to make when they married: there was a basket that his wife had brought with her from the sky, and she had made the man promise that he would not look into it until she gave him permission. But that very day when his wife was out in the fields working, he became so curious that he snatched the lid off and looked inside. For a moment, he just stood there looking into the basket; then he burst out laughing.

When his wife returned home, she sensed immediately what had happened, and she put her hand on her heart and with tears in her eyes she said, "You've looked in the basket." The man laughed and said, "You silly woman. You silly, silly creature. Why have you made such a fuss about this basket? There's nothing in it at all."

"Nothing?" she asked hardly above a whisper.

"Yes, nothing," he stated.

The beautiful woman from the sky turned around, walked away, and vanished. She was never seen on the earth again.

Then van der Post's old servant told him that the woman did not vanish because the man looked into the basket, but she vanished because he had found the basket empty. Then she added: the basket "was full of beautiful things of the sky she had stored there for them both, and because he could not see them and just laughed, there was no use for her on earth any more and she vanished."[11]

Just as the Queen of Heaven in Western culture also vanished so long ago.

The man, like my Knight, was *blind* to the *presence* of soul. The story is timeless, for it reflects both the African people's profound sensitivity to the loss of soul and Western culture's arrogant dismissal of the basket's starry contents as "just a silly illusion" or *fantasy proneness*. How different it was, says van der Post, with the early people of Africa who regarded the loss of soul "as the greatest calamity that could come to human beings." **For them the preservation of soul was the greatest, the most essential task of life. They created elaborate rituals, stories, music, and dance that nurtured meaning and the creativity of the soul.**[12] And as we have seen with the painters of the temple caves in Europe, it appears that they too knew that the preservation of soul was their greatest and most urgent task.

The stories of the Bushmen as well as those of many other African races had been fashioned out of thousands of years of soul experience and they were told to inform, to awaken, and to preserve this ancient wisdom. Van der Post tells us that stories were the greatest containers of soul for the Bushman. They were the baskets "wherein his own lady of the starry sky stored the rare and dynamic intimations of his soul."[13]

There is little wonder that the Bushmen were reluctant to share their stories with Westerners. What we do know of their stories comes mainly from the Bushmen interviewed by Bleek and Lloyd during the nineteenth century when, in Hancock's words, their "declining remnant" was still struggling "to preserve their Stone Age culture."* To understand many of their stories we have to give the same kind of attention to detail that we give to a dream, but in addition we also need to know the animals, insects and birds, the world of the Kalahari Desert, and we need to have a deep love for and attunement with nature. And, most important, we need to know all we can about the Bushmen and their culture. Of course, as with all art forms in Western culture, there exists an abundance of theories of how to interpret their stories.

---

* Now there are the more recent teachings from Namibia and Botswana.

In *The Heart of the Hunter* van der Post tells several of these stories and discusses what he understands of their meaning, especially those about mantis. I have used his responses and impressions of the stories not only because of his sensitivity to the Bushmen but because he has a deep understanding of the "creative substratum" of the human psyche. He knows that the symbolic/mythic structures or archetypes of this substratum constitute a heritage that is potentially present in every person and that the Bushmen's "local embodiment" of these archetypes reflects a "particular pattern of the imagination" that we, in our estrangement from nature, have lost.

This "particular pattern" in the mantis stories reflects the soul on its journey through life to experience, learn, make mistakes, and grow. In story after story we see how mantis must struggle to find balance and become whole. He is always willing to play the fool in order to become more than he is. Through all of the adventures of mantis, says van der Post, we begin to realize that he is a symbol of *being* and *becoming*, of the mystery of life emerging out of death, of the wholeness of life, and of matter and spirit as mysterious manifestations of this wholeness.[14] Step by step, adventure by adventure, mantis is initiated into the ground of soul and this ancient "pattern of the imagination" that allows him to experience his own wholeness.

In Western terms mantis reflects the journey of the soul in that deep, natural and poetic mode of the imagination that Vico would have called the pre-reflective, symbolic, mythic mode of consciousness. It is important to remember that Vico would have stressed the *logic* of this mode of the imagination, for it is out of the *poetic logic* of this mode of dreaming and imagining that reflective, conceptual consciousness emerges. So it is here in the Stone Age that Vico would have found the symbolic artifacts, the rituals, the poetic-mythic documents that mirror back to us our spontaneous journey into consciousness.

The word *spontaneous* does not mean that the Bushmen came to these principles without effort or trial and error. They became aware of them through extensive experience and the nurturing of soul in all of their rituals and art forms. They were trackers, hunters of great meaning, which is another way of saying that they, like most indigenous people, sought to be in harmony with the laws or spontaneous principles of their own development. This is how they discovered in their own lives the patterns that trigger the flow of energy and integrate the various brain components—including the heart.

Vico was convinced that what he called ricorso, that *historical* journey into the depths of our mind's origins to understand these principles *conceptually,* is "the greatest spiritual effort" an individual or a culture can make. He believed that once we developed conceptual, rational consciousness, we would be able to "grasp anew, in idea, the principles of [our] own spontaneous life and power."[15] We have seen, however, just how difficult it has been "to grasp," in idea *or* imagination, the life and power of our early ancestors. Since our logical, conceptual minds have been *uprooted* from our symbolic, archetypal experience, we have lost our vision. We have denigrated and censored the dreaming, visionary mind, not only in ourselves, but in all people who nurture it. Vico envisioned a ricorso that would bring into conceptual consciousness the symbolic, archetypal heritage of our origins. But we have not yet accomplished this.

It is important to remember that for Vico the symbol was not to be thought of as undeveloped or as something we had outgrown, for he clearly understood that the symbolic mind exists as a fully developed mode of the mind in and of itself, as does the conceptual mind. Vico does not mention the heart as a part of the brain, nor does he mention the right or left brain, but he does focus on the functions that we have come to identify with the various components of the brain. What is especially important is that he recognized the *equal value of symbolic and conceptual language,* an equality that would permit no repression, no censorship, and no dominance of one mental function over the other. The symbol could not be reduced to the idea, nor could the idea be reduced to the symbol. Vico envisioned the life of the mind as an integral and dynamic continuum of movement between the past and the present, the symbol and the idea. He thought of this movement between the major energy fields of the human mind as a *relationship* that is "the most intimate and self-generative process of the human subject."[16]

We have not yet achieved a cultural understanding that both symbolic and conceptual language are equal, and we do not yet know quite how to achieve the dynamic continuum of movement between them that Vico envisioned. When Vico speaks of the mind's experience of its own wholeness, he is thinking in Western terms. It appears that there are different ways to experience wholeness: we know that ritual and other techniques practiced by our ancestors trigger "an 'integrative' mode of consciousness." Van der Post's deep admiration of the Bushmen was rooted in what he perceived as the most admirable sense of wholeness he had ever experienced.

We don't yet know what our lives would be like if we valued feeling, intuition, and symbolic, mythic language as we now value conceptual language — and if we could learn how to achieve that dynamic continuum of movement between them. *Will the collected artifacts of our ricorso open the door to our lost selves who are still alive in the depths of us? And will we allow the recent decades of brain research to inform us?* The research of the Institute of HeartMath alone shows us the kind of damage the split between our feeling and thinking does to our physical body and our entire emotional system. The Institute has developed techniques to achieve a heart-centered *coherence* among all the brain components, all the body's physical and emotional systems, and the electrical and magnetic fields of energy in which we live. They have shown that it is *the intelligence of the heart* that makes this integration possible. But we now also know that it is our *intention* to know, our *intention* to live fully that will determine our development.

As mentioned earlier, a major responsibility of our ricorso is to translate into conceptual language what the symbolic artifacts, rituals, and poetic-mythic documents, in this case from the San Bushmen, mirror back to us about this deep "creative substratum" of the human psyche. How can we understand conceptually that "particular pattern of the imagination"?

We will keep in mind that it is through dreams, visions, stories, relationships, rituals, dances, and painting that *soul experience* is possible. It was true for our ancestors and it is true for us. *Our conceptual language is* not an attempt to reduce the experience but rather to allow the principles present within the experience to be perceived conceptually. What follows are some of the major principles that are derived from the thousands of years of our ancestors' spiritual experience. Some we find expressed in the cave paintings of western Europe and others are derived from the Bushman's life and art. They are also found in all the shaman-mystic-scientist cultures:

Everything in the visible world is rooted in the invisible, spirit world, which is the source of all life; human beings must remain in communication with this invisible world in order to live life fully, co-create with nature, and become all that one is; to lose communication with this world is "the greatest calamity" that human beings can experience; therefore, nurturing this relationship, the preservation of soul, is "the greatest, most urgent of all [our] tasks"; communication with the spirit world can take many forms, such as altered states of consciousness, dreams, intuition, symbolic/archetypal events, synchronistic events, rituals and other art forms; since spirit flows through and is in all things, spirit and matter are one; both being and becoming are essential to life; death is not an end but rather birth, death, and rebirth are movements from one dimension to another; all life is a part of the whole, and the whole is in every part; this allows for a deep sense of equality and belonging; it also allows for an awareness that there is infinite power in the small; balance is necessary for growth and development; human feeling and intention, such as trust in the universe and respect for all life, are powerful energy forms that transform life; love is necessary for life, as is joy, laughter, and celebration; when we live our lives in harmony with these principles, which reflect the essential structure of the universe, we grow and thrive and experience the sacred in all things.

When we state these principles conceptually, we see that they are basically the principles of all ancient wisdom traditions. In fact, these principles, in Aldous Huxley's words, form "the perennial philosophy" of all those who eat the Fruit from the Cosmic Tree. This, of course, confirms the reality of their existence in the "creative substratum" of the human psyche.

Many of these principles are found in the mantis stories. One is seen in the image of mantis itself: *the power of the small*. Van der Post tells us that mantis was an image of the Bushman's God. Of all the magnificent creatures of Africa that the Bushman could have chosen as an image of the divine, says van der Post, he "chose the physically insignificant."[17] In our culture, we tend to overlook the significance of the small, whether it is in the outer world or the inner world. Van der Post talks about **"the immense significance of the tiny, tentative first movements in the individual heart and imagination."[18] These tiny movements need to be noticed and nurtured.** Often these very small movements of soul will be captured in a dream. As I mentioned above, my son had a dream in which he was told that we must nurture "everything that is coming into being." This is an imperative principle of growth and development. But we must first be able to *see* and to *honor* the infinitesimally small before we are able to nourish it.

This ability often comes when we realize that there is something missing in our lives and we begin to *look* for something that holds meaning for us. The recognition of something lacking, something missing, says van der Post, is a dynamic force within the human heart. This awareness is the first step toward the realization of our greater self. It has the power to move mountains. **When we are able to rescue "the significance of the small from the tyranny of the great," we are able to renew life not only within our own psyche but in our culture as well.**[19]

Van der Post insists that the theme not only of *being* but of *becoming* is woven into the Bushmen's stories, music, dancing, and art: life is an unending process of becoming and it is this recognition that gives life its joy and meaning. This is especially true in the mantis stories. Mantis is related to a strange array of creatures, such as rock-rabbit; Porcupine, who is married to the Rainbow; Mongoose; and the Blue Crane. In fact, it appears, says van der Post, that part of the significance of mantis is that he is related to all of the vast and complex life of early Africa. In all his relationships, he reflects "people of the early race," which meant, says van der Post, that they were all aspects of "the first spirit" or soul. It appears that the Bushmen also had a concern for those first principles of soul that their earliest ancestors experienced.[20]

For those of us who did not grow up in the midst of insects and animals, we have very little knowledge of their individual characteristics.

But the Bushmen had thousands of years of experience living among them, so they knew their modes of behavior and their particular characteristics. Since this world was also familiar to van der Post, he came to realize that the characters and the roles they played in the Bushman's stories were never accidental. He had complete respect for the Bushman's precision in choosing an animal to play a particular role. He knew that the Bushman's choice reflected his knowledge that no other image could reflect the intention of the story as well.[21]

For example, in an early story about mantis, he appears as a dead hartebees. The Bushmen loved and, only with the exception of the eland, gave the highest honors to the hartebees. According to van der Post, the hartebees was considered cultured, civilized, and among the highest in the society of animals in Africa. By paying homage to the hartebees in this manner, the Bushman was nurturing his own potential "to become the human equivalent of what the Hartebees was among the beast of bush and veld." So the story is told about how mantis appeared to the people of the first spirit as a dead hartebees. They happily cut it up and looked forward to the feast ahead. But much to their surprise, the severed parts of the animal began to merge back together until he was whole and alive once again. This, says van der Post, demonstrates that **mantis symbolizes the spirit that makes whole all that has been separated, that brings life again out of death, and that reflects the unity of matter and spirit.**[22]

It seems that there are stories for almost every aspect of development, but there is one story about mantis with the baboons that seems to speak directly to our experience today. It illustrates mantis' desire to pursue knowledge and become more than he is. According to van der Post, baboons represent the critical mind, the intellectual in the animal world. Since cultivation of the mind is the *most* important goal for them, they are emotionally immature, easily provoked, and quickly violent. But mantis knows that the baboons have an important contribution to make to life. So, in order to become more of who he is capable of being, mantis feels he must develop his critical abilities.[23]

In this pursuit mantis is both the father, the old vision, and the son, the new vision that is coming into being. The father sends his son out to gather the wood for the arrows that he must use in the battle with the baboons. It appears that the terms *battle* and *arrows* are used symbolically for *argument* and *intention*. "The arrows," says van der Post, "are an image of Mantis's *will* to bring about a greater expression of himself."

However, mantis is naive and does not yet have the skill to deal with intellect that lacks the foundation of inner maturity and, like Parsifal, he finds himself in the role of the fool. The baboons quickly become suspicious of mantis' intentions and end up killing him and battering his head until an eye falls out. They then play ball with the eye and later begin to argue over the possession of it. It is clear that young mantis, in his effort to develop his critical faculties, symbolizes a vision of his future self. But since mantis is in the process of learning from the baboons, his vision as yet is not fully developed. And it is this potential vision that is almost destroyed by his opponents. I suppose we all learn sooner or later that a debate between the purely rational and an emerging vision of life is dangerous at best. At this point in the story van der Post exclaims: "If there is any better image of what the over-critical faculty, the one-sided mind of pure reason, does to new creation, I have yet to meet it."

Back home mantis' father has a dream of what has happened to the "new vision" of his son and he goes out to do battle with the baboons himself. The father symbolizes that deeper aspect of the psyche whose instinctive, intuitive wisdom is called into action by the potential death of his own becoming. Perhaps it is our own potential extinction that will most quickly awaken us to these spontaneous principles of soul. In the father's struggle with the baboons to save the new vision, he too is almost killed, but finally he is able to rescue the eye.

The father's solution to this problem is *to withdraw from the argument*, wrap the eye in a bag made of hartebees' skin and go deep into nature. He entrusts the eye—the new vision—to the hartebees, the image of all that he wishes to become. This protective container reflects that deeper substratum of the natural, instinctive psyche. Once again, we see the part become whole: the father places the eye of the young mantis in water so that nature, along with his love and attention to the process, can restore the wholeness of the child. And indeed, mantis is made whole again, his *vision* is reborn, and he is renewed and wiser from his experience.[24]

Van der Post is surely correct when he says that the Bushmen's stories were their greatest containers of soul. These stories and the millions of images they painted and etched in stone throughout southern Africa and the Sahara form the sacred texts of their 27,000 years of spiritual experience. And this is equally true of the 25,000 years of spiritual experience reflected in the hundreds of painted caves in western Europe as well as at other sites around the world.

It has taken many decades since the discovery of these ancient traditions to realize that this art is the first known sacred texts of our species. In their stories and in these texts spread out across the world we have before us the flower and the fruit of millions of years of nature's struggle to evolve its capacity and ability to perceive the source of its own becoming, to bring that invisible source into visible, sensuous form, and to participate in the miracle that nature has achieved in us. It is these texts—both within their physical forms and in their living existence deep within the human psyche— that can help us to "bring back to life the deepest levels of the psyche from which our present consciousness has evolved."

Van der Post felt that our survival depended on bringing back into consciousness the Bushmen's wisdom, their love of and respect for life and their joy in being and becoming. In *A Story Like the Wind* he wrote,

> *The older I have become, the greater has grown my awareness of the debt I owe to this fast vanishing world of Africa and the greater my conviction that somehow it must be recorded, so that it should always be there to help thaw the frozen imagination of our civilised systems so that some sort of spring can come again to the minds of men.*[25]

Wherever van der Post went to talk about the Bushman, there was great interest and often people wrote to him to tell him they had dreamed about the Bushman. He took this as the psyche's *recognition* of that unacknowledged aspect of itself.

In *The Heart of the Hunter* van der Post tells of one such dream. It was the dream of a man from Spain who said he had not dreamed for years, but after hearing about the Bushman, that evening he dreamed he was in an old dilapidated castle. Somewhere inside this old castle he heard a woman crying "as if her heart would break." The man rushed from room to room, up and down stairs, through hallways, but he could not find her. The woman's weeping grew louder and more heartbreaking, but still he could not find her. Then suddenly a Bushman appeared in one of the windows and indicated that he would lead the man to the woman. The man started to follow but was horrified to realize that one of the fiercest of the wolfhounds, which he lets loose every evening to guard his house, went straight for the Bushman. The man wanted to call the dog back, but he could not find his voice.[26]

When I first read this dream, I had to put the book down. The symbolic structure was tragically clear. This man's dream belongs not only to him but to Western culture. The birth-giving, nurturing feminine in ourselves and in our culture *is* weeping as if her heart would break—and we cannot find her. The Bushman in us knows he can help us, but to our horror there is also something in us that we think is for our protection but which, in fact, once let loose, will kill the Bushman and prevent our finding the woman.

Van der Post's response to the dream was an acknowledgment that even though the Bushmen and their Stone Age culture barely exist in the physical world, they are making their appearance in the dreams of people in the West. And, he adds, anything that awakens the dreaming heart is of great value.[27]

But to move mountains we need to nurture the dreaming heart and everything it brings into being. We need to go beyond *recognition* to actively tracking down our lost selves. This is the moment when we become the hunter of great meaning in the small and seemingly insignificant. And as we become skillful trackers, we discover that there is a universe tracking us. Like mantis, we are on a journey of *being* and *becoming: just as mantis wove her basket wherein she stored the eggs of her future self in my jasmine bush, we too are in the process of remembering, containing, and nourishing the seeds of our own becoming.*

This journey, this hope, as it weaves a sacred container for our dreams and for all the stories of our heart, will be our basket where we will store our gifts from the starry sky — those "rare and dynamic intimations of [our] soul." And we will protect this basket from ourselves by remembering that we have within us both the woman of the starry sky and the man who cannot *see*. And we will not forget that the man who cannot see owns fierce wolfhounds who will destroy our path to the woman from the starry sky *and* to the Bushman whose most urgent task it is to protect the soul — if we cannot find our voice to call them back.

Chapter Twenty-Nine

Our focus is on the continuation of the shaman-mystic tradition of soul that flowered among our Stone Age ancestors. And there is now evidence not only of the continuation of this tradition but of a powerful and pervasive development.

The Shaman-Mystic-Scientist Tradition of the Megalithic Builders (12,000–3000 BCE)

Not until the twentieth century was there enough archaeological evidence from the Stone Age and the cultures that followed to verify a continuation of development. As mentioned earlier, the Mesolithic or transitional period is usually considered to have taken place between 10,000 and 8000 BCE, depending on the area, and was followed by the Neolithic or farming period. Many mysteries remain about the great builders of the megalithic monuments that we now know were built during the late Stone Age, the Mesolithic period, and the Neolithic period. Some of the well-known structures, such as Stonehenge and Newgrange, were built around 3000 BCE and later. But, as mentioned earlier, the lowest level of a megalithic structure presently being excavated in Indonesia, Gunung Padang (Mountain of Enlightenment), might prove to have been constructed as early as 20,000 BCE, and Göbekli Tepe in Turkey has been dated between 12,000 and 10,000 BCE.[1]

Our focus is on the continuation of the shaman-mystic tradition of soul that flowered among our Stone Age ancestors. And there is now evidence not only of the continuation of this tradition but of a powerful and pervasive development. It is now known that the builders of these megalithic monuments were both shaman-mystics and scientists who constructed their monuments to "access and read" the rhythms of the cosmos so that life could be lived in harmony with the laws of the universe. They "placed their highest value on the objectivity of geometry," and achieved a "remarkable balance between the intuitive and the logical." These builders understood that human consciousness can co-create with the Divine Mind or *Cosmic Consciousness* and, since we have this ability, we have the responsibility to be the mediators between the invisible, spiritual world and the visible, material world. These builders, says Critchlow, were fully committed to the spiritual dimension and its integration into the life of the individual and the physical world of time and space.[2]

The existence of these megalithic monuments around the world suggests an earlier, worldwide civilization that might have been destroyed by a cataclysmic event that occurred between 10,900 and 10,800 BCE. Some of the structures would have been built before the catastrophe while the majority, using the same highly developed technology, would have been built after the event. According to Hancock, there is evidence of a comet that fragmented and hit the earth in various places, each with a devastating impact.[3] This view is gaining credibility, but not yet accepted by many scholars.

If this proves to be the case, it could explain how such advanced knowledge of the laws of nature and the techniques of expanding consciousness were lost, except for pockets of survivors. It is true that legends and myths throughout the world tell about a great flood and how, after the destruction, "gods" traveled around the globe to bring back the knowledge of civilization.[4] This "mysterious legacy of knowledge" did survive, whether it was from catastrophic events or the vicissitudes of time, and it did flower again in various places around the world. We have focused only on those places and times that are specifically important to Western culture. And, of course, many indigenous cultures have continued to maintain profound knowledge of these principles and techniques.

The Shaman-Mystic Tradition of Old Europe (6500–2500 BCE; in Crete 1400 BCE)

From the work of Marija Gimbutas and Carl Kerényi presented in the "Introduction," we know that at least parts of this ancient spiritual tradition existed in the Neolithic cultures of what Gimbutas called Old Europe, and it achieved an exquisite flowering on the island of Crete. The designs and symbols in these cultures reflect a long and unbroken shaman-mystic tradition all the way back to the Stone Age. The feminine Source of Life and its cycles of birth, death, and rebirth were celebrated, and the ancient labyrinth was held sacred as the path to this Source, the holy of holies. The Divine Feminine was honored as the Mistress of the Labyrinth, a *Way to the Light*, and the many sacred rituals and dances associated with the labyrinthine journey were part of the Mystery Schools of Crete and Eleusis in Greece. These practices were related to the mysteries of the caves and were structured to trigger altered states of consciousness that would allow the initiate to receive the knowledge of immortality — the fruit of the Cosmic Tree of Life.

We had no comprehensive knowledge of these cultures until the twentieth century work of Gimbutas. Her conclusions were supported by tens of thousands of artifacts yet initially rejected by a shocked profession of predominantly male archaeologists. The artifacts speak for themselves, however, especially when these cultures are seen in the historical context of the spiritual tradition that preceded and followed them. With the waves of invasion and destruction from 4500 BCE to 1400 BCE, the cultures of Old Europe were lost and forgotten — until their recent discovery.

The Shaman-Mystic-Scientist Tradition of Ancient Egypt (3000–1000 BCE)

As I mentioned earlier, it is quite understandable to lose the knowledge of a past that had been buried for thousands of years, but it is not as easy to understand how we could lose our imagination for the power and grandeur of a civilization whose remaining structures reflect a knowledge we ourselves do not have. But we did lose this imagination in the early nineteenth century when the Egyptian hieroglyphs were deciphered, and the discipline of Egyptology was born. The materialistic worldview blinded scholars to the real achievements of Egyptian culture, and it was not until the twentieth century that a different perspective began to emerge among Egyptologists, but it did not bear fruit until the end of that century and the beginning of this one.[5]

An earlier giant in the development of our understanding of ancient Egypt, as mentioned above, was R. A. Schwaller de Lubicz, but he was "virtually ignored by the Egyptological establishment." During the twentieth century, his many books on ancient Egyptian culture revealed the depths of Egyptian mathematical, architectural, medical, and spiritual development. His work made it exceedingly clear that Egypt was a major source of Western science and culture. The ancient writers had expressed the same conclusion, but the Egyptologists ignored both Schwaller de Lubicz and the ancient writers.[6]

What is important from the perspective of this book is that Schwaller de Lubicz gave to the world an understanding of the shaman-mystic consciousness within a highly developed and sophisticated civilization. It now appears that ancient Egypt was the continuation and beautiful culmination of our species' spiritual evolution from the Stone Age shaman-mystic experiences of the cave cultures in Europe, the San people of Africa, and the great shaman-scientist-builders of the megalithic monuments around the world. This is still true even when we take into consideration the Edfu texts' claim that the Egyptians originally came from an island home after a great cataclysm. The Egyptian culture remains a stunning culmination of that "mysterious legacy of knowledge" from our ancestors around the world.

The sacred paintings that our earlier ancestors had made on the walls of caves or the surfaces of rocks were now painted on the inner walls of temples and pyramids. These paintings reflect highly developed rituals that were structured to elicit *direct experience* just as the architecture was structured to attract and hold cosmic and earth energies that also played their part in the Egyptian transformative rituals and celebrations. **Important for our focus is that the Egyptian rituals reflect in detail the development of what the megalithic builders saw as the human ability to mediate between the invisible, spiritual world and the visible, material** world. These great Egyptian visionaries accepted and developed their role as co-creator with the Divine Mind or Cosmic Consciousness.

In *Serpent in the Sky: The High Wisdom of Ancient Egypt,* John Anthony West presents the discoveries Schwaller de Lubicz was able to accomplish during his fifteen years of research and fieldwork in Egypt. This civilization, according to Schwaller de Lubicz, was, in fact, based on the principles of cosmic consciousness. The great shaman-mystic-scientist builders had profound knowledge of the creative principles of the universe, and it was these principles that determined the form and structure of all their sacred works:[7]

> *the complex of Egyptian temples contain a global lesson of which each temple is a chapter where a particular theme of the Sacred Science is developed. Thus no pharaonic temple is the replica of another, but each edifice speaks through its overall plan, its orientation, the layout of its foundations, the choice of materials used, and the openings in its walls.*[8]

The Temple of Luxor, for example, is the only temple that represents an architectural figure of the human being. Schwaller de Lubicz discovered in the structure of the Temple "such esoteric knowledge as the location of the ductless glands, of the Hindu energy chakras, and of the Chinese acupuncture points." The Temple's astronomical orientation, the geometry of its construction, its art and inscriptions all point to the human being who has achieved Cosmic Consciousness.[9]

Even though ignored by the Egyptologists, Schwaller de Lubicz was a major scholar in the breakthrough of our understanding of ancient Egypt, not only in the sacred geometry underlying their megalithic temple structures but in the "Sacred Science" that formed the foundation of every aspect of Egyptian culture. The discovery of this Sacred Science by Schwaller de Lubicz was the discovery of the earliest known extensive source of what is now called "the Perennial Philosophy," whose fragments are kept alive among the Gnostics, Kabbalists, Hermeticists, Alchemists, Sufis, and "a series of enlightened and clairvoyant masters."[10] This is, of course, the shaman-mystic-scientist tradition we are tracking.

The more recent work of Alison Roberts and Jeremy Naydler explores some of the many Egyptian rituals for the transformation of consciousness through its contact with and integration of cosmic conscious forces. Just as with the earlier megalithic builders, human consciousness, now symbolized by the King, is the mediator between the timeless, invisible forces and the visible earth forces of time and space.

In *Hathor Rising: The Power of the Goddess in Ancient Egypt* and *My Heart My Mother: Death and Rebirth in Ancient Egypt* Roberts examines the Egyptian art of living, the art of death and rebirth, and the fiery serpent goddess (the feminine dimension of the divine) who exists in love and harmony with her husband, the fiery solar god. And Naydler in *Shamanic Wisdom in the Pyramid Texts: The Mystical Tradition of Ancient Egypt* shows how the Pyramid Texts reveal the shaman-mystic foundation of the civilization of ancient Egypt. Both scholars show how the rituals are structured to ignite altered states of consciousness and direct experience in the spirit world. Each of these scholars reveals how the Egyptian *heart-centered experiential consciousness* opens the mind to the ecstasy and beauty of life in time and space as well as connects the mind to cosmic dimensions of reality.

Roberts explores the multifaceted images of the goddess Hathor and her central place in the spiritual tradition of ancient Egypt. She is the power both in nature and in the human being to create or destroy—an energy that must be desired and loved by an equal force, symbolized by the sun god Re, if it is to be channeled creatively. The individual, symbolized by the king, had to learn how to harness and channel the energy and power of Hathor so that he—and Egypt—could achieve the fullness of being. In order to achieve this balance of energy, the king had to know how to die, be reborn, and become the Solar King.[11]

Only then would he be able to achieve within himself the marriage of the sun god to the fiery and powerful goddess Hathor. This marriage reflected wholeness: it was a union of the creativity of the night with the achievements of the day. It was the union of the moon and the sun, of death and rebirth, of our ancestors and ourselves, of the cosmos and the earth, of the spirit realm and the physical world of time and space. *It was a marriage of the head and the heart, since thought, duty and responsibility could only be effective when they were inspired by attraction, beauty, and desire.* Once this balance had been achieved, the Solar King was able to channel the powerful creative forces of Hathor. This achievement was symbolized by the embrace of Hathor in the form of the fiery serpent goddess who rises up the spine of the king and appears on his brow.[12]

In *Shamanic Wisdom in the Pyramid Texts*, Naydler shows how the Pyramid Texts depict in detail the Sed Festival, which encompasses the shamanic rituals the king must undergo in order to become the Solar King. Naydler points out that the Pyramid Texts in the pyramid of Unas are around 4,350 years old and are the earliest ancient Egyptian sacred literature. In fact, he says, they are the earliest "extended" writing worldwide. **Unfortunately, the Egyptologists failed to recognize that these texts on the inner walls of this pyramid reflect the continuation of a powerful shaman-mystic tradition.**[13] Similar initiatory traditions, says Naydler, existed throughout the ancient world and were practiced long before they were committed to writing.[14] Both Roberts and Naydler make it clear that the Egyptian rituals were not empty structures nor, in the case of the Sed Festival, were the rituals limited to the dead king or simply the coronation of a new king, as many Egyptologists have assumed. Naydler presents convincing evidence that the Sed Festival Rituals were shamanic initiation and renewal rites that altered consciousness and ignited direct experience of the spirit world. *Its rituals reflect the actual inner events in the consciousness of the king.*[15]

The Sed Festival took place at varying intervals and lasted several days. The activities were highly charged shamanic rituals whose "central rite involved the king crossing the threshold between worlds in order to stand in direct relationship to the normally hidden spiritual powers." At its core, says Naydler, was "a mystical ritual that served the purpose of bringing the king into a conscious relationship with the spirit world."[16] Thus, the living king as Horus entered the Cosmic spirit realm and embraced Osiris, the dead king. These two archetypes of life and death, Horus and Osiris, become *fused* in the king's consciousness. *This, says Naydler, is the foundation of the entire Festival and the source of the king's power.*[17]

I have mentioned several times that for our ancestors nothing was more important than living in harmony with the laws of nature. In order to do this, a conscious connection between the physical world and the spirit dimension was absolutely necessary, and all rituals were structured to achieve and maintain this connection. Without this, there could be no true power. Osiris was symbolic of this spirit dimension. He was the dead king, but we have to be cautious here, for what we think of as *the dead* or *the land of the dead* was not what the Egyptians experienced. For them the Osirian realm was actually the vital source of everything that comes into being in the physical world. It was the land of the ancestors who were "the guardians of the forces of life, and hence the well-being of the whole land of Egypt." They were "the conduits of this inner spiritual vitality to the outwardly manifest world." **And it was the king's role to keep these worlds connected and to be the mediator between them.** The realm of the ancestors or what we call the land of the dead was not a passive state, says Naydler, but rather "a state of energized inwardness, poised to burst forth again into manifestation."[18]

One of the most significant symbols of this "energized inwardness" was the body of the Cosmic goddess, Nut.[19] During the Sed Festival, it was her body that the king entered, for she is, says Roberts, "the fiery Egyptian matrix" of all life. She is "the sacred vessel of transformation which renews the Egyptian king."[20] In this matrix the king becomes one with Osiris and journeys through the body of the great Cosmic goddess where he undergoes purifications, becomes a creative partner with the formerly destructive Seth, unites all opposites, and is reborn from the body of Nut at dawn as the sun god Re.[21]

Earlier I said that the king must undergo the rituals of the Sed Festival to be able to channel the fiery creative force of the serpent goddess Hathor. This is true, but now we can see that during the rituals of the Sed Festival, the king is contained within the body of the Cosmic goddess who, in her many forms, nurtures the king throughout his entire journey. She is mother, beloved, and daughter who offers the king the gifts needed for each aspect of his life. She gives the king a new body, feeling, heart, laughter, spontaneity, fecundity, sexual power, and mystical illumination. Horus and Osiris are *One*. The entire journey to become the solar king is contained in and nurtured by the fiery life force, or kundalini energy, that can now rise up and settle on the king's brow as his third eye.[22]

Now all Egypt can prosper. The king has died and is reborn. He has risen from his sarcophagus; he is the *resurrected* king. The djed pillar [the Sacred Tree of Life] can be raised, the king can be crowned with the crowns of both upper and lower Egypt, and the Solar King can dance to the four corners of the land in recognition of the unity and fruitfulness of his kingdom. The Festival ends with a public feast and the celebration of all Egypt.[23]

We can easily see the similarities between the Sed Festival Ritual in Egypt and the Jewish First Temple Ritual of Day One. Both are shaman-mystic rituals of entering the Other world: the Egyptian King enters the realm of Osiris, and the Jewish High Priest enters Day One, the Holy of Holies. For each tradition, this realm is the vital source of everything that comes into being in the physical world. Here the secrets of creation, of birth and death, are experienced. The King or the High Priest achieves within himself a delicate balance through the loving fusion of all opposites. Both experience the sacred marriage: in love and intimacy the King embraces Hathor, the fiery life force, and in love and intimacy the High Priest embraces Wisdom, the radiant, divine archetypal High Priestess, the Queen of Heaven.

At dawn the King is reborn from the body of Nut, and since the High Priestess gives birth in the Holy of Holies, we know that the High Priest is also reborn—both are *resurrected*. The King returns to the material realm, is crowned as the balancing force and mediator between the realms of spirit and matter for all Egypt. The High Priest passes back through the veil and reenters the material realm. Each of these rituals was the heart of the ancient Egyptian and Jewish Mysteries—and they would become the heart of the later movement that became Christianity in which Jesus was the High Priest and initiate of this sacred tradition.

It is clear that all three traditions were rooted in the ancient shaman-mystic wisdom of our ancestors. The sacred knowledge of each tradition was the ability to initiate altered states of consciousness so that the individual could have a Near (Actual)-Death Experience. In other terms, the initiate could enter the spirit realm, die to the limited consciousness of time and space, experience Cosmic Consciousness, the depth of love, feeling, joy, the sacredness of all life, and be reborn, that is, return to the realm of time and space renewed and whole. Roberts makes it clear that "the ancient Egyptian ritualists were initiates of the highest order in the heavenly mysteries of death and rebirth, steeped in knowledge of the afterlife during their lifetime on earth."[24] And Barker's research shows this to be true for the Jewish First Temple mystics as well as the mystics who were the early Christians. These ancestors were truly Masters of Life and Masters of Light.

In ancient Egypt, this knowledge of the mysteries of death and rebirth and the wisdom of the fiery serpent goddess were lost during the reign of King Akhenaten, 1349–1334 BCE. Roberts explains that while his reign maintained the vision of the unity of all life, in the later phase of his reign, there was a rejection of the dark side of life, of death, of the feminine, and of everything connected with the night-time journey of the sun/king in the realm of darkness. The light—the sun god Re, alone prevailed, and the connection to the earth and the feminine *wisdom of the heart* was lost.[25]

However, during the Ramesside Nineteenth Dynasty, especially during the reign of King Seti I, 1291–1278 BCE, there was a return of these ancient archetypal patterns of spiritual knowledge, and this return was enshrined forever in stone and in the beauty of Egyptian art. If the so-called Akhenaten revolution had not taken place, says Roberts, Seti might never have initiated the great works of art that give us explicit knowledge of Egypt's ancient spiritual tradition. Seti brought back *the wisdom of the heart*, and the balance of the past was reborn in the present.[26]

We have seen how this sacred tradition of *the wisdom of the heart* was also lost in Judaism in 621 BCE under Josiah and the Deuteronomists and, once again, how it was reborn in the early movement of Christianity and then lost again with the establishment of the Church of Rome. This wisdom tradition went underground and was maintained in the various forms of Alchemy, Gnosticism, the Hermetic arts, the Kabbalah, and Mystic Christianity. Later we will look briefly at how this wisdom tradition emerges repeatedly in European consciousness but is always repressed.

We now know that the Egyptian initiates experienced what we have lost and devalued—the feminine power of the heart in each of us to birth a *feeling* world. They understood that, *without feeling, we cannot bring justice into being. In fact, without the integration of all that the feminine symbolizes, creation cannot continue to unfold.*[27] This could not be more profound: the heart holds the fiery, feminine, divine, creative energy of love that we need in order to create in the material world. When we are attracted to this energy, desire it, and embrace it, this energy becomes the *eye*; it becomes *vision*.

Part of the beauty of the Egyptian wisdom is that *love* and *desire* for this life force are needed to achieve a balanced integration and to give birth to a *feeling* world. This is far more important than it might at first appear. For the king—or the knight—to marry the fiery serpent goddess with love and desire reflects a true union of spirit and matter: *the energies of both the body and the mind are integrated in and channeled through the heart.* There is no rejection of the body or the feminine as occurs in so many of the later spiritual traditions. *This is the wisdom of the heart.*

There are many images in Egypt of *the divine wisdom of the heart.* For example, Hathor is sometimes a sacred cow, the Milky Way, a beautiful woman, or the desirable, fiery serpent energy—but she can also appear as the Cosmic Tree. She is the Lady of the Sycamore who "rises forth from the branches of this much-loved tree." The fruit of her tree has a milky white liquid and the same liquid oozes forth from its leaves. This juice is called the "milk of the sycamore."[28] In other words, she and the fruit are one, and in some depictions of this tree, the goddess appears within its branches and offers her *milk* to all those who are reaching for it with the will and readiness to receive it.

At other times, she appears as a bare sycamore tree in contrast to the tree flowing with milk. But even in the tree's skeletal form, dried up and burned out, the goddess still rises up "like the rising sap of life" and is able to give her gifts from this tree as well, for she is the life force itself.[29]

This image reflects the eternal power of the heart/soul even within a wasteland. These sacred Egyptian rituals reveal the original meaning of the goddess, the tree, the rising kundalini serpent energy, and the fruit freely given—all aspects of the sacred experience of cosmic consciousness.

Chapter Thirty

The Shaman-Mystic Jewish Tradition
(832–621 BCE)

In the "Introduction," we explored the Hebrew shaman-mystic tradition of the First Temple and how these archetypal symbols of the goddess, the tree, the rising, kundalini serpent energy, and the fruit freely given were politically manipulated and degraded in the hands of the Deuteronomists in 621 BCE. The date for the building of the First Temple is uncertain, but it was probably sometime between 957 and 832 BCE, later, of course, than the flourishing of the highly developed and sophisticated shaman-mystic tradition in Egypt. What is important for us to realize, however, is that the entire ancient world was rooted in this shaman-mystic tradition.

The Shaman-Mystic-Scientist Anatolian Greek/ Presocratic Tradition
(500 BCE to the Birth of Christ)

In the "Introduction," I discussed the Presocratic Greek shaman-mystic tradition discovered by Kingsley. These Greeks, from the western coast of Anatolia, settled in Italy around 538 BCE. Recent excavations in Italy reveal that the shaman-mystic tradition they brought with them from Anatolia had endured for more than 500 years, right up to the birth of Christ. And we will see that Kingsley's research shows us how this tradition continued to influence the West long after the birth of Christ—even after the establishment of the Church of Rome.

In fact, says Kingsley, this tradition of shaman-mystic healers is at the very roots of Western culture. Men such as Pythagoras and Parmenides, whom we have known as philosophers, were actually masters of entering altered states of consciousness, of experiencing other dimensions of reality for long periods of time, of initiating others and teaching techniques of ecstasy, of healing, and of giving laws that were healing for entire cities. **Through their *visionary* abilities "they laid the foundation for disciplines that were to make the West what it now is: chemistry, physics, astronomy, biology, rhetoric, logic."**[1] These shaman-mystic visionaries were practical technicians, scientific thinkers, lawgivers, and ambassadors. And they, like the shaman-mystics before them, held a unified vision of spirit and matter, of the mystic and the scientist.

It would be impossible to overstate the gift of Kingsley's work to our understanding of the ancient world. Not only does he reveal the depth of inner experience and the intellectual genius of the Greek shaman-mystics, but he reveals the continuity of ancient shamanic traditions so vast that they stretched from southern Spain through Greece and Crete, northern Africa (including, of course, Egypt) to Lebanon and Syria, Babylonia, Anatolia, Persia, and all the way into Central Asia, the Himalayas, Mongolia, Tibet, Nepal and India.[2] **This lost wisdom of our ancestors forms the very roots of who we are. Yet the West has severed itself from its own source—until now.**

In Kingsley's work, *In the Dark Places of Wisdom*, he discusses some of the techniques these Greek shamans used for healing and for achieving powerful states of consciousness. They, like the Egyptians before them, honored death and birth, the darkness *and* the light, for they also understood that the light comes into being out of darkness. They used the dark places, such as caves, for their journeys into altered states of consciousness. When they entered the darkness of the labyrinthine cave, they were met by the Great Goddess who was their guide, for here too she was known as *a Way to the Light*.

Their healing rituals also took place in the darkness of caves where those who needed healing lay down, remained motionless, and hardly breathed, sometimes for days. Eventually, they completely surrendered to their condition. Then the healing dream would come or they would "enter a state described as neither sleep nor waking—and eventually they'd have a vision." This method of healing was called *incubation*. It was understood that healing came from another dimension of reality, and these healers were highly skilled in achieving the state of consciousness that would allow the flow of healing energy from deeper orders of reality. They also knew how to create the conditions conducive to the patient's achieving this consciousness. Sometimes, however, the priest would dream for the patients and receive the knowledge of what they needed for healing. These priests were called "the masters of dreams, lords of the lair."[3]

Apollo was the god of these shamans, for he was the god of darkness, death, and nonbeing. *And* he was the sun god, for the light is born only out of darkness. It was said that Apollo slept with the goddess Persephone in the Holy of Holies of darkness and death, and he was birthed out of this darkness as the Sun King, the eternal god Apollo. This is Apollo in his wholeness. We have seen how the Sun King in Egypt is also born out of the darkness of the great goddess of Night. This experience and understanding of the creative relationship of death and birth is the foundation of shaman-mystic wisdom. When direct experience does not exist and knowledge of this relationship is lost, death and darkness are feared, censored, and repressed. This loss is why we now know Apollo only as a god of light, reason, and rationality.[4]

And this is why today our dreams and our visions are urging us to visit the darkness once again. The visionary life allows us to experience the creativity of death and darkness, to lose our fear, to know that all life is immortal—because all life dies and is reborn. One afternoon István returned from a powerful vision with the joyous knowledge of this eternal truth. He had had several visionary experiences of dying and resisting death, only to realize that once he surrendered to the force of life, he had no fear and he himself became one with the flow of this force. This was the kind of surrender those in incubation must have experienced—to flow with the life force, to become one with it. In István's attempt to express this, he looked at me with the eyes of one from another world and said:

> *Death is as Divine as Life.*
> *Hold them in both hands.*
> *Play with them.*
> *Balance them.*
> *This is the Divine Game.*

These words continue to hold poetic power and magic for me. This is true of all speech that is born in the world of vision. Kingsley tells us that these shaman-mystic healers used musical language and poetic incantations during their journeys to other dimensions of consciousness. The shaman poets, says Kingsley, "explained how the words in their poems were seeds that were meant to be absorbed so they could grow and transform the nature of the hearer, give rise to a different awareness." Kingsley points out that it has long been recognized that Greek epic poetry has its roots in shamanic poetic language—and we might add, so does much of later spiritual literature.[5]

The power of poetic language was well known among the Celtic bards: through their musical and poetic incantations they were able to ignite altered states of consciousness in their listeners. This could be true wherever the shamanic tradition existed. Altered states of consciousness often activate the bubbling spring of poetic words, phrases, and even total poetic expression. The body often flows or dances with the music of the words. And these words *are* seeds that grow in us and transform us. Vico was quite right when he said that our first language is poetry and that poetry perfectly reflects the inner structure of consciousness itself. And the shaman knew that the inner structure of our consciousness is related to the essential structure of the universe.

Every individual has the necessary brain components to experience altered states of consciousness and to participate in the wholeness of her or his own inner wisdom. This is how we bring forth what is within us so that we will not destroy ourselves and our world. *The shaman-mystic is simply the name for the individual who participates in the available dimensions of consciousness and is able to teach others to do the same.* Their techniques activate the poetic, symbolic well of spiritual knowledge within us so that we can remember who we are and why we're here. And this appears to be precisely what the Presocratic shaman-mystics were capable of accomplishing.

The Greek shaman-mystics, as well as the shaman-mystic tradition that spread all the way from Spain to Central Asia, had roots that stretched back into the Stone Age when modern consciousness emerged around the world. For thousands of years our ancestors created and used methods of altering consciousness and entering higher dimensions of reality. Such experiences were their gifts to all who followed, not just through historical connections but through the treasured deposits they made in the collective psyche of our species. Those ancestors planted the seeds of shamanic-mystic consciousness in the collective mind of our species, and the tradition Kingsley speaks of is a beautiful flowering of those seeds.

Kingsley tells us about Parmenides, who, as mentioned earlier, was one of the most notable philosophers and healers in this tradition. He explains how profoundly Parmenides influenced Plato but, at the same time, how profoundly Plato *distorted* and *rationalized* the great tradition that Parmenides—and Pythagoras before him—represented. Plato, says Kingsley, was not the father of Western philosophy after all. The true father of Western philosophy was a shaman, and it was this shaman, not Plato, who invented logic. But it was Plato's rationalization of the Presocratic shamans that was to dominate Western cultural development. Logic was severed from its roots in the deep inner structure of visionary consciousness.[6]

It is this rationalization that has allowed us to skate on the surface of the mind for almost two thousand years, to construct an entire worldview that consists only of this surface, and to construct a fiction of our superiority that has blinded us to the true story of our past. We could say that the discoveries of the twentieth century are calling us home, but we could also say that we are calling ourselves home. For is it not our own longing for this something that has been missing that is allowing the earth to release these gifts of our ancestors?

For all too long we have been led to believe that it was the birth of Christianity that saved us from this *pagan* world of our ancestors. **What** is brilliantly clear now is that the teachings of Jesus about Christ Consciousness are a continuation of the shaman-mystic tradition of our ancestors. But it was this ancient tradition that the Church did everything it could to destroy, including its attempt to reduce all that had come before it to ignorance and sensuous, material pleasures.

The Continuation of This Shaman-Mystic Tradition After Christianity

Kingsley tells us that the Greek shaman-mystic tradition lasted right up to the time of Christ. His research also shows how this tradition continued to influence the West long after the birth of Christ—even after the establishment of the Church of Rome. And with the work of Roberts and Naydler we are able to see that the shaman-mystic-visionary tradition of Egypt continued to exist in different forms throughout the ancient world— through the Greek and later Roman rule of Egypt, the birth of Christ, the establishment of the Church of Rome, and much later. Roberts tracks the continuation of this Egyptian mystery tradition while Kingsley tracks the continuation of the Presocratic mystery tradition. Both of these traditions come together in Egypt at Akhmim in the shaman-mystic mystery tradition of Alchemy. Roberts illustrates convincingly how the emergence of Alchemy in Akhmim had roots in the ancient Egyptian mysteries of death and rebirth. And Kingsley traces the influence of the Presocratic mysteries of death and rebirth from southern Italy to Alexandria in Egypt and then down the Nile to Akhmim in southern Egypt.[7]

It was in Akhmim that the ancient Egyptian shaman-mystic death and rebirth mysteries, the Presocratic shaman-mystic tradition (especially the work of Pythagoras and Empedocles), and Greek, Jewish, and Arabic alchemical works merged. As the intolerance of the Church of Rome after the fourth century became too oppressive for this tradition to openly survive and develop, it went underground or fled to safer havens in Mecca, Baghdad, and Persia.

It is important for us to remember that by 750 CE the Muslim world had conquered the old Persian empire, most of the Roman world, which included Egypt, Spain, and north Africa, and they were still on the move in their attempt to conquer more of Europe and other territories all the way to Asia. By 1095 CE the Christian Crusades against the Muslims and other non-Christians began. This is the military side of the picture, but what is often excluded in the history of the West is the intellectual and spiritual development in the Islamic world during this same period.

During the latter part of the 700s the House of Wisdom was founded in Baghdad. Muslim scholars, along with Jewish and Christian scholars, both men and women, studied the humanities and sciences there, including mathematics, astronomy, medicine, alchemy, chemistry, zoology, geography, cartography, the arts, and literature. Translations were made into Arabic from many languages, such as Farsi, Aramaic, Hebrew, Syriac, Greek and Latin. Egyptian alchemical texts were translated, and, according to recent discoveries by Dr. Okasha El Daly at the Institute of Archaeology, University College London (UCL), a ninth century Arabic Alchemist, almost a thousand years before the West, successfully deciphered hieroglyphic signs. By the ninth century the House of Wisdom had accumulated the largest collection of books in the world. In addition to the extensive scholarship initiated by the House of Wisdom, the first universities were established, and hospitals available to everyone were developed throughout the Arab world. There were also many advances in architecture, engineering, and food production during this period, as well as discoveries such as the cause of infectious diseases by microorganisms and the development of algebra and ophthalmology.[8]

While the Church of Rome was destroying much of the ancient world, the Arabic culture was attempting, through their translations, to preserve it. Timothy Freke and Peter Gandy in *The Hermetica: The Lost Wisdom of the Pharaohs* tell us that many so-called "Pagan scholars and sages fled to the newly emerging Arab culture," where by the ninth century, as we have seen, the Muslims had "created an empire whose learning and scientific achievements were unsurpassed."[9]

However, Persia had been a center for Greek, Jewish, and Persian studies long before the intolerance of the Church or the later Arab conquest. It was, therefore, also a natural haven for foreign scholars when Christian intolerance made the continuation of their work impossible. Minou Reeves, in *Europe's Debt to Persia: Religion, Philosophy, Astronomy, Mathematics, Medicine and the Sciences*, tells the story of how the Persian kings opened the doors of their academies to all scholars whose work was threatened by the growing intolerance of the Church of Rome. As the terrifying darkness spread, scholars fled to Persia with what manuscripts they could take with them. The Persian kings sponsored the translations of their manuscripts into many languages and invited these scholars to teach in their academies. As we have seen, this open and scholarly tradition continued after the Arab conquest, and it was the Persian academy that became the model for the later centers of learning in Baghdad. **It would be, to a large extent, Persia and later the Muslim culture that preserved the intellectual and spiritual genius of the West. And it was they who created the model for men and women from all fields of study and from all ethnic groups to work together to nurture the growth and development of civilization.**[10]

It was within this powerful intellectual and spiritual tradition of Persia that the ancient shaman-mystic-alchemists from Akhmim merged with Sufism. Later, during the twelfth century, this ancient tradition from Akhmim within Sufism would be revived by the great Sufi Al-Suhrawardi. He recognized the authenticity of the Akhmim tradition because he understood, says Kingsley, that there is essentially "only one true wisdom," or in Al-Suhrawardi's words, one "true leaven."[11] **This wisdom, known by many names and existing in many places, always carries the secrets of our evolution and our place in the universe.**

This ancient wisdom tradition, deeply enriched by the Sufi tradition of Islam, found its way back to Europe through contact with the Sufis during the Crusades. But even before the Crusades, as early as the ninth century, the Islamic culture of Spain was influencing the great minds of Europe. Cordova became the intellectual, sophisticated, and tolerant center of the continent. Jews, Christians, and Muslims lived in harmony and shared their knowledge with each other and with those who came to learn from them. Islamic culture and this ancient wisdom tradition inspired some of Europe's greatest creativity during the High Middle Ages, and, as we will see, this inspiration was renewed during the

Italian Renaissance, the Rosicrucian period, the German and English Romantic period, and the twentieth century.

PART V

THE PROMISE OF THE PAST:
FIVE WAVES OF REMEMBERING

Chapter Thirty-One

The High Middle Ages
The First Wave of the Renaissance
(1000–1300 CE)

*This "twelfth century Renaissance" realized "the centrality of the heart"
in the development of a higher consciousness.*[1]
— Christopher Bamford

Let's look at these periods. We have noted how, with the establishment of the Church of Rome, this wisdom tradition remained underground in Europe for several hundred years — from the fourth century until the eleventh or twelfth century — when it — the carrier of our true stories — burst forth during the **High Middle Ages** in the legends of the Holy Grail; the honoring of the feminine and the land; the poetry of the troubadours that praised woman as soul; the Courts of Love; and the building of the great Gothic cathedrals in honor of "Our Lady."

And there were yet other powerful streams of awakening and creativity. Alchemical texts were being translated from Arabic into Latin for the first time; the ancient Jewish shaman-mystic tradition reemerged in Europe with the appearance of the Zohar; and the incredibly independent and creative Beguine women appeared on the scene, among whom were some of Europe's great female mystics. Many of the Beguine women along with Cistercian monks and nuns began developing an understanding of love that heals, transforms, and unites the individual heart with the heart of the world. At the same time the troubadours and the Cathars in southern France were also creating a path of love that drew people together from many diverse traditions.[2]

In "The Meaning of the Rose Cross," Christopher Bamford shows how the "initiatory wisdom streams" of this "twelfth century Renaissance" realized "the centrality of the heart" in the development of a higher consciousness. We have seen that the ancient shaman-mystic traditions as well as modern brain research place the heart in a central position. The heart is soul, the feminine ground of being. Bamford insists on an extremely important point: all these traditions (and he includes the Cathars) arrive at "a new understanding of non-dualism, or the complete interpenetration of the individual soul and the world soul,..." They were all working, he says, to create a new "culture for the transformation of the world in the human soul...." They understood that each person's spiritual journey was also *a journey* to spiritualize the world.[3]

And it was *this journey* that inspired all Europe: the quest for the Grail itself was a quest for direct experience and communion with the Otherworld through love, respect, and loyalty to the Queen of that world, the Sovereign of the Land, *Our Lady*, the soul of the world. Out of the European wasteland emerged an incredible blossoming of soul. There must have been a profound longing for spiritual meaning that was ignited by contact with the great intellectual and sophisticated cities of Muslim Spain and through contact with the Sufis during the Crusades. And this new focus, in turn, ignited the underground traditions in Europe. This period was in actuality our first European Renaissance—which could not have occurred without contact with the highly developed and tolerant Arabic culture.

This incredible awakening prepared the way for the later Italian Renaissance. It is now clear that the various creative periods in Europe were powerful waves of this first renaissance during the High Middle Ages. What amazes me is that after hundreds of years of repression by the Church of the ancient mysteries of death and rebirth—our true wisdom— this soul knowledge reemerged into the consciousness of Western culture along with a clear image of the damage done to the Western psyche during these years of repression.

The Grail stories reveal that the wasteland of Europe had come about because we had lost contact with the Otherworld, the spirit realm. This is symbolized in the world of time and space by King Arthur's loss of Guinevere's love and, in a broader sense, the story of the evil King and his followers who refused the cosmic fruit and, instead, raped the spirit women at the sacred sites on the earth where they could be contacted. These were the Voices at the Wells who had offered the sacred water (that is, the sacred fruit) to all who sought it. Their sacred bowl or grail was stolen, the maidens disappeared, the water dried up, and the abundance of the land was reduced to a wasteland. There could not be a clearer description of what had happened during the centuries of denial, disregard, and repression of the knowledge of direct experience of the spirit world. *The symbolism of the Maidens' offering of the sacred Grail is parallel with the Tree of Life and the goddess who gives the gift of higher consciousness.*

When we look at the sources of the Grail stories, we immediately realize that we are in touch once again with the indigenous shaman-mystic traditions, now of Ireland, Wales, and Brittany, as these traditions are carried to the courts of France, England, and Germany by the great bards of the time. The underground traditions, such as Alchemy, Kabbalah, and Mystic Christianity, also found expression in the stories along with the mysticism of the Sufis. And we must keep in mind that this was the Sufism that had merged with our own Presocratic shaman-mystic tradition, the earlier Egyptian mysteries of death and rebirth, and the later alchemical developments. It is now clear that this ancient tradition frames the Grail stories.

If we remember for a moment the Egyptian mysteries of death and rebirth enacted by the Pharaoh during the Sed Festival, we see immediately that the Grail King is unable to participate in such a Festival, for this King cannot die. *He and Western culture have lost the knowledge of how to connect to the spirit world.* We will remember that Naydler has told us that the core of the Sed Festival was "a mystical ritual that served the purpose of bringing the king into a conscious relationship with the spirit world."[4]

Through this ritual the living king as Horus entered the Cosmic spiritual realm and embraced Osiris, the dead king. These two archetypes of life and death, Horus and Osiris, became *fused* in the king's consciousness. *This, says Naydler, is the foundation of the entire Festival and the source of the king's power.*[5] The Grail King has lost this ability to fuse life and death, and thus he has lost the source of his power.

Since the Grail King cannot enter the realm of death to achieve the fusion of death and life in his own consciousness, we know that he has also lost his ability to relate to the feminine ground of being, through whom and with whom the King is transformed and empowered. And thus the Grail King is impotent and is no longer able to channel the fiery power of the feminine to create or destroy. And, as Roberts tells us, the feminine is an energy that must be desired and loved by an equal force if this energy is to be channeled creatively. *The King must love her, desire her, be willing to die to integrate her fiery force within himself — and thus the land.*[6]

The Great Mysteries have been lost; Queen Guinevere's love has been lost; the connection to the spirit dimension and soul has been lost — and death appears everywhere. The King is impotent and the land is a wasteland. This reflects the spiritual condition of European culture, *but it also reflects the awareness of this loss*. And this is always where the journey begins. The moment we become aware of what we have lost, we can begin the journey to find it. As I mentioned in the "Introduction," it is when we become aware that we are "dreaming a terrible dream," that we begin our journey to awaken to a higher consciousness.

And so it is with the Grail King. The old consciousness is no longer capable of ruling. He finds himself in a wasteland and realizes that he and the land are one. The King knows that the only thing that can save him and the culture is for someone, or some larger aspect of himself, to become conscious enough to ask the crucial question of what ails the king. Once the Question is asked, the new consciousness of the King begins his Quest. He plunges into the labyrinthine journey to heal himself and his culture. *The Great Mysteries of death and rebirth must be rediscovered.* Our hero must learn once again what his culture has lost: how to relate to Nature, to the feminine, to spirit, to death, to other men, and to the world.

The Round Table of King Arthur's Court is a symbol for the wholeness, equality, and loyalty to each other that the knights seek. **Within the labyrinthine journey the knights have the opportunity to learn how to relate to the feminine, how to love her, to be sensitive to her, and to serve her. This was what my own journey required of me: my Knight had to learn how to relate to the visionary feminine within me.** As we progress in the journey, we understand that our relationship with our visionary partner opens us to the Otherworld. Through love, respect, and loyalty to our visionary, the Queen of that world, we are able to communicate with the spirit dimension of reality. Our journey teaches us that She is soul, the Sovereign of the Land, *Our Lady*, the soul of the world. We learn that without this relationship to soul, we and our world become a wasteland.

When a person who is able to ask the question does appear before the King, it is strangely comforting to know that he is clueless—as so many of us are when we start out on our journey. But he does have the *desire* and the ability to learn. His task is nothing less than his own transformation, and it is *this* transformation that can heal civilization. As in all such journeys, once the seeker asks the question and enters the labyrinth, she/he meets precisely the experiences needed to teach us what we need to know. We follow Baba Yaga's threads throughout the labyrinthine journey, and we know that the path is also the goal, for the path transforms our lives and thus our civilization. From Chrétien de Troyes to Robert de Boron to Wolfram von Eschenbach and later to the great journey of Dante Alighieri, the focus during this creative period is on the evolution of our consciousness through the Great Mysteries.

Unfortunately, the Grail stories gradually became Christianized and the hero Galahad, like Jesus, became the all-light, one-sided, not-of-this-world man who could never have a physical relationship with a woman if he is to achieve the Grail. **This is tragically incongruous since the Grail is, and always has been, associated with learning how to relate to the feminine, how to love her, desire her, and how to live in harmony with her to create a feeling and just world.** It is about the energies of the body *and* the mind, of matter *and* spirit, integrated and channeled through the heart. It is the feminine who gives the king a new body, feeling, heart, laughter, spontaneity, fecundity, sexual power — and mystical illumination.[7] There is no rejection of the body or the feminine: this is the wisdom of the heart and the essence of the Grail. *And this is what the Church rejected once again.*

The Grail stories flourished for fifty years, from 1175 to 1225, and then they ceased to be written. The fountain of inspiration, says medieval scholar, Jesse Weston, "seems suddenly to have run dry.... May it not be that it was because the origin of the Grail.... bore the impress, of a body of thought and idea, which, known by the name of Gnosticism, was already under the Church's ban?" Even as early as 1913 Weston understood that "There is a stream of tradition, running as it were underground, which from time to time rises to the surface, only to be relentlessly suppressed."[8]

The twentieth century discoveries have proven this statement to be true. It could hardly be clearer that the Great Mysteries of death and rebirth surfaced during the High Middle Ages along with the consciousness of our loss of soul and the desire to relate once again with the Sovereign of the Land. Western European consciousness had lost its relationship with Nature and no longer knew how to live in harmony with her laws or how to be the mediator between the cosmos and the earth. It had lost its connection to the spirit dimension of reality, and it no longer honored the feminine source of life. When we remember the depth and beauty of the great rituals of Egyptian spirituality, especially the Sed Festival Rituals, we can see that the Grail King reflects the West's loss of such rituals. But the Grail stories are gifts, like Baba Yaga's threads, to guide us back into these great mysteries. These Grail stories are still alive in Western culture today, and they are calling us to redeem the *whole* knowledge of our deepest potential.

The awakening during the High Middle Ages manifested on so many different levels that many of its goals and accomplishments are yet to be discovered on a scale that could bring about their integration into Western culture. What is important for our purpose is the recognition that it was the underground shaman-mystic-scientist tradition, developed and enriched by Mystic Christianity and its relationship with Islam, that gave birth to this new consciousness in Europe.

There is so much that could be said about each of the manifestations of this renaissance, but my focus is on the Grail journey and the great cathedrals that were built to Our Lady because (1) the Grail clearly delineates the West's loss of the great mysteries of death and rebirth and the labyrinthine journey we must take to find Soul—the lost and exiled Queen of Heaven; and (2) the great cathedrals, especially the cathedral at Chartres, bring into focus Our Lady of Soul who nurtures and gives birth to all those who long for the cosmic fruit and are willing to take the labyrinthine journey to achieve it. **In fact, we will see that Chartres is a living text that celebrates the birth of Christ/Cosmic consciousness and is itself a form of initiation into the mysteries of that consciousness.**

Chartres belonged to the sacred feminine and the mysteries of birth from the beginning. One thousand years before Christianity, the Celts felt the sacredness of this place and their Druid priests created an altar to the Black Madonna who was destined to give birth to a child.[9] The wisdom of the Druids is said to be rooted in the Old Irish (Hibernian) Mysteries whose initiates were poets and visionaries who anticipated the birth of Christ Consciousness. It was to this birth of the higher self that the altar of the Black Madonna was dedicated.

Legend tells us that after the death of Christ, a group of Christians led by Joseph of Arimathea brought the Holy Grail to Chartres and dedicated the sacred ground to the Virgin Mary.[10] The Holy Grail was understood as a form of the feminine, her gift of the sacred fruit of consciousness. The Black Madonna/the Virgin is the soul of the world, perpetually giving birth to the higher, eternal consciousness of the divine. She is the sacred energy of the earth, which is said to reach its highest point at Chartres, and she is the womb that nurtures evolutionary consciousness, love, and light in every individual who seeks her wisdom. At Chartres she gives birth to a son who symbolizes Christ Consciousness.

In the 1940s a French monk presented the idea that the cathedrals built in northern France and dedicated to "Our Lady of Light" (Notre Dame de Lumiere) during the High Middle Ages were strategically located on the ground to replicate the constellation Virgo (the Virgin). The pattern of the Virgo constellation had traditionally been associated with the female, the Earth Goddess of bountifulness—again, she who gives birth to all life. The building of these cathedrals in the pattern of Virgo was a way, says Critchlow, of sacralizing a nation, of creating heaven on earth, of following the Hermetic law of as above, so below.[11]

If the builders did in fact have such a cosmic plan in the construction of these cathedrals dedicated to Our Lady, it would not have been unusual within the tradition of the sacred builders. It is worth pausing for a moment to look more closely at the *builders* or architects of the cathedrals. **Builders were known from earliest times to be initiates of the mysteries. It is said that the initiates of the Hibernian Mysteries were the great builders of the Megalithic structures in the Celtic countries.**[12] **And in Egypt, to be a builder meant following "the path of rebirth through the mother goddess."**[13] There are stories about Solomon being an initiate of the Egyptian mysteries of death and rebirth, that his temple (the First Temple of Judaism) had held the ancient secrets of the builders, and that during the High Middle Ages the Knights Templar went to Jerusalem to retrieve this secret knowledge. While the builders of Chartres are not known by name, the cathedral itself reveals that they were, in fact, great initiates in the mysteries of death and rebirth.

From the megalithic builders to the builders of the cathedrals, there appears to be a continuum of knowledge rooted in the great mysteries and sacred geometry. Nothing was more important to the builders than knowing and understanding the laws of nature—of the earth, the human being, and the cosmos—*so that they could create structures in harmony with those laws*. Critchlow tells us that from megalithic times the square symbolized the stability of the earth and our experience in the physical world; the triangle symbolized the human being "as the harmonizing human consciousness"; and the circle/hexagon symbolized the cosmos.[14] These archetypal forms and their many manifestations continue to exist in cathedrals and temples around the world. *What is so important for us to know is that human consciousness is the mediator between the cosmos and the earth and that the builders had the knowledge of how to enhance this ability to mediate through the geometric structures themselves.*

Those who know the Gothic cathedrals well say that they are designed to awaken the spirit. They are an alembic that is finely tuned to bring about the transformation of human consciousness. They have been called living alchemical texts in stone. In fact, the mysterious Fulcanelli writes in *The Mysteries of the Cathedrals* that the Gothic cathedrals depict the Great Work of Alchemy. In the "Introduction" to Fulcanelli's book Walter Lang states that "It has long been believed that the Gothic cathedrals were secret textbooks of some hidden knowledge;..." This is now known as fact: "the Gothic cathedrals have for seven hundred years offered European man a course of instruction in his own possible evolution."[15]

We now know that this instruction is from the sacred texts of our shaman-mystic-scientist traditions in which the Celts, Egyptians, Jews, Greeks, Christians, Arabs and others have played a vital role. The entire iconography of Chartres is a library of knowledge from the Celtic, Hermetic, Kabbalistic, Christian, Alchemical, and Sufi wisdom of our evolution toward cosmic consciousness. One of the more familiar stories that is depicted in stone at Chartres is the Christian story of paradise lost and paradise regained in the holy of holies of the New Jerusalem, the city of Heaven on Earth. The cathedral itself is a symbol of the New Jerusalem. And throughout the cathedral is depicted the Christian story of the birth of the child — *the holy child who brings a consciousness that can save the world.* These cathedrals are the culmination in stone of our heritage from our ancestors who discovered and kept alive the sacred path to higher consciousness.

I must admit that before I began this research, I had no real knowledge about the Gothic cathedrals — and I am still not quite over the shock and surprise that the sacred streams of knowledge I had been tracking merged and found their magnificent expression in these vast architectural structures of stone and glass. I thought often of how my dreaming mind had taken me to Chartres to show me how our culture had allowed Our Lady, the soul of the world, to be entombed in stone outside the great cathedral, but that she was still alive in nature and perpetually coming into being.

I had simply to stand amazed at my ancestors' journey from the exquisite paintings on stone in the caves of Europe and around the world, the carvings on the vast rock canvases in Africa, the megalithic monuments that also appear around the world, the painting and writing on the stone walls of the pyramids and temples, and finally to the stone and glass of the Gothic cathedrals. *All of these are sacred texts painted, etched, and written in symbol, geometry, and earth/cosmic energies.* They reveal our ancestors' ability to use symbolic language, arithmetic, and geometry, not only to understand the laws of the cosmos but also to co-create with those laws.

These texts reveal our ancestors' vast spiritual experience all the way from their early ability to enter altered states of consciousness and commune with other dimensions of reality to their awareness that the human species is capable of cosmic consciousness. This knowledge and experience, in Critchlow's words, allow them to make "a full commitment to a spiritual reality which is invisible to the material or sensorial world."[16] That full commitment to the spiritual reality they had experienced and could understand both intuitively and logically expressed itself in the creation of small and large civilizations whose earthworks, temples/observatories, rituals, and patterns of behavior initiated and maintained a conscious relationship and balance with that reality. Our ancestors understood that losing this relationship would result in the very wasteland that the Grail stories so vividly depict. The consciousness behind these stories knew what the West had lost — and they knew what had to be done to regain it. *So they created structures for our transformation. In the words of Sir Ronald Fraser, the cathedrals are "an instrument of high initiation."*[17]

The mysteries of these cathedrals dedicated to Our Lady, especially at Chartres, are complex and profoundly interconnected. We must enter those mysteries in our own way and in our own time, but there are a few specific characteristics that at least suggest what might be in store for us. In relation to the continuum of knowledge from the megalithic builders to the architects of Chartres, Gordon Strachan in *Chartres: Sacred Geometry, Sacred Space* tells of a legend that on this same sacred site there was a dolmen dating back to megalithic times around 2000 BCE. Strachan states that there is no evidence that a dolmen was ever there, yet other scholars take it for granted that megalithic structures clearly exist within the structure of Chartres. And Strachan himself says that in spite of this lack of evidence from his perspective, "there are certain anomalies in the Gothic cathedral which are strangely reminiscent of megalithic monuments, particularly Stonehenge." He mentions the orientation, the solar and lunar cycles, and the proportional measurements of the two monuments.[18]

Strachan also explains how the cathedral's spires symbolize the sun and the moon and are two complementary cycles that are "ingeniously built into the fabric of the design in the form of two slightly different axes, which run the length of the building, creating as it were, a *vibrato* effect on the resonance of the Cathedral." He also tells us that "certain shapes and volumes set up certain vibratory patterns" that profoundly affect the human mind and body.[19] And Louis Charpentier, in his book, *The Mysteries of Chartres Cathedral*, writes an entire chapter on how the "geometry of the plan of elevation of the cathedral" is musical.[20]

Fraser, in his discussion of Charpentier's book, asks who were these builders who knew "how to balance weight and counterweight, to arrange masses of stone so that the building vibrates to the tap of a fingernail?" Everything, he tells us, is designed to have an effect on the human being. Chartres, according to Fraser, is like an ancient megalithic menhir: it is built on the earth where the earth energies are powerful and can be drawn upward through the structure of the cathedral while the spires of the cathedral can pull down power from the sky. "One can think of the cathedral as such a stone."[21]

At least a few words need to be said about the light in the cathedral. It is said that people are usually impressed with the quality of light, how it seems to emerge out of the darkness. Charpentier states that "The stained-glass window and true gothic are inseparable. Like true gothic, the window is a product of high science, a product of alchemy." The Alchemists add something else that is difficult for the West to understand: they say that the "staining" that creates colors is a result of allowing the Spiritus Mundi to flow through the material. This is an integral part of the Great Work of Alchemy—the conscious integration of the spirit of the universe into matter. Charpentier says that around 1140 "when all the windows at Chartres were in place, the 'source' of stained glass began to dry up, probably through the Adept's disappearance, his work being finished."[22]

Critchlow explains how, with the use of sacred geometry, the cathedral was constructed according to cosmic laws in proportion to the human body. This creates the possibility for the human being to experience a sense of eternity, timelessness, spacelessness, unity and grandeur—that is, to experience the depth within and without. And in this way, says Critchlow, we can begin to experience our own sacredness. Once we experience our own sacredness, he says, we are much less likely to destroy life. The cathedral is designed to open us up.[23] It is the *Opener of the Way*.

Beginning around 1000 CE, even before the final construction of the cathedral at Chartres between 1194 and 1250 CE, much of the wisdom that would be expressed in the new architecture was already being taught and experienced. René Querido in *The Golden Age of Chartres: The Teachings of a Mystery School and the Eternal Feminine,* says that the master teachers at the famous School of Chartres sought to bring together in their teaching the major streams of thought that from early on had met and mingled at Chartres. There was, he says, "an ancient Greek stream penetrated with Platonism" that brought "a profound knowledge and practice of esoteric Christianity." For two hundred years, Querido tells us, the master teachers of Chartres "sought to reconcile Celtic and Greek mysteries, Arthurian and Grail streams, with a Christianity based not on belief but on the possibility of man's direct experience of Christ and the spiritual hierarchies."[24]

"Chartres," he says, "was the spiritual meeting point of many streams so that it might become an active center from which a special message would ring out." **At the core of all these streams was the knowledge of Christ Consciousness and how to achieve it. And this is why, says Querido, the emphasis at Chartres has always been on birth, "the birth of the higher self."** This birth of higher consciousness was called the **Mary Mysteries**. The child that is birthed at Chartres "is the potential in each of us of the higher self seeking to emerge so that we may become co-creators with the gods. This is the image of the Virgin bearing the Child that imbues the entire cathedral."[25]

Querido tells us that Chartres was a healing center that focused on three crucial questions: (1) How do we heal the soul? (2) How do we heal our culture? (3) How do we heal our planet?[26] As these questions reveal, the School of Chartres had the same goal as all of the "initiatory wisdom streams" throughout the culture—to heal the soul, our culture, and the planet. And these were the very questions that my own journey had forced me to ask again and again.

Yet I had known very little about the actual history of Chartres. It was not until my friend Anne Baring had been invited in July of 2014 to the New Chartres Academy to present seminars on her recently published book, *The Dream of the Cosmos: A Quest for the Soul*, that my new awareness began to unfold. I had not known that a New Chartres Academy/School had been established by Ubiquity University with the aim of opening once again "the wellspring of wisdom developed by the wise ones of civilizations long past."[27] Anne and I talked on the phone when she returned from Chartres and she gave me the titles of some of the books I have used here.

This new information resulted in one of those amazing moments in the labyrinthine journey when major pieces of the puzzle fall into place. In my dream of Chartres so long ago I had seen the miracle of Our Lady, the Soul of the world, perpetually coming into being, and I had realized that it was this birth that could heal civilization. And now I was learning that the very heart of Chartres had always been about this miraculous birth.

It was especially appropriate that Anne had been invited to present seminars at the New Chartres Academy since *The Dream of the Cosmos* is focused on the same three questions asked by all the ancient "initiatory wisdom streams": how do we heal the soul, our culture, and our planet? Anne's life work is rooted in her own visionary experiences which initiated *A Quest for the Soul* that has lasted a lifetime. She would find that it was our loss of connection to Soul, the feminine **heart** of the divine, that has held back our planetary evolution—the achievement of Christ/Cosmic Consciousness, or, in the words of the Alchemists, *The Great Work*. As we face the resulting "collective insanity" that is spreading around the world, Anne's *The Dream of the Cosmos* provides an understanding of this loss and how we can get back on track.[28]

The master teachers at Chartres made it clear that these questions are answered by entering a path of *direct inner experience* where "we discover our inherent harmony with the cosmos, with the earth, and with the deepest core of our being." Symbolically speaking, they sought and experienced the fruit from the Cosmic Tree. These questions, says Querido, "are exceedingly alive today, and their answer can be found at Chartres." Querido tells us that during the two hundred years that the School of Chartres was blessed with these great teachers, they and their students "practiced a path of initiation leading to an active communion with the world of the spirit." These masters were intellectual giants, but they were not content with knowledge alone. While they taught the Seven Liberal Arts as a path of inner development, they knew that healing could only be achieved through the direct inner experience of soul–gnosis. Everything at Chartres, he says, was rooted in the mysteries of gnosis–the birth of the new consciousness, the new human being. And it was the path of these great masters that paved the way for the full manifestation of the cathedral of Chartres.[29]

It is surprising that at the time of the actual building of the cathedrals to Our Lady there was complete cooperation among the clergy, the political leaders, and the people. Critchlow says that the entire community was involved in the building of Chartres, which was completed in twenty-six years. It was thought, he says, to be a great blessing to build a sacred place for the Virgin.[30] But the building in France alone of eighty cathedrals and many large churches and abbeys in less than a hundred years required more than cooperation; it required organization, vision, money, master craftsmen, and *builders*.[31] It is known that during the early phases of building, captured Islamic masons were brought back to Europe for their expertise.[32] Most people assume that the only organization capable of such projects was the Knights Templar.

What gave birth to such intense and passionate creativity during those years between 1000 and 1300 CE? Critchlow says that it was "a matter of life or death." It was, he says, "a matter of civilization."[33] As I watched the DVD on Chartres and heard Critchlow say "a matter of civilization," I paused the DVD. The power of this moment was profound and certainly emotional as I thought again of my dream of Chartres so many years ago in which I knew that what I was seeing *could heal civilization*. And what had I seen?

> *As I walk away from the cathedral, I witness a miracle taking place in nature. On both sides of the road there is a continuous line of large silver wombs in the earth, each one opening to the road as I pass by and each one giving birth to the most exquisitely beautiful silver woman. She is "Our Lady" – the soul of the world. Her birth is like a graceful dance as her head and arms emerge out of the wombs and onto the road I am traveling.* **I realize that I am experiencing the miracle that can heal our civilization.**

I would not know for decades that, in fact, the great Cathedral of Chartres did hold within its history *the miracle that can heal our civilization*. And, just like the Grail legend, I was shown where I was on my labyrinthine journey toward healing: my rational mind was severed from my visionary mind. My rational self had found no answer for healing in the Christianity of my culture, for we had constructed a sarcophagus for Our Lady and made an unseemly attachment of her tomb to the front of the great cathedral. **When the Church repressed the deeper shaman-mystic knowledge that the Christ was a symbol of the achievement of Christ/Cosmic Consciousness, we lost Our Lady, the womb of our becoming.**

We cannot achieve Cosmic consciousness if we project it out onto someone else: we have to know that our work is not just to follow the Christ but to become the Christ. When I was so desperate to find spiritual meaning in my life, I experienced in a great dream the wombs in nature at Chartres. And so many years later I would discover that the cathedral itself is a great alembic or womb. This dream showed me that the mystery of birth is still alive at Chartres—and that the healing of self, culture, and planet would come with the birth of our higher self—with the birth of soul—that is, with the birth of our own Christ Consciousness.

Bucke knew this through his own experience in the 1800s. "The Saviour of man," says Bucke, "is Cosmic Consciousness—in Paul's language—the Christ."³⁴ The early mystics who initiated Christianity knew this—as did the shaman-mystic tradition that kept this knowledge alive. Bucke discovered that it was precisely those people who had had such an experience who not only had created the world's great religions but *whose consciousness had seeded modern civilization*.³⁵

Since the source of all religions is rooted in a higher consciousness, it is clear that those who had achieved this consciousness would want the rest of us to be able to experience it as well. *They would have no need to be worshiped*; they would simply want to show us the path toward this consciousness. This has been the aim of the initiators of all religions. But when the path to higher consciousness is taken over by institutions/churches, men almost always construct doctrines—rules and regulations—to control our behavior and place us in a subordinate position to their structures. We are told we must believe, not experience— and the techniques for achieving higher consciousness are repressed.

However, the great cathedrals of the High Middle Ages seem to have dissolved this repression effortlessly as they appeared on the French landscape in alignment with the constellation Virgo as "Our Lady of Light," the soul of the world, returned to birth the new consciousness. These shaman-mystic builders were Masters of Light who knew how to construct magnificent alembics for the distillation of our darkness into the light of cosmic consciousness. For two hundred years at the School of Chartres the master teachers "practiced a path of initiation" that opened the world of spirit for themselves and their students.³⁶ While they engaged the intellect, the ultimate goal was gnosis—direct experience of Christ/ Cosmic consciousness.

The labyrinth was a symbol of this path. I had not known that twenty-two of the eighty Gothic cathedrals built in France had labyrinths. I had only known about the one at Chartres. Unfortunately, many of these beautiful labyrinths were later destroyed by the Church clergy during the seventeenth and eighteenth centuries,³⁷ but the labyrinth at Chartres remains today in all its beauty and symbolic significance. As we have seen, the labyrinth reaches deep into our ancient spiritual history as a symbol of our individual path to higher consciousness. As we enter

Chartres Cathedral, a great womb itself, we immediately see yet another womb: the great labyrinth. The now retired Rector of the Cathedral, Chanoine François Legaux, says that the labyrinth has the same number of stones as the days an infant spends in the mother's womb. It is, he says, symbolic of the Earth Womb, our second womb that gives birth to our higher consciousness.[38] As we walk the labyrinth of our life journey and finally arrive at the center of our new birth, we have also arrived at the center of the rose window, which is exactly the same size as the labyrinth. As we look up, we see that Our Lady is at the center of the rose holding the newborn child—our new consciousness.

What happened during the High Middle Ages is one of the most phenomenal events in the history of the West. Christianity began, as do all great religions, in an experience of higher consciousness—gnosis. This is precisely what the Church had denied and what it had spent so much of its time, energy, and money to destroy—and seven hundred years later, this knowledge emerged like the great phoenix out of the fire of its destruction within the very heart of the Church itself! Everything at Chartres, says Querido, was rooted in the mysteries of gnosis—the birth of the new consciousness, the new human being.[39]

Here at last we see the true story of Christianity. Scholars today often say that there were many different streams of early Christianity, and this is true. But that does not prevent us from knowing that the *origin of Christianity*, as in all religions, was in gnosis—direct experience of a higher consciousness. And it is *this consciousness* that is the Savior of our species. It is this consciousness that gives us the answers to the healing of soul, culture, and planet.

But Chartres, as we have seen, is not the story of Christianity alone. For Chartres is the heart of all the West's true stories from our shaman-mystic-scientist past as it appeared in the megalithic monuments and continued to develop through the Egyptian mysteries, the Hebrew First Temple shaman-mystic tradition, the later Jewish/Christian mysteries, the Celtic and Greek mysteries, the Grail mysteries, and the Islamic/Sufi alchemical mystical tradition. Clearly, the story of our journey to Cosmic consciousness is universal. Everyone who has experienced this higher consciousness of the heart, even for a moment, knows that the living center of all sacred traditions is One. Chartres is a magnificent symbol that continues to radiate this message to the world.

The message of our potential for cosmic consciousness so beautifully present at Chartres is a message about our wholeness. For here we see the development of our intellect *and* our soul, of the masculine and the feminine. The cathedral is a celebration of the West's rediscovery of soul: Jesus is joined once again with Mary, his beloved. For, as we have seen, Jesus had always walked with Mary, his mother, his sister, and Mary of Magdala, who is his beloved. Here is Christ Consciousness achieved in the wholeness of the sacred marriage. When this happens, there is no division between the material and the immaterial world: each partakes of and participates in the other. In this state of consciousness, the Light of Our Lady and the Light of Christ are One and inherent in this world.

What happened to this creative energy of the High Middle Ages (1000–1300 CE) as it appeared to diminish is a complex story that is still being discovered and the details are beyond the scope of our purpose. What we do know is that it continued to live underground in spite of the overwhelming reaction of the Church. We will see how the evolutionary ideas of heart consciousness and of a love that dissolves all dualisms will reemerge during what is called the Northern Renaissance or the Rosicrucian Enlightenment.

However, it was during this same time period of approximately two hundred years that the Church organized the devastating Crusades to conquer the Holy Land. In the First Crusade, German Jews were massacred in the Rhineland under the belief that "the battle against Christ's enemies ought to begin at home."[40] Some historians estimate that only about one in twenty crusaders actually survived long enough to see the Holy Land, and that hundreds of thousands of men, women, and children were slaughtered. **And it was also during this same time period that the Church reacted against the Renaissance of the High Middle Ages and brutally destroyed all other forms of resistance to the Church:**

(1) The Grail stories were written for about fifty years (from 1175 to 1225 CE) to the great enthusiasm of all Europe. Then, as mentioned above, (a) the Grail hero became Christianized, and (b) there was a complete cessation of the stories. The hand of the Church was clear in both cases. (2) In southern France between 1209 and 1229 CE, the Church, with the aid of French leaders, slaughtered the Cathars by the tens of thousands. After 1229 CE the Inquisition was established to kill any remaining Cathars as well as any other group not in agreement with the Church. Between 1243 and 1244 CE the Cathar fortress of Montsegur was attacked and the remaining Cathars were brutally massacred. The sophistication, independence, wealth, and creativity of this "heretical" culture were destroyed. This has been called the first European genocide. (3) In the early 1300s the French king, with the help of a reluctant pope, destroyed the Knights Templar. (4) During the 1400s the Church would initiate the witch trials that would last for centuries.

Chapter Thirty-Two

>―↔―О―↔―<

The Italian Renaissance
The Second Wave of the Renaissance
(1460–1527 CE)

The newly discovered Corpus Hermeticum – texts about direct inner experience – was at the very heart of the Italian Renaissance.

In spite of this kind of repression, the shaman-mystic tradition did survive underground, and was ignited during the Italian Renaissance by ancient manuscripts from Macedonia and Byzantium. In *Giordano Bruno and the Hermetic Tradition*, Frances Yates tells us that around 1460 one of the agents that Cosimo de' Medici had employed to collect manuscripts arrived in Florence from Macedonia with a manuscript that contained a copy of the *Corpus Hermeticum*. These Hermetic texts embodied precisely the kind of teaching the Church had hoped to destroy. *The texts were about gnosis – direct inner experience, and it was this discovery that was at the very heart of the Italian Renaissance.*[1]

With the fall of Constantinople in 1453, Byzantine scholars and treasured Greek manuscripts began to flow into Florence, but Cosimo insisted that Marsilio Ficino translate the Hermetic texts first, even before the works of Plato and Plotinus. Ficino finished the translations of the Hermetic texts around 1464 before Cosimo died.² Only then did he translate the works of Plato, Plotinus, and other Greek writers, all of which were clearly influenced by Ficino's previous translations of the Hermetic texts. Ficino viewed the Hermetic texts not only as texts about gnosis but of ancient Egyptian gnosis. Hermes Trismegistus was thought to be the author of these texts and, in Ficino's mind, the source of the ancient wisdom tradition that led directly to Plato.³

When in 1614 the Greek scholar Isaac Casaubon dated the Hermetic texts as having been written during Christian times, it was thought that he eliminated the possibility that they were ancient texts from Egypt. Many scholars believed that this information shattered the very impetus of the Italian Renaissance. There were those, however, who simply ignored the dating because they were convinced that the knowledge in the texts did in fact come from ancient Egypt. Yates puts it in different language: "there were many who ignored it, or refused to believe it, and clung obstinately to the old obsessions."⁴

However, present research such as Alison Roberts' and Jeremy Naydler's reopens the question. Roberts' detailed study of Egyptian symbols, temple paintings of rituals, and papyri on the death and rebirth rituals and Naydler's translation of the death and rebirth mysteries in the pyramid texts present us with new evidence of the Egyptian influence in Hellenistic Egypt. So extensive is this evidence that Roberts is able to state that "now we begin to see that it was Casaubon and his followers who were the deluded ones, dazzled by the Greek philosophical style and unaware of the ancient Egyptian death and rebirth mysteries which were sometimes obscured by later non-Egyptian modes of expression."⁵

So we can be grateful that there were those during the Italian Renaissance and later who valued the Hermetic texts as reflecting authentic Egyptian shaman-mystic experience. Their ability to value these texts must surely have been rooted in their own shaman-mystic experience as well as in the achievements of the first renaissance during the High Middle Ages. While later scholars negated the authenticity of the Hermetic texts and the reality those texts reflected, the tradition not only survived but flourished during what Yates calls the Rosicrucian Enlightenment during the late 1500s and early 1600s.

While it is true that the Hermetic texts were at the heart of the Italian Renaissance, this great awakening could never have occurred without the economic and political changes that had been taking place in Northern Italy. It is well known that even during the late Middle Ages, the cities of Florence, Venice, and Milan in northern Italy were important trading centers that connected them to the Byzantine Empire and the surrounding Muslim cultures that included the old Persian culture. The Medicis in Florence were not only powerful bankers but capable politicians whose wealth and connections to the pope and Rome made Florence the strongest center for trade, finance, art, and ideas. Contact with other cultures, some beyond the reach of the Church, and the wealth that supported a sense of independence, nurtured new ways of perceiving life and the individual's role in it.

But there were also other reasons that had deeper, less perceptible roots. We have seen how the modern mind can be affected by the soul experience of our Stone Age ancestors when an American therapist's recurring dream of mantis awakened her to the "creative substratum" within her own psyche. Jung understood that our psyche is millions of years old and that we carry within us the history of our evolution. And, when Gimbutas discovered the previously unknown symbolic system of Neolithic Old Europe, she too realized that the Western psyche still carried the imprint of its life-sustaining energy.

Since we now know that our human experience lives deep within the psyche while more recent events lie just beneath the surface of individual consciousness, it is appropriate to explore historical movements as events in the labyrinthine journey of our conscious evolution—or regression. We have observed the tendency of the human psyche to fulfill its potential wholeness, but we have also observed the tendency to repeatedly destroy all that has been achieved. The Jesus of the Nag Hammadi texts would explain this destruction as the reaction of those among us who have not yet brought forth what is within them.

During the Italian Renaissance, there was an explosion of soul energy that attempted to discover and manifest its true self, but there was also an equal force from the Church and State that sought to destroy it. Since European consciousness had been largely shaped by the Church from the fourth century, let's quickly review some of the major events of the European experience since the establishment of the Church of Rome. We have already seen how the violence and censorship of the Church forced the intellectual and spiritual genius of Europe to go underground or to escape to Persian and Muslim cities in order to survive and continue their development. And we have also seen how Europe lay in darkness for hundreds of years. All of the dreams, aspirations, stories, and myths, in the words of Godwin, had been "subsumed" by the "male-dominated Church of Rome" into "its own grand scheme."[6]

European consciousness had lost its soul stories: it had been severed from "Our Lady," its visionary partner and soul. And *this* had left Europe in a spiritual wasteland. Thankfully, the Celtic countries, deeply rooted in the Hibernian Mysteries, had been able to maintain their own stories through an oral tradition of poetry and music that had been kept alive by their bards. We know that it was these stories that inspired the Grail Quest of the High Middle Ages. Their stories had traveled from court to court, from Ireland to Wales, south to Brittany and west to France and Germany. And the stories were certainly known in northern Italy as well as in Cordova and the Holy Lands. These stories were told, retold, and written in creatively different narratives, but they all became *the one true leaven*, that is, the wisdom that heals the soul. These stories were written for fifty years, beginning in 1175 and ending in 1225. It is assumed they were silenced by the Church. However, their reverberations remained imprinted on the European psyche.

Around the same time, from 1000–1200 CE, the master teachers and students at Chartres worked with these same social and spiritual themes in their effort to fulfill the Grail Mystery within themselves and their culture. **One of the great gifts of the Chartres masters is their integration of Europe's soul stories**: they honored the ancient Celtic Druids' dedication of the land of Chartres to the Sacred Feminine in the form of the Black Madonna, and they allowed this feminine energy from deep within the soil of Chartres to guide them in the development of the **Mary Mysteries, the birth of Christ Consciousness.** They integrated the Celtic soul stories of Arthur and the Round Table and the new code of masculine behavior along with the stories of the Grail Quest, and they integrated the Greek mysteries with the Platonic and Aristotelian streams of knowledge.[7]

In addition, they integrated the great wave of Platonic, Mystic Christianity that had originated in Athens through the Christian initiate, Dionysius the Areopagite. In 48 CE, when he was thirty-eight years old, Dionysius heard the apostle Paul speak in Athens. It is said that "Paul arrived in Athens like a fiery spirit." Since Dionysius had been initiated into the Mysteries at Eleusis, Ephesus, and Heliopolis ("the place of the light"), he understood Paul's Damascus experience of the Christ as light and love. Paul and Dionysius became intimate friends and co-workers, Paul in the Mediterranean and Dionysius in Athens.[8]

It was in Athens that Dionysius founded "the esoteric school of Paul," which was a center for esoteric wisdom and training in *the heart-centered consciousness of Christianity*.[9] Similar teachings would exist elsewhere as the *secret tradition* until the Church forced it underground. These particular teachings of Dionysius the Areopagite were transmitted orally by initiates through the centuries until the sixth century when the teachings were written down in Greek. Each student/teacher was called Dionysius because each taught what the original Dionysius had taught. These teachers would later be referred to as pseudo-Dionysius.[10] What is important for our purpose is that these teachings moved through western Europe and into Paris where on Montmartre a school was founded on the teachings of Dionysius the Areopagite. Querido tells us that this school was still active during the ninth century when the writings of Dionysius the Areopagite were translated from Greek into Latin. This tradition found its way from Montmartre to Chartres where it was received and understood by the great masters of Chartres. **These masters, says Querido, knew that they were sowing the seeds for what might take centuries to come into being.**[11]

And, as discussed earlier, the very architecture of the cathedral at Chartres holds the wisdom of the ancient Egyptian death and rebirth mysteries along with the Alchemical and Sufi traditions. **What we have at Chartres is the sacred text of the European soul—and this text remains imprinted on the European psyche.** Most of this wisdom remains below consciousness, but it has not been lost. During each wave of the renaissance, this consciousness would surface in unexpected ways.

If we assume that the great period of awakened consciousness during the High Middle Ages ended around 1300 with the violent reactions of the Church, then it would only be about one hundred and sixty years later that the Italian Renaissance began to flourish. But something happened during the 1300s that may well have shaped that awakening. And this was the vast sweep of the Bubonic Plague that ravaged Europe and Asia during that century. Some writers speculate that the plague killed one-half to one-third of the population. It brought many social, economic, political, and religious changes, especially in Italy. I do not want to focus on the consequences of this nightmare other than simply to speculate on how this confrontation with death on such a massive scale might have shaped the European mind to more deeply value life in the material world. The Church had attempted to focus the mind on the other world and to denigrate the world of matter. This was about to change.

There was a gradual but decisive shift from the divine and the world to come to the human and this world. While the poet and philosopher Petrarch is usually credited with this shift, it was a perspective whose time had come. Petrarch lived during the 1300s, and, while he remained spiritual and loyal to the Church, it was his introduction to the classical literature the Church had banned that awakened him to the limitations of his own time and place in history. He became an ardent collector and scholar of classical literature. The more he read about the classical world, the more convinced he became that *the human being is creative* and fully capable of achieving such a world once again. This subtle shift from thinking solely within the "grand scheme" of the Church to other possibilities would later be called *humanism* and would be considered a *bridge* from the Middle Ages to the Italian Renaissance. As knowledge of the classical world became more available, scholars, poets, philosophers, scientists, artists, musicians, and architects crossed that bridge into a world of magnificent discovery and creativity.

We can clearly see in Petrarch the emerging image of the creative power *in the individual*. And it is especially important to know that Petrarch's own creativity, like Dante's before him, was inspired and guided by the image of a woman he loved. While Petrarch's Laura, again like Dante's Beatrice, was a real woman, he only knew her from afar. Yet she became the symbol of the Soul that inspired in Petrarch the depths of love. The illuminating presence of Beatrice for Dante and Laura for Petrarch continues the thread of love that was developed during the High Middle Ages. While Laura inspired the joy of ideal love, she also inspired desire and anguish in the very real human heart of the poet.

There is certainly a high degree of irony in the fact that Petrarch's work *for* the Church allowed him to travel throughout Italy and most of Europe where he could search for classical texts that had survived the Church's purge of that world centuries earlier. In this way, he was able to discover the intellectual and spiritual world that had existed, and he never doubted that this world could coexist with Christianity.

This shift to human creativity—and even the sense of individual divinity, while often still within the framework of the Christian myth, continues throughout the Italian Renaissance. In Michelangelo's painting of *The Birth of Adam* on the ceiling of the Sistine Chapel in Rome, the divine creativity of God is being *given* to Adam in a single touch of the finger. Michelangelo also captures the growing focus on the human being in his larger-than-life nude statue of *David* who is a surprising celebration of both the beauty of the human body and its readiness to confront the Goliath of life with his simple sling-shot. The concentrated focus in David's eyes and the strength in his body and hands elicit admiration and confidence in his ability to create his world. It is difficult for us today to realize just how much energy and genius it would take to release the European mind from the exclusive images of the Christian Church.

However, the images of the Renaissance artist would depend to some degree on whether the Church or an independently wealthy family had commissioned the art. For example, earlier than the works of Michelangelo mentioned above are Botticelli's *The Birth of Venus* and *Primavera (Spring)*. Both were commissioned by the wealthy Medici family and both are outside the framework of the Church and within the world of classical mythology. Both paintings celebrate the beauty and sensuousness of the female body and even of nature herself. And both celebrate divine beauty and illumination in the tradition of Dante's Beatrice or Petrarch's Laura.

The major myth of the Church, of course, is the birth of Christ, the savior of the world. As we have seen, the Church identifies this event as a singular historical event in time and space, but Mystic Christianity understands the event as the announcement by spirit to consciousness that the individual has conceived and will give birth to Christ/Cosmic Consciousness. Paintings of the Annunciation during both the Middle Ages and the Italian Renaissance use the Church myth but, at the same time, they often reveal the deeper myth of the soul.

As we have seen, it was this myth of the soul that had flowered at Chartres. It was the sacred "birth of the higher self," says Querido, "that imbues the entire cathedral."[12] Since this soul myth had been so potently activated during the High Middle Ages, the archetypal structure of the story itself could ignite in the artist, consciously or unconsciously, a deeper wisdom that often manifested in the work of art.

Artists were obviously captivated with the theme of Mary, a human being, suddenly confronted with the presence of divine consciousness. She is usually startled and sometimes even fearful or resistant in the presence of such a force. As this divine consciousness appears before Mary in the form of the angel Gabriel, their eyes lock into an intense, concentrated gaze. This divine intensity is not only portrayed in the conscious, visual connection, but it is often portrayed in golden light streaming from the cosmos into Mary.

In Simone Martini's painting of *The Annunciation* during the 1300s, still the Middle Ages, the entire scene is illuminated with the golden light of cosmic consciousness. Everything is imbued with this light, yet there are also two streams of light that flow into Mary from the dove, the Holy Spirit, and from the angel Gabriel's golden words that can be seen emanating from the cosmic Mind of Gabriel and flowing into the human consciousness of Mary. The golden light enters Mary as the consciousness that she will give birth to a child, the savior of the world.

This theme persists during the Italian Renaissance. During the 1400s one of Fra Angelico's paintings of the Annunciation depicts Mary's momentous encounter with divine consciousness in a simpler setting but retains the intense focus between the angel and Mary. In other paintings of the Annunciation, he depicts a cosmic stream of light flowing into Mary, and sometimes he shows the golden light of language flowing from Gabriel's mind into the consciousness of Mary. **All the Annunciation paintings, however, reflect the awareness of a divine presence that suddenly appears to human consciousness. We cannot ignore the possibility that this theme is the same as that celebrated at Chartres: the birth of Christ Consciousness within the individual.**

In fact, we know that the return of this sacred wisdom was at the heart of the Italian Renaissance. The seeds of this wisdom were sown not only in the Grail legends and at Chartres during the High Middle Ages, but also in the translated alchemical texts and the Jewish Zohar. And the Beguine mystics, along with the troubadours and the Cathars in southern France, developed the path of love that heals, transforms, and unites the individual heart with the heart of the world. **All of these seeds were germinating just below the surface of consciousness.**

And in the outer world, what the Church had attempted to destroy during the fourth century returns with renewed strength. It is, in fact, the so-called *pagan* world, the intellectual and spiritual genius of Europe, that returns. We have already seen how Petrarch collected every classical text he could find and discovered in these texts a world he wished to recreate in his own time. Gemistus Pletho, a Greek scholar from Byzantium, was also influential in the return of classical studies to Italy. He reintroduced Plato to Europe, met Cosimo de' Medici and encouraged him to found a new Platonic Academy in Florence. Marsilio Ficino was placed at its head, and it was here that Ficino translated the *Corpus Hermeticum* that had arrived in Florence around 1460 and later the works of Plato, Plotinus, and the Neoplatonists. With these works, European consciousness was confronted with the shaman-mystic tradition of the Egyptian death and rebirth mysteries, the Presocratic philosophers, Alchemy, and Kabbalah.

But, of course, there is more to the story of recovery. Much more. And it is this part of the story that Europe loves to forget. Let's imagine for a moment that we are looking at a map of Italy during the time of the Italian Renaissance. We see that it is a long southern peninsula of Europe that juts down into the Mediterranean Sea with the Adriatic Sea to the east and the Tyrrhenian Sea to the west. Greece lies to the southeast, and east of Greece between the Aegean Sea and the Black Sea is Byzantium, what is now Istanbul. As our vision moves south from Byzantium through Anatolia, we see that a semicircle is formed around Italy by the remarkable cultures of Persia (now Islamic), Baghdad, Mecca, and west to Cairo, Alexandria, and Cordova. Except for Byzantium, these are all Islamic cultures whose Golden Age was between the eighth and thirteenth centuries. Italy is right in the middle of the great Byzantine and Muslim cultures. **Without these cultures, the Italian Renaissance could not have existed.**

It is said that the Islamic Empire was "the first truly universal civilization," which attracted "the Chinese, the Indians, the people of the Middle East and North Africa, black Africans, and white Europeans." Muslim, Jewish, and Christian intellectuals, including women and men, pursued knowledge through rational, scientific, and spiritual discourse. Since these scholars and philosophers had freedom of speech and thought, they too developed a form of *humanism* in their search for "knowledge, meaning and values."[13] These cultures had a profound influence on Europe during the Middle Ages and the Italian Renaissance. Unfortunately, there has been an unhealthy tendency in European thought to ignore its debt to these cultures.

The other culture, not Islamic, that was decisive in the development of the Italian Renaissance was, of course, Byzantium. According to Judith Herrin in *Byzantium: The Surprising Life of a Medieval Empire,* Europe also failed in acknowledging the debt it owed Byzantium. Her book delineates this debt. **The "modern western world,"** she says, **"which developed from Europe, could not have existed had it not been shielded and inspired by what happened further to the east in Byzantium."**[14] We need to know just what did happen in this Eastern Empire.

It was an old civilization, says Herrin, one that had lasted a thousand years during which it made its influence felt in Western Europe, the Balkans, and the eastern Mediterranean. It had been founded by Greeks from Megara in 667 BCE, and what would be especially important for the Italian Renaissance, it never censored its roots in the so-called *pagan* world of ancient Greece and Rome. Later, in 330 CE, when Constantine made Byzantium the new capital of the Roman Empire, it would adopt Christian ideas, but as an old, well-established culture, it was able to maintain and nurture its ancient identity and, at the same time, integrate the new Christian beliefs. While it had its flaws as all empires do, says Herrin, it "never developed an Inquisition and generally avoided burning people at the stake."[15]

The roots of the culture were embedded in the Greek world, its language, and its intellectual and spiritual accomplishments. "Byzantium's imperial identity was strengthened by a linguistic continuity that linked its medieval scholars back to ancient Greek culture, and encouraged them to preserve texts by major philosophers, mathematicians, astronomers, geographers, historians and doctors by copying, editing and commenting on them."[16]

They valued Homer's *Iliad* and *Odyssey*, and they "produced the first critical editions" of his poems. The Greek plays and speeches were studied and committed to memory "by generations of schoolchildren." They also studied and learned the dialogues of Plato. In these ways, "A strong element of ancient pagan wisdom was incorporated into Byzantium."[17] Not only were the Byzantines able to bring to Italy the actual well-preserved classical texts with commentaries, many were able to arrive in Italy with these living texts held within their own memories. And come they did with the wisdom that Italy needed most.

It was after Byzantium was sacked and pillaged by the Fourth Crusade in 1204 that many fled to Italy. During the 1300s Byzantine teachers of Greek were given positions in Italian universities where the teachers also lectured on Plato, whose work was basically unknown, and with their students, they translated classical works. Pletho, mentioned earlier, was one of these influential scholars.[18] And again, after the Byzantine Empire fell to the Ottoman Turks in 1453, a flood of scholars, artists, scientists, mathematicians, philosophers, poets, architects, and craftsmen came to Europe.

It appears, however, that this knowledge of the ancient world was desired and accepted, as well as resisted and devalued. While the Islamic world and Byzantium gave Italy much of what it needed to awaken from the controlled worldview of the Church, Europe often looked upon its benefactors as inferior. Herrin speaks of a "clear line of systematic hostility" and "a western antagonism to Byzantium" that has existed from the eighth century onward.[19]

The reasons for this are not entirely clear. Was it that the daughters as well as the sons of ruling families in Byzantium were educated and that women could participate "in the highest levels of society," or was it that their classical training, in Herrin's words, "penetrated every part of the empire across the centuries" and this allowed the Byzantines to be associated with *pagans* and the pre-Christian world? As late as the 1500s Erasmus noted that "an aptitude for Greek excited suspicion in the Church."[20] Europe, says Herrin, accepted the scholarship and achievements of Byzantium "with the same sense of superiority" that was evident in the pillaging of the city by the Crusaders in 1204. "The West's gain was not a measure of Byzantium's contribution but further evidence of its intrinsic inferiority."[21]

This disturbing observation must be taken seriously since the same can be said about Europe's attitude toward the debt it owes to Persia and the Muslim world. As I said earlier, these are debts that Europe loves to forget. Since we have concerned ourselves throughout this book with what has decayed in our culture, we need to question the possible cause for such a response.

Unfortunately, even today, superiority and privilege are deeply embedded in Western consciousness. These characteristics allow taking from others without respect or gratitude, and they are always symptoms of failed development. There can be many reasons for such failure, but a significant reason, in this case, is the fact that for centuries Europe was a brutally censored culture. The Church programmed the European mind to believe in the superiority of Christian culture, and it demeaned and destroyed the ancient spiritual paths of inner development.

The Church denied our most sacred heritage: the knowledge of our divinity and creativity. This was the heritage that could heal Europe—the very heritage that the Renaissance scholars and artists were now rediscovering. But it would take time to heal, and time was not a gift that Europe would receive.

Of course, we know that not all Europe was unconscious and ungrateful.

So, on the one hand, we have to recognize that the severe and violent censorship of the Church impaired the capacity of many to experience gratitude for the breadth of Persian and Islamic scholarship, the power and beauty of their art, and the depths of their spiritual experience. Nor could the European "Soul clap its hands and sing" or sail "To the holy city of Byzantium" to contemplate "Monuments of unageing intellect" or to learn "Of what is past, or passing, or to come."[22]

But, on the other hand, there were those who could—and did. The return of the classical world, profoundly enriched by the earlier Golden Age of Persian and Islamic cultures, and still alive in the memory of the Byzantines, ignited the beginnings of a dramatic transformation in the consciousness of those willing and able to receive it. And, as mentioned earlier, the translation, printing, and study of the works of Plato, the Neoplatonists, and the Hermetic texts at the new Academy in Florence marked the return of the shaman-mystic-scientist tradition—**a tradition of direct inner experience.**

And it was this that the European mind so needed to heal the wounds of censorship and denial. This new awareness drew to itself other aspects of the underground tradition, such as Kabbalah while Alchemy and various other forms of Gnosticism were just about to surface. In *The Dream of the Cosmos*, Baring tells us that Kabbalah "flourished briefly in Renaissance Italy" and this allowed the ancient knowledge of the Cosmic soul and the divinity of the individual to be revived. She relates how

Marsilio Ficino and Pico della Mirandola had "hoped to create a fusion of Kabbalism and Christianity." But, she adds, "these ideas could not take root and flourish."[23]

This was particularly evident when the exceptionally brilliant Pico della Mirandola not only sought to bring together Kabbalah and Christianity, Plato and Aristotle, but "all schools of thought in a single symphony of philosophies." He planned a conference in Rome for 1487 with the intention of bringing together the philosophies of the "ancient and medieval, pagan and Christian, Moslem and Jewish" traditions. In preparation for the conference, he wrote 900 theses or what he called *Conclusions* from different authorities and had them printed in Rome in 1486. **The Church denounced the work, blocked the conference, and jailed Pico.**[24]

Pico had also written an introduction to this plan, his now famous *Oration on the Dignity of Man*. This is often called the manifesto of the Renaissance because of its vision of the unlimited potential of the human being. **Pico celebrated what he saw as the creative and mystical potential within the human being to achieve divine consciousness.** Each of us, he wrote, has both the choice and the responsibility to work toward this goal. He did not view any one philosophy or tradition as the only or absolute truth. All philosophies, he said, must be studied and debated to find the true leaven. This was to have been his goal for the conference.

It's worth pausing for a moment to reflect on the life—and death—of this young man who was brilliant far beyond even the standards of the Italian Renaissance. He knew Latin, Greek, Hebrew, Arabic, Aramaic, and Chaldean. He was known for his photographic memory, and it is said that he had committed to memory every Greek and Latin text he had ever read. Even stranger is the story that he could recite Dante's *Divine Comedy* backward.[25] His vision of bringing together all philosophies and religions reflected the depth of his own understanding and the inspiration of the time, but it was also due to the earlier work of the master teachers at Chartres. Within the vast scope of Pico's reading was the work of Dionysius the Areopagite, whose Platonic, mystic, heart-centered Christianity had been a part of the teachings at Chartres.[26] Pico's quest for mystical experience and the realization of his higher self was, at least in part, due to the influence of Dionysius the Areopagite and the seeds these master teachers had sown in the European psyche.

One can only wonder what a mind like Pico's might have achieved had the Church allowed him to develop rather than denounce his thinking as heretical, scandalous, offensive, and pagan.[27] Pico was only twenty-three years old when he wrote the 900 theses, *Conclusions*, and had them printed in Rome. He was young, flamboyant, and lacked diplomacy. Unfortunately, he was not given the freedom or the time to develop. He was only released from prison through the intercession of Lorenzo de' Medici and several Italian princes who had been persuaded by Lorenzo to argue in Pico's favor. The pope agreed to release Pico under the protection of Lorenzo. But Pico was not cleared by the pope until 1493, only one year before his death at thirty-one years of age.[28]

It is known that Pico died a horrible death from poisoning. It was thought by many that the pope was responsible, but others thought it more likely to have been Pietro de' Medici, the son of Lorenzo, who objected to Pico's support of Girolamo Savonarola, the fiery fundamentalist Dominican monk who was an influential critic of the corruption of the Church as well as the secular power of the Medici family.[29] It is not entirely clear who poisoned Pico, but it is clear that the Church had already poisoned the possibilities of Pico's development. **Pico had held in his hands for one brief moment the pure clay of who we are and why we're here, and he wanted to explore the unlimited possibilities of human consciousness with the great minds of Europe. This was not to be.**

Had Pico been allowed to continue his quest, he might not have been so profoundly influenced by the fanatical Savonarola. Pico would naturally feel the need of support from a man of the Church who could, at the same time, condemn the corruption of the Church. And Savonarola's support for the poor and the right of people to govern themselves would probably also have been attractive to Pico. Unfortunately, under Savonarola, these rights could only exist within a puritanical, Christian worldview. Pico would die just before Savonarola would gain the power in Florence to try to realize his Christian theocracy.[30]

At the height of the Italian Renaissance, Savonarola became a persuasive force in Florence against the corruption of the Church *and* what he considered the *secular* accomplishments of the artists and thinkers of this period. Some of the artists, influenced by his preaching, destroyed their paintings. Botticelli stopped painting for years, and Pico burned some of his poetry. Savonarola organized young street people to patrol the streets and report inappropriate dress and conduct. His followers searched homes and public places for what Savonarola condemned as sinful and worldly art. He also organized a large bonfire to destroy secular art, such as paintings, sculptures, and books. Cosmetics, mirrors, jewelry, and even musical instruments were also destroyed. Within four years, an opposition party in alliance with the pope brought about the imprisonment, torture, and death of Savonarola. However, his ideas would influence the coming Protestant Reformation.[31]

Pico stands as a symbol of brilliant potential, the spiritual and mystical longing to achieve a higher consciousness, and the passion to find the true leaven in all religions, but he was destroyed by both the censorship of the Church and the censorship of fanatical reform. It would be this battle between these two forms of censorship that would consume Europe for the coming centuries.

The seeds of consciousness that had been sown during the High Middle Ages could not be nourished in such an environment. The principles of direct inner experience taught in the Hermetic texts and in the newly discovered Kabbalah could not survive. Yet, it had been these evolutionary principles that had been at the very heart of the Italian Renaissance from the beginning.

In spite of this pervasive censorship, however, there were those who were able to survive and continue their work in their own way. Perhaps no artist was actually able *to manifest* the unlimited potential of the human being better than Leonardo da Vinci, who was not only a great painter but a sculptor, architect, inventor, and explorer in all fields of knowledge. He was the true Renaissance Man. His simple sketch of the *Vitruvian Man* became a symbol of the human ability to encompass the universe: man stands fully inside the square of the earth and the circle of the cosmos, revealing himself to be the microcosm of the macrocosm. He, like Goethe later, understood that the laws of nature organize energy and manifest themselves in the various forms of nature.

The Italian Renaissance was a spectacular awakening of the intellectual and spiritual legacy whose roots stretch all the way back to the beginnings of modern consciousness, but it did not have the time or the freedom needed to fully develop. When the conditions that had made the Renaissance possible began to change and the 1527 destruction of Rome occurred, the Italian Renaissance began to wane. But the new seeds that had been planted did not entirely die out; they continued to grow in less visible ways, both in culture and in the human psyche. Connections with the underground traditions would be strengthened, and the movement would emerge again in the North.

There would be a dynamic flow of ideas and creativity in the early 1600s between England, Germany, northern Italy, and Bohemia. The underground traditions of Alchemy, Kabbalah, Hermeticism, and Mystic Christianity would surface and find a haven in Bohemia. This was the Northern Renaissance that Yates would call the Rosicrucian Enlightenment. But the Church and the Hapsburgs would so completely destroy this world that it would not be until the twentieth century that Frances Yates would discover that it had even existed.

Chapter Thirty-Three

The Northern/Rosicrucian Enlightenment
The Third Wave of the Renaissance
(1600–1620 CE)

This Northern Renaissance was "more a radical and innovative continuer of the medieval traditions" than it was a follower of the Italian Renaissance traditions. It was "a last attempt, before going completely underground, to recapture the high ground and realize" what the great Italian Renaissance masters "had only dreamed of some hundred and fifty years before."[1]

—Christopher Bamford

The story of the survival of this Renaissance tradition was lost until the last half of the twentieth century when Yates discovered this lost story beneath the known history of the early seventeenth century. Yates describes her experience in *The Rosicrucian Enlightenment* as being like that of an archaeologist, digging down through layer after layer of historical material until just before the Thirty Years War there emerged "a whole culture, a whole civilization," that had been "lost to view."[2] Yates realized that this culture was a continuation of the Hermetic tradition that had given such strength to the Renaissance in Florence around 1460 when Cosimo de' Medici insisted that Marsilio Ficino translate the newly recovered *Corpus Hermeticum*. **And it was, but Christopher Bamford has helped** us realize that it was also a continuation of the beautiful flowering of consciousness that had occurred during the High Middle Ages.

Yates had assumed that the impact of the discovery of the Hermetic texts during the Italian Renaissance had begun to lose its power during the early seventeenth century until her research revealed that instead of losing its influence, there had been a rebirth and expansion of the tradition. During the years since the Italian Renaissance, this movement's open and inclusive atmosphere had made it possible to absorb the wisdom of other underground Western traditions, such as Alchemy and the Jewish Kabbalah. This brought about a creative and intellectual activity that spanned the distance between England and Prague. This movement, which Yates called the Rosicrucian Enlightenment, was "concerned with a striving for illumination, in the sense of vision, as well as for enlightenment in the sense of advancement in intellectual or scientific knowledge." *Yates discovered that—in fact—it was this underground tradition that had nurtured a mathematical approach to nature and had given the impetus and direction to the scientific revolution.*[3]

Bamford in "The Meaning of the Rose Cross" shows how this underground tradition also nurtured the evolutionary ideas and experiences developed during the High Middle Ages: *heart consciousness and a love that dissolves all dualisms*. While the great Cathedrals were being built during the High Middle Ages to "Our Lady" who perpetually gives birth to our higher self—Cosmic Consciousness—there were those whose actual day-to-day work was the transforming of the world by transforming the heart. *The heart was perceived as the center of consciousness—and the center of the world.* Their concern, says Bamford, was "not only a personal mysticism of union with the divine, but a cosmic transformation, a work of regeneration."[4] This wisdom of love, Sophia or Our Lady, was thought of as the "cosmic glue" that unites the divine, the human, and the earth. And this, we can now see, is a rebirth of the wisdom of the Megalithic Builders. *This unity was symbolized by the Rose while the Rose Cross symbolized the merging of all nature with human nature in the heart of love.*[5] **Just as the master teachers at Chartres, these groups were working for a true healing of soul, the culture, and the world.**

Bamford tells us that among the Beguines, women mystics, troubadours, knights, Platonists, Franciscans, Sufis, Hermetists, Cathars, lay people, monks, nuns, and others, the focus was on achieving this unity and higher consciousness through love. It was through the experience of profound love that one becomes "an organ of creative, loving perception—no longer blind, deaf, and dumb.... This is the heart as the whole person, the person as an organ of perception."[6] It is this perception that had been achieved during the High Middle Ages, says Bamford, that was still alive and active at the heart of the Rosicrucian Enlightenment. The Fraternity of the Rose Cross itself, says Bamford, was "more a radical and innovative continuer of the medieval traditions" than it was a follower of the Italian Renaissance traditions.[7] **It was "a last attempt, before going completely underground, to recapture the high ground and realize" what the great Italian Renaissance masters "had only dreamed of some hundred and fifty years before."[8]**

This movement, says Yates, had held great expectations for the coming of a true Enlightenment—one rooted in both mystical experience and scientific exploration. Those who were part of the movement had a keen awareness of the dangers of scientific knowledge without inner experience. They realized that society, education, and religion would have to be reformed, and that such a reformation could take Europe beyond conflicting religious doctrines to a new sense of individual dignity and purpose. They knew that freedom from the repressive tendencies of Church and State was absolutely necessary for such an Enlightenment to occur, and they made a remarkable attempt to gain political power over the dominant forces of the Hapsburg-Jesuit alliance.

They failed, and with that failure came the destruction of their world, successive waves of political propaganda against them, repression, witch-hunting, and the Thirty Years War between Protestants and Catholics. It was in this "exquisite Renaissance culture," says Yates, that the potential existed for the culmination of the most creative and intelligent tendencies of the entire Italian Renaissance—and we now know that this includes the Renaissance of the High Middle Ages. But both the vision and the movement "slipped out of history."[9] *A whole world disappeared and with it the hopes of the shaman-scientists who had envisioned an evolutionary leap for the whole world.*

During the 1700s, after the "convulsions of witch-hunting"[10] and the long, violent years of war, the French Enlightenment would occur, but it would be a very different Enlightenment from the one envisioned by the shaman-scientists of the early seventeenth century. **The visionary force that had given birth to the mathematical, scientific exploration of the world had been shattered and silenced. Abstract reasoning now dominated and inner experience once again was devalued and repressed.**

When the Royal Society for the advancement of science was formed in 1660 in London, it had visible roots stretching back into this earlier movement but, as Yates explains, "in order to preserve its delicate existence great caution was required."[11] Only the science of outer exploration could survive. Political and religious control, misinformation, fear tactics, lack of adequate education, and years of repressing the human ability for visionary experience made this marriage of reason and vision impossible.

Western culture has always valued the French Enlightenment, and there are good reasons to do so: it was a qualitative leap in the development of differentiated, independent thinking and a move away from authority and doctrine. But few realize that its roots were in a movement whose aim was to include the whole mind in its striving for understanding — the rational, conceptual mind *and* the symbolic, visionary mind. This was certainly not part of the later French Enlightenment thinkers' worldview. So little did they understand the symbolic, visionary, heart-centered mind that they thought of their rational achievements as superior to all that had come before them. They thought of themselves as modern, civilized men in contrast to their earlier, *primitive*, mythic-minded ancestors.[12]

There were those, of course, who were not so sure and who sought to understand the mind on a much deeper level. It was the age, after all, of Vico himself who had a profound understanding of the two great dimensions of the mind: the rational, conceptual mind and the symbolic, visionary mind. Vico knew very well that symbolic language is our first language: it is not irrational but possesses a poetic logic that gives birth to the logic of conceptual consciousness. Vico insisted that the symbol cannot be reduced to the idea, nor can the idea be reduced to the symbol. The mind's wholeness depends on an integral and dynamic continuum of movement between the symbol and the idea.

This age would have been the time, in Vico's thinking, to return to our past to discover how the mind had developed so we could, in his words, discover the principles of the mind's own spontaneous development. But this did not happen. Vico was ignored. His contemporaries were captivated by the belief that the true life of the mind only began with the emergence of reflective, conceptual consciousness. All that preceded this historical event was irrational and potentially destructive—thus the need for censorship and repression. As mentioned earlier, the notion that the logical brain could develop out of a component of the brain that lacked logic is in itself irrational.

It is as though the French Enlightenment philosophers had no real understanding of the three waves of the European Renaissance. They dismissed the past and focused on what they viewed as *progress*. All that came before their own high achievement was considered primitive and savage. Clearly, such a view could not allow for a tension and dialectic to exist between the great polarities of the mind. The only aspect of the mind that was valued was the rational; all the other brain components were devalued, dismissed, and repressed. **The Knights of the Western world had *lost their vision*—once again—and they rode away from Wisdom to construct a brilliant, rational universe whose repression of its own polarity was as ruthless as any form of repression that had preceded it.**

Once again Yahweh had abandoned Wisdom, and he lost the happiness that she gave him. No longer did he honor his equal partner in the creativity of the universe, and this left him alone, superior to all, but without the joy of the Queen of Heaven, for "She is the tree of life to those who lay hold of her / and those who hold her fast are called happy."[13] But once again, all that the Queen, Our Lady, had symbolized was devalued and repressed. No longer was she able to offer her fruit from the Cosmic Tree, for the highest evolutionary achievement was now the Man of Reason.

In no way would we want to give up the movement away from the authority of the Church and State and the movement toward individual thinking. Nor would we want to give up the great ideas of liberty, justice, equality, and human rights so brilliantly put forth by the French Enlightenment. But the earlier Rosicrucian Enlightenment had worked toward the same ideals and we must remember that they, unlike the French Enlightenment, had held the vision of *wholeness*, which included the rational, scientific mind *and* the visionary, experiential mind. Our Rosicrucian ancestors understood that *without feeling, we cannot create a just world*. They knew that *without the experiential wisdom of the heart, creation could not continue to unfold.*[14] They knew that with the abandonment of Wisdom, that is, with the devaluing of feeling, vision, dream, and the experience of higher states of consciousness — our ancient shaman-mystic tradition — we could not achieve or maintain our highest ideals for long.

Chapter Thirty-Four

The German and English Reaction
The Fourth Wave of the Renaissance
(1775–1850 CE)

In spite of the efforts of the Romantic poets to give us the blueprint for the development of the Self and to show us how the repeated repressions of this blueprint had produced the Faustian split in Western consciousness, it was the worldview of the French Enlightenment and the new, one-sided science that won the day.

By the early 1800s a powerful reaction against the one-sided French Enlightenment came from Germany and England. This resistance spread quickly throughout Europe and beyond. The movement emphasized the creativity of wholeness, which included both the rational *and* the visionary. The artists and thinkers of this period also resisted the authority of the Church and State and sought individual freedom and the liberty to think and act authentically and responsibly. The English visionary, poet, and printmaker, William Blake, exemplified the radical creativity of the individual who seeks to free himself and society from all systems and imposed beliefs in limits. He understood that the evolutionary journey is guided by the divine within, not by any Church or religion. The major Romantic writers did not reject the rational mind, but they did reject an exclusive rational approach to understanding the world. In Blake's words, they rejected the "single vision" of the French Enlightenment philosophers and material science.

The French Enlightenment philosophers had emphasized only the rational mind, but the Romantic writers sought to integrate rational consciousness into the creativity of visionary consciousness/the creative Imagination. For many of these writers the creative Imagination was similar to Corbin's description of the *organ of soul*, the organ that allows us to perceive and co-create with the subtle/spirit world. They valued the dreaming, visionary, mystic mind and knew, as did the ancient Egyptian initiates, that justice cannot exist without *feeling*. Many of these writers were well aware that without the integration of all that the feminine symbolized, creation could not continue to unfold.

Among the Romantics there was the reemergence of a unified, non-exploitative view of nature. This attitude toward nature ranged from a deep appreciation of nature to Goethe's understanding of the unity of nature and human consciousness since they both had their roots in Universal Mind or what we today might call the quantum field. He understood that the laws of nature organize energy and manifest themselves in all the various forms of nature, including human consciousness, art, and our deepest aspirations. Many of the Romantic writers simply experienced peace and renewal in nature and resisted the exploitation of the Industrial Revolution.

So when both Germany and England reacted against the Enlightenment during the Romantic period, they were not reacting against reason, but against the movement's exclusiveness. They understood the dangers of the intellect acting without feeling. Many of the Enlightenment ideals were much admired, but in both countries there was a movement to explore and experience what had been omitted during the Enlightenment. As M.H. Abrams makes clear in his *Natural Supernaturalism: Tradition and Revolution in Romantic Literature*, "Romantic philosophy is thus primarily a metaphysics of integration, of which the key principle is that of the 'reconciliation,' or synthesis of whatever is divided, opposed, and conflicting."[1]

There were brilliant philosophers, scientists, poets, visionaries, painters, and musicians in many countries, but I will focus on Goethe and Novalis in Germany since both had deep roots in the work of the Alchemists, Hermeticists, and Rosicrucians, and both exemplified the key principles of the age. The story is well known of how the young Goethe returned home from the University in Leipzig in 1768, sick "more in mind than in body," met Fräulein von Klettenberg who was a Pietist, and began to study Alchemy.[2] The roots of Pietism were in Alchemy, religious reform, and Rosicrucianism. Goethe, and later Novalis, absorbed the knowledge of the Rosicrucians who were forced underground in 1620, and both integrated that knowledge into their own work.

The Rosicrucians understood that it is the transformation of soul that transforms society. Each of us can transform the world by transforming ourselves. Goethe had been deeply influenced by the Rosicrucian development of this theme in *The Chemical Wedding of Christian Rosenkreutz*, which was published in 1616. This is a symbolic story of the soul's labyrinthine journey to transform itself by bringing into consciousness those aspects of the mind that had been repressed. The individual soul is invited to attend a wedding of the King and Queen by a beautiful, angelic woman, who becomes the Mistress of the Labyrinth, the organizing principle in nature that guides the soul on its *Way to the Light* at the center of the labyrinth. During the journey, the soul confronts the opposing principles within the personality, along with the experiences that bring about their intensification and balance. The heightening, balancing, and stabilization of these opposing principles create the foundation for the Sacred Marriage of the King and Queen. This "metaphysics of integration" reveals the roots of the Rosicrucian Enlightenment in the ancient shaman-mystic tradition of the Great Mysteries of death and rebirth. And it would be the role of the Romantic poets to continue that work.

In 1795 Goethe wrote *Das Märchen*, a tale similar to *The Chemical Wedding of Christian Rosenkreutz*. It too is a symbolic tale of the soul's journey to transform itself. The structure of the Märchen is a circular, labyrinthine journey in which the Light at the center activates a circular movement of all the fragments of the personality around itself and, at the same time, initiates a spiral movement of intensification and elevation of these fragments onto a higher plane of being. Only at the center of Light can these now highly developed aspects of the personality be integrated. This is reflected in the Sacred Marriage of opposing principles. In Jung's words, the center is a "central point within the psyche, to which everything is related, by which everything is arranged, and which is itself a source of energy. The energy of the central point is manifested in the almost irresistible compulsion and urge *to become what one is,* just as every organism is driven to assume the form that is characteristic of its nature, no matter what the circumstances."[3]

Later, Novalis, influenced by the Alchemists and Goethe, wrote a tale similar to *Das Märchen* within his novel, *Heinrich von Ofterdingen.* Novalis' Märchen, told by the poet Klingsohr in the ninth chapter of the novel, has the same theme as Goethe's Märchen: the transformation of the human soul. Novalis, like Goethe, had been ill "more in mind than in body"[4] when he began his studies at the Bergakademie at Freiberg just a few months after the death of Sophie von Kühn, the woman he loved. It was there that Novalis began reading the Alchemists and the natural philosophers of the sixteenth and seventeenth centuries, and it was there that he also read many of the books that Goethe had read under the guidance of Susanne von Klettenberg. Later, Novalis would read Goethe's works. While Novalis did not have a living Susanne von Klettenberg to guide him, he did have the image of Sophia, who had become for him a spiritual symbol equal to Christ.[5] Thus both men suffered from a "wounded" consciousness; both discovered a mode of self-healing in the underground tradition; and both were guided through their labyrinthine journey by the image of a woman.

All of Goethe's works, both literary and scientific, were informed and shaped by this earlier tradition and his own healing experience.[6] The same is true of Novalis: all of his work following his Freiberg studies and the reading of Goethe bear the imprint of their healing influence. Novalis was the first serious interpreter of Goethe's *Das Märchen.*[7] He understood *that its intention was to reflect the dynamic process of the development of the Self.* Both Goethe and Novalis felt that **the true role of the poet was the intensification and elevation of human experience.**[8]

Every person, says Novalis, should become a poet so we can all accomplish the task of every true poet: the writing of the sacred text of our own labyrinthine journey. The poet pursues *the intensification of experience, the evolution of life.* The most significant kind of history, says Novalis, is the *complete* human history — the history of every single person's life journey toward wholeness. This kind of history would not be indifferent to the life of a single individual. Thus, the true historian is also a poet, but, says Novalis, every true poet is also a historian.[9]

Novalis understood that when we spiral down deep into our own individual mind and our own historical past, we begin to participate in the history of the human species and to discover the spontaneous principles of the mind's development. It was these principles that both Goethe and Novalis experienced and reflected symbolically in their work, especially in the form of the Märchen. These principles open us to our own personal history and connect us to the history of our species. These words were another confirmation of my own journey, for it was the inner journey to soul that had led me to the outer journey of history.

This is the Vician ricorso. Novalis does not use Vico's term, but ricorso is a precise expression for Novalis' intention. This understanding was a major breakthrough for Novalis, for it was his realization that the history of the human race can rise to consciousness only in the mind of the person who is simultaneously in the process of becoming conscious of his or her own personal history. Only through our personal ricorso are we able to enter into the ricorso of the human species. Novalis believed Goethe to be such a historical poet, and this was the work that Novalis himself hoped to accomplish. Unfortunately, Novalis died when he was twenty-eight years old. Yet it was Novalis who gave the Romantic period its major symbol: the alchemical *sapphire blue flower* that depicts the labyrinthine journey toward the light from the perspective of darkness and thus the completion of the Great Mysteries, the sacred marriage of the King and the Queen.

Goethe's work in Alchemy, science, and his own personal ricorso allowed him to observe and study on a very deep level *the spontaneous principles of development* at work in nature, human consciousness, and art.

Each particular form, according to Goethe, must be observed as *process*—a process of the gradual realization of inborn potentialities. This process reflects the tendency in nature to evolve: it is the first principle or law of nature, but it exists as potential until activated.

Once activated, the principles initiate a growth process, a heightening or intensification process that Goethe called *Steigerung*. The principle of Steigerung manifests itself in a polarity of opposing forces, *Polarität*, but, says Goethe, the principle of growth prevents the continual movement between these opposing forces on the same level. The tendency in nature to evolve, in a healthy organism, urges a movement toward a more heightened or differentiated level. Thus, normal growth takes on *a spiral movement*. Opposed to this constant metamorphosis is the tendency in nature to maintain a particular form once it is achieved. Goethe called this *Specificationstrieb*. This allows form to stabilize itself before the tendency to evolve sets in once again. If stabilization is not sufficiently allowed, the organism can suffer from a lack of full development. However, if the overall process of Steigerung reaches its completion at every level of development, that is, if all potentialities have been developed and the greatest possible balance of opposing tendencies achieved, this would be what Goethe called *Ganzheit* or *Wholeness*. This would be the goal of the evolutionary process.[10]

The symbolic structure of the Märchen became the main literary form in which these spontaneous principles of growth and development could be poetically and symbolically reflected. As mentioned earlier, both Goethe and Novalis felt that it was the work of the poet to reflect and intensify this dynamic process within the human psyche. This poetic reflection of the development of the Self became *"the new mythology."*[11] This *new mythology* was the ancient blueprint for cosmic consciousness rooted in the shaman-mystic-scientist tradition. With this blueprint, each of us could become the poet of our own labyrinthine journey.

Goethe's life journey to understand the organizing principles in all life forms and to understand his own personal development allowed him to become conscious of the history, if not of the human race, certainly of Western consciousness. **Faust, Parts I and II, is an extended Märchen that** reflects the failure in Western culture to understand the dynamic process of the development of the Self. By severing the rational mind from feeling and the creative imagination, our journey toward wholeness has been thwarted. Goethe is telling us what we now know was central to the Egyptian Mysteries: without *feeling* the development of the Self cannot unfold. In fact, without the integration of feeling and all that the feminine symbolizes, life itself cannot continue to unfold. **We have lost the Wisdom of the Heart, and Faust is the personification of that loss.**

In this last wave of the European Renaissance, Goethe gives us the image of what our great knights have become after hundreds of years of repression. Western consciousness has split itself off from feeling, from the heart, from the feminine world of experience, and we have become the dissociated Faust, unable to recognize the dark, violent, unfeeling Mephistopheles as self. This Faustian split is the manifestation of our not having brought forth what was within us, and what we have not brought forth is destroying us.

Faust is a German scholar who has spent his life in intellectual pursuits, yet his achievements have not brought him fulfillment. He is a man of reason, but so detached from feeling that he stands on the brink of dissociation. His lack of feeling and compassion is reflected in the negative, cynical, materialistic, and ultimately violent Mephistopheles. And it is this dark side of Faust who leads him in his pursuits of fulfillment. Western culture knows this Mephistopheles well, for we see him everywhere in positions of power: he is a wheeler-dealer, sometimes sophisticated and witty, but always negative, dismissive, violent — and completely incapable of believing in anything not related to his own self-interest.

In Part I Faust ventures out in the world in search of happiness through emotional involvement with a woman. But he is basically guided by his own personal desires and instincts, that is, Mephistopheles, and he ends up bringing about the destruction of Gretchen, the woman he has pursued. In Part II he once again pursues a relationship with a woman, this time Helen of Troy. They have a son, Euphorion, who, through his own rash pursuit of too much too fast, is destroyed. Helen leaves Faust to follow her son into the Otherworld.

Alchemically speaking, Faust's continued attempts to integrate the feminine dimension of his own psyche blow up in the alembic. He has not yet learned how *to relate* to his feminine visionary. He is still the great, independent knight who unconsciously leaves his visionary soul behind as he rides out into the world to accomplish his own goals. But now, without her, he has become the dark, negative Mephistopheles who is narcissistic, unfeeling, and violent. As long as Faust is unconscious of this darkness as his own, no growth can take place and thus no integration.

Finally, Faust decides he will attempt to fulfill himself through public accomplishments. He enters into a project of reclaiming vast areas of land submerged under water. This certainly is symbolic of Faust's attempt to bring his own unconscious aspects into consciousness. But even here his own ambition activates Mephistopheles and allows Faust to betray and destroy others. He has received all the world has to offer him rationally and materially, but nothing brings him the fulfillment or the understanding he seeks.

Mephistopheles maintains power over Faust until the end when Faust is finally able to reject the cynical, materialistic, nihilistic schemes of his own darker, detached self. Faust is now aware that Mephistopheles is his own darkness and violence, and this consciousness allows him to take responsibility for the destruction and deaths he has brought about. **But Goethe makes it very clear that Faust is only able to reject Mephistopheles and take responsibility because of his growing ability to feel the depths of sorrow and remorse for what he has done.** This leads Faust to commit the rest of his life to his project of reclaiming the land so that others can have a better future. When Faust, at the end of his life, is able to see what he has accomplished for others, he experiences the fulfillment he has sought all his life.

There is yet a deeper level of Faust's reclaiming vast areas of land whose soil is green and fertile. Faust thinks of this land as **a new Earth** where people in the future will be free to create their lives. **On one level, reclaiming this land is the reclaiming of those vast aspects of the mind that have been split off by the West's continual repression of its own wholeness. On another level, it is land that Faust—humankind—can

retrieve from the misconceptions, the doctrines, the distortions, and the lies of the past. It is the *pure clay* for our children.

Faust is able to retrieve this land, certainly not because he is a saint, but because his deep longing for fulfillment never allows him to give up. *This is land free from the Mephistophelian shadow of Western culture* — a belief system that almost destroyed Faust, just as it is surely destroying the Western mind. It was Faust's terrible life-long struggle with this shadow — his intense longing, his failures, his crimes, his remorse — and his growing ability to feel, to love, and finally to reject Mephistopheles — that made it possible for him *to reclaim the pure soil for all of us.*

The intensification of experience and the evolution of consciousness that are possible in this new soil are depicted at the end of the poem with Faust's physical death and the continuation of his consciousness and creativity on a higher plane of being. Because Faust has allowed feeling and love to blossom within him, he is met by love and forgiveness. Through this love, he is finally able to realize a higher frequency of being that *opens the way* to the Divine Feminine, the Holy of Holies.

I had taught Faust I and II when I was in my early thirties, long before I was able to understand the depths of Faust's struggle. Now I know that all of us who take the labyrinthine journey into the depths of our own being must confront our own negations of life, our own wounded consciousness. But we must also remember that it is the **Light** at the center, the **Mistress of the Labyrinth**, that guides us to her. At the center, we discover *this green and fertile soil*, this loving, creative universe with infinite possibilities. This is the *pure clay* we want to bequeath to all our children and to all future generations.

During this Romantic Renaissance in the West, a generation of poets made an extraordinary effort to retrieve this *pure clay* for all of us. When I was able to see this effort within its historical context, I was deeply moved by the persistent and continual urgency within the Western psyche to heal itself. Both Goethe and Novalis experienced what Kingsley has called "that vast missingness deep inside us." They understood, as did Kingsley, that the most extraordinary threat that we face is "the extinction of our knowledge of what we are."[12]

Through their own wounded consciousness, both poets faced this threat and discovered the path of their ancestor shaman-mystics — a path that was still very much alive in Germany in spite of the fact that it could only be active underground. They realized that the missing, dormant, and repressed pieces of soul could only be found and experienced by going within, so they spiraled down into the depths of their own experience. Their deep inner focus on soul intensified their experience and activated the circular/spiral movement of the soul's energy from the circumference to the center of wholeness. Their poetry reflects this dynamic process of the soul's attempt to retrieve all that had been lost.

In spite of the efforts of these poets to give us the blueprint for the development of the Self and to show us how the repeated repressions of this blueprint had produced the Faustian split in Western consciousness, it was the worldview of the French Enlightenment and the new, one-sided science that won the day. No longer was military force necessary to maintain the Mephistophelian worldview that there is nothing but matter and life is a fluke without meaning or purpose. Science had established itself as the sole arbiter of truth — and this, we have to remember, was a science that only had the tools to explore the material world. And, as a result, the assumption arose that there was nothing else to explore.

Chapter Thirty-Five

The Twentieth and Twenty-First Centuries
The Fifth Wave of the Renaissance

When we change the narrative, we change the world.

It would not be until the early twentieth century and the discovery of quantum physics that a more inclusive vision would begin to return to the scientific world. When the pioneers of quantum physics realized they had stepped out of the old materialistic view of reality and into a world strangely similar to the descriptions of the shaman-mystic, they began to read the same kind of texts that had ignited the work of the earlier shaman-scientists before the Thirty Years War. During the decades following the discovery of quantum physics, there were remarkable scientists who were also visionaries working to reconcile inner and outer realities. Yet it would not be until Fritjof Capra experienced what he had been studying as a theoretical physicist and published his work about the parallels between modern physics and mysticism that the scientist and the mystic could openly begin once again to form a respectful and complementary relationship.

Throughout this book we have seen how the discoveries of the twentieth century are changing everything we thought we knew about our inner and outer reality. To review briefly, the twentieth century discoveries include: (1) the quantum field; (2) extensive knowledge about the emergence of shamanism and its integrative rituals around the world by 40,000 BCE; (3) the magnificent shaman-mystic, artistic tradition of the cave cultures in Europe and around the world; (4) the spiritual development of many of our indigenous ancestors, such as the San people in southern Africa and around the world; (5) the Dead Sea Scrolls that brought a greater understanding of the Jewish shaman-mystic tradition of the First Temple; (6) the Nag Hammadi texts that reveal a Christ who teaches the shaman-mystic path to Christ Consciousness; (7) Old Europe with its extensive Neolithic cultures that were peaceful, egalitarian, sedentary, artistic, visionary, and rooted in the shaman-mystic dimension of reality; (8) the highly developed, sophisticated shaman-mystic, heart-centered culture of Egypt; (9) the Anatolian Presocratic shaman-mystics who, like the Egyptians before them, were powerful creators of culture as technicians, scientific thinkers, lawgivers, and ambassadors; (10) the existence and continuity of shaman-mystic traditions that spanned the distance from southern Spain to Central Asia; (11) a greater knowledge of the underground traditions, such as Alchemy, Hermeticism, Kabbalah, and Mystic Christianity, that have kept the knowledge of our evolutionary potential alive in spite of its continual repression by mainline culture; (12) an awareness of the creative periods, such as the High Middle Ages, the Italian Renaissance, the Rosicrucian period, and the German and English Romantic period, as successive waves of the renaissance of this underground tradition; (13) a psychology that recognizes the value of symbolic language and the dreaming, visionary, mystical mind; (14) the understanding that the heart is a major component of the brain and that wholeness requires all the brain components; (15) the discovery that the brain has the neurological mechanism for altered states of consciousness ranging from mild visionary experiences to a total mystic state of consciousness, that is, Cosmic/Christ Consciousness.

Other developments include: (16) millions of people who are having Near-Death Experiences, or more accurately stated, Actual-Death Experiences, while the brain is dead, which offers evidence of the existence of consciousness beyond the brain; (17) many others who are experiencing communication with loved ones who are no longer in the physical dimension; (18) people who are experiencing anomalous events that simply do not make sense within the context of a material worldview; (19) scholars, scientists, and artists who have discovered and experienced deeper orders of reality *spontaneously* as well as through the use of sacred medicine and newly developed techniques to initiate altered states of consciousness; and (20) indigenous people who are sharing their ancient wisdom for the healing of all life.

When we change the narrative, we change the world. These discoveries and developments of the twentieth century offer us that new/ancient narrative—and it is a narrative supported by quantum physics: we live in a world of infinite potential. We are a multidimensional, co-creative species with the evolutionary potential for Cosmic Consciousness. Our ancestors made the leap into modern consciousness when they developed symbolic language and the ability to communicate with the spirit dimension—the quantum field, the source of all reality. There must have been spontaneous experiences with this dimension that led our ancestors to develop methods they could use to ensure communication between the realms.

Through their experience, they learned the primary importance of developing and maintaining a relationship with this cosmic dimension of reality. For thousands of years they observed the laws of nature and lived in harmony with those laws—and this relationship allowed them to experience the unity of all life. They were able, metaphorically speaking, to eat the fruit from the Cosmic Tree of Life.

They knew that we are immortal, we are divine, and we are creators. All our intentions, thoughts, feelings, and actions are manifested in our bodies and in our world. **This knowledge of who we really are is the green and fertile soil, the pure clay that our ancestors have reclaimed for us again and again. Yet every time this "new Earth" emerges, the floodgates are opened and it is submerged once again with a worldview that negates the Gift of our ancestors.**

But this time is different.

Chapter Thirty-Six

Why is this time different?

The consciousness of the world is being reframed to include a greater reality.

1. The New Science Revolution has exploded the myth of matter and its horrifying worldview of a meaningless, purposeless universe. Quantum physics has revealed that matter and spirit are one energy and that we are all an integral part of a vast, creative universe of "pure potential, of infinite possibility."[1]

2. Our consciousness affects the cosmos. Within this quantum field of "infinite possibility," we are all creators: what we think and what we do matters. It is how we create our world. In fact, each of us has a responsible role to play in the destiny of our planet.

3. The New Science Revolution and the Shaman-Mystic Revolution are merging into one revolution: each confirms the other's knowledge of the unity of matter and spirit and of a universe of "pure potential" and "infinite possibility." Both revolutions have confirmed the wisdom of the Sacred Fruit from the Cosmic Tree of Life: we are divine, immortal, and creative.

4. Various anomalous events, such as the UFO phenomenon, are structured in such a way that they continually expand our consciousness even though we may remain unaware of this process.

5. The discovery that some of our ancestors as early as the Stone Age had experienced Cosmic Consciousness radically transforms our view of the past as well as our potential for the present.

6. Our ancestors' knowledge of the HEART as central not only to our development but to our ability to perceive reality parallels twentieth century brain research that the heart has intelligence, transforms perception, heals, and connects us to other dimensions of reality. Heart consciousness expands our world through love and meaning. We now know that the integration of the heart is essential to our evolution.

7. With the surfacing of the Underground Traditions of Alchemy, Kabbalah, Hermeticism, Gnosticism, and Mystic Christianity, the ancient legacy of our ancestors is being integrated into mainline consciousness.

8. We now know that Western civilization attempted to integrate this knowledge into consciousness during the Renaissance Movements: the High Middle Ages, the Italian Renaissance, the Rosicrucian Enlightenment, and the German and English Romantic period. Knowledge of these movements can inform our own efforts of integration today.

9. Scientists confirm the existence of *an intelligent and highly organized energy field* that supports our work to transform what has decayed into new, creative forms. This work ignites a wave of organization, the ML Code, that moves through us and, cell by cell, creates a completely new being. Scientists today call these cells Imaginal cells, since they "contain the imagining or blueprint of a whole new being."[2] It is encouraging to know that when we work in harmony with the laws of nature, we ride the wave of universal creativity.

10. Visionary experience confirms that *this highly organized principle of transformation is more easily accessible to all of us today* because an energy field of light has been drawn to the earth and connected with the earth's energy field.

11. The decayed forms of our culture have now violently surfaced into consciousness and are forcing us to acknowledge our shadow side.

While this seems negative, it may not be, since the decayed must surface for us to be fully conscious of its existence and its power to destroy everything that supports and sustains life.

12. The political and social movements of the twentieth century have supported an inclusive, fairer social structure, and today, with the Internet, millions of people around the world are informed and supportive of the principles that support all life.

13. Indigenous people around the world are coming forward to urge us to *see* that our planet is dying—and that we have the power to do something about it. They want us to awaken from the *terrible dream* that is destroying all life on the planet. They are communicating with us in whatever way they can, but they are also meditating on deep levels for us and for the healing and balancing of the earth. These indigenous groups have kept alive that "mysterious legacy of knowledge" that we have lost.

There are many creative indigenous voices here in our country and around the world, but I will briefly mention only four indigenous groups: (1) the San Bushmen of the twentieth and twenty-first centuries in Namibia and Botswana, one of the oldest living cultures on earth; (2) the Kogi people of South America, "the last surviving high civilization of pre-conquest America;"[3] (3) the spirit voices of the Yanomami from the rainforests of South America; and (4) some of the voices of Native Americans in the United States.

San Bushmen in Namibia and Botswana

Just as I was finishing this book, I discovered the work of Bradford and Hillary Keeney, both scholars with an intimate, participatory knowledge of the shaman-mystic tradition *still alive* among the San Bushmen in Namibia and Botswana. I had been extremely cautious about studies from anthropologists who had reported as outside observers on the traditions of the San. In an earlier chapter, I used the work of Laurens van der Post, not because he had participatory experience in the San spiritual traditions, but because his heart had been opened to their love of soul, their joy and authenticity. Van der Post knew that the San people nurtured and kept alive their connection to soul and the loving consciousness of the cosmos. They embodied the living, radiant reality that we had lost. And van der Post, like Jung, also knew that this gift from some of our earliest ancestors was still within us and that, if we want to live fully, "we have to reach down and bring back to life the deepest levels of the psyche from which our present consciousness has evolved."[4] I had asked, "*How* do we reach down and bring this consciousness back to life within ourselves?" There are several answers to this question, but the San Bushmen have heard our question, and they have sent *their* answer to us through the Keeneys.

Bradford and Hillary Keeney have an amazing story to tell—a story that brings to us the actual San spiritual teachings and practices as told by the tribal elders of northeastern Namibia. Bradford tells us that at age twenty he had a spontaneous experience of the vast love and infinite joy of the cosmos while he was playing the piano. The music, he says, pierced his heart open. He saw before him a large luminous egg that "was a fountain of love that poured ecstatic happiness and deep meaning into my heart all night long." **He experienced what Bucke and others call Cosmic Consciousness and, as Bradford would later discover, the San Bushmen call "the deliverance of God's ostrich egg," an initiation that "brings the know-how for entering and navigating the mysteries of the spiritual universe."** Bradford didn't know quite what to do with this experience, so he continued his education with a scholarship to MIT, a doctorate from Purdue University, and a successful academic career. In 1992, he was invited to the University of South Africa as a visiting professor.[5]

The week before this invitation, Bradford had a dream that he was visiting a group of San Bushmen in the Kalahari Desert. The dream even presented a map of the location of the San people, whom he did, in fact, visit that same year. On his arrival, he saw the Kalahari Bushmen running across the desert to greet him. Yes, they had dreamed of his arrival just as he had dreamed of visiting them. He was greeted with, "Welcome to your home. We have been waiting for you."[6]

Bradford returned to the Kalahari many times during the next twenty years, for he truly had found his home as well as the spiritual home of our species. He also spent many years traveling around the world to study shamanic healing traditions and to conserve their wisdom and practices. "In the Kalahari," he states, "I discovered original spirituality. Its tracks lead to cultural traditions all over the planet."[7]

While with the San Bushmen, Bradford was taught by them, participated in their spiritual practices, was recognized by them as a person who possesses and controls a "supernatural essence or power that can be harnessed to heal…physical and social ills," and was allowed "to delve deeper and deeper until he became an accepted holder of their [the San's] most important truths."[8]

The Bushman elders also acknowledged Hillary Keeney as a healer and teacher of the Bushman way of life. The Keeneys were encouraged by the San to take the San's "spiritual medicine" to the world.[9] In 2010 Bradford Keeney's *The Bushman Way of Tracking God: The Original Spirituality of the Kalahari People* was published, and in 2015 Bradford and Hillary Keeney presented the San practices in *Way of the Bushman As Told by the Tribal Elders: Spiritual Teachings and Practices of the Kalahari Ju/'hoansi*. Bradford Keeney has also written on the shamanic-mystic tradition at the roots of Christianity in *Shamanic Christianity: The Direct Experience of Mystical Communion*.

"In the beginning," says Bradford, "we were all Bushmen—people inseparable from the wild of nature." The San Bushmen have "the oldest genetic lineage," the greatest genetic diversity in their DNA, and the earliest form of language. They are "the descendants of the ancestors for all modern humans." Earlier I gave the generally accepted dates of the San Bushman culture as 33,000 BCE to 1800 CE. However, the continual discoveries of artifacts and rock art push the date to earlier times. Bradford says that their rock art indicates "that they have been practicing **an extraordinarily potent form of spirituality** for over sixty thousand years."[10] And the San Elders in Namibia and Botswana carry this "potent form of spirituality" into the present.

As I also indicated earlier, it is generally accepted that the western European cave culture was a few thousand years earlier than the San culture, yet we cannot be absolutely certain since the dates are determined by what has been discovered. Some scholars suggest that the Stone Age culture might have begun in Africa and later moved north into western Europe. As discussed earlier, the existence of the San Bushmen has been severely threatened, and in some areas they are extinct, including the areas where Wilhelm Bleek and others did their extensive interviews in the 1800s. The Keeneys' work presents the teaching of the few remaining Bushmen Elders of northeastern Namibia.[11] The collective work done by Bleek and others has been referred to by Lewis-Williams as the "Old Testament" of Bushmen spirituality while the later work with the Kalahari Bushmen in Namibia and Botswana he referred to as the "New Testament."[12]

And now we must ask ourselves just what is this **"potent form of spirituality"** still practiced by our few remaining ancestors in the Kalahari Desert? Before I answer this, I want to state once again that our Stone Age ancestors had achieved a high level of symbolic language and the ability to experience other dimensions of reality through altered states of consciousness. Their experience was the breakthrough into modern consciousness. When I started writing this book, I did not know with any degree of certainty whether our Stone Age ancestors had experienced what Bucke called Cosmic Consciousness—the light and love of the creative universe that Bucke experienced only for a few moments but which transformed his life forever. **Now we know that our Stone Age ancestors not only experienced cosmic consciousness, but they knew how to initiate it in themselves and others.**

The present-day San shamans in Namibia still hold this knowledge which, they tell us, goes all the way back to the beginning of the Bushmen. These shamans are, in fact, **Masters of the Life force of the universe.** They experience the light and love and joy and ecstasy of the fruit of the Cosmic Tree, which for them is experienced as the Divine Ostrich Egg. They knew, just as our later ancestors who received the gifts from the Queen of Heaven, the Great Tree of Life, that "those who lay hold of her / and those who hold her fast are called happy."[13] Not only do the San know how to initiate the experience of this divine consciousness, but they are also able to hold its energy in their bodies as it intensifies to what they describe as a "boiling" point. The elders tell us that,

> *This life force is called in and expressed by enthusiastic singing, drumming, and dancing. When our healers feel the intense heat of n/om [the non-subtle, vibratory life force] boil inside of them as a result of the sincere and prayerful singing and dancing, they can deliver God's "thorn" of n/om. When your heart is pierced by this kind of celebrated relationship with...God,... all manner of spiritual gifts may spring forth, including divine guidance, heightened joy, and the gifts for healing and teaching.*[14]

This is gnosis, direct communication with and participation in the divine life force. The singing, drumming, and dancing become a community affair. They dance together as a group. They touch or hold each other as they intensify and transfer this energy. The shamans are able to shape this powerful energy into thorns, needles, nails, or arrows of concentrated, intense cosmic energy/kundalini and send it into another's body to awaken that body to this vital healing life force.

In San rock art and western European cave art there are images of figures whose bodies are being pierced by just such thorns, needles, nails, or arrows of what we can now with some confidence call kundalini energy. This remained a mystery for Western scholars until the San shamans explained this sacred process of awakening and healing.

This wisdom of the San shamans still living today is yet another gift of the twentieth and twenty-first centuries. As mentioned earlier, I did not know this when I wrote the chapter on the San Bushmen. However, the deep appreciation for the San people that van der Post expresses in his writing and talks throughout the West has played an important role in awakening the Western psyche to something deep and forgotten from our Stone Age past. Was it the work of **Mantis** to appear synchronistically in our dreams or in our lives to prepare us for the actual teachings of the San Bushmen? And was it the work of the San Bushmen themselves to appear in the dreams of those who heard the talks or read the books van der Post brought to the West?

What about the man who dreamed of the woman crying "as if her heart would break"? Remember how the dreamer rushed from room to room to look for her? Then suddenly a Bushman appeared in one of the windows and indicated that he would lead the man to the crying woman. The man started to follow but then was horrified to realize that one of the fiercest of the wolfhounds, which he let loose every evening to guard his house, went straight for the Bushman. The man wanted to call the dog back, but he could not find his voice. Have such dreams helped us to find our voice?

These teachings that come directly to us from the San Bushmen form a basket "full of beautiful things of the sky" that they have stored there for all of us. This basket is filled with ecstatic joy, cosmic love, music, dance, song, story, heart, soul, and ropes to the vital force of life. Will we be like the man who could see nothing in the basket of gifts his bride from the sky had prepared for both of them? Will we be blind to these cosmic gifts from the San? Will the San people vanish from the earth along with their sacred knowledge because we do not have the ability to *see* or the ability to call back the wolfhounds of our severed rational minds?

We now know that, once we achieved self-consciousness and symbolic language, it was possible not only to experience altered states of consciousness but also to experience Cosmic Consciousness—the light, love, creativity, and joy of the source of all life and consciousness. This is the experience of the San Bushmen and, as Bradford states, this *is* our original spirituality whose "tracks lead to cultural traditions all over the planet." It *is* the "mysterious legacy of knowledge" that our ancestors worked so hard to preserve and pass on to all future generations.

The Kogi

The Kogi have maintained their isolation high in the mountains of Colombia for the last four hundred years. They view themselves as the guardians of the world, the elder brothers of our species, while we are the younger brothers who have lost our connection to the laws and heart of nature. As a result of this loss, they see us as the destroyers of the earth with our construction of nuclear weapons, dams, deforestation, strip mining— and our general disregard for the integrated earth systems. In the past, they have accepted what they see as their responsibility to maintain balance and health for our planet, but they now say that our actions are making this impossible. They have broken their isolation to try to communicate to us that our actions are destroying all life forms. The world is dying because of us, and they can no longer maintain the balance necessary for life.

After much negotiation among themselves, they agreed to allow Alan Ereira, a filmmaker, to enter their world, film their way of life, and relate their urgent message to us, their "Younger Brother." Ereira's film, *The Heart of the World: Elder Brother's Warning*, and the book, *The Elder Brothers: A lost South American people and their message about the fate of the earth*, were the result of this encounter. And now, more than twenty years later, the Kogi called Ereira back to them once again to make another film, *Aluna*, with a message even more urgent than the first. Then, in 2015, the Kogi came to the United States to speak once again about the condition of the earth. According to a friend who attended, the Elder who spoke appeared to remain in meditation most of the time. His message was clear: *the mother sent him; the mother is suffering; all her seeds are dying; extinction is now clear.* Then the Elder asked: "What are the seeds? **The seeds are the wisdom, the knowledge...of the Mother Earth."**[15]

It is absolutely amazing that the Kogi still exist in spite of the destruction we have caused all around them. They, like the San Bushmen, are carriers of the *living* shaman-mystic-scientist tradition of our past. They understand the laws of nature, her integrated energy systems, and what happens when we disregard her laws. They relate to nature with love, respect, and gratitude. Nature is a living being, the Great Mother, the source of all life.

The Kogi have a clear understanding of what quantum physicists are just beginning to understand: *thought creates the material world.* **"The Kogi themselves say that thought is the scaffolding of matter; that without thought, nothing could exist." But even more poignantly, they say we, the younger brother, are "not just plundering the world," but we are "dumbing it down, destroying both the physical structure and the thought underpinning existence."**[16]

In the film *Aluna* the Kogi attempt to teach their healing earth science to younger brother by demonstrating the sacred interrelationships within all of nature. Scientists who observe the Kogi demonstrations state that the Kogi knowledge may actually be at the "cutting edge." The film follows one of the Kogi shamans who goes to London as part of his demonstration. The shaman visits the observatory at the University of London, meets the Steele Professor of Astronomy, Professor Richard Ellis, but the shaman makes it clear that he is not interested in learning Western knowledge. Yet he inadvertently reveals his own knowledge of the solar system to the amazement of those present.[17]

How do the Kogi obtain their scientific and spiritual knowledge? They receive it from Aluna. This is a very important word for the Kogi. Aluna is Mind, the Mind of the Universe; it is the energy in and behind nature and all life; it is intelligence; and it is pure potential. The Kogi also call Aluna the Mother, her Essence, her Unity, and the Source of all life and wisdom. They also speak of Aluna as the Sea, the origin of the laws of the universe, the cosmic organizing principles of life. The human mind in concentrated thought, say the Kogi, is the doorway between this world and Aluna.

The Kogi understanding of Aluna is similar to the understanding of ancient shaman-mystic-scientists when they speak of the Otherworld; or of modern physicists when they speak of the quantum field; or of NDErs when they speak of the sea of light and love. And we will remember that scientist Gustaf Strömberg said that "Matter and life and consciousness have their 'roots' in a world beyond space and time.... In this non-physical realm lies the ultimate origin of all things, of energy, matter, organization and life, and even consciousness itself."[18]

We might ask how the Kogi, who have remained isolated from the world since the Conquest, know what we consider to be advanced knowledge? The answer is that they receive their knowledge from Aluna. Their shaman-mystic-priests are trained from birth to live in Aluna, to understand her laws and her wisdom. They remain isolated in a cave or forest for nine years; others remain in training for yet another nine years. These shaman-mystic-priests who have been in Aluna for eighteen years live high in the mountains and have contact only with those priests who have trained for nine years. No one in the physical world teaches these shamans. They learn everything in Aluna: they become attuned to Aluna and learn by listening, "listening spiritually." **In Aluna they talk with the masters of the world, and they listen to the "inner music of the universe"—and then, we are told, they begin to dance. All knowledge, all wisdom, comes from within, from Aluna.[19] And this is Cosmic Consciousness.**

We do not have this wisdom. We do not know how to experience the interconnectedness and sacredness of all life. We do not know how to be the mediator between the cosmos and the earth. We do not know how to develop the whole mind and experience the loving consciousness of the heart. We do not know our potential for cosmic consciousness or how to achieve it. **And our not knowing is the result of our own sacred shaman-mystic-scientist tradition being repressed again and again by those in power.**

The isolated Kogi shaman-mystic-priests of the high Sierras live continuously in Aluna, the Holy of Holies, in order to keep the world in balance and harmony. Their message to us is that our "dumbing the world down" is now making it impossible for them to maintain this balance. Their message of the horrific consequences of Western thought is an urgent and sacred call for us to reclaim our lost knowledge.

The Yanomami

The spirit voices of the indigenous Yanomami people first manifested in 1994. The Yanomami people have been reduced to 30,000–40,000 people who live in a few hundred villages in the Amazon rainforest in northern Brazil and southern Venezuela. The story of these voices is a strange and beautiful one. Janet Mayer tells her story in *Spirits...They Are Present*. She explains how she spent so much of her early life experiencing tragedies before they happened but was unable to prevent them. In her effort to shift her energies, she decided to try a technique for entering altered states of consciousness called Holotropic Breathwork, which had been developed by Stanislav Grof. It was during her second session that "the impossible, the unimaginable," happened:

> *I felt pressure in my chest, which moved to my throat and out of my mouth with a force of its own.... I began spontaneously*

> *speaking a language I had never heard before.... Words flew off my tongue, the power of them staggering.... I felt elated, overjoyed as if something wonderful was taking place within. My voice was thunderous, vibrating as I shouted and screamed, laughing and crying as I rejoiced! I began slowing down, taking a breath, then once again building, gaining speed and incredible strength – like the force of an arrow shot from a bow, the unknown words flew from my lips, propelling me into a sitting position so that the language could run its course through my upper body.... I somehow knew that the words formed a message whose purpose I felt but couldn't explain. My tongue was moving so fast, but I had no idea what was being said....*
>
> *Abruptly my tongue would halt, and then begin a chant that was poetic.... On and on, I voiced a message that needed to be set free, to be released from its origins.... I wanted to feel this way forever and share whatever was being said with everyone.*[20]

For more than four years Janet sent tapes of her speaking this language to people and organizations that might be able to tell her if it was a known language and, if so, what language, who was speaking, and what was the message. Finally, she was directed to Ipupiara, an indigenous South American shaman who held a Ph.D. in Anthropology and Biology and who taught classes on South American culture at the Smithsonian Institute. He immediately recognized the language that Janet was speaking as Yanomami and agreed to translate some of the tapes for her.[21]

Finally, the translation came: *We need to be more Earth-Honoring People*. And it was repeated twenty-three times. Then another line: *Messages will be released: Honor Fire, Water, Air, Mother Earth*. This was repeated seventeen times. Then Ipupiara told Janet that some of what she said was a prayer about healing Mother Earth and it was in the form of a chant. As Ipupiara continued to translate the tapes, he discovered both male and female voices and three other languages: in addition to Yanomami, he heard Fulnio, Tucano, and Canamari. Ipupiara concluded that there were a number of Spirits speaking through Janet, each with a similar message about the need to honor the earth. When Janet spoke in Canamari, Ipupiara told her that she was speaking a sacred healing ceremony "as if from one Shaman to another." Later, a female speaker stated in Fulnio, "Very powerful moments are coming." Ipupiara took the tapes to Brazil and played them for several tribes who were absolutely astounded that a white woman was speaking their languages.[22]

All of the messages had to do with the earth—honoring the earth and healing the earth. One tape focused on the Pachacuti prophecy that the Eagle of the North and the Condor of the South will come together to share experience and wisdom. I had heard this prophecy from shamans when I was in South America, and I was so pleased to know this was actually occurring between Janet and the Yanomami. The voices also insisted on their need to communicate and that "more channels" would emerge; that there is a need to bridge spirit, the human being, and the earth; and that *this language is a loving language of wisdom that opens the heart.*[23]

The way Janet learned from the Yanomami that they view their language as a language of wisdom was in itself remarkable. One day Janet felt an urgent need to write a poem with the title, "This Language of Wisdom." Later, when Ipupiara called her with the translation of the last tape he had been working on, he said that this tape was a poem whose first line was "This, the language of wisdom." Her poem and the Yanomami poem were very much alike. Janet felt that "Somewhere along the line, the Yanomami language crossed over to my thoughts in English."[24]

The Yanomami voices made it clear that Janet must get their messages out to people. One message was addressed to Janet personally: "Release the Messages." The spirit speaker then urged Janet to allow this spirit energy to flow through her. Ipupiara's translation was, in part, "You are a teacher, such a powerful master. Don't chase it away, go to it beloved one. Don't be shy, your spirit adjusts yourself to your powerful energy...." Janet knew this was a message urging her to allow their energy to flow through her and to release their messages to the world. She understood and felt their urgency and their sacredness.[25]

I had heard about Janet's experience from my friends, Bob and Phran Ginsberg, founders of Forever Family Foundation. Then I met Janet at FFF's Conference in San Diego a few years ago. I heard her speak this language and later talked with her about her experience. I was impressed with Janet's openness, modesty, and respect for the Yanomami and other spirit voices. When I heard her speak the language, I felt that it truly is a loving language of wisdom that opens the heart. The frequencies of the language and the urgency of the spirit speakers are as powerful as their message. These Yanomami ancestors and other voices from the spirit dimension are doing everything they can to communicate with us and to open our hearts to what is happening to our earth. We at least owe them the respect to listen – and to listen with our hearts.

In July of 2017 I spoke with Janet again about the recent activity of the Yanomami spirit voices. She told me that they are occurring more frequently and are assisting her in her healing work with others. **Before the presidential elections in November 2016, Janet said the voices increased, and it became very clear to her that we are entering a time of intense change.** Since her translator, Ipupiara, is no longer alive, she does not have a translation of the voices, but she does *feel* their messages. After they speak, she allows herself to go into a meditative state and feel their intention.

She and I discussed how interesting it was that she did find a translator fairly early on who could let us know that the loving messages from the spirit voices were deeply and urgently concerned about the earth and how now, with Ipupiara's passing, *we are left to feel the frequencies of the language.* Janet thinks that these frequencies elicit different feelings in each person. In other words, we each feel what we need to feel for our own growth and development. **In this way, the Yanomami Spirit Voices are building and strengthening the Bridge between the spirit/cosmic dimension and the earth through the mediating consciousness of the individual. Again, just as with our earlier ancestors, it is the individual who mediates between the cosmos and the earth.**[26]

Healing Hearts at Wounded Knee

What happened at Wounded Knee? On December 29, 1890 the United States Seventh Cavalry massacred approximately 300 Lakota Sioux people, including children, babies, women, men, and elders. Around twenty-five years ago the Lakota Birgil Killstraight received a dream that moved him to organize the Chief Big Foot Memorial Ride on the one hundredth anniversary of the massacre at Wounded Knee. The first ride had nineteen horseback riders; over the last twenty-five years the number has increased to the hundreds. These riders retrace the steps of Chief Big Foot and those with him to Wounded Knee in an effort to create community and healing—and in memory of a dream that died at Wounded Knee.[27]

To join the Memorial Ride and Meditation for the healing of all humanity, several Native American groups formed a global organization called *Healing Hearts at Wounded Knee*. Their goal is to bring attention to the worldwide human trauma and suffering brought about by war, genocide, holocaust, massacre, and racism. Their pledge is to end all of these forms of violence. The focal point is Wounded Knee, but, they say, we all have wounded knees and we all have wounded hearts. They are aware that there can be no real peace or joy until we address this worldwide grief and suffering. "Where," they ask, "is that rage, grief and deep suffering in our collective psyche and soul?" The year 2015 inaugurated the Call to end all war and to awaken to the suffering that blocks healing and peace. They invite all people to commit to ending violence and to join them in this yearly global meditation.[28]

I was deeply moved by the Native American Call for the healing of all humanity. Their worlds have been destroyed by racism, war, dishonesty, massacre, and genocide. Their rage, grief, and suffering are present and real. Yet they go beyond the belief that we cannot heal our collective grief. They understand so well that there can be no peace until we become conscious—**heart conscious**—of the grief and suffering around the world. **When we work on that which has decayed, our path will lead us to this kind of healing—for both the victims and the perpetrators of these crimes.**

How has our species been able to participate in genocides, holocausts, and massacres? How did we ever justify these actions to ourselves? How did we ever think one group of people could be superior to any other? How were we ever able to think that mass killing could resolve anything? We need to recognize that this kind of thinking is undeveloped, wounded, and unconscious. Another form of wounded consciousness is the belief that the goal of ending this violence is naive and impossible. **From the perspective of the *heart*, it *is* possible. When we know it is possible, we will achieve it.**

The voice that ripped through my throat that night in Death Valley was the voice of our collective rage, grief, and deep suffering. And it was the voice of the collective belief that we can never end war or the suffering it causes. It was the voice of our children who have experienced the worlds constructed out of the toxic clay we have given them. **But Healing Hearts at Wounded Knee is born out of a consciousness that has gone beyond this belief.**

When I began the meditation with Healing Hearts at Wounded Knee on their Memorial day in December 2015, I immediately remembered the voice that said: **"You have drawn to yourselves this day/All those on your planet/Who are creating worlds/Of Love and Peace."** These were the words communicated to me in the vision of the disk of light and love—a disk vibrating with the frequencies of cosmic consciousness. It is important for us to remember that this is the healing consciousness that we attract to ourselves when we commit to healing the "rage, grief and deep suffering in our collective psyche and soul."

Chapter Thirty-Seven

>—◦—<

The "great saints and sages have given us glimpses into our evolutionary future. Their spiritual accomplishments are thought to have created the psychic blueprints that are functioning as strange attractors to focus the collective wave erupting within human awareness."[1]

— Christopher Bache

As our planet goes through what may well be the greatest crises we have faced as a species, it is important to remember that we cannot evaluate our evolutionary future adequately from our present perspective. If we choose to work on what has decayed both within us and without, we need to **trust the process.** We are both the caterpillar and the emerging butterfly. From the perspective of the caterpillar, the entire world is being destroyed. And this is true in the sense that everything the caterpillar identified as reality is breaking down. It is also true that a new reality is coming into being, but the new form is not yet clearly visible to us.

This is where trust comes in, but it is trust in a known and scientifically confirmed law of nature. As we have discussed before, our intention to enter the labyrinthine journey toward a higher consciousness activates an evolutionary law of nature. This invisible, highly organized principle begins to move through us as it creates new *Imaginal cells* that will transform our entire being. The old structures are destroyed because the scaffolding of our thought will no longer support the decaying forms.

Our intention and longing for new myths of meaning are creating new forms of thinking whose scaffolding attracts the new cells that contain the blueprint of our evolutionary future.

The caterpillar's story truly is an appropriate metaphor for our own transformation. As a caterpillar, it crawls around and around and up and down. It consumes and consumes—and then it consumes more. One day this simply is not enough for the caterpillar, so it weaves a lovely silken chrysalis and begins the journey to create a new life. I like to think of the silken chrysalis as the labyrinth we enter when we choose to confront the personal and planetary crises with a higher consciousness. This silken intention protects us during our journey, it creates a sacred womb for our gestation, and it attracts a higher organizing principle to us.[2]

Years ago, I had read Christopher M. Bache's *Dark Night, Early Dawn* and had been deeply moved by his visionary experiences of our evolutionary future. When I was almost finished writing this book, I decided to look through his work again. I was surprised to find a statement about our ancestors that I had not remembered: "**the great saints and sages have given us glimpses into our evolutionary future. Their spiritual accomplishments are thought to have created the psychic blueprints that are functioning as *strange attractors* to focus the collective wave erupting within human awareness.**"[3]

This is an accurate and eloquent statement of what is occurring with the twentieth century discoveries of the shaman-mystic-scientist cultures. The accomplishments of these ancestors are indeed the psychic blueprints for what we are attempting to achieve today. In *The Passion of the Western Mind*, Richard Tarnas says that the modern mind is attempting "to rediscover its intimate relationship with nature and the larger cosmos."[4] **By holding in consciousness our ancestors' evolutionary achievements, we strengthen their power to function as *strange attractors*. If we allow ourselves to be sensitive to the archetypal patterns underlying these cultures, these patterns can inform and ignite our own development, and we can become the *psychic bridges* between the blueprint of the past and its manifestation in the future.**[5]

Let's look once again at the underlying archetypal patterns in these ancient cultures. The ancient Mayan oracle mentioned earlier reflects the basic patterns not only of these cultures but of all growth and development: "Polarity is the loom on which reality is strung." Our ancestors understood that creativity takes place **within** *the unified energy field of opposing principles*. We can move to the extreme of either one of these poles to explore and experiment, but our survival and well-being depend on achieving a conscious balance between such opposing principles as mind and matter, spiritual experience and scientific understanding, female and male, and birth and death. It was the role of the Great Mystery Schools in these cultures to initiate individuals into this sacred knowledge.

While all shaman-mystic-scientist cultures know this and share the same underlying archetypal pattern for our evolutionary future, the evidence of these patterns varies from culture to culture. One of the most comprehensive and exquisite renderings of our ancestral practices to maintain the balance of all opposing principles is found in Egypt during the Ramesside period, the Nineteenth and Twentieth Dynasties, c. 1293–1070 BCE. In *My Heart My Mother: Death and Rebirth in Ancient Egypt*, Roberts tells us that a major focus of this period was to reestablish the complete archetypal pattern of spiritual development that had existed before the reign of Akhenaten.

In spite of the fact that Akhenaten had a clear vision of the profound unity of all life, during his reign emphasis and power began to shift away from the feminine toward the masculine and away from death and darkness toward the light. There was also a rejection of the many female and male deities that symbolized specific aspects of cosmic and human realities. Akhenaten ignored Hathor, the fiery serpent goddess who had been so crucial in the Pharaoh's achievement of cosmic consciousness. Had there not been such a powerful effort to reestablish and "enshrine forever in stone" the complete archetypal constellation, says Roberts, we might never have had such an extensive and artistically beautiful rendering of the evolutionary blueprint.[6]

During the Ramesside period, this blueprint is revealed in the many Egyptian rituals that are preserved in papyri, temple structures, carved reliefs, paintings on temple walls and ceilings, sarcophagi, and other art forms. And Naydler has shown us how the heart of this blueprint had existed earlier in the Pyramid Texts near the end of the Fifth Dynasty, c. 2350 BCE. These texts, says Naydler, "are the earliest example of any piece of extended writing worldwide."[7]

In spite of what at first appears as an abundance of evidence from the Ramesside period, Roberts laments that even this is "only a small fraction of the rituals which must once have been performed in the secrecy of Egyptian temples," and "only fragments remain of the vast temple libraries."[8] But the rituals we do have from these Egyptian Mysteries beautifully and profoundly reflect the archetypal dance of balance between death and birth, darkness and light, the moon and the sun, female and male, the heart and the head, the ancestors and the living, duty and desire, sexual power and mystical illumination, the earth and the cosmos, and spirit and matter. The achievement of this balance of opposing principles was symbolized by the Solar King's ability to channel the creative forces of the fiery serpent goddess, Hathor. Her energies lovingly rise up the King's spine and settle at his third eye. **This symbolic constellation reflects the achievement of cosmic consciousness, the Wisdom of the Heart.**

Unfortunately, Western culture has severed the energy fields of the great loom of life right down the middle. We have cut the threads connecting the polarities. We honor the male but exclude the female; we glorify the rational brain but reject the feeling wisdom of the heart; we celebrate birth but fear death; and we acknowledge matter but deny spirit. We praise the French Enlightenment that valued only the rational mind and appeared not to know about the earlier Enlightenment that valued the mind's wholeness. We praise modern "objective" science and appear not to know that it was a limited science (until quantum physics) that could only explore the physical world because its earlier attempts to explore both inner and outer reality were destroyed by the Church and State. The scaffolding of this kind of thinking cannot support the complete loom, and this has brought the West—and now the world with us—to the brink of extinction.

Tarnas describes the journey of the Western mind as "an overwhelmingly masculine phenomenon." He succinctly states, "The masculinity of the Western mind has been pervasive and fundamental, in both men and women, affecting every aspect of Western thought, determining its most basic conception of the human being and the human role in the world." Tarnas accepts this as necessary for the achievement of "an autonomous rational human self." He further states, "This masculine predisposition in the evolution of the Western mind, though largely unconscious, has been not only characteristic of that evolution, but essential to it." Tarnas does not accept that the masculine dominance of Western history is because women are less intelligent, nor does he accept that this phenomenon is simply a result of "social restriction." He thinks it is *archetypal*. He sees the evolution of the Western mind as "driven by a heroic impulse to forge an autonomous rational human self by separating it from the primordial unity with nature."[9]

This position, held by many Western scholars, must now be reevaluated in light of the discoveries of the twentieth century. **If we accept that the spiritual accomplishments of the great saints and sages—our ancestors—are the psychic blueprints for our evolution, it becomes painfully clear that the Western *heroic* model is an aberration of that blueprint. The great saints and sages of our past did not discover the principles of achieving higher consciousness by severing themselves from nature or from all that the feminine symbolizes.**

The ancestral blueprint is clear, especially in the Egyptian rituals: without the feminine power of the heart to birth a *feeling* world, we cannot bring justice into being; without the integration of all that the feminine symbolizes, creation cannot continue to unfold;[10] and without a deep respect for the laws of nature, inner and outer development is thwarted. The consequence is a spiritual and material wasteland.

This masculine Western phenomenon was creatively interrupted during each renaissance of Western history. In the first Renaissance during the High Middle Ages, all that had been repressed and censored for hundreds of years rose to the surface of consciousness in powerful and creative attempts to integrate with the masculine mind. This deep soul longing and the underground shaman-mystic-scientist tradition merged and nourished each other. **One of the great gifts each of these periods of awakening gave to Western culture is a clear view of the nature of Western illness and the dangers of the split-off masculine endeavor.**

The Grail stories, for example, reflect the spiritual and material loss within Western culture. The king has lost his power: he is impotent, and he cannot die, yet death is everywhere, and his kingdom is a wasteland. The Great Mysteries of death and rebirth have been lost. This king does not know how to enter the realm of death to confront the energies of the Otherworld and fuse death and life in his own consciousness. And he has also lost his relationship with the feminine, that fiery power in nature and himself to create or destroy. Without a loving, desiring, respectful relationship with her, he cannot channel her energies creatively and thus destruction is everywhere. **There could hardly be a clearer picture of the failure of the Western heroic impulse.** However, the Grail stories are also an invitation to the Western hero to be initiated into the ancient Mysteries of his own Wholeness.

It is important at this point to focus briefly on the archetypal structure of the *heroic impulse*. Joseph Campbell's famous study, *The Hero With a Thousand Faces*, delineates the basic stages of the hero's journey. *The archetypal hero sets out on his journey alone, but he does not sever himself from nature or the feminine.* The stages of his journey are similar to those in the labyrinthine journey, and they are characteristic of all conscious development. The archetypal hero receives the Call to adventure. He separates from the world of time and space to embark on a long inner journey to gain greater knowledge and to forge his own independence and autonomy.[11]

He encounters great obstacles, fights many battles, endures many tests, experiences supernatural wonders, and receives the aid of helpers all along the way. He suffers the death of all he thought he knew about life, symbolized by his dismemberment or crucifixion. He goes through a dark night of the soul, symbolized by being swallowed by or contained in a larger being, such as the great womb of the feminine, the cave, or the body of Nut in the Egyptian ritual, or like Jonah in the belly of the whale.

This is a supreme ordeal that allows the hero to experience himself as part of a greater force. He emerges, once again, with many helpers from nature.[12]

He has struggled with his own limitations, fought the dark monsters within himself, developed lifesaving skills, attracted nature's help, maintained his integrity, and—at last—achieved his independence and autonomy. These achievements enable him to meet the opposing forces on equal ground. The Sacred Marriage of the masculine and the feminine—the balanced union of opposites—can now take place. He is resurrected, that is, he returns to the world of common day, transformed and empowered to bestow gifts on his community.[13] **The archetypal hero's achievement of independence and autonomy takes place within the Great Loom of Polarities. And this is crucial: nature and the feminine support the hero's journey to independence and autonomy.**

This is not the journey of the Western hero whose culture has denied him every path to the inner world. **We must never forget that the Western repressive *heroic impulse* is the consequence of the persistent repression and censorship of the complete archetypal constellation of our evolution.** It is the consequence of losing our true stories. This Western hero is like my knight/priest at Chartres who was demoralized by World War II and the failure of the Church or any other aspect of culture to provide meaning. He left the priesthood and the Church, but he also abandoned nature and his feminine visionary.

His visionary also left the Church, but she remained close to nature and was able to experience the miracles that appeared with each step she took. She knew that these were the miracles that could heal her knight—and civilization. She was an intimate part of the knight, but he did not know this. She was the organ of soul, his connection to the subtle world, but he did not know this. She was Wisdom, the Queen of Heaven, the Cosmic Tree, the flowing waters of life, the bright and radiant one who gives birth in the holy of holies. But he did not know this.

My Knight had been stripped of his true heritage too many times and had been inundated by false claims to meaning far too often. He was on his own with only his rational mind to serve him. He believed nothing, trusted nothing, and chose to explore nothing but the material world so visible before him. We have to admire his insistence to discover and understand the world on his own terms. However, his separation from nature and from his visionary feminine counterpart rendered him unstable and fearful: he distrusted both because he knew neither. *He was like a shooting star, all on its own, streaking across the night sky until it burned out.*

This Western model of achieving freedom and autonomy is not a model for our evolutionary future, nor was it a creative model for our past. **However, it is not surprising that such a repressive model for achieving freedom and autonomy would arise in a culture that had repeatedly repressed and destroyed the full blueprint of its own evolutionary future.** But that future now depends on us recognizing our "terrible dream" about reality. We need to be able to *see* the suffering we cause when we sever our rational mind from nature and the feminine visionary within us. The Jesus of the Nag Hammadi texts was well aware of the consequences of our failure to bring forth what is within us: it destroys us. When we do not believe there is anything within to bring forth, the ego flips wrong side out in a desperate attempt to reflect something—anything—that might be acclaimed as meaningful. This aberration in our mental development distorts our ability to think rationally and renders our highest ideals volatile. When Josiah destroyed the Wisdom tradition in Judaism, those who understood the consequences lamented that their hearts had forsaken Wisdom, and they had lost their vision. They knew their kingdoms would be burned and their people scattered.

But, as we have seen, there were those within Judaism and Christianity who understood this Wisdom and kept it alive for us. They have watered the sacred tree, "perfumed with the incense of the holy of holies" whose "fruit is for all to eat." When we eat of this fruit or enter the alembic of transformation, or travel the labyrinth to the center of our deepest selves, *we confront the divine, the cosmic Mind, the Christ—not as Other, but as Self.* And the ego flips right side in to reflect the meaning it was always seeking.

The discoveries of the twentieth century have revealed that the masculine heroic model of Western mainline culture was challenged multiple times and in various ways throughout the history of Western civilization. Jung has shown how the shaman-mystic-scientist tradition, in the form of Alchemy, always included a working partnership with the feminine. Alchemy existed underground for more than seventeen centuries in its attempt to both compensate for and challenge the incomplete and unbalanced heroic model of consciousness.[14] Many fairy tales and dreams were also manifestations of this same compensatory effort on the part of the human psyche.

These historical challenges reflect the immense struggle within the Western mind, and they reveal the persistence of **the archetypal undercurrent of balanced mental development.** This undercurrent of development has risen to the surface of consciousness in five waves of awakening. **Each renaissance has challenged the Western heroic model of mental development with a more complete archetypal pattern for our evolutionary future. This is the core challenge of each renaissance in Western history.**

We can meet this challenge. We now understand that nature is working with us. This is our moment. As systems theorist, Ervin László, has said, "When a human society reaches the limits of its stability, it becomes supersensitive and is highly responsive to the smallest fluctuation. Then the system responds even to subtle changes in values, beliefs, worldviews, and aspirations."[15] Our society has definitely reached the limits of its stability, and this means that our individual thoughts and feelings and longings can significantly affect our future. In Bache's words, "At such times our individual choices may have enormous ramifications if they reflect our highest potential and seek the greatest good of humanity as a whole."[16]

Each one of us is the alembic for transforming what has decayed in our culture. This decay is presently rising to the surface, to the forefront of our culture, so we can see it reflected back to us in its horrifying clarity. This is our work, and this is the work of the earth. As we become conscious of our own darkness and work on distilling this darkness into light, we change and the world changes. This is our moment to bring forth what is within us to heal the collective psyche. As we seek to transform this darkness within ourselves, we attract the Merchants of Light—and we draw to ourselves all those on our planet who are creating worlds of Love and Peace. Our ancestors' psychic blueprints for Cosmic/Christ Consciousness are within us, informing us and igniting our own development. This is how we become the *psychic bridges* between the evolutionary blueprint of the past and its manifestation in the future.[17]

Interestingly, symbols of this blueprint for Cosmic Consciousness are all around us. The Greek Key, the stylized image of the labyrinth, is everywhere. For example, it appears on the walls of public buildings, drapery, decorative pillows, furniture, clothing, dishes, and dozens of other art objects. Even the Western calendar begins with the birth of an individual who had achieved Cosmic Consciousness. And the Christian celebration of this birth of consciousness is at the time of the winter solstice, nature's rebirth of light.

In the Christian tradition, it is interesting that this archetypal symbolism persists but is not usually recognized: the birth of divine consciousness is celebrated with the cosmic tree and the lights of consciousness spiraling to the top, culminating in the bright light of the star—the achievement of Cosmic/Christ Consciousness. Judaism also has the cosmic tree, the Menorah. While the celebration of lighting the lamps of the Menorah has historical meaning today, the earlier Jewish images of the tree were symbolic of the Queen of Heaven, Wisdom, immortality, and joy. Wisdom was "the Lady in the burning bush," the Lady of the fiery tree who gave birth in the holy of holies.[18] From this earlier perspective, to light the lamps of the Menorah is to bring consciousness and wisdom into the world. In both Judaism and Christianity, the archetypal tree of Cosmic Consciousness is still alive.

We have seen throughout this book that (1) our longing for an inclusive myth of meaning has activated an energy field that made possible the discoveries of the psychic blueprints for our evolutionary future; (2) these psychic blueprints, in turn, are functioning as *strange attractors* to ignite, inform, and focus our attention on our transformation; and (3) this focus attracts to us nature's organizing principle that moves through us and creates Imaginal cells that contain the blueprint of a whole new being.

This truly is *our moment*.

We are involved both individually and collectively in the great mysteries of death and rebirth. The entire planet has become a Mystery School. We are both caterpillar and emerging butterfly, and we need to understand the darkness and death of the old even as we participate in creating the new.

The 18th Hexagram in *The I Ching*[19] states:

> *WORK ON WHAT HAS BEEN SPOILED*
> *Has supreme success.*
> *It furthers one to cross the great water.*

Conclusion

I

Throughout this book we have explored the Gift that our ancestors have worked so hard to preserve for us and to pass on to future generations. Symbolically, it is the gift of the fruit from the Cosmic Tree of Life, and literally, it is the knowledge that we are immortal, divine, and creative. This knowledge is the *pure clay* we need to create our worlds in harmony with the laws of the universe.

We have seen how this knowledge, this Gift, has been repressed again and again, yet never entirely lost. And now, in this moment in our history, this knowledge, as part of a highly organized energy field, has risen to the surface of awareness and is bringing about a reframing of our consciousness. It has initiated (1) the discoveries of cultures that nurtured this knowledge in the past; (2) two major revolutions: the shaman-mystic revolution and the scientific revolution of quantum physics; (3) visionary experiences of people around the world; (4) anomalous events, including UFO and crop circle phenomena; (5) social and political movements for equality and freedom; and (6) **the release into consciousness of *what has decayed* throughout the centuries of repression.**

The emergence of this decay into consciousness is an urgent call for us to realize that we have failed to participate in our own evolution. When a culture negates the power of the mind and the reality of the soul, people lose their inner compass. This loss flips the focus outward and causes an unbearable sense of emptiness. This emptiness has aptly been called a "metaphysical malnutrition,"[1] and it results in what Kingsley has called that terrible "missingness" within.

This vacuum within the psyche is the root cause of the desperate and addictive search to fill this empty space. When there is no attraction to or knowledge of how to draw all the aspects of the psyche toward its inner, coherent center, the focus, as mentioned above, shifts outward. When this shift occurs, the ego does not have a deep center to reflect, so it seeks meaning or significance in the outer world. This desperate move results in an ego that cannot be fulfilled. In extreme cases, such an egotistic or narcissistic personality can never have enough attention, admiration, power, or control. *And since there is no inner stability, violence is inevitable.*

In the 1980s I met a scientist who had been involved in research on an extreme form of the narcissistic personality. This condition is called *alexithymia: the hormones from the heart simply cannot flow to the brain.* Such a person is dysfunctional emotionally and socially. The research also indicated that a person with alexithymia has a weak imaginative faculty and difficulty using symbolic language. There is an inability to understand or describe one's own emotions or be aware of the emotions of others, thus the lack of compassion and empathy. When I checked more recent research, I read that alexithymia is prevalent in approximately ten percent of the population, but the same characteristics can exist in other forms of mental disorder. The insatiable need for power in such dysfunctional personalities accounts in large measure for their excessive presence in political and financial positions throughout the world.

The existence of this and other types of dysfunction is not surprising given the fact that our Western materialistic worldview has devalued, repressed, and forgotten our symbolic, imaginative abilities and the earlier wisdom of the heart. Our culture has denied feeling as a valid way of knowing and dismissed soul as a religious fiction. This loss has expressed itself in many forms, such as addiction, indifference, fundamentalism, fanaticism, and violence, along with the extreme forms of the egotistic, narcissistic personality who craves power, has no compassion for others, feels superior to everyone, cannot discern or speak the truth, and is hell-bent to destroy what cannot be controlled.

*The blatant rise to power in the U.S. of these decayed forms of thwarted development is intensely alarming, but **it allows us to see what has been an underlying condition in our culture for centuries**.* For several hundred years, most Americans have not been aware of what this aspect of our government has been willing to do to force its will on the world, nor have most of us been aware of the fact that this behavior, whose roots go all the way back to the original invasions, was encouraged and condoned by the Church. I had not realized until recently that the European Christian Monarchs, who supported the discovery, invasion, and colonization in the Americas, were supported in their genocide by what is called the Doctrine of Discovery/Domination that was issued by several papal bulls from the Vatican, beginning in 1493.[2]

According to Steven Newcomb (Shawnee/Lenape), Co-Director of the Indigenous Law Institute, as well as other scholars, these documents declared war on the non-Christian world by instructing Christians to invade, capture, vanquish, subdue, and reduce all non-Christian people to perpetual slavery. Further, these papal bulls demanded that the invaders take all lands and possessions of the vanquished people. If these people were to refuse to merge themselves into the "superior race" of the Christian conquerors, they should be destroyed. These are the deep roots of the shadow of our culture—roots that extend into our European past. And, if we think that this is no longer relevant, we need to know that this Doctrine of Discovery, in relation to land ownership, was accepted as law by the United States Supreme Court in 1823 in the case of *Johnson v. M'Intosh*.[3]

> *This doctrine of ancient Christendom, supported by papal edicts, continues to serve as the conceptual foundation of the political and legal system of the United States, and as the conceptual foundation of other dominating political systems elsewhere in the world in relation to original nations.*[4]

Even through the twentieth and twenty-first centuries, Supreme Court decisions concerning Native Americans have upheld the Doctrine of Discovery/Domination, that is, all rights to the land belong to the United States. The original peoples have only the right of occupancy.[5]

This is our legacy. We must know it, so we can transform it. There are millions of people in the United States and elsewhere, including many Catholics, who oppose this law of prejudice, privilege, and superiority, yet these toxic attitudes continue to live and incite violence within the national psyche. During our more than two hundred years of history, our government has been involved in numerous invasions, and we are presently conducting warfare in seventy-six countries.[6] There have been murders, coups, torture, and assassinations both within this country and abroad. From 1946 to 2000, our country interfered in eighty elections in other countries, and this is not counting the invasions or coups backed by our government.[7] We are now in perpetual war, and we are supporting the slaughter of hundreds of thousands of civilians, including children, destroying entire cultures, and allowing disease and starvation to kill the ones we have failed to bomb.

And now as we watch our Congress refuse to do anything to stop the slaughter of our children in their schools, we are horrified with this loss of soul. Yet, it is this same loss of soul that has allowed our government to murder the first peoples of this land, the Native Americans, to separate them from their children, and to brutally deny their civil rights. And it is this same loss of soul that has allowed the separation of African American children from their parents during slavery, as well as the continuous murder and denial of the human rights of African Americans and other minority cultures in this country. And it is this same loss of soul that is presently separating children from their parents who are fleeing the violence this country has seeded in their home countries for decades. Those who have suffered injustice from this Mephistophelian shadow of our culture have always known about our loss of soul. **Now that this shadow has established itself in the most powerful positions of our government, we are able to see more clearly what it means for a culture to lose its soul.**

The name, Mephistopheles, is definitely the correct name for this shadow self as it actually means **liar** and **destroyer**.[8] Our government has always lied to us, but never before have we witnessed on a daily basis the destruction of reality through incessant and compulsive lying from the president, those around him, a major media outlet that amplifies the deception, and various forms of social media. This persistent lying destroys the liar, but it also destroys the intellectual scaffolding of our culture and demeans the national and international discourse. But even more important, it brings about the deterioration of our mental and physical health and threatens all life on the planet. This is the ultimate price for selling our souls. Unfortunately, our culture has not been aware of the creative or destructive effects of what we think and feel.

We will remember that Goethe's Faust did, in fact, sell his soul to the deceptive Mephistopheles, who had no ability to feel or love. Faust could only become conscious of his own complicity in the crimes he attributed to Mephistopheles when he began to *feel* sorrow for the suffering around him, and he could only take responsibility when he realized that Mephistopheles was his own shadow. It was through his growing ability to feel, and eventually to love, that Faust was able to redeem his soul.

I often think of my dream of the jackals at the North Pole stirring the contents of a great cauldron so that the contents will not spill out and cover the earth with disaster. My son Pisti is in the dream, and he tells me that **"The time is critical."** When I ask what is in the cauldron, Pisti says, "Shit. Unclaimed shit." I understand that it is the work of each of us to claim our own "shit" from the cauldron. We do not have to claim what is not ours, but we do have to be acutely conscious of just what does, in fact, belong to us. **We have to become conscious of our own shadow.** Had each of us done our work daily, the planet would not now be threatened. I feel sorrow and remorse for my own unconsciousness, but I also feel the transformative potential in each of us once we are willing to do this sacred work. For it becomes clear that working on what has decayed can open us to feeling and love — and, ultimately, to the redemption of our own souls.

We are living in a time when we are forced almost hourly to observe the decayed forms of Western culture now that they are in full view: in addition to the egotistic/narcissistic personality's drive for power and money, his sense of privilege and superiority, his dishonesty and his lack of feeling, we are also watching his disdain for the law and legal institutions, his flagrant greed, incompetence, vulgarity, brutality, ignorance, lack of respect, racism, misogyny, and violence. And we are also forced to see this shadow's willingness to demonically play with the destinies of the peoples and countries of the world for his own gain. **These characteristics are symptoms of failed development. We need to see this for what it is—not just a few dangerously undeveloped individuals, but the unconscious shadow of our culture.**

What we are witnessing is the full-blown pathology of the Western worldview. We no longer need to ask what has caused this pathology. We know.

And knowing this is our strength. We know that we lost our soul when we lost our true stories of experiencing a higher consciousness within. **As we navigate these difficult times of change and transformation, we also know that there is a cosmic intelligence working with us.** The shocking thrust of these decayed forms into the spotlight with the 2016 elections as I was still writing this book on the major cause of this decay was both startling and confirming. The visionary world and *The I Ching* had made it clear to me that this book was to be about the work we need to do on these decayed forms. The synchronicity was evident. And even one instance of synchronicity is the manifestation of a cosmic law that reflects the relationship of the outer world to the inner world in a non-causal, meaningful way. All such events, says *The I Ching*, are the results of the "immutable, eternal law at work in all change."[9]

In no way do I want to give the impression that I understand the philosophical and mathematical science of *The I Ching*. But what I do know is that we have received an urgent message that now is the time to work on what has decayed. The condition of decay is advanced, but it can still be turned around—if we choose to do this work on ourselves and the culture. **In the commentaries on *The I Ching*, Richard Wilhelm explains that by doing this work, the world can be set in order once again, but, he says, LOVE must prevail throughout the entire work.**[10]

Along with the message of the 18th Hexagram, we received the healing code of ML, which is the highly organized energy field that our longing for a just and peaceful world has activated. So, we know the work we need to do, and we know that as long as we are doing this work, we are within the field of infinite possibilities.

II

This same illness has risen to power elsewhere in the world and is presently threatening other countries. Our work on what has decayed is urgent: this work requires us (1) to know in what ways these decayed forms reflect us, so we can do the inner work to heal ourselves and, at the same time, (2) to know in what ways we can politically and socially block the destructive consequences of this decay.

It is important to recognize that the consciousness of the world is not the same as it was during the 1930s when similar forms of thwarted development rose to power in Europe. We are now part of the highly organized energy field that has reframed our consciousness through the discoveries of our past, the social and political movements, and the spiritual and scientific revolutions. We have already seen that large numbers of people in our country and around the world are energized and focused in their rejection of the egotism, narcissism, racism, misogyny, disregard for children, the poor and the sick, the lack of respect for nature, the denial of reality, censorship, and the unabashed disrespect for life itself.

And we are now reclaiming the sacred knowledge of *how* we evolve. We are realizing that the true role of civilization is to discover and nurture this knowledge. Our ancestors understood that *civilization cannot develop unless it is rooted in the power of the heart to give birth to a feeling world.* They knew that without feeling, we cannot bring *justice* into being. And they understood that *without the inward journey to develop soul, creation cannot continue to unfold.* The message is clear: without the creative energy of love, we cannot create a true civilization. And when we cannot create, we destroy.

And this is what Jesus of the Nag Hammadi texts meant when he said, "If you bring forth what is within you, what you bring forth will save you. If you do not bring forth what is within you, what you do not bring forth will destroy you."[11] Jung has frequently reminded us that just as the goal of the acorn is to become an oak tree, so is it the goal—the blueprint—of the soul to fulfill its own unique form of wholeness—*to bring forth what is within*. Given the necessary conditions for development, the individual, just as the acorn, will eventually achieve wholeness. **It is our responsibility as individuals and as a civilization to know, create, and maintain the necessary conditions for *the evolution of life*. This is the true role of civilization.**

We have not yet achieved this. Most of us have not been aware of our potential to evolve, to bring forth our own uniqueness, or to achieve Cosmic Consciousness. And most—not all—of our politicians do not feel the responsibility to "Protect everything that is coming into being." Many people do insist, however, that every child has the right to be born, but they seldom acknowledge other, equally important rights, such as the right to be loved, wanted, and healthy, to live in a just, safe, equitable and non-polluted world. And (it should go without saying) that all our children have the right to an education and health care. In addition, as our ancestors understood, all children have the right to receive their true stories—*the pure clay* of who they are and why they're here. This is the responsibility of a true civilization. **Anything less is not civilized.**

The shaman-mystic revolution and the new science revolution are helping us to remember this and realize once again that *civilization should be both a poetic and a scientific endeavor* to intensify and elevate human experience. Every person, says Novalis, should become a poet *so we can all accomplish the task of every true poet: the writing of the sacred text of our own labyrinthine journey*. The poet pursues *the intensification of experience and the evolution of life*. The Celtic bards used music and poetic incantations to ignite intensified states of consciousness in their listeners. And the San people use dance to intensify and elevate their experience of deeper orders of reality. Our ancestors painted caves and temples, etched the surfaces of rock, created rituals, music, dance, and built megalithic structures that are both temples and observatories to engage and harmonize human consciousness with the consciousness of the universe. These ancestors were shaman-mystics who were also artists and scientists. They understood that it was their role in civilization to create "spiritual technologies" to assist the development of soul.

The new science of quantum physics is beginning to awaken this same consciousness in modern scientists. Physicist Amit Goswami tells us that the new science of quantum physics "is producing its own technology" that can help us expand consciousness. Once we understand "the primacy of consciousness," he explains, we realize that consciousness, our subjective experiences, feelings, love, and spirituality "can all be included within the purview of science." Goswami further states that the universe has a purpose, we have a purpose, and science has a purpose. Then he adds what we never thought we would hear a modern scientist say: *the purpose of science is to pursue what it means to be human, "which is to pursue, to discover, the soul."*[12]

Our main goal as human beings, says Goswami, is to "work on ourselves to transform into that bigger consciousness." We are able to expand consciousness, he says, through the "journey to the heart," through feeling, emotion, and love. We need to come down from the head and bring the energy into the heart.[13] This is the wisdom of the heart that all the ancient shaman-mystic-scientist cultures nurtured, and it is now being nurtured by the new science.

The discoveries of our past and the new science are helping us to remember that a true civilization creates structures that initiate, nurture, guide, and intensify the evolution of the species. Marija Gimbutas tells us that in the Old European cultures, "The emphasis...was on technologies that nourished people's lives." The creative foundation of any civilization, she adds, "lies in its degree of artistic creation, aesthetic achievements, nonmaterial values, and freedom which make life meaningful and enjoyable for all its citizens." War, says Gimbutas, *is not endemic to the human species.*[14] No weapons of war have been found in these cultures, nor were any depictions of violence, war, or torture found in their art. They were peaceful, egalitarian, and artistic. Their art celebrated the joy of Life, and their technologies supported this way of life. Can we even begin to imagine what the great technicians of the West might create—if they fell in love with Soul, the Sovereign of the Land, and realized that they can only rule the land by right of their union with her and their championship of her freedom?

Falling in love with Soul, however, begins by nurturing *respect*—for all life. Nothing of value is possible without *respect*. Without it, we cannot love, for *respect* is the foundation of all relationships, knowledge, and creativity. We have seen such respect in the Native Americans at Standing Rock and the hundreds of tribes who joined them in their resistance to the Dakota Access Pipeline. Their *respect* for the land, the air, the water, themselves, future generations, and all life reflects their love for Soul, the Sovereign of this Land. They have always known that their rights to the land are born out of this respect and love and their willingness to champion her freedom. Where are the laws, the courts, and the people who can prevent King Amangon from raping their land and stealing the golden bowls from the Maidens at the Wells?

The answer to this question is developing out of social and political movements. The latest movements, such as the Black Lives Matter Movement, the Me Too and Never Again Movements, are demanding accountability for disrespectful and criminal behavior. The mission of Black Lives Matter, a civil rights movement, is to develop the political power capable of reducing the violence against Black communities. In the Me Too Movement, women who have experienced disrespect and sexual assault from men who had power over them are bringing this injustice into the spotlight and demanding that these men be held accountable. And the Never Again Movement is a youth movement born out of the experience of the mass murder of their high school friends and teachers. They are committed to gun control and the reduction of violence in this country. Some of these young people in this ethnically diverse movement have been deeply influenced by Native American and Black leaders, who have long been committed to an ethical and feeling world. One young spokesperson from the Never Again Movement has stated explicitly that **our culture is in need of soul.**

The new Poor People's Campaign: A National Call for Moral Revival **is a response to this urgent need of soul in America.** This movement began in 2017 but has its roots in the Poor People's Campaign of 1968, organized by Reverend Dr. Martin Luther King, Jr. King had been acutely aware of our loss of soul. **He knew that our illness was spiritual, and he** was bold enough to speak openly about racism, poverty, and militarism as interrelated systems of violence.[15]

The new Poor People's Campaign was organized by Reverend Dr. William Barber II and Reverend Dr. Liz Theoharis to unite people across the country to create a new narrative in which the dignity and equality of all people are acknowledged and respected.[16] This is a comprehensive campaign that directly addresses the pathological, Mephistophelian shadow of American culture and the tragic consequences of its cruelty. It is a call for an awareness — a new consciousness — of our historical treatment of others, beginning with a call for equality and justice for all First Nations that have suffered and continue to suffer from the Doctrine of Discovery and the denial of their rights, resources, culture, and wealth. It addresses the attacks on democracy in the forms of anti-immigrant, anti-Muslim, anti-African American, anti-Hispanic, and anti-LGBTQ prejudice and violence. It addresses poverty (almost half the population in the U.S. lives in poverty), systemic racism, the destruction of the environment, an economy based on war, and the "distorted moral narrative."[17]

Just what is this distorted moral/religious narrative that views the 2016 presidential election as an answer to prayer? In "A Moral Agenda Based on Fundamental Rights," this dysfunctional narrative is defined as the "extremist religious and Christian nationalist agenda [that] deliberately diverts attention from the key issues and challenges facing the majority of Americans." This narrative frames the "moral crisis" in the U.S. as a battle between "progressive atheist values and God." This framing is rejected by the Poor People's Campaign. "Indeed," they point out, "there are profound consequences to a moral narrative that ignores poverty, healthcare, decent jobs, and other crises facing the poor today…. The truth is that a morality that claims to care for the souls of people while destroying their bodies and communities is deeply immoral."[18]

This movement developed out of many years of organizing and meeting with thousands of people in more than thirty states. It consists of poor people, moral leaders, and people of conscience who are aware of the devastating consequences of these problems and are committed to working for the development of a moral consciousness that will inform and structure all our public policies and budget allocations. **This is a consciousness that is beyond political parties and individual religions because it is rooted in our deepest spiritual and Constitutional commitments to a just and feeling world.**[19]

All of these movements are committed to a very different kind of civilization. They are rooted in a clear view of the dishonest, immoral and unethical agendas of our government—and they are demanding change. They are not tolerating inaction, disrespect, or lies.

We are watching a new consciousness that is developing from all walks of life and all ethnic groups—and it is a consciousness that can change our world.

Not long after Pisti's death, István had a vision about respect and love. "I realized," István said, "that love is the Key to everything." But then he quickly added that he also realized that love is not possible without respect:

> *respect allows us to be more conscious of love, but I have to say that I never experienced respect like I did today. It has a completely new meaning for me. I respected myself and everyone and everything else to such a degree that the whole world was sacred.*[20]

It is *respect* that opens the heart, and it is the heart that births a **feeling** and **just** world. We have longed for a myth of meaning—a great myth that gives meaning to our individual, temporal struggles for survival, love, and creativity. *And the universe has responded.* The wisdom of our ancestors has emerged out of the earth and the past to instruct us. Quantum physicists are discovering spirit and the human soul. Our dreams, visions, and anomalous experiences are awakening and guiding us. Our ancestors and beings from other worlds are working with us in both the subtle *and* the physical worlds. Baba Yaga's balls of yarn are rolling out in front of us, and nature herself is participating through her highly organized energy fields that are intensifying our experience and elevating our consciousness.

We now have everything we need to confront the collective darkness that has risen into our consciousness and is parading across our national — and world — stage. Each day we see what the lack of respect looks like, how it behaves, and how it destroys everything it touches. This darkness is not disguised with intelligence or superior ability: it is revealing with every word and gesture precisely what it is and what it seeks to accomplish. We cannot be fooled. And this, at least, is a good thing.

Writer Paul Levy describes our present condition as "a state of fragmentation deep within the collective unconscious itself that has seemingly spilled outside of our skulls and has taken the form of collective events playing themselves out en masse on the world stage."[21]

Our soul is calling out for us to observe this incredibly obvious display of darkness and violence that is revealing itself before us, for as Levy adds,

> *One of the most destructive dynamics in the human psyche is when the darkness of the unconscious becomes visible and makes itself available for being made conscious... and we choose to ignore it.*[22]

At the same time, however, our soul is also calling out to us to be conscious of the forces of light that are emerging in our world. While it is true that our darkness is becoming painfully visible to us, it is important to remember that the light can be found within this terrible dream that we have been dreaming. As the Gnostic Jesus taught, this light is hidden within the darkness of our unknowing, and as Jung continually reminded us, "One does not become enlightened by imagining figures of light, but by making the darkness conscious."[23] And, says poet and playwright Christopher Fry, "there is an angle of experience where the dark is distilled into light."[24] We are just beginning to realize that this *angle* can only be achieved through the *feeling heart*. It is the wisdom of the heart, the power of love, that is the agent of distillation.

As we work with these opposing principles, it is important to remember that our higher consciousness, Christ/Cosmic Consciousness, is rooted in a unified field that includes but transcends opposing forces.

Jung and Goethe would tell us to hold this tension of opposites with the knowledge that it is nature's tendency to evolve, to achieve a new, a third, a completely unanticipated consciousness that transcends this split of opposites that we are now experiencing.

Between 1989 and 1992, I was part of a small group of therapists and professors who met once a month to practice methods of entering altered states of consciousness. The first information that came to us had to do with the existence of points of energy around the earth. We didn't know what they were, but we did know that we needed to meditate on them and draw their energy into the earth. About a year later, we received information through another vision that these points of energy around the earth were nexus points in a great web around the earth and throughout the universe. And, to the astonishment of all of us, we were told that our ancestors knew how to consciously travel from one nexus point to another within this great web of light.

So many unexpected things happened during those three years, both within the group and within my own life, that I didn't think much more about the web. It wasn't until 1992, one year after Pisti's death, that I had a vision in which he showed me the planet covered by a radiant net of light. It was breathtakingly beautiful. As I was taking in its beauty, Pisti told me that the nexus points of light within this net needed to be activated and grounded by individual souls on the earth.

That was over twenty years ago, but a few months ago, I experienced several synchronistic events that related to Pisti until suddenly I felt his presence and heard him say that the net around the earth has been strengthened and we would be moving to a new level of our work on the earth.

Later, I realized that this net of light had been described as Indra's net in the ancient cosmology of the Vedas in the East. It was seen as an infinite web whose nodal points were jewels, each of which reflected all the other nodal points throughout the universe. I was also to learn that many people had experienced this net in dreams or visions. Anne Baring shares her experience of this net in *The Dream of the Cosmos*. In a vision, she sees "a great web or net made of gossamer filaments of light; they sparkle with jewels like a spider's web in the sun. At the jeweled points where these filaments meet there are vortices of swirling energy." Then Anne hears this radiant net of light speak to her as the Consciousness of the Cosmos, as Soul and Spirit: "My dream, the Dream of the Cosmos, is for you to know Me again, to realize that you live within My Being, My Light and My Love."[25]

A few years ago, a friend introduced me to Sharon McErlane, who has also experienced this net of light. She was initiated into the reality of the net through continuous visions with a group of spirit women who called themselves the Great Council of the Grandmothers. Through these experiences, Sharon learned that the net of light is heart energy that we are able to connect with through our own heart. This allows a giving and receiving between the individual heart and the heart centers or nodes of the net, which she also describes as jewels. When we hold this energy in our hearts, we are connected to all others who are holding this light. This is another way of saying that each jewel reflects within itself all the other jewels.

I had always assumed that this net of light existed only in the spirit dimension, but Sharon pointed out that in 2014, through the use of the Hubble telescope, scientists discovered that there is, in fact, a "cosmic web" that exists in the physical world, not only around the earth but throughout the entire universe.

For several years Sharon has been traveling around the world to work with thousands of women who are connecting with the net of light and grounding this heart energy in themselves and the earth. The Grandmothers said that the work with the net of light was especially important for women to do since the heart/soul is feminine energy that is urgently needed to heal the out-of-balance masculine energy on the earth. Symbolically, we can say that the Queen of Heaven is returning to the earth through the hearts of women who are working with the great net of light. When I told Sharon about the information from Pisti that the net has been greatly strengthened, she said that she had received this same message from the Grandmothers.[26]

István also experienced this net of light in a vision with Pisti in 1992, but from a somewhat different perspective. He saw a radiant light just above the earth's surface all around the globe. Pisti told István that this light was attracted to the earth by everyone on the planet who had ever loved. "The power of this love," Pisti told his Dad, "can do anything. It is infinite." **It appears that as our heart consciousness develops, we are able to attract higher frequencies of light from the universe into the nexus points of the earth's net, and then, through meditation, we are able to draw this light into our hearts and into the earth.** Light is consciousness and love, and each has a magnetic quality that attracts and connects the light throughout the universe.

István seemed to understand this instantly, as is common in visionary experience. But he then realized that just beneath the light, there was what appeared to be an impenetrable layer of pollution that encrusted the earth like cement. As he began to feel the negative energy of this pollution, he heard Pisti say, "Only love can pierce the pollution of forgetfulness, separation, and despair that covers the earth."

Then Pisti asked his Dad, "Can you see those points of light all around the globe?" When István looked closer, he could see individual points of concentrated light right on the earth. Pisti then explained that these points of light were formed by souls who were able to receive, hold, and transmit the light of love. In this way, Pisti explained, they were transforming the pollution into light. These souls, said Pisti, are like high-voltage power stations that ground the light in the earth and send it around the planet. Then Pisti added that "everyone who loves is dreaming a dream to pierce that pollution and carry this light to the center of the earth."[27]

It took some time for me to put all the pieces of this puzzle together. (l) The group that was working on altered states of consciousness received information that there are points of energy around the earth that we need to meditate on and draw their energy into ourselves and the earth. (2) Then the group learned that these points of energy are nexus points in the great web around the planet and throughout the universe. (3) One year after Pisti's death, I actually *saw* the radiant net of light around the earth in all its luminous beauty. And, once again, I learned that the nexus points of light within this net need to be activated and grounded by individual souls on the earth. (4) Then there were István's visions in which he was told that the light was drawn to the earth by love and that there are souls who are drawing this light into themselves and the earth. They were described as high-voltage power stations capable of grounding the light of love into the earth and sending it around the planet. Through this process, *they are distilling the darkness into light.* (5) I discovered the existence of Indra's net in the ancient Vedas. (6) I learned that Western scientists had discovered this cosmic web through the Hubble telescope. (7) I heard of other individuals who had experienced visions of the cosmic web. And (8) I learned about the wisdom of the Great Council of the Grandmothers concerning the net of light and the work being done with this net by groups around the world.

(9) There was one more piece of the puzzle that I had not fully integrated with all of the above instances, most of which came later. This was my experience in 1990 with the disk of light, which I discussed earlier. This occurred at a time when I was still under the influence of the Western worldview, and I doubted every visionary experience I had. But *not* this one. I had never had a more powerful experience in my entire life. The energy was so intense that it took hours after the experience to reestablish my normal balance. When my Western mind tried to assess all that was taking place in my life in the years before Pisti's death, it was this vision that forced me to *know* that there are, in fact, other dimensions of reality.

At the time, of course, I knew I was experiencing the light that we and so many others on the planet had called because the Voice made it clear that they were a response to this call:

> *We are the Light.*
> *We are the Light*
> *Circling around your planet.*
>
> *You have called us*
> *And we are here*
> *To be with you all three.*

> *Can you feel us?*
> *You have called us*
> *And we are here.*
>
> *Can you feel us?*
> *Your planet has called us*
> *And we are here.*

Then there was a moment in which the consciousness of the disk told us that they were ready to connect to our planet. Somehow, we knew what to do: as the three of us sat on the floor, we suddenly made a circle and embraced. Then we felt the energy descend and flow through us and into the planet. Each of us had a strange feeling that we had been born for this moment. Later, I would realize that people all over the earth were doing exactly what we were doing: they were loving and longing for a world of love and peace, and, in so doing, they were drawing this light to the planet and then allowing it to descend and connect to the earth through them.

> *You have drawn to yourselves this day*
> *All those on your planet*
> *Who are creating worlds*
> *Of Love and Peace.*

It seems strange to me now that I did not realize for some time that we had experienced what all the later visions were instructing us to do: to allow the light energy to flow through our hearts and into the earth. I simply had not been fully aware of the tremendous creative *potential* in this process. Yet István's visions with Pisti had shown us how the darkness, the terrible spiritual pollution on the earth, was being distilled by individuals who could receive the light of love, hold this light, and then transmit it around the world.

It was now clear to me that all we have to do is open our hearts, focus on a nodal point in the net of light and allow that light and love to flow through us, into the earth, and around the world. We might not even feel the energy at first, but eventually we will. Those who love are doing this whether they are conscious of it or not. When we love, we attract the light of love everywhere, and the power of love distills darkness into light. However, it appears that now we all need to focus that love by *consciously* connecting with the nexus points in the great net of light, *consciously* grounding that light in the earth beneath us, and then *consciously* sending that light around the world.

Our every thought, feeling, and act, whether constructive or destructive, sends ripples throughout the entire universe and is reflected in all the jewels of this divine net. This is the wisdom of Indra's cosmology, quantum physics, and modern visionaries. *We are creative beyond anything we have ever allowed ourselves to imagine.* Our ancestors knew this, and they wanted us to have the sacred knowledge that we are immortal, divine, *and creative.* This is the fruit from the Cosmic Tree of Life. Once we know this, we know we *can* create a loving and peaceful world.

When the various pieces of this puzzle came together, I was overwhelmed with the incredible reality that is taking place on the earth. Collectively, we had called this highly organized energy field of light to the earth—*and it is here.* This energy field of cosmic consciousness has its source in a love that is infinite. It carries the blueprint for our spiritual evolution. I now know that when we called this consciousness and love to ourselves, we were renouncing the terrible dream and awakening to the Dream of the Cosmos.

This is the consciousness that is changing our world.

Appendix 1: Timelines

(Dates are approximate)

Twentieth Century Discoveries of Our Evolutionary Heritage

I. Stone Age (Upper Paleolithic) (40,000–10,000 BCE)

    Cave Cultures in Western Europe (40,000–10,000 BCE)
    San Culture in Africa (33,000 BCE, possibly earlier, through the 1800s CE)
    The Remaining San Shaman Elders Today in Namibia and Botswana

II. Age of the Megalithic Builders (12,000–3000 BCE)
    Mesolithic, Neolithic Periods, possibly much earlier

III. Neolithic Period in Old Europe and Crete (6500–2500 BCE; in Crete until 1400 BCE)

IV. Egypt (3000–1000 BCE, possibly much earlier)

V. Jewish First Temple Tradition (832–621 BCE)

    Dates for the First Temple construction vary widely. The construction date from rabbinic sources is 832 BCE, and the destruction of the tradition under Josiah, not the Temple, is 621 BCE.

VI. Anatolian Greek/Presocratic Tradition (500 BCE to the Birth of Christ)

Five Waves of Awakening to Our Evolutionary Heritage

I. High Middle Ages (1000–1300 CE)

II. Italian Renaissance (1460–1527 CE)

III. Rosicrucian Enlightenment (1600–1620 CE)

IV. English and German Romantic Movement (1775–1850 CE)

V. Present Time

Appendix 2: Dreams/Visions

Description	Person	Page
The I Ching/ML Experience	István	44-45
"Our brothers and sisters on the earth are dreaming a terrible dream."	Betty	45-46
Addiction to Rational Consciousness	Betty	60
A Physicist's Vision of the Cosmic Dance	Fritjof Capra, Ph.D.	66-67
Cosmic Consciousness	Richard Maurice Bucke, M.D.	70
The New Planetary Consciousness/DNA	István	72
Cosmic Consciousness	Elisabeth Kübler-Ross, M.D.	72-73
North Pole/Cauldron of Shit	Betty	93-94
Dream Visit with Jung	Betty	97-98
Fear of Death vs. Force of Life	István	104-105
The Woman in Blue and the Spiral of Life	Betty	117-118
The Knight/The Visionary and the Birth of "Our Lady" at Chartres Cathedral	Betty	130-131
The Women in Blue and the University	Betty	197-198
The Living Womb of Yin-Yang and the Birth of the Feminine	Betty	198-199
History Cries through me	Betty	226-229
The San Pedro Experience	Betty	235-237
The Cosmic Tree of Life and the Holy of Holies	Betty	239-241
"Protect everything that is coming into being."	Pisti	243-244
Death Valley/Desert Mother of Grief and Rage	Betty	245-246
Pure Clay for Our Children	István	245-246
Disk of Cosmic Consciousness	Betty	248-250
The Queen of Heaven Embraces the Desert Mother of Rage and Grief	Betty	253-254
"Death is as Divine as Life."	István	340
Cosmic Consciousness	Bradford Keeney, Ph.D.	410
Cosmic Consciousness	The San Bushmen	412-413
Aluna/Cosmic Consciousness	The Kogi	416-417
Respect/Sacred World	István	446
Net of Light 1992, 2017	Betty	448
Net of Light/Consciousness of the Cosmos	Anne Baring	448-449
Net of Light/Heart Energy	Sharon McErlane	449
Net of Light, Consciousness and Love	István	450

Appendix 3: The Complete Gospel of Mary Magdalene

The Gospel of the Beloved Companion: The Complete Gospel of Mary Magdalene by Jehanne de Quillan (2011) is the first translation into English of a previously unpublished gospel from the first century. This gospel was originally written in Alexandrian Greek, brought from Egypt to the Languedoc in southern France during the early to middle first century, and preserved to the present day by the families and community of that region, which is de Quillan's own spiritual community. It was translated into Occitan, the language of that area, in the early twelfth century, but de Quillan has used the original Alexandrian Greek as the basis for her translation.

The author does not reveal the location of the original manuscript, which she explains is a matter of trust with those in her spiritual community who have protected and valued this text, often with their lives, for over a millennium but always with the hope that its message could one day be known by others. The original manuscript uses no punctuation, no chapter or verse, but de Quillan punctuates her translation and divides it into chapters and verses for clarity and reference. However, in addition to this translation, she adds an Appendix with a translation of the entire text as it appears in the original manuscript. She also adds a commentary comparing *The Gospel of the Beloved Companion* with the Canonical and Gnostic Gospels. The majority of her community has welcomed this translation, but de Quillan relates the fear of the traditional minority that knowledge of this manuscript could open the community once again to the wrath of the Church.

I do not refer to this complete Gospel of Mary in Part I because I did not discover it until *Merchants of Light* had entered the process of publication. However, this text appears to be further confirmation of the sacred relationship between Jesus and Mary Magdalene *and* Jesus as a spiritual teacher of the way of an ancient mystical tradition.

Appendix 4: Kundalini

Throughout this book I have discussed the creative energy of the universe — an energy that exists in each one of us. It is the loving, conscious, eternal, creative, and transformative source of all life. Our ancestors discovered this energy either spontaneously or through developed techniques and became master visionaries, mystics, healers, and scientists who discovered the sacred laws of the universe within and without. Some experienced the full development of this energy as it rises from the base of the spine, flows up through the chakras, opens the heart, unfolds fully in the brain, and physically transforms the body and mind. This energy, in all its forms, has been called by many names: in the Kalahari Desert it is N|om; in the East it is Kundalini; in the West it is the vital force of life, Wisdom, the Queen of Heaven, the Holy Spirit, Cosmic Consciousness or Kundalini.

In a recent conversation with Andrew Harvey, mystical scholar, he mentioned the increase in people who are spontaneously experiencing this energy in its kundalini form of rising and moving through the body. He introduced me to an American woman, Dorothy Walters, who has experienced the full rising of kundalini and who, he says, is the greatest living mystical poet. Since I had not mentioned this particular form of experience occurring today in Western culture, Dorothy's work is very helpful: *Unmasking the Rose: A Record of a Kundalini Initiation* and *The Kundalini Poems: Reflections of Radiance and Joy*. For other perspectives, see the anthology, *Kundalini Rising: Exploring the Energy of Awakening*.

Two videos of Andrew Harvey and Dorothy Walters (YouTube, Oct. 31, 2016, Nov. 13, 2018) are important for descriptions of (1) the kundalini experience; (2) Dorothy's conviction of an imminent "exponential increase" in people experiencing kundalini and other forms of spiritual awakening; (3) how all these experiences are creating a morphogenetic Field that makes it easier for others to experience this new consciousness; and (4) how the decayed and collapsing structures of our time are preparing the way for the birth of "a new, divine, embodied humanity."

Endnotes

Introduction/Overview

1. Joseph Campbell, *The Masks of God, Vol. 3: Occidental Mythology* (London: Arkana, 1991), 14.
2. Michael Winkelman and John R. Baker, *Supernatural as Natural: A Biocultural Approach to Religion* (Upper Saddle River: Pearson Prentice Hall, 2010), 85, 96.
3. Joanna Eede, "Uncontacted Tribes: The Last Free People on Earth," *National Geographic*, April 1, 2011, http://voices.nationalgeographic.com/2011/04/01/uncontacted-tribes-the-last-free-people-on-earth/.
4. Anne Baring and Jules Cashford, *The Myth of the Goddess: Evolution of an Image* (London: Viking, 1991), 38–40.
5. Campbell, *The Masks of God, Vol. 1: Primitive Mythology* (London: Arkana, 1991), 328.
6. Marija Gimbutas, *The Language of the Goddess* (San Francisco: Harper & Row, 1989), 89.
7. Carl Kerényi, *Dionysos: Archetypal Image of Indestructible Life*, trans. Ralph Manheim (Princeton: Princeton University Press, 1976), 89–95. See also Kerényi, "Labyrinth-Studien," in *Humanistische Seelen-Forschung* (München: Langen Müller, 1966), 226–288. So powerful and all pervasive was the labyrinthine journey that its stylized symbol, often called the Greek key, is still seen today throughout Western culture, but now the knowledge of its once profound meaning is lost and it appears only as ornament.
8. Mircea Eliade, *Patterns in Comparative Religion*, trans. Rosemary Sheed (Cleveland: Meridian Books, 1970), 267, 286, 269, 283.
9. Manly Palmer Hall, "Golden Chain of Homer That Binds Heaven and Earth," Promienie Gwiazd, YouTube video, posted May 8, 2013, https://youtu.be/v_eu2uKGCf4.
10. William Butler Yeats, "The Two Trees."
11. Margaret Barker, *The Great Angel: A Study of Israel's Second God* (Louisville: Westminster/John Knox, 1992), 58.
12. Barker, *The Great High Priest: The Temple Roots of Christian Liturgy* (London: T&T Clark, 2004), 243.
13. Barker, *Great High Priest*, 243–246.
14. James M. Robinson, gen. ed., "On the Origin of the World," in *The Nag Hammadi Library*, trans. Members of the Coptic Gnostic Library Project of the Institute for Antiquity and Christianity (San Francisco: Harper & Row, 1977), 169.
15. Barker, *Great Angel*, 65.
16. Barker, *Great Angel*, 58.
17. Roger Cook, *The Tree of Life: Symbol of the Centre* (London: Thames & Hudson, 1974), 107.

[18] Barker, *The Revelation of Jesus Christ* (Edinburgh: T&T Clark, 2000), 15-17 and "What Did King Josiah Reform?," Thinly Veiled, accessed May 1, 2016, http://www.thinlyveiled.com/barker/josiahsreform.htm.
[19] Exodus 20:4-6.
[20] Barker, *Great Angel*, 15.
[21] John White, "The Doomsday Fallacy," *Atlantis Rising*, May/June 2010, 59.
[22] Elaine Pagels, *The Gnostic Gospels* (New York: Vintage Books, 1981), xiii-xiv.
[23] Rainer Maria Rilke, *Briefe an einen jungen Dichter* (Leipzig: Insel-Verlag, 1932), 46.
[24] Bradford Keeney, *The Bushman Way of Tracking God: The Original Spirituality of the Kalahari People* (New York: Atria Books, 2010), xix.
[25] Graham Hancock, *Magicians of the Gods: The Forgotten Wisdom of Earth's Lost Civilization* (New York: Thomas Dunne Books, 2015), 35-36 and Hancock, introduction to *Göbekli Tepe: Genesis of the Gods*, by Andrew Collins (Rochester: Bear, 2014), 1-3.
[26] Hancock, *Magicians of the Gods*, 9-11.
[27] Keith Critchlow, *Time Stands Still: New Light on Megalithic Science* (Edinburgh: Floris Books, 2007), 10, 13, 19, 21, 20.
[28] Critchlow, *Time Stands Still*, 14.
[29] Gimbutas, *The Goddesses and Gods of Old Europe: Myths and Cult Images* (Berkeley: University of California Press, 1982), 16.
[30] Gimbutas, *Goddesses and Gods*, 9-10 and *The Civilization of the Goddess: The World of Old Europe*, ed. Joan Marler (New York: HarperSanFrancisco, 1991), vii-xi.
[31] Gimbutas, *Civilization of the Goddess*, vii-xi and *Language of the Goddess*, xv-xxi.
[32] Joan Marler, "The Circle Is Unbroken: A Brief Biography," in *From the Realm of the Ancestors: An Anthology in Honor of Marija Gimbutas*, ed. Joan Marler (Manchester: Knowledge, Ideas & Trends, 1997), 7.
[33] Gimbutas, *Language of the Goddess*, 321.
[34] Barker, *Great Angel*, 58.
[35] Kerényi, *Dionysos*, 6, 10.
[36] Kerényi, *Dionysos*, 14-28.
[37] Gimbutas, *Goddesses and Gods*, 117-135 and *Language of the Goddess*, 25-29.
[38] Kerényi, "Kore," in *Essays on a Science of Mythology: The Myths of the Divine Child and the Divine Maiden*, by C.G. Jung and C. Kerényi, trans. R.F.C. Hull (New York: Harper TorchBooks, 1963), 154. See also Kerényi, "Labyrinth-Studien," 226-288.
[39] Kerényi, *Dionysos*, 95.
[40] Gimbutas, *Language of the Goddess*, 3-29.
[41] Gimbutas, *Goddesses and Gods*, 9-10.
[42] Baring and Cashford, *Myth of the Goddess*, 40.
[43] Jeremy Naydler, *Shamanic Wisdom in the Pyramid Texts: The Mystical Tradition of Ancient Egypt* (Rochester: Inner Traditions, 2005), 20-47.
[44] Naydler, *Shamanic Wisdom*, 31.
[45] John Anthony West, *Serpent in the Sky: The High Wisdom of Ancient Egypt* (Wheaton: Theosophical Publishing House, 1993), ix.

[46] Naydler, *Shamanic Wisdom*, 31 and West, *Serpent in the Sky*, ix.
[47] West, *Serpent in the Sky*, xviii.
[48] West, *Serpent in the Sky*, 9.
[49] West, *Serpent in the Sky*, 16-23.
[50] West, *Serpent in the Sky*, xv.
[51] West, *Serpent in the Sky*, 25.
[52] West, *Serpent in the Sky*, ix.
[53] Naydler, *Shamanic Wisdom*, 148-149.
[54] Naydler, *Shamanic Wisdom*, 3.
[55] See Barker, *Great High Priest* and *Great Angel*.
[56] Stephan A. Hoeller, *Jung and the Lost Gospels: Insights into the Dead Sea Scrolls and the Nag Hammadi Library* (Wheaton: Theosophical Publishing House, 1993), 16-17, 25.
[57] Marvin Meyer, ed., *The Gnostic Gospels of Jesus: The Definitive Collection of Mystical Gospels and Secret Books About Jesus of Nazareth* (New York: HarperSanFrancisco, 2005), xx-xxi, 47.
[58] Barker, *Great Angel*, 51.
[59] Peter Kingsley, *In the Dark Places of Wisdom* (Inverness: Golden Sufi Center, 1999), 55-60.
[60] Kingsley, *Dark Places of Wisdom*, 101-105, 108-115, 7, 36.
[61] Kingsley, *Dark Places of Wisdom*, 113-114.
[62] Kingsley, *Dark Places of Wisdom*, 202-206.
[63] Kingsley, *Dark Places of Wisdom*, 207-208.
[64] Kingsley, *Dark Places of Wisdom*, 43-45.
[65] Kingsley, *Dark Places of Wisdom*, 115.
[66] Eliade, *A History of Religious Ideas, Vol. 1: From the Stone Age to the Eleusinian Mysteries*, trans. Willard R. Trask (Chicago: University of Chicago Press, 1978), xv.
[67] See Aldous Huxley, *The Perennial Philosophy* (New York: Harper Colophon Books, 1970).
[68] Frances A. Yates, *The Rosicrucian Enlightenment* (Boulder: Shambhala, 1978), xii.
[69] See Gimbutas, *Goddesses and Gods*; *Language of the Goddess*; and *Civilization of the Goddess*. For an excellent study of the feminine image from the Upper Paleolithic to the present, see Baring and Cashford, *Myth of the Goddess*.
[70] See Thomas Goddard Bergin and Max Harold Fisch, *The New Science of Giambattista Vico*. Unabridged Translation of 3rd ed. (1744). (Ithaca: Cornell University Press, 1984) and A. Robert Caponigri, *Time and Idea: The Theory of History in Giambattista Vico* (London: Routledge and Kegan Paul, 1953).
[71] Andrew Newberg, Eugene D'Aquili, and Vince Rause, *Why God Won't Go Away: Brain Science and the Biology of Belief* (New York: Ballantine Books, 2001), 169, 156.
[72] Lynne McTaggart, *The Field: The Quest for the Secret Force of the Universe* (New York: HarperCollins, 2002), 21, 11, 33.
[73] Fred Alan Wolf, "Mind and the New Physics/Taking a Quantum Leap in Consciousness: An Interview with Fred Alan Wolf, Ph.D.," by Ronald S. Miller, *Science of Mind*, October 1985, 85, 81.

[74] Amit Goswami, Richard E. Reed, and Maggie Goswami, *The Self-Aware Universe: how consciousness creates the material world* (New York: G. P. Putnam's Sons, 1995), 2.
[75] McTaggart, *The Field*, xiii.
[76] Rilke, *Briefe an einen jungen Dichter*, 46.
[77] Jacques Vallee, *The Invisible College: What a Group of Scientists Has Discovered About UFO Influence on the Human Race* (San Antonio: Anomalist Books, 2014), 5, xii–xiii.
[78] Vallee, *Invisible College*, 2, 13, 12.
[79] Vallee, *Invisible College*, 16, 5, 6, 174–178, 194–206.
[80] Vallee, *Invisible College*, 153–154, 140, 203, 208.
[81] Vallee, *Invisible College*, 18, 123, 199, 200.
[82] Vallee, *Invisible College*, 11.
[83] Freddy Silva, *Secrets in the Fields: The Science and Mysticism of Crop Circles* (Charlottesville: Hampton Roads, 2002), Back Book Cover, xvii, xiv.
[84] Rilke, *Briefe an einen jungen Dichter*, 46.
[85] See "Temporary Temples: The Latest UK Crop Circles," Temporary Temples, http://temporarytemples.co.uk/.
[86] Silva, *Secrets in the Fields*, xiii, xiv.
[87] Silva, *Secrets in the Fields*, xiv.
[88] Vallee, *Invisible College*, 28, 196.
[89] Jessica Roemischer, introduction to "Comprehensive Compassion, Part 1" and "The Divinization of the Cosmos, Part 2," by Brian Swimme, *What is Enlightenment*, September–December 2006, 70–71.
[90] Brian Swimme, "Comprehensive Compassion, Part 1" and "The Divinization of the Cosmos, Part 2," *What is Enlightenment*, September–December 2006, 79.
[91] See Candace B. Pert, *Molecules of Emotion: The Science Behind Mind-Body Medicine* (New York: Simon & Schuster, 1999).
[92] Charles Eisenstein, "Aluna: A Message to Little Brother," *Tikkun*, May 26, 2015, https://www.tikkun.org/nextgen/a-message-to-little-brother. See also Alan Ereira, *The Elder Brothers: a lost South American people and their message about the fate of the earth* (New York: Alfred A. Knopf, 1992) and Ereira, *Aluna*, film (United Kingdom: Columbia, 2012).
[93] Swimme, "Comprehensive Compassion," 73–92. See Swimme, "Awakening the Impulse to Evolve: The Birth of Evolutionary Spirituality," interview by Craig Hamilton. Teleseminar Audio Archives: www.evolutionaryspirituality.com (website discontinued).
[94] Swimme, "Comprehensive Compassion," 73–92.
[95] Swimme, "Comprehensive Compassion," 73–92.
[96] Pisti's words to his father in a vision after Pisti's death.
[97] Richard Wilhelm, trans., *The I Ching* or *Book of Changes*. Translated into English by Cary F. Baynes (Princeton: Princeton University Press, 1975), lv. I discuss this event in more detail in my book, *The Miracle of Death: There is Nothing But Life* (Claremont: Kamlak Center, 2003), 115–125.
[98] Yates, *Rosicrucian Enlightenment*, 179–180.
[99] Graham Hancock and Santha Faiia, *Heaven's Mirror: Quest for the Lost Civilization* (New York: Three Rivers Press, 1998), 314–315. See also Hancock, *Magicians of*

the Gods; Charles H. Hapgood, *Maps of the Ancient Sea Kings: Evidence of Advanced Civilization in the Ice Age* (Kempton: Adventures Unlimited Press, 1996); and Richard Firestone, Allen West, and Simon Warwick-Smith, *The Cycle of Cosmic Catastrophes: How a Stone-Age Comet Changed the Course of World Culture* (Rochester: Bear, 2006).

[100] Hancock and Faiia, *Heaven's Mirror*, 314–315. See also Hancock, *Magicians of the Gods*.

[101] Hancock and Faiia, *Heaven's Mirror*, 314–315.

[102] Winkelman and Baker, *Supernatural as Natural*, 85.

[103] See Hancock, *Fingerprints of the Gods: The Evidence of Earth's Lost Civilization* (New York: Crown Trade Paperbacks, 1995).

[104] Hancock, *Magicians of the Gods*, 169–171, 177.

[105] West, *Serpent in the Sky*, 1, xiv.

[106] Gustaf Strömberg, *The Soul of the Universe* (North Hollywood: Educational Research Institute, 1948), 303–306.

[107] Saryon Michael White, "An Imaginal Journey of Peace," May 22, 2007, www.saryon.com.

[108] Barker, *Great High Priest*, 246.

[109] Edgar J. Goodspeed, trans., "The Wisdom of Solomon," 7:27, in *The Apocrypha* (New York: Modern Library, 1959), 191.

Chapter One

[1] Sue Monk Kidd, *The Secret Life of Bees* (New York: Viking, 2003), 107.

[2] Kovács, *Miracle of Death*, 65.

Chapter Two

[1] McTaggart, *The Field*, xiii.

[2] McTaggart, *The Field*, xviii.

[3] Michael Harner, *The Way of the Shaman: A Guide to Power and Healing* (New York: Bantam Books, 1986), 45.

[4] McTaggart, *The Field*, xv–xvi.

[5] Fritjof Capra, *The Tao of Physics: An Exploration of the Parallels Between Modern Physics and Eastern Mysticism* (Boulder: Shambhala, 1975), 11.

Chapter Three

[1] Elisabeth Kübler-Ross, *On Life After Death* (Berkeley: Celestial Arts, 1991), 67.

[2] Kenneth Ring, *Heading Toward Omega: In Search of the Meaning of the Near-Death Experience* (New York: William Morrow, 1985), 9.

[3] Ring, *Heading Toward Omega*, 53.

[4] Ring, *Heading Toward Omega*, 226.

[5] Richard Maurice Bucke, *Cosmic Consciousness: A Study in the Evolution of the Human Mind* (New York: E.P. Dutton, 1969), 9–10.

[6] Bucke, *Cosmic Consciousness*, 7, 11, 6.

[7] Bucke, *Cosmic Consciousness*, 5.

8. Bucke, *Cosmic Consciousness*, 11.
9. Kovács, *Miracle of Death*, 96–97.
10. Kübler-Ross, *On Life After Death*, 64–65.
11. Kübler-Ross, *On Life After Death*, 67–68.
12. Ring, *Heading Toward Omega*, 75.
13. Ring, *Heading Toward Omega*, 53–54, 71–72.
14. Ring, *Heading Toward Omega*, 227–228.
15. Ring, *Heading Toward Omega*, 10, 255.
16. James Owen, "Near-Death Experiences Explained?," *National Geographic*, April 10, 2010, http://news.nationalgeographic.com/news/2010/04/100408-near-death-experiences-blood-carbon-dioxide/.
17. McTaggart, *The Field*, 21, 11, 25, 29, xvii, 94.
18. McTaggart, *The Field*, 26, 174.
19. McTaggart, *The Field*, 33.
20. Wolf, "Mind and the New Physics," 85, 81.
21. Goswami, Reed, and Goswami, *Self-Aware Universe*, 2.
22. McTaggart, *The Field*, xiii.

Chapter Four

1. Swimme, "Comprehensive Compassion," 85, 76.
2. McTaggart, *The Field*, xix.
3. Ervin László, *Macroshift: Navigating the Transformation to a Sustainable World* (San Francisco: Berrett-Koehler, 2001), 11.
4. Swimme, "Comprehensive Compassion," 85.
5. Swimme, "Comprehensive Compassion," 85.
6. McTaggart, *The Field*, xiv.
7. Swimme, "Comprehensive Compassion," 85, 76 and "Awakening the Impulse to Evolve."
8. Haridas Chaudhuri, *California Institute of Integral Studies: Fall 98 Public Programs* (San Francisco: CIIS, 1998), 25.
9. Elizabeth M. Wilkinson and L.A. Willoughby, *Goethe: Poet and Thinker* (New York: Barnes & Noble, 1962), 29.
10. Wilkinson and Willoughby, *Goethe: Poet and Thinker*, 140–141.
11. Wolf, "Mind and the New Physics," 85, 81.
12. Eliade, *History of Religious Ideas*, xiii.
13. Eliade, *History of Religious Ideas*, xiii.
14. Eliade, *History of Religious Ideas*, xvi, xv.
15. Bucke, *Cosmic Consciousness*, 7.
16. Eliade, *History of Religious Ideas*, xvi.
17. Eliade, *History of Religious Ideas*, xiii.
18. Swimme, "Comprehensive Compassion," 76–79 and "Awakening the Impulse to Evolve."
19. Gregg Braden, *The Divine Matrix: Bridging Time, Space, Miracles, and Belief* (Carlsbad: Hay House, 2007), 114.
20. Swimme, "Comprehensive Compassion," 74, 76.

Chapter Five

1. Pagels, *Gnostic Gospels*, xiii–xiv.
2. Veronica Anne Goodchild, *Songlines of the Soul: Pathways to a New Vision for a New Century* (Lake Worth: Nicholas-Hays, 2012), 16–17, 269.
3. Pagels, *Gnostic Gospels*, xiii–xiv.
4. Stanley Krippner, "The Epistemology and Technologies of Shamanic States of Consciousness," *Journal of Consciousness Studies* 7, no. 11-12 (January 2000): 93.
5. Kovács, *Miracle of Death*, 118–119.
6. C.G. Jung, *Alchemical Studies*, vol. 13 of *The Collected Works*, trans. R.F.C. Hull (Princeton: Princeton University Press, 1967), 265–266.
7. Karen Armstrong, *The Battle for God: A History of Fundamentalism* (New York: Random House, 2001), 136–137.
8. Armstrong, *Battle for God*, 136–137.
9. Robert Fisk, *The Great War for Civilisation: The Conquest of the Middle East* (New York: Alfred A. Knopf, 2005), xviii.
10. Baring and Cashford, *Myth of the Goddess*, 623–624.

Chapter Six

1. Caponigri, *Time and Idea*, 130–143, 164–187. See also Bergin and Fisch, *New Science of Giambattista Vico*.
2. Kovács, *Miracle of Death*, 140–141.
3. Caitlin Matthews, "The Voices of the Wells: Celtic Oral Themes in Grail Literature," in *At the Table of the Grail: No one who sets forth on the Grail Quest remains unchanged*, ed. John Matthews (London: Watkins, 2002), 3–25.
4. Caponigri, *Time and Idea*, 130–143, 164–187.
5. Caponigri, *Time and Idea*, 165.
6. Caponigri, *Time and Idea*, 170–171.
7. Caponigri, *Time and Idea*, 136.
8. Caponigri, *Time and Idea*, 1, 139.

Chapter Seven

1. Novalis [pseud.], *Henry von Ofterdingen*, trans. Palmer Hilty (New York: Frederick Ungar, 1974), 84.
2. Pagels, *Gnostic Gospels*, xviii.
3. Barker, *Great High Priest*, 1–33.
4. Pagels, *Gnostic Gospels*, xx.
5. Barker, *Great Angel*, 58 and *Great High Priest*, 243.
6. Eliade, *History of Religious Ideas*, xv.
7. Eliade, *History of Religious Ideas*, xvi.
8. Yates, *Rosicrucian Enlightenment*, 231.
9. Peter J. French, *John Dee: The World of an Elizabethan Magus* (London: Routledge and Kegan Paul, 1984), 66.
10. Yates, *Rosicrucian Enlightenment*, xiv.
11. Yates, *Rosicrucian Enlightenment*, xii, xiv.

12 Yates, *Rosicrucian Enlightenment*, 232–233.
13 Yates, *Rosicrucian Enlightenment*, 14, xiii.
14 Yates, *Rosicrucian Enlightenment*, 224.
15 Yates, *Rosicrucian Enlightenment*, 190.

Chapter Eight

1 Jean Markale, *Cathedral of the Black Madonna: The Druids and the Mysteries of Chartres* (Rochester: Inner Traditions, 2004), 78–80.
2 Henry Adams, *Mont-Saint-Michel and Chartres* (New York: New American Library, 1961), 195, 197–198.
3 Malcolm Godwin, *The Holy Grail: Its Origins, Secrets & Meaning Revealed* (London: Bloomsbury, 1994), 9.
4 Godwin, *Holy Grail*, 22.
5 Markale, *Cathedral of the Black Madonna*, 146–147.
6 Barbara G. Walker, *The Woman's Dictionary of Symbols and Sacred Objects* (San Francisco: Harper & Row, 1988), 206 and *The Woman's Encyclopedia of Myths and Secrets* (New York: HarperSanFrancisco, 1983), 1048–1049.
7 Barker, *Great High Priest*, 241.
8 Walker, *Woman's Encyclopedia*, 1049.
9 Godwin, *Holy Grail*, 20.
10 Jesse L. Weston, *The Quest of the Holy Grail* (London: Frank Cass, 1964), 3, 135–136.
11 John Boswell, *Christianity, Social Tolerance, and Homosexuality: Gay People in Western Europe from the Beginning of the Christian Era to the Fourteenth Century* (Chicago: University of Chicago Press, 1981), 271–273.
12 Walker, *Woman's Encyclopedia*, 1049.
13 Hoeller, *Jung and the Lost Gospels*, 16–17, 25.
14 Pagels, *Gnostic Gospels*, xiii–xiv.

Chapter Nine

1 Jean-Yves Leloup, *The Sacred Embrace of Jesus and Mary: The Sexual Mystery at the Heart of the Christian Tradition* (Rochester: Inner Traditions, 2006), 6–7.
2 Barker, *Great High Priest*, 1–33.
3 Leloup, *Sacred Embrace*, 6–7.
4 Michael S. Russo, "The Hellenistic Age: From Alexander to Augustus," Molloy College, accessed March 2, 2010, https://www.molloy.edu/sophia/ancient_lit/hellenisticage1.htm (web page discontinued); Burton L. Mack, *The Lost Gospel: The Book of Q & Christian Origins* (New York: HarperSanFrancisco, 1994), 54–55; and Chester G. Starr, *A History of the Ancient World*, 4th ed. (New York: Oxford University Press, 1991), 410.
5 "Royal Road," Wikimedia Foundation, last modified June 8, 2010, http://en.wikipedia.org/wiki/Royal_Road; "Silk Road," Wikimedia Foundation, last modified June 8, 2010, http://en.wikipedia.org/wiki/Silk_Road; "Travelers on the Silk Road," Silk Road, accessed June 9, 2010, http://www.silk-road.com/artl/srtravelmain.shtml; and "Silk Road," Crystal Links, accessed June 19, 2010, http://www.crystalinks.com/silkroad.html.

6. Kingsley, *Return to Eternity: A transformational workshop with Peter Kingsley* (www.PeterKingsley.org 2006) CD.
7. Richard Hooker, "Hellenistic Greece: The Three Empires," Washington State University, http://www.wsu.edu/~dee/GREECE/3EMPIRES.HTML (web page discontinued).
8. Erwin R. Goodenough, *By Light, Light: The Mystic Gospel of Hellenistic Judaism* (Amsterdam: Philo Press, 1969), 2.
9. Ervin László, Stanislav Grof, and Peter Russell, *The Consciousness Revolution: A Transatlantic Dialogue*, ed. Ervin László (Boston: Element Books, 1999), 17 and Kerényi, *Eleusis: Archetypal Image of Mother and Daughter*, trans. Ralph Manheim (New York: Bollingen Foundation, 1967), 10, 16.
10. Kerényi, *Eleusis*, 17.
11. Kerényi, *Eleusis*, 10–16.
12. Kerényi, *Eleusis*, 37.
13. Kerényi, "The Mysteries of the Kabeiroi," in *Papers from the Eranos Yearbooks, Vol. 2: The Mysteries*, ed. Joseph Campbell (Princeton: Princeton University Press, 1971), 37–40.
14. Pagels, *Beyond Belief: The Secret Gospel of Thomas* (New York: Random House, 2003), 56.
15. Kerényi, "Kore," 154.
16. Kerényi, "Kore," 120.
17. Kerényi, "Kore," 123.

Chapter Ten

1. Goodenough, *By Light, Light*, 7.
2. Goodenough, *By Light, Light*, 7–8, 241–242.
3. Barker, *Great Angel*, 48.
4. Goodenough, *By Light, Light*, 262–263.
5. Timothy Freke and Peter Gandy, *Jesus and the Lost Goddess: The Secret Teachings of the Original Christians* (New York: Harmony Books, 2001), 12.
6. Theodor H. Gaster, ed., *The Dead Sea Scriptures*, 3rd ed. (Garden City: Anchor Books, 1976), 5.
7. Charles Francis Potter, *The Lost Years of Jesus Revealed: Newest Revelations of the Dead Sea Scrolls and the Nag-Hammadi Discoveries* (New York: Fawcett, 1962), 16–17.
8. Gaster, *Dead Sea Scriptures*, 6 and Potter, *Lost Years of Jesus*, 17.
9. Gaster, *Dead Sea Scriptures*, 6–8.
10. Lawrence H. Schiffman, "Judaism, Christianity and the Dead Sea Scrolls," University of California Television (UCTV), YouTube video, posted August 7, 2008, https://youtu.be/92hyhBXLaWE.
11. Schiffman, "Judaism, Christianity."
12. Leloup, *Sacred Embrace*, 6–7.
13. Potter, *Lost Years of Jesus*, 144, 10, 9, 12–14.
14. Potter, *Lost Years of Jesus*, 17–18.
15. Potter, *Lost Years of Jesus*, 18–19.
16. Barker, *Great Angel*, 12–15.

Chapter Eleven

1. Barker, *Great High Priest*, 236.
2. Barker, *Great High Priest*, 229-261.
3. Barker, *Great Angel*, 12.
4. Barker, *Great Angel*, 13, 16-17.
5. Barker, *Great High Priest*, 236.
6. Barker, *Great Angel*, 64. For more on Wisdom, see Barker, *Great High Priest*, 229-261 and *Great Angel*, 48-69.
7. Godwin, *Holy Grail*, 22.
8. Barker, *Great Angel*, 66, 52-53.
9. Barker, *Great Angel*, 58 (Genesis 6:6-7 and Proverbs 3:18).
10. Exodus 20:4.
11. Barker, 1 Enoch 93, "Where Shall Wisdom Be Found?," Orthodox Europe, accessed April 9, 2017, http://orthodoxeurope.org/page/11/1/7.aspx.
12. Barker, *Great High Priest*, 234 (Jeremiah 44:16-17).
13. Barker, *Great Angel*, 14 and 1 Enoch 42, "Where Shall Wisdom Be Found?"
14. Campbell, *Masks of God: Occidental Mythology*, 13-14.
15. Barker, *Great Angel*, 58 (The Wisdom of Sirach 24:13-22).
16. Barker, *Great High Priest*, 238 (1 Enoch 32:3), 243-244 (1 Enoch 24:4).
17. Barker, *Great High Priest*, 243-246.
18. Robinson, "Origin of the World," 169.
19. Barker, *Great Angel*, 48-69.
20. Barker, *Great Angel*, 64.
21. Barker, *Great Angel*, 51.
22. Leonard Shlain, *The Alphabet Versus The Goddess: The Conflict Between Word and Image* (New York: Viking Penguin, 1998), 73.
23. Barker, *Great High Priest*, 26.
24. Barker, *Great Angel*, 15.

Chapter Twelve

1. Meyer, "The Gospel of Philip," in *Gnostic Gospels of Jesus*, 57.
2. Barker, *Great Angel*, 51.
3. Pagels, *Gnostic Gospels*, xx.
4. Barker, *Great High Priest*, 26.
5. Robinson, *The Nag Hammadi Codices: A general introduction to the nature and significance of the Coptic Gnostic Library from Nag Hammadi*, 2nd rev. ed. (Claremont: Institute for Antiquity and Christianity, 1977), 3-4.
6. Robinson, *Nag Hammadi Library*, 9, 7.
7. Robinson, *Nag Hammadi Library*, 12.
8. Robinson, *Nag Hammadi Library*, 2, 5-6.
9. Pagels, *Gnostic Gospels*, xv-xvi.
10. Meyer, *Gnostic Gospels of Jesus*, xx-xxi.
11. Pagels, *Beyond Belief*, 57.
12. Pagels, *Beyond Belief*, 56-57.

13 The Gospel of Mary was not found with the Nag Hammadi texts, but was earlier discovered in the late 19th century near Akhmim in upper Egypt. According to The Gnostic Society Library, it was purchased by a German scholar and taken to Berlin, where it was called the *Berlin Gnostic Codex*. It is sometimes referred to as the *Akhmim Codex*. It is thought to date to the second century and copied around the fourth century, which is around the time the Nag Hammadi texts were buried. This Codex contains Coptic translations of two other texts that were also found among the Nag Hammadi texts. Two world wars and other unfortunate occurrences prevented the publication of the Gospel of Mary until 1955.

> "Two other small fragments of the *Gospel of Mary* from separate Greek editions were later unearthed in archaeological excavations at Oxyrhynchus, Egypt…. **Finding three fragments of a text of this antiquity is extremely unusual, and it is thus evidenced that the *Gospel of Mary* was well distributed in early Christian times and existed in both an original Greek and a Coptic language translation.**"

"Gnostic Scriptures and Fragments: The Gospel According to Mary Magdalene," The Gnostic Society Library, accessed April 2, 2017, http://www.gnosis.org/library/marygosp.htm.

14 Markale, *Cathedral of the Black Madonna*, 146–147.
15 Meyer, "The Gospel of Philip," in *Gnostic Gospels of Jesus*, 63 and Leloup, *Sacred Embrace*, 9.
16 Meyer, "The Gospel of Philip," in *Gnostic Gospels of Jesus*, 57.
17 Leloup, *Sacred Embrace*, 9.
18 Leloup, *Sacred Embrace*, 130–131.
19 Barker, *Great Angel*, 3–4.
20 Barker, *Great Angel*, 51.

Chapter Thirteen

1. Marvin Meyer and Esther A. De Boer, *The Gospels of Mary: The Secret Tradition of Mary Magdalene, the Companion of Jesus* (New York: HarperSanFrancisco, 2004), xvi–xvii.
2. Meyer and De Boer, *The Gospels of Mary*, 20–21.
3. Henri Corbin, "Mundus Imaginalis or the Imaginary and the Imaginal," Hermetic Library, accessed November 4, 2017, https://hermetic.com/moorish/mundus-imaginalis.
4. Meyer and De Boer, *The Gospels of Mary*, xvi–xvii.
5. Meyer, "The Gospel of Mary," in *Gnostic Gospels of Jesus*, 39. In *The Gospel of Mary Magdalene*, translated from the Coptic by Jean-Yves Leloup and translated into English by Joseph Rowe (Rochester: Inner Traditions, 2002), the word *mind* is translated as *nous*.
6. Corbin, "Mundus Imaginalis."
7. Corbin, "Mundus Imaginalis."
8. Corbin, "Mundus Imaginalis."

9. Pert, *Molecules of Emotion*, 187.
10. McTaggart, *The Field*, 26.
11. Walter T. Stace, ed., *The Teachings of the Mystics: Selections from the Great Mystics and Mystical Writings of the World* (New York: Mentor Books, 1960), 14-15.
12. Corbin, "Mundus Imaginalis."
13. Meyer, "The Gospel of Philip," in *Gnostic Gospels of Jesus*, 60.
14. Meyer and De Boer, *The Gospels of Mary*, 20.
15. Corbin, "Mundus Imaginalis."
16. Barker, *Great High Priest*, 155, 146-162.
17. Barker, *Christmas: The Original Story* (London: The Society for Promoting Christian Knowledge, 2008), 5.
18. Strömberg, *Soul of the Universe*, 253, 303.
19. Barker, *Great High Priest*, 246.
20. Barker, *Great High Priest*, 147.
21. Barker, *Christmas*, 5.
22. Barker, *Christmas*, 5 and Hebrews 10:20.
23. Barker, *Christmas*, 167.

Chapter Fourteen

1. Goodenough, *By Light, Light,* 230, 244, 264.
2. Goodenough, *By Light, Light,* 233-234, 241, 255.
3. Goodenough, *By Light, Light,* 236.
4. Goodenough, *By Light, Light,* 201, 212, 230-233.
5. Goodenough, *By Light, Light,* 233.
6. Goodenough, *By Light, Light,* 212, 201.
7. Goodenough, *By Light, Light,* 222, 233.
8. Goodenough, *By Light, Light,* 221.
9. Goodenough, *By Light, Light,* 216, 244.
10. Margaret Starbird, *Magdalena's Lost Legacy: Symbolic Numbers and the Sacred Union in Christianity* (Rochester: Bear, 2003), 32.

Chapter Fifteen

1. Freke and Gandy, *The Jesus Mysteries: Was the "Original Jesus" a Pagan God?* (New York: Three Rivers Press, 2001), 195.
2. Freke and Gandy, *Jesus Mysteries*, 116.
3. Starbird, *Magdalena's Lost Legacy*, 29, 46, 42-43.
4. Barker, *Great Angel*, 51.
5. Joan Chamberlain Engelsman, *The Feminine Dimension of the Divine* (Philadelphia: Westminster Press, 1979), 102-103.
6. Karen Jo Torjesen, *When Women Were Priests: Women's Leadership in the Early Church and the Scandal of Their Subordination in the Rise of Christianity* (New York: HarperSanFrancisco, 1993), 7.
7. Torjesen, *When Women Were Priests*, 7, 11, 19.
8. Freke and Gandy, *Jesus and the Lost Goddess*, 7.
9. Starbird, *Magdalena's Lost Legacy*, 42-43.

[10] Starbird, *Magdalena's Lost Legacy*, 54–56.
[11] Starbird, *Magdalena's Lost Legacy*, 57–59.
[12] Meyer, "The Gospel of Philip," in *Gnostic Gospels of Jesus*, 67.
[13] Barker, *Christmas*, 49. "To Jesus alone as our high priest were the secret things of God committed," is quoted by Barker from Ignatius, Letter to the Philadelphians, 9. The quotation, "by drawing aside the curtain," is quoted by Barker from Clement Miscellanies 7.17.
[14] Barker, *Christmas*, 7–8.
[15] Pagels, *Beyond Belief*, 56–57.
[16] Meyer, "The Gospel of Philip," in *Gnostic Gospels of Jesus*, 47, 60.
[17] Pagels, *Beyond Belief*, 55–56.
[18] Tom Huston, "A Brief History of Evolutionary Spirituality," *What is Enlightenment*, January–March 2007, 80.
[19] Pagels, *Beyond Belief*, 56.
[20] Freke and Gandy, *Jesus Mysteries*, 22–23.

Chapter Sixteen

[1] Goodspeed, "The Wisdom of Solomon," 7-8, in *The Apocrypha*, 189–193.
[2] Saryon Michael White, "*An Imaginal Journey of Peace*."
[3] Barker, *Great Angel*, 64.
[4] Goodspeed, "The Wisdom of Solomon," 7:27, in *The Apocrypha*, 191.
[5] Saryon Michael White, "*An Imaginal Journey of Peace*."
[6] Strömberg, *Soul of the Universe*, 304.
[7] I owe this connection between the Imaginal cells and the archetypes to my friend, Reverend Dr. Christopher Rubel, an Episcopalian minister and therapist.

Chapter Seventeen

[1] Meyer, "The Gospel of Thomas," in *Gnostic Gospels of Jesus*, 67.
[2] Alvin Boyd Kuhn, *Who is This King of Glory? A Critical Study of the Christos-Messiah Tradition* (Bensenville: Lushena Books, 2006), 90–91.
[3] Goodspeed, "The Wisdom of Solomon," 8:2-3 and 8:17-18, in *The Apocrypha*, 192, 193.
[4] Kuhn, *King of Glory*, 111–112.
[5] Barker, *Great Angel*, 13.
[6] Campbell, *Masks of God: Occidental Mythology*, 137–139.
[7] Kuhn, *King of Glory*, 90–91.
[8] Kuhn, *King of Glory*, 109. See also Freke and Gandy, *Jesus Mysteries*; Tom Harpur, *Pagan Christ*; and Gerald Massey, *Ancient Egypt: The Light of the World* (Sioux Falls: NuVision, 2008).
[9] Kuhn, *King of Glory*, 116, 119.
[10] Freke and Gandy, *Jesus Mysteries*, 25–26, 111.
[11] Tom Harpur, *Pagan Christ: Recovering the Lost Light* (New York: Walker, 2004), 29.
[12] Freke and Gandy, *Jesus Mysteries*, 63.
[13] Harpur, *Pagan Christ*, 29.
[14] Harpur, *Pagan Christ*, 27.

[15] Harpur, *Pagan Christ*, 28.
[16] Barker, *Great High Priest*, 1–7.
[17] Kuhn, *King of Glory*, 137–139, 141, 168.
[18] Kuhn, *King of Glory*, 136, 143.
[19] G.R.S. Mead, *Fragments of a Faith Forgotten* (Whitefish: Kessinger, 1930), 18, 12 and Kuhn, *King of Glory*, 143.
[20] Charles B. Waite, *History of the Christian Religion to the Year 200* (Chicago: C.V. Waite, 1908), 487.
[21] Waite, *History of the Christian Religion*, 487.
[22] Freke and Gandy, *Jesus Mysteries*, 27–28.
[23] Kuhn, *King of Glory*, 169.

Chapter Eighteen

[1] Kingsley, *Dark Places of Wisdom*, 10.
[2] Kingsley, *Dark Places of Wisdom*, 9.
[3] Pagels, *Gnostic Gospels*, xx.
[4] Kingsley, *Dark Places of Wisdom*, 34.
[5] Swimme, "Comprehensive Compassion," 73–92.
[6] Barker, *Great Angel*, 58.

Chapter Nineteen

[1] Rilke, *Briefe an einen jungen Dichter*, 46.
[2] I had earlier been impressed with an article written by a feminist literary theorist in which she presented Lavinia as a symbol of the feminine in a patriarchal world. More specifically, I now thought of Lavinia as an appropriate symbol of what we have all done to the feminine visionary—the soul—within us. I have not been able to find the original article.
[3] Kovács, "Journey of the Mothers," in *Earthwalking Sky Dancers: Women's Pilgrimages to Sacred Places*, ed. Leila Castle (Berkeley: Frog, 1996), 199.
[4] Rilke, *Briefe an einen jungen Dichter*, 46.
[5] Kidd, *Secret Life of Bees*, 107.

Chapter Twenty

[1] Jorge Luis Delgado with MaryAnn Male, *Andean Awakening: An Inca Guide to Mystical Peru* (San Francisco: Council Oak Books, 2006), 38–39.
[2] Huxley, *The Doors of Perception* (New York: Harper & Row, 1954), 22–23.
[3] Huxley, *Doors of Perception*, 25.
[4] Swimme, *The Hidden Heart of the Cosmos: Humanity and the New Story* (Maryknoll: Orbis Books, 1996), 108–109. Swimme tells how "Indians of South America teach that to become human 'one must make room in oneself for the immensities of the universe'"; otherwise, "we cannot find our true nature."

Chapter Twenty-Two

[1] Kovács, *Miracle of Death*, 34.

2. Kovács, *Miracle of Death*, 101.
3. Kovács, *Miracle of Death*, 110–114.
4. Strömberg, *Soul of the Universe*, 303–305 and Saryon Michael White, "*An Imaginal Journey of Peace.*"
5. Yates, *Rosicrucian Enlightenment*, 179–183.
6. Patricia Cota-Robles, "Celebration of a Special Life," The Galactic Free Press, January 8, 2011, http://soundofheart.org/galacticfreepress/content/patricia-cota-robles-celebration-special-life.
7. Kovács, *Miracle of Death*, 153–155.
8. William Irwin Thompson, *Beyond Religion: The Cultural Evolution of the Sense of the Sacred from Shamanism to Religion to Post-Religious Spirituality* (Great Barrington: Lindisfarne Books, 2013), 44–48.
9. David Lorimer, ed., *The Circle of Sacred Dance: Peter Deunov's Paneurhythmy* (London: Vega, 2002), 7.
10. Lorimer, ed., *Prophet for Our Times: The Life and Teachings of Peter Deunov* (London: Vega, 2002), 17, 31, 17; *Circle of Sacred Dance*, 7; and *Prophet for Our Times*, 34.
11. Lorimer, *Prophet for Our Times*, 37.
12. Lorimer, *Circle of Sacred Dance*, 15–25.
13. Beinsa Douno (Peter Deunov), *Gems of Love: Prayers and Formulas*, trans. and ed. David Lorimer (Surrey: Grain of Wheat Trust, 1994), x–xi.
14. Barker, *Great Angel*, 51.
15. Barker, *Great Angel*, 51, 64.
16. Jung, *The Structure and Dynamics of the Psyche*, vol. 8 of *The Collected Works*, trans. R.F.C. Hull (Princeton: Princeton University Press, 1969), page number not located. This is a frequently quoted statement from C.G. Jung.

Chapter Twenty-Three

1. Jung, *Symbols of Transformation: An Analysis of the Prelude to a Case of Schizophrenia*, vol. 5 of *The Collected Works*, trans. R.F.C. Hull (Princeton: Princeton University Press, 1967), xxiv.
2. Jung, *Structure and Dynamics of the Psyche*, page number not located.
3. Jung, *Symbols of Transformation*, xxix.
4. Jung, *Structure and Dynamics of the Psyche*, page number not located.
5. McTaggart, *The Field*, xiii.
6. Goodspeed, "The Wisdom of Solomon," 7:27, in *The Apocrypha*, 191 and Saryon Michael White, "*An Imaginal Journey of Peace.*"
7. Jung, *Structure and Dynamics of the Psyche*, page number not located.

Chapter Twenty-Four

1. Paul G. Bahn and Jean Vertut, *Journey Through the Ice Age* (Berkeley: University of California Press, 1997), 16–18.
2. Richard Rudgley, *Secrets of the Stone Age: A prehistoric journey with Richard Rudgley* (London: Century, 2000), 184–185.
3. Rudgley, *Secrets of the Stone Age*, 178, 191.

4. Hancock, *Supernatural: Meetings with the Ancient Teachers of Mankind* (Toronto: Doubleday, 2005), 28.
5. Rudgley, *Secrets of the Stone Age*, 183.
6. Rudgley, *Secrets of the Stone Age*, 179–182.
7. "100,000-Year-Old Ochre Toolkit and Workshop Discovered in South Africa," Science Daily, October 18, 2011, https://www.sciencedaily.com/releases/2011/10/111013141807.htm.
8. Stan Gooch, *Cities of Dreams: When Women Ruled the Earth* (London: Aulis Books, 2001), 8–9. Gooch's information comes from the work of Adrian Boshier and Peter Beaumont, published in the journal *Optima*, 1972. Their discoveries, says Gooch, revealed one of the largest sites that "evidenced the removal of a million kilos of ore [ocher]. At another site half a million stone-digging tools were found, all showing considerable wear. All of the sites in fact produced thousands of tools and involved the removal of large quantities of ore; and while some were open quarries, others had true mining tunnels. In all cases, however, these excavations had been painstakingly refilled when the site was abandoned."
9. Rudgley, *Secrets of the Stone Age*, 155–156.
10. Rudgley, *Secrets of the Stone Age*, 154–157.
11. Hancock, *Supernatural*, 28 and Blake Edgar, "Home of the Modern Mind: Did culture begin with the color red and a Stone Age clambake?," *Archaeology*, March/April 2008, 59–65.
12. Campbell, *Masks of God: Primitive Mythology*, 358.
13. Campbell, *Masks of God: Primitive Mythology*, 358–359.
14. Campbell, *Masks of God: Primitive Mythology*, 359.
15. Jean Clottes and David Lewis-Williams, *The Shamans of Prehistory: Trance and Magic in the Painted Caves*, text by Jean Clottes, trans. Sophie Hawkes (New York: Harry N. Abrams, 1998), 81.
16. Stanley Coren, "Do Dogs Dream?," *Psychology Today*, October 28, 2010, https://www.psychologytoday.com/us/blog/canine-corner/201010/do-dogs-dream.
17. Wolf, "Mind and the New Physics," 85, 81.

Chapter Twenty-Five

1. Baring and Cashford, *Myth of the Goddess*, 39.
2. Baring and Cashford, *Myth of the Goddess*, 6.
3. Baring and Cashford, *Myth of the Goddess*, 39.
4. Baring and Cashford, *Myth of the Goddess*, 38–39.
5. Laurens van der Post, *A Mantis Carol* (Washington, DC: Island Press, 1975), 114.
6. Baring and Cashford, *Myth of the Goddess*, 36.
7. Armstrong, *The Case for God* (New York: Anchor Books, 2010), 10.
8. Campbell, *Masks of God: Primitive Mythology*, 307–310.

Chapter Twenty-Six

1. Campbell, *Masks of God: Primitive Mythology*, 307–310 and *The Way of the Animal Powers, Vol. 1: Historical Atlas of World Mythology* (San Francisco: Harper & Row, 1988), 73–77.

2. Hancock, *Supernatural*, 157, 156.
3. David Lewis-Williams, *The Mind in the Cave: Consciousness and the Origins of Art* (London: Thames & Hudson, 2002), 8.
4. Lewis-Williams, *Mind in the Cave*, 8.
5. Lewis-Williams, *Mind in the Cave*, 136–138 and Hancock, *Supernatural*, 170–172.
6. Hancock, *Supernatural*, 170–172.
7. "Africa's Rock Art," Trust for African Rock Art, accessed April 9, 2017, http://africanrockart.org/rock-art-in-africa/africas-rock-art/.
8. Lewis-Williams, *Mind in the Cave*, 138–139.
9. Lewis-Williams, *Mind in the Cave*, 139.
10. Richard Gray, "Stone Age man ate mushrooms: Oldest evidence for fungi in the human diet discovered in 19,000-year-old tooth plaque," Daily Mail, April 21, 2015, https://www.dailymail.co.uk/sciencetech/article-3048678/Stone-Age-man-ate-mushrooms-Oldest-evidence-fungi-human-diet-discovered-19-000-year-old-tooth-plaque.html.
11. Hancock, *Supernatural*, 29–30.
12. Winkelman and Baker, *Supernatural as Natural*, 85.
13. Hancock, *Supernatural*, 30.
14. Joseph Chilton Pearce, *The Biology of Transcendence: A Blueprint of the Human Spirit* (Rochester: Park Street Press, 2002), 41, 50.
15. Pearce, *Biology of Transcendence*, 51.
16. Pearce, *Biology of Transcendence*, 51.
17. See Doc Childre and Howard Martin with Donna Beech, *The HeartMath Solution: The Institute of HeartMath's Revolutionary Program for Engaging the Power of the Heart's Intelligence* (New York: HarperSanFrancisco, 2000). See also www.heartmath.com.
18. Pearce, *Biology of Transcendence*, 49.

Chapter Twenty-Seven

1. Charles D. Laughlin, "Archetypes, Neurognosis and the Quantum Sea," Biogenetic Structuralism, September 21, 2012, http://www.biogeneticstructuralism.com/docs/archetyp_sse.rtf.
2. Clottes and Lewis-Williams, *Shamans of Prehistory*, 14–17.
3. Clottes and Lewis-Williams, *Shamans of Prehistory*, 19.
4. Hancock, *Supernatural*, 199.
5. Hancock, *Supernatural*, 167 and Clottes and Lewis-Williams, *Shamans of Prehistory*, 33, 23.
6. Lewis-Williams, *Mind in the Cave*, 290.
7. Newberg, D'Aquili, and Rause, *Why God Won't Go Away*, 146, 140, 145.
8. Newberg, D'Aquili, and Rause, *Why God Won't Go Away*, 146.
9. Newberg, D'Aquili, and Rause, *Why God Won't Go Away*, 146–147, 52, 152.
10. Stace, *Teachings of the Mystics*, 14–15.
11. Newberg, D'Aquili, and Rause, *Why God Won't Go Away*, 120, 169, 156.
12. Hancock, *Supernatural*, 36–37.
13. Hancock, *Supernatural*, 36–37.

¹⁴ Lewis-Williams, *Mind in the Cave*, 291.
¹⁵ Winkelman and Baker, *Supernatural as Natural*, 84–85.
¹⁶ Winkelman and Baker, *Supernatural as Natural*, 85.
¹⁷ Michael Winkelman, *Shamanism: A Biopsychosocial Paradigm of Consciousness and Healing* (Santa Barbara: Praeger, 2010), 118–119.
¹⁸ Winkelman and Baker, *Supernatural as Natural*, xxi, xxiii.
¹⁹ Wolf, "Mind and the New Physics," 85, 81.
²⁰ Laughlin, "Archetypes, Neurognosis and the Quantum Sea."
²¹ Laughlin, "Archetypes, Neurognosis and the Quantum Sea."
²² Laughlin, "Archetypes, Neurognosis and the Quantum Sea."
²³ McTaggart, *The Field*, 21.
²⁴ Swimme, "Comprehensive Compassion," 73–92.
²⁵ McTaggart, *The Field*, xiv.
²⁶ Chaudhuri, *California Institute of Integral Studies*, 25.

Chapter Twenty-Eight

¹ van der Post, *The Heart of the Hunter: Customs and Myths of the African Bushman* (San Diego: Harcourt Brace, 1989), 141.
² See van der Post, *Heart of the Hunter* and *Mantis Carol*.
³ van der Post, *Mantis Carol*, 110, 114.
⁴ van der Post, *Mantis Carol*, 110, 114.
⁵ van der Post, *Mantis Carol*, 17–21.
⁶ van der Post, *Mantis Carol*, 17–21.
⁷ van der Post, *Mantis Carol*, 18–20.
⁸ Jung, *Structure and Dynamics of the Psyche*, page number not located.
⁹ van der Post, *Mantis Carol*, 23–24.
¹⁰ van der Post, *Mantis Carol*, 20, 19.
¹¹ van der Post, *Heart of the Hunter*, 141–145.
¹² van der Post, *Heart of the Hunter*, 141.
¹³ van der Post, *Heart of the Hunter*, 170–171.
¹⁴ van der Post, *Heart of the Hunter*, 200, 181, 183.
¹⁵ Caponigri, *Time and Idea*, 136.
¹⁶ Caponigri, *Time and Idea*, 170–171.
¹⁷ van der Post, *Heart of the Hunter*, 163, 166–167.
¹⁸ van der Post, *Heart of the Hunter*, 132.
¹⁹ van der Post, *Heart of the Hunter*, 132, 189.
²⁰ van der Post, *Heart of the Hunter*, 200, 179–180.
²¹ van der Post, *Heart of the Hunter*, 184.
²² van der Post, *Heart of the Hunter*, 181–183.
²³ van der Post, *Heart of the Hunter*, 200–201.
²⁴ van der Post, *Heart of the Hunter*, 200–206.
²⁵ van der Post, *A Story Like the Wind: An Epic Novel of Contemporary Southern Africa* (New York: Harvest/Harcourt edition, 1972), x.
²⁶ van der Post, *Heart of the Hunter*, 135.
²⁷ van der Post, *Heart of the Hunter*, 135.

Chapter Twenty-Nine

1. Hancock, *Magicians of the Gods*, 35-36 and introduction to *Göbekli Tepe*, by Andrew Collins, 1-3.
2. Critchlow, *Time Stands Still*, 10, 13-14, 20, 101-119.
3. Hancock, introduction to *Göbekli Tepe*, by Andrew Collins, 5.
4. See Hancock, *Fingerprints of the Gods*.
5. Naydler, *Shamanic Wisdom*, 27-32, 45-47.
6. Naydler, *Shamanic Wisdom*, 31.
7. West, *Serpent in the Sky*, vii, ix, 17.
8. West, *Serpent in the Sky*, ix.
9. West, *Serpent in the Sky*, ix.
10. West, *Serpent in the Sky*, viii.
11. Alison Roberts, *Hathor Rising: The Power of the Goddess in Ancient Egypt* (Rochester: Inner Traditions, 1997), 8-13.
12. Roberts, *Hathor Rising*, 8-50.
13. Naydler, *Shamanic Wisdom*, 148.
14. Naydler, *Shamanic Wisdom*, 56, 66.
15. Naydler, *Shamanic Wisdom*, 68.
16. Naydler, *Shamanic Wisdom*, 85-86.
17. Naydler, *Shamanic Wisdom*, 68.
18. Naydler, *Shamanic Wisdom*, 84, 375.
19. Naydler, *Shamanic Wisdom*, 84.
20. Roberts, *Hathor Rising*, 28.
21. Naydler, *Shamanic Wisdom*, 166.
22. Roberts, *Hathor Rising*, 24-32, 58-64.
23. Naydler, *Shamanic Wisdom*, 166.
24. Roberts, *My Heart My Mother: Death and Rebirth in Ancient Egypt* (Rottingdean: NorthGate, 2000), 156.
25. Roberts, *My Heart My Mother*, 2.
26. Roberts, *My Heart My Mother*, 2-6
27. Roberts, *My Heart My Mother*, 26.
28. Roberts, *My Heart My Mother*, 26.
29. Roberts, *My Heart My Mother*, 27.

Chapter Thirty

1. Kingsley, *Dark Places of Wisdom*, 7.
2. Kingsley, *Dark Places of Wisdom*, 114.
3. Kingsley, *Dark Places of Wisdom*, 79-83.
4. Kingsley, *Dark Places of Wisdom*, 91, 90.
5. Kingsley, *Dark Places of Wisdom*, 120, 123.
6. Kingsley, *Dark Places of Wisdom*, 115.
7. Roberts, *My Heart My Mother*, 192-225 and Kingsley, *Ancient Philosophy, Mystery, and Magic: Empedocles and Pythagorean Tradition* (Oxford: Clarendon Press, 1996), 59-68, 371-391.

8. See Okasha El Daly, *Egyptology: The Missing Millennium: Ancient Egypt in Medieval Arabic Writings*, University College London Institute of Archaeology Publications, vol. 33 (London and New York: Routledge, 2016). See also Cem Nizamoglu, "The House of Wisdom: Baghdad's Intellectual Powerhouse," Muslim Heritage, accessed April 9, 2017, http://www.muslimheritage.com/article/house-of-wisdom; "1001 Inventions: Discover the Golden Age of Muslim Civilization," Muslim Heritage, accessed April 9, 2017, http://www.muslimheritage.com/article/house-of-wisdom; and Daly, "Hieroglyphics cracked 1,000 years earlier than thought," University College London, October 3, 2004, http://www.ucl.ac.uk/news/news-articles/news-releases-archive/Hieroglyphics.
9. Freke and Gandy, *The Hermetica: The Lost Wisdom of the Pharaohs* (New York: Jeremy P. Tarcher/Putnam, 1999), 10.
10. Minou Reeves, *Europe's Debt to Persia: Religion, Philosophy, Astronomy, Mathematics, Medicine and the Sciences* (Reading: Ithaca Press, 2013), 246, 260, 269, 287, 368, 264–265, 317–328.
11. Kingsley, *Ancient Philosophy*, 388.

Chapter Thirty-One

1. Christopher Bamford, "The Meaning of the Rose Cross," in *The Rosicrucian Enlightenment Revisited*, ed. Ralph White (Hudson: Lindisfarne Books, 1999), 51.
2. Bamford, "Meaning of the Rose Cross," 51.
3. Bamford, "Meaning of the Rose Cross," 47, 51–52.
4. Naydler, *Shamanic Wisdom*, 85, 86.
5. Naydler, *Shamanic Wisdom*, 68.
6. Roberts, *Hathor Rising*, 8–13.
7. Roberts, *Hathor Rising*, 58–62.
8. Weston, *Quest of the Holy Grail*, 135–137.
9. René Querido, *The Golden Age of Chartres: The Teachings of a Mystery School and the Eternal Feminine* (Hudson: Anthroposophic Press, 1987), 14, 28.
10. Querido, *Golden Age of Chartres*, 29.
11. *Chartres Cathedral: A Sacred Geometry* (Golden Age Productions, 2003) DVD.
12. B.C.J. Lievegoed, *Mystery Streams in Europe and the New Mysteries* (New York: Anthroposophic Press, 1982), 27.
13. Roberts, *My Heart My Mother*, 196–197.
14. Critchlow, *Time Stands Still*, 103.
15. Fulcanelli [pseud.], *The Mysteries of the Cathedrals: Esoteric Interpretation of the Hermetic Symbols of the Great Work / A Hermetic Study of Cathedral Construction*, trans. Mary Sworder (Las Vegas: Brotherhood of Life, 2005), 30–31.
16. Critchlow, *Time Stands Still*, 14.
17. Ronald Fraser, "The Mysteries of Chartres Cathedral," Research Into Lost Knowledge Organisation, accessed 2016, http://www.rilko.net/EZ/rilko/page106.php?PHPSESSID=a7oi1hh7enpoabmr07fqceubo4 (web page discontinued).
18. Gordon Strachan, *Chartres: Sacred Geometry, Sacred Space* (Edinburgh: Floris Books, 2011), 10–13.

19 Strachan, *Chartres: Sacred Geometry*, 12, 85.
20 Louis Charpentier, *The Mysteries of Chartres Cathedral*, trans. Ronald Fraser (Haverhill: Rilko Books, 1997), 129.
21 Fraser, "Mysteries of Chartres Cathedral."
22 Charpentier, *Mysteries of Chartres Cathedral*, 138, 141, 140.
23 *Chartres Cathedral: A Sacred Geometry*, DVD.
24 Querido, *Golden Age of Chartres*, 14–15.
25 Querido, *Golden Age of Chartres*, 16–17, 37.
26 Querido, *Golden Age of Chartres*, 16.
27 "Inclusive Spirituality – New Age Transformation (Part 2)," Discernment Group, May 7, 2006, http://www.crossroad.to/articles2/006/discernment/inclusive-spirituality-2.htm.
28 Anne Baring, *The Dream of the Cosmos: A Quest for the Soul* (Dorset: Archive, 2013), 3–5.
29 Querido, *Golden Age of Chartres*, 16, 18, 71, 18.
30 *Chartres Cathedral: A Sacred Geometry*, DVD.
31 Charpentier, *Mysteries of Chartres Cathedral*, 13, 81.
32 Strachan, *Chartres: Sacred Geometry*, 19.
33 *Chartres Cathedral: A Sacred Geometry*, DVD.
34 Bucke, *Cosmic Consciousness*, 7, 6.
35 Bucke, *Cosmic Consciousness*, 11.
36 Querido, *Golden Age of Chartres*, 18.
37 "The Virgo Cathedrals of Northern France," Library of Halexandria, May 19, 2006, http://www.halexandria.org/dward758.htm.
38 *Chartres Cathedral: A Sacred Geometry*, DVD.
39 Querido, *Golden Age of Chartres*, 17.
40 "Islam and Europe Timeline (355–1291 A.D.)," The Latin Library, accessed December 29, 2017, http://www.thelatinlibrary.com/imperialism/notes/islamchron.html.

Chapter Thirty-Two

1 Yates, *Giordano Bruno and the Hermetic Tradition* (Chicago: University of Chicago Press, 1964), 12–13.
2 Yates, *Giordano Bruno*, 12–13.
3 French, *John Dee*, 66.
4 Yates, *Giordano Bruno*, 398.
5 Roberts, *My Heart My Mother*, 224–225.
6 Godwin, *Holy Grail*, 8.
7 Querido, *Golden Age of Chartres*, 14–15, 24, 37.
8 Querido, *Golden Age of Chartres*, 99–100, 103.
9 Querido, *Golden Age of Chartres*, 97.
10 Querido, *Golden Age of Chartres*, 106–107.
11 Querido, *Golden Age of Chartres*, 32, 104, 97–107.
12 Querido, *Golden Age of Chartres*, 17.
13 "Islamic Golden Age," Islamic History, accessed January 9, 2018, http://islamichistory.org/islamic-golden-age/.

14. Judith Herrin, *Byzantium: The Surprising Life of a Medieval Empire* (Princeton: Princeton University Press, 2008), xiv.
15. Herrin, *Byzantium*, xiv–xv.
16. Herrin, *Byzantium*, xvi.
17. Herrin, *Byzantium*, xvi.
18. Herrin, *Byzantium*, xix–xx.
19. Herrin, *Byzantium*, 331.
20. Herrin, *Byzantium*, 330–332.
21. Herrin, *Byzantium*, 333.
22. William Butler Yeats, "Sailing to Byzantium."
23. Baring, *Dream of the Cosmos*, 42, 366.
24. "Giovanni Pico della Mirandola," Stanford Encyclopedia of Philosophy, revised August 3, 2016, https://plato.stanford.edu/entries/pico-della-mirandola/.
25. Luke Slattery, "A Renaissance Murder Mystery," *The New Yorker*, July 22, 2015, https://www.newyorker.com/culture/culture-desk/a-renaissance-murder-mystery.
26. Walter Pater, "Pico Della Mirandola," in *The Life of Pico Della Mirandola* by Giovanni Della Mirandola, trans. Sir Thomas More (David Nutt in the Strand, 1890), 8.
27. "Giovanni Pico della Mirandola," Wikimedia Foundation, last modified February 3, 2018, https://en.wikipedia.org/wiki/Giovanni_Pico_della_Mirandola.
28. Wikimedia, "Giovanni Pico della Mirandola."
29. Slattery, "Renaissance Murder Mystery."
30. "Savonarola's Preaching Got Him Burned," Christianity.com, April 28, 2010, https://www.christianity.com/church/church-history/timeline/1201-1500/savonarolas-preaching-got-him-burned-11629883.html.
31. "Girolamo Savonarola (1452–98): Influence on Florentine Art," Visual Arts Cork, accessed February 3, 2018, http://www.visual-arts-cork.com/history-of-art/savonarola.htm.

Chapter Thirty-Three

1. Bamford, "Meaning of the Rose Cross," 46.
2. Yates, *Rosicrucian Enlightenment*, 231.
3. Yates, *Rosicrucian Enlightenment*, xiv, xii.
4. Bamford, "Meaning of the Rose Cross," 51, 55.
5. Bamford, "Meaning of the Rose Cross," 56, 62.
6. Bamford, "Meaning of the Rose Cross," 53.
7. Bamford, "Meaning of the Rose Cross," 65.
8. Bamford, "Meaning of the Rose Cross," 46.
9. Yates, *Rosicrucian Enlightenment*, 14, xiii.
10. Yates, *Rosicrucian Enlightenment*, 224.
11. Yates, *Rosicrucian Enlightenment*, 190.
12. See Frank E. Manuel, *The Eighteenth Century Confronts the Gods* (Cambridge: Harvard University Press, 1959).
13. Barker, *Great Angel*, 58 (Proverbs 3:18).
14. Roberts, *My Heart My Mother*, 26.

Chapter Thirty-Four

1. M.H. Abrams, *Natural Supernaturalism: Tradition and Revolution in Romantic Literature* (New York: W.W. Norton, 1973), 182.
2. Ronald D. Gray, *Goethe the Alchemist: A Study of Alchemical Symbolism in Goethe's Literary and Scientific Works* (Cambridge: Cambridge University Press, 1952), 4.
3. Jung, *The Archetypes and the Collective Unconscious*, vol. 9, part 1 of *The Collected Works*, trans. R.F.C. Hull (Princeton: Princeton University Press, 1969), 357.
4. Ronald D. Gray, *Goethe the Alchemist*, 4.
5. Frederick Hiebel, "Goethe's 'Maerchen' in the Light of Novalis." *PMLA* 63 no. 4 (1948): 920 and *Novalis: German Poet-European Thinker-Christian Mystic*, 2nd ed. (Chapel Hill: University of North Carolina Press, 1954), 24–27.
6. See Ronald D. Gray, *Goethe the Alchemist*.
7. Hiebel, "Goethe's 'Maerchen,'" 918.
8. Hiebel, "Goethe's 'Maerchen,'" 922.
9. Hiebel, "Goethe's 'Maerchen,'" 926 and Novalis, *Henry von Ofterdingen*, 84–85.
10. Wilkinson and Willoughby, *Goethe: Poet and Thinker*, 192–197.
11. Hiebel, "Goethe's 'Maerchen,'" 916.
12. Kingsley, *Dark Places of Wisdom*, 34, 9.

Chapter Thirty-Six

1. McTaggart, *The Field*, 33, 11.
2. Saryon Michael White, "An Imaginal Journey of Peace."
3. Ereira, *Elder Brothers*, 1.
4. Jung, *Structure and Dynamics of the Psyche*, page number not located.
5. Keeney, *Bushman Way of Tracking God*, xiv–xv.
6. Keeney, *Bushman Way of Tracking God*, xv, xvii.
7. Keeney, *Bushman Way of Tracking God*, xvi, xvii, xvi, xviii.
8. Keeney, *Bushman Way of Tracking God*, xix.
9. Keeney, *Bushman Way of Tracking God*, xvi.
10. Keeney, *Bushman Way of Tracking God*, ix, viii, x and Bradford Keeney and Hillary Keeney, eds., *Way of the Bushman As Told by the Tribal Elders: Spiritual Teachings and Practices of the Kalahari Ju'hoansi* (Rochester: Bear, 2015), x.
11. Keeney and Keeney, *Way of the Bushman*, xvi.
12. Keeney and Keeney, *Way of the Bushman*, x–xi.
13. Barker, *Great Angel*, 58 (Proverbs 3:18).
14. Keeney and Keeney, *Way of the Bushman*, 4.
15. Mamo Palia, "Dialogue for the Restoration of the Original Seeds," The Mother Earth Restoration Trust, accessed April 2, 2017, http://www.themotherearthrestorationtrust.world/dialogue_for_the_restoration_of_the_original_seeds.
16. Eisenstein, "Aluna: A Message to Little Brother."
17. Eisenstein, "Aluna: A Message to Little Brother."
18. Strömberg, *Soul of the Universe*, 253, 303.
19. Ereira, *Elder Brothers*, 126–129.

20. Janet Mayer, *Spirits...They Are Present* (Bloomington: AuthorHouse, 2011), 32-33.
21. Mayer, *Spirits*, 59-60.
22. Mayer, *Spirits*, 65-66, 69-70, 93-94.
23. Mayer, *Spirits*, 74-83.
24. Mayer, *Spirits*, 81-84.
25. Mayer, *Spirits*, 87-89.
26. The severed rational mind tends to denigrate and dismiss this kind of unusual phenomenon, often without a thorough investigation. I read on the Internet a "skeptic's" dismissal of Janet's experience by suggesting that Janet could have learned the languages from the Internet. This would be highly unlikely since Ipupiara identified four languages that were sometimes spoken in a male dialect, sometimes in the form of a prayer or chant, sometimes in the form of speech from one shaman to another, sometimes in words that were taboo for a woman to speak, and sometimes in the words of a female. Anyone who has studied languages knows how difficult it is to become fluent in any language, much less four languages, without hearing them or conversing with native speakers. However, those who know Janet know this kind of hoax would be completely alien to her.
27. Sarah Sunshine Manning, "Healing Continues 125 Years After Wounded Knee Massacre," Indian Country Today, December 28, 2015, http://indiancountrytodaymedianetwork.com/2015/12/28/manning-healing-continues-125-years-after-wounded-knee-massacre-162895 (web page discontinued); edited December 28, 2016, accessed October 21, 2018, https://newsmaven.io/indiancountrytoday/archive/manning-healing-continues-125-years-after-wounded-knee-massacre-Mg4_WasDAkGnPnFs7x63Ew/.
28. "Healing Hearts at Wounded Knee, Local and Global Ceremonies: 125th Year Memorial of the Massacre at Wounded Knee." Healing the Heart of Humanity, November 14, 2015, https://healingheartsatwoundedknee.com/22-29-december-2015-wounded-knee-south-dakota-healing-hearts-at-wounded-knee-local-and-global-ceremonies/.

Chapter Thirty-Seven

1. Christopher M. Bache, *Dark Night Early Dawn: Steps to a Deep Ecology of Mind* (New York: State University of New York Press, 2000), 245.
2. See Norie Huddle and Charlene Midland, *Butterfly: A Tiny Tale of Great Transformation* (New York: Huddle Books, 1990).
3. Bache, *Dark Night Early Dawn*, 245.
4. Richard Tarnas, *The Passion of the Western Mind: Understanding the Ideas That Have Shaped Our World View* (New York: Ballantine Books, 1993), 440.
5. Bache, *Dark Night Early Dawn*, 245.
6. Roberts, *My Heart My Mother*, 2-6.
7. Naydler, *Shamanic Wisdom*, 148.
8. Roberts, *My Heart My Mother*, 4.
9. Tarnas, *Passion of the Western Mind*, 441.

10. Roberts, *My Heart My Mother*, 26.
11. Campbell, *The Hero With a Thousand Faces* (Novato: New World Library, 2008), 210–211.
12. Campbell, *Hero With a Thousand Faces*, 210–211.
13. Campbell, *Hero With a Thousand Faces*, 210–211.
14. Jung, *Psychology and Alchemy*, vol. 12 of *The Collected Works*, trans. R.F.C. Hull (Princeton: Princeton University Press, 1968), 22–23.
15. László, *Macroshift*, 11.
16. Bache, *Dark Night Early Dawn*, 241, 244.
17. Bache, *Dark Night Early Dawn*, 245.
18. Barker, *Great High Priest*, 246.
19. Wilhelm, *The I Ching* or *Book of Changes*, 75.

Conclusion

1. Joseph M. Felser, *The Way Back to Paradise: Restoring the Balance Between Magic and Reason* (Charlottesville: Hampton Roads, 2005), 50.
2. *The Doctrine of Discovery: Unmasking the Domination Code* (38 Plus 2 Productions, LLC, 2015) DVD.
3. *Doctrine of Discovery*, DVD.
4. *Doctrine of Discovery*, DVD.
5. *Doctrine of Discovery*, DVD.
6. Seymour Hersh, *Democracy Now*, KPFK, June 20, 2018, https://www.democracynow.org/shows/2018/6/20.
7. Stephen Kinzer, "Overthrow: 100 Years of U.S. Meddling & Regime Change, from Iran to Nicaragua to Hawaii to Cuba," *Democracy Now*, KPFK, March 12, 2018, https://www.democracynow.org/2018/3/12/100_years_of_us_interference_regime. See also Kinzer, *Overthrow: America's Century of Regime Change from Hawaii to Iraq* (New York: Times Books, 2006).
8. Dictionary.com, s.v. "Mephistopheles," accessed April 1, 2018, http://www.dictionary.com/browse/mephistophelian?s=t. According to Goethe scholar K.J. Schröer (1886), Memphistopheles "is a compound of Hebrew mephitz 'destroyer' and tophel 'liar.'"
9. Wilhelm, *The I Ching* or *Book of Changes*, lv.
10. Wilhelm, *The I Ching* or *Book of Changes*, 477–478.
11. Pagels, *Gnostic Gospels*, xiii–xiv.
12. Amit Goswami, in *Consciousness: Bridging the Gap Between Conventional Science and the New Super Science of Quantum Mechanics*, chap. 4, by Eva Herr (Faber: Rainbow Ridge Books, 2013), 117, 94, 104.
13. Goswami, in *Consciousness: Bridging the Gap*, by Eva Herr, 106.
14. Gimbutas, *Civilization of the Goddess*, vii–xi.
15. Reverend Dr. William J. Barber II, "America's Moral Malady," *The Atlantic*, accessed June 22, 2018, https://www.theatlantic.com/magazine/archive/2018/02/a-new-poor-peoples-campaign/552503/. The new Poor People's Campaign's "Moral Agenda Based on Fundamental Rights" can be found at https://www.poorpeoplescampaign.org.

16. Greg Kaufmann, "The New Poor People's Campaign Wants to Change How We Think About Poverty," Talk Poverty, May 14, 2018, https://talkpoverty.org/2018/05/14/new-poor-peoples-campaign-wants-change-think-poverty/.
17. Barber, "Moral Agenda Based on Fundamental Rights."
18. Barber, "Moral Agenda Based on Fundamental Rights."
19. Barber, "Moral Agenda Based on Fundamental Rights."
20. Kovács, *Miracle of Death*, 61–62.
21. Paul Levy, "Rebirth in an Age of Polarization," Awaken in the Dream, accessed April 2, 2017, http://www.awakeninthedream.com/rebirth-in-an-age-of-polarization/.
22. Levy, "When the Most Awake Among Us Fall Asleep: Marc Gafni, His Supporters and Seiko," Awaken in the Dream, accessed April 9, 2017, http://www.awakeninthedream.com/marc-gafni/.
23. Jung, *Alchemical Studies*, 265–266.
24. Christopher Fry, "Comedy," in *Comedy: Meaning and Form*, ed. Robert W. Corrigan (San Francisco: Chandler, 1965), 16.
25. Baring, *Dream of the Cosmos*, 56.
26. See Sharon McErlane, *A Call to Power: The Grandmothers Speak* (Net of Light Press, 2006); *Our Love is Our Power: Working with the Net of Light That Holds the Earth* (Net of Light Press, 2009); and *Casting the Net* (Net of Light Press, 2015). See also www.netoflight.org.
27. Kovács, *Miracle of Death*, 160–161.

Selected Bibliography

Abrams, M.H. *Natural Supernaturalism: Tradition and Revolution in Romantic Literature*. New York: W.W. Norton, 1973.

Adams, Henry. *Mont-Saint-Michel and Chartres*. New York: New American Library, 1961.

Armstrong, Karen. *The Battle for God: A History of Fundamentalism*. New York: Random House, 2001.

–. *The Case for God*. New York: Anchor Books, 2010.

Bache, Christopher M. *Dark Night Early Dawn: Steps to a Deep Ecology of Mind*. New York: State University of New York Press, 2000.

Bahn, Paul G., and Jean Vertut. *Journey Through the Ice Age*. Berkeley: University of California Press, 1997.

Bamford, Christopher. "The Meaning of the Rose Cross." In *The Rosicrucian Enlightenment Revisited*, edited by Ralph White, 43–72. Hudson: Lindisfarne Books, 1999.

Barber II, Reverend Dr. William J. "America's Moral Malady." *The Atlantic*, accessed June 22, 2018. https://www.theatlantic.com/magazine/archive/2018/02/a-new-poor-peoples-campaign/552503/. See also the new Poor People's Campaign's "Moral Agenda Based on Fundamental Rights" at www.poorpeoplescampaign.org.

Baring, Anne. *The Dream of the Cosmos: A Quest for the Soul*. Dorset: Archive, 2013.

Baring, Anne, and Jules Cashford. *The Myth of the Goddess: Evolution of an Image*. London: Viking, 1991.

Barker, Margaret. *Christmas: The Original Story*. London: Society for Promoting Christian Knowledge, 2008.

–. *The Great Angel: A Study of Israel's Second God*. Louisville: Westminster/John Knox, 1992.

–. *The Great High Priest: The Temple Roots of Christian Liturgy*. London: T&T Clark, 2004.

–. *The Revelation of Jesus Christ*. Edinburgh: T&T Clark, 2000.

Bergin, Thomas Goddard, and Max Harold Fisch, trans. *The New Science of Giambattista Vico*. Unabridged Translation of Third Edition (1744). Ithaca: Cornell University Press, 1984.

Boswell, John. *Christianity, Social Tolerance, and Homosexuality: Gay People in Western Europe from the Beginning of the Christian Era to the Fourteenth Century*. Chicago: University of Chicago Press, 1981.

Braden, Gregg. *The Divine Matrix: Bridging Time, Space, Miracles, and Belief.* Carlsbad: Hay House, 2007.

Bucke, Richard Maurice. *Cosmic Consciousness: A Study in the Evolution of the Human Mind.* New York: E.P. Dutton, 1969.

Campbell, Joseph. *The Hero With a Thousand Faces.* Novato: New World Library, 2008.

–. *The Masks of God, Vol. 1: Primitive Mythology.* London: Arkana, 1991.

–. *The Masks of God, Vol. 3: Occidental Mythology.* London: Arkana, 1991.

–. *The Way of the Animal Powers, Vol. 1: Historical Atlas of World Mythology,* San Francisco: Harper & Row, 1988.

Caponigri, A. Robert. *Time and Idea: The Theory of History in Giambattista Vico.* London: Routledge and Kegan Paul, 1953.

Capra, Fritjof. *The Tao of Physics: An Exploration of the Parallels Between Modern Physics and Eastern Mysticism.* Boulder: Shambhala, 1975.

Charpentier, Louis. *The Mysteries of Chartres Cathedral.* Translated by Ronald Fraser. Haverhill: Rilko Books, 1997.

Chartres Cathedral: A Sacred Geometry. Golden Age Productions, 2003, DVD.

Childre, Doc, and Howard Martin with Donna Beech. *The HeartMath Solution: The Institute of HeartMath's Revolutionary Program for Engaging the Power of the Heart's Intelligence.* New York: HarperSanFrancisco, 2000.

Clottes, Jean, and David Lewis-Williams. *The Shamans of Prehistory: Trance and Magic in the Painted Caves.* Text by Jean Clottes. Translated by Sophie Hawkes. New York: Harry N. Abrams, 1998.

Cook, Roger. *The Tree of Life: Symbol of the Centre.* London: Thames & Hudson, 1974.

Corbin, Henri. "Mundus Imaginalis or the Imaginary and the Imaginal." Hermetic Library, accessed November 4, 2017. https://hermetic.com/moorish/mundus-imaginalis.

Critchlow, Keith. *Time Stands Still: New Light on Megalithic Science.* Edinburgh: Floris Books, 2007.

Currivan, Jude. *The Cosmic Hologram: In-formation at the Center of Creation.* Rochester: Inner Traditions, 2017.

Daly, Okasha El. *Egyptology: The Missing Millennium: Ancient Egypt in Medieval Arabic Writings.* University College London Institute of Archaeology Publications, vol. 33. London: Routledge, 2016.

–. "Hieroglyphics cracked 1,000 years earlier than thought." University College London, October 3, 2004. http://www.ucl.ac.uk/news/news-articles/news-releases-archive/Hieroglyphics.

Delgado, Jorge Luis, with MaryAnn Male. *Andean Awakening: An Inca Guide to Mystical Peru.* San Francisco: Council Oak Books, 2006.

Doctrine of Discovery: Unmasking the Domination Code. 38 Plus 2 Productions, 2015, DVD.

Douno, Beinsa (Peter Deunov). *Gems of Love: Prayers and Formulas.* Translated and edited by David Lorimer. Surrey: Grain of Wheat Trust, 1994.

Eisenstein, Charles. "Aluna: A Message to Little Brother." *Tikkun*, May 26, 2015. https://www.tikkun.org/nextgen/a-message-to-little-brother.

Eliade, Mircea. *A History of Religious Ideas, Vol. 1: From the Stone Age to the Eleusinian Mysteries.* Translated by Willard R. Trask. Chicago: University of Chicago Press, 1978.

—. *Patterns in Comparative Religion.* Translated by Rosemary Sheed. Cleveland: Meridian Books, 1970.

Engelsman, Joan Chamberlain. *The Feminine Dimension of the Divine.* Philadelphia: Westminster Press, 1979.

Ereira, Alan, dir. *Aluna.* 2012; UK: Columbia. Film, 89 min.

—. *The Elder Brothers: A lost South American people and their message about the fate of the earth.* New York: Alfred A. Knopf, 1992.

Felser, Joseph M. *The Way Back to Paradise: Restoring the Balance Between Magic and Reason.* Charlottesville: Hampton Roads, 2005.

Firestone, Richard, Allen West, and Simon Warwick-Smith. *The Cycle of Cosmic Catastrophes: How a Stone-Age Comet Changed the Course of World Culture.* Rochester: Bear, 2006.

Fisk, Robert. *The Great War for Civilisation: The Conquest of the Middle East.* New York: Alfred A. Knopf, 2005.

Freke, Timothy, and Peter Gandy. *The Hermetica: The Lost Wisdom of the Pharaohs.* New York: Jeremy P. Tarcher/Putnam, 1999.

—. *Jesus and the Lost Goddess: The Secret Teachings of the Original Christians.* New York: Harmony Books, 2001.

—. *The Jesus Mysteries: Was the "Original Jesus" a Pagan God?* New York: Three Rivers Press, 2001.

French, Peter J. *John Dee: The World of an Elizabethan Magus.* London: Routledge and Kegan Paul, 1984.

Fry, Christopher. "Comedy." In *Comedy: Meaning and Form*, edited by Robert W. Corrigan, 15–17. San Francisco: Chandler, 1965.

Fulcanelli [pseud.]. *The Mysteries of the Cathedrals: Esoteric Interpretation of the Hermetic Symbols of the Great Work / A Hermetic Study of Cathedral Construction.* Translated by Mary Sworder. Las Vegas: Brotherhood of Life, 2005.

Gaster, Theodor H., ed. *The Dead Sea Scriptures.* 3rd ed. Garden City: Anchor Books, 1976.

Gimbutas, Marija. *The Civilization of the Goddess: The World of Old Europe.* Edited by Joan Marler. New York: HarperSanFrancisco, 1991.

—. *The Goddesses and Gods of Old Europe: Myths and Cult Images.* Berkeley: University of California Press, 1982.

—. *The Language of the Goddess.* San Francisco: Harper & Row, 1989.

Godwin, Malcolm. *The Holy Grail: Its Origins, Secrets & Meaning Revealed.* London: Bloomsbury, 1994.

Gooch, Stan. *Cities of Dreams: When Women Ruled the Earth.* London: Aulis Books, 2001.

Goodchild, Veronica Anne. *Songlines of the Soul: Pathways to a New Vision for a New Century.* Lake Worth: Nicholas-Hays, 2012.

Goodenough, Erwin R. *By Light, Light: The Mystic Gospel of Hellenistic Judaism.* Amsterdam: Philo Press, 1969.

Goodspeed, Edgar J., trans. *The Apocrypha.* New York: Modern Library, 1959.

Goswami, Amit. In *Consciousness: Bridging the Gap Between Conventional Science and the New Super Science of Quantum Mechanics*, chap. 4, by Eva Herr. Faber: Rainbow Ridge Books, 2013.

Goswami, Amit, Richard E. Reed, and Maggie Goswami. *The Self-Aware Universe: how consciousness creates the material world.* New York: G. P. Putnam's Sons, 1995.

Gray, Richard. "Stone Age man ate mushrooms: Oldest evidence for fungi in the human diet discovered in 19,000-year-old tooth plaque." Daily Mail, April 21, 2015. https://www.dailymail.co.uk/sciencetech/article-3048678/Stone-Age-man-ate-mushrooms-Oldest-evidence-fungi-human-diet-discovered-19-000-year-old-tooth-plaque.html.

Gray, Ronald D. *Goethe the Alchemist: A Study of Alchemical Symbolism in Goethe's Literary and Scientific Works.* Cambridge: Cambridge University Press, 1952.

Hancock, Graham. *Fingerprints of the Gods: The Evidence of Earth's Lost Civilization.* New York: Crown Trade Paperbacks, 1995.

—. Introduction to *Göbekli Tepe: Genesis of the Gods*, by Andrew Collins, 1–8. Rochester: Bear, 2014.

—. *Magicians of the Gods: The Forgotten Wisdom of Earth's Lost Civilization.* New York: Thomas Dunne Books, 2015.

—. *Supernatural: Meetings with the Ancient Teachers of Mankind.* Toronto: Doubleday, 2005.

Hancock, Graham, and Santha Faiia. *Heaven's Mirror: Quest for the Lost Civilization.* New York: Three Rivers Press, 1998.

Hapgood, Charles H. *Maps of the Ancient Sea Kings: Evidence of Advanced Civilization in the Ice Age.* Kempton: Adventures Unlimited Press, 1996.

Harner, Michael. *The Way of the Shaman: A Guide to Power and Healing.* New York: Bantam Books, 1986.

Harpur, Tom. *The Pagan Christ: Recovering the Lost Light.* New York: Walker, 2004.

Harrison, Jane Ellen. *Prolegomena to the Study of Greek Religion.* Princeton: Princeton University Press, 1991.

Herrin, Judith. *Byzantium: The Surprising Life of a Medieval Empire.* Princeton: Princeton University Press, 2008.

Hiebel, Frederick. "Goethe's 'Maerchen' in the Light of Novalis." *PMLA* 63, no. 4 (1948): 918-934.

–. *Novalis: German Poet-European Thinker-Christian Mystic.* 2nd ed. Chapel Hill: University of North Carolina Press, 1954.

Hoeller, Stephan A. *Jung and the Lost Gospels: Insights into the Dead Sea Scrolls and the Nag Hammadi Library.* Wheaton: Theosophical Publishing House, 1993.

Huddle, Norie, and Charlene Midland. *Butterfly: A Tiny Tale of Great Transformation.* New York: Huddle Books, 1990.

Huston, Tom. "A Brief History of Evolutionary Spirituality." *What is Enlightenment,* January-March 2007.

Huxley, Aldous. *The Doors of Perception.* New York: Harper & Row, 1954.

–. *The Perennial Philosophy.* New York: Harper Colophon Books, 1970.

Jung, C.G. *Alchemical Studies.* Vol. 13 of *The Collected Works.* Translated by R.F.C. Hull. Princeton: Princeton University Press, 1967.

–. *The Archetypes and the Collective Unconscious.* Vol. 9, Part 1 of *The Collected Works.* Translated by R.F.C. Hull. Princeton: Princeton University Press, 1969.

–. *Psychology and Alchemy.* Vol. 12 of *The Collected Works.* Translated by R.F.C. Hull. Princeton: Princeton University Press, 1968.

–. *The Structure and Dynamics of the Psyche.* Vol. 8 of *The Collected Works.* Translated by R.F.C. Hull. Princeton: Princeton University Press, 1969.

–. *Symbols of Transformation: An Analysis of the Prelude to a Case of Schizophrenia.* Vol. 5 of *The Collected Works.* Translated by R.F.C. Hull. Princeton: Princeton University Press, 1967.

Keeney, Bradford. *The Bushman Way of Tracking God: The Original Spirituality of the Kalahari People.* New York: Atria Books, 2010.

Keeney, Bradford, and Hillary Keeney, eds. *Way of the Bushman As Told by the Tribal Elders: Spiritual Teachings and Practices of the Kalahari Ju'hoansi.* Rochester: Bear, 2015.

Kerényi, Carl. *Dionysos: Archetypal Image of Indestructible Life.* Translated by Ralph Manheim. Princeton: Princeton University Press, 1976.

–. *Eleusis: Archetypal Image of Mother and Daughter.* Translated by Ralph Manheim. New York: Bollingen Foundation, 1967.

–. "Kore." In *Essays on a Science of Mythology: The Myths of the Divine Child and the Divine Maiden,* by C.G. Jung and C. Kerényi, 101–155. Translated by R.F.C. Hull. New York: Harper TorchBooks, 1963.

–. "Labyrinth-Studien." In *Humanistische Seelen-Forschung,* 226–273. München: Langen Müller, 1966.

–. "The Mysteries of the Kabeiroi." In *Papers from the Eranos Yearbooks, Vol. 2: The Mysteries,* edited by Joseph Campbell, 32–63. Princeton: Princeton University Press, 1971.

Kidd, Sue Monk. *The Secret Life of Bees.* New York: Viking, 2003.

Kingsley, Peter. *Ancient Philosophy, Mystery, and Magic: Empedocles and Pythagorean Tradition.* Oxford: Clarendon Press, 1996.

–. *In the Dark Places of Wisdom.* Inverness: Golden Sufi Center, 1999.

–. *Return to Eternity: A transformational workshop with Peter Kingsley.* www.PeterKingsley.org, 2006, CD.

Kinzer, Stephen. *Overthrow: America's Century of Regime Change from Hawaii to Iraq.* New York: Times Books, 2006.

–. "Overthrow: 100 Years of U.S. Meddling & Regime Change, from Iran to Nicaragua to Hawaii to Cuba." *Democracy Now,* KPFK, March 12, 2018. https://www.democracynow.org/2018/3/12/100_years_of_us_interference_regime.

Kovács, Betty J. "Journey of the Mothers." In *Earthwalking Sky Dancers: Women's Pilgrimages to Sacred Places,* edited by Leila Castle, 195–211. Berkeley: Frog, 1996.

–. *The Miracle of Death: There is Nothing But Life.* Claremont: Kamlak Center, 2003.

Krippner, Stanley. "The Epistemology and Technologies of Shamanic States of Consciousness." *Journal of Consciousness Studies* 7, no. 11–12 (January 2000): 93–118.

Kübler-Ross, Elisabeth. *On Life After Death.* Berkeley: Celestial Arts, 1991.

Kuhn, Alvin Boyd. *Who is This King of Glory? A Critical Study of the Christos-Messiah Tradition.* Bensenville: Lushena Books, 2006.

László, Ervin. *Macroshift: Navigating the Transformation to a Sustainable World.* San Francisco: Berrett-Koehler, 2001.

László, Ervin, Stanislav Grof, and Peter Russell. *The Consciousness Revolution: A Transatlantic Dialogue.* Edited by Ervin László. Boston: Element Books, 1999.

Laughlin, Charles D. "Archetypes, Neurognosis and the Quantum Sea." Biogenetic Structuralism, September 21, 2012. http://www.biogeneticstructuralism.com/docs/archetyp_sse.rtf.

Leloup, Jean-Yves. *The Sacred Embrace of Jesus and Mary: The Sexual Mystery at the Heart of the Christian Tradition.* Rochester: Inner Traditions, 2006.

Levy, Paul. *The Quantum Revelation: A Radical Synthesis of Science and Spirituality*. New York: Select Books, 2018.

–. "Rebirth in an Age of Polarization." Awaken in the Dream, accessed April 2, 2017. https://www.awakeninthedream.com/rebirth-in-an-age-of-polarization/.

–. "When the Most Awake Among Us Fall Asleep: Marc Gafni, His Supporters and Seiko." Awaken in the Dream, accessed April 9, 2017. http://www.awakeninthedream.com/marc-gafni/.

Lewis-Williams, David. *The Mind in the Cave: Consciousness and the Origins of Art*. London: Thames & Hudson, 2002.

Lorimer, David, ed. *The Circle of Sacred Dance: Peter Deunov's Paneurhythmy*. London: Vega, 2002.

–, ed. *Prophet for Our Times: The Life and Teachings of Peter Deunov*. London: Vega, 2002.

Mack, Burton L. *The Lost Gospel: The Book of Q & Christian Origins*. New York: HarperSanFrancisco, 1994.

Manuel, Frank E. *The Eighteenth Century Confronts the Gods*. Cambridge: Harvard University Press, 1959.

Markale, Jean. *Cathedral of the Black Madonna: The Druids and the Mysteries of Chartres*. Rochester: Inner Traditions, 2004.

Marler, Joan. "The Circle Is Unbroken: A Brief Biography." In *From the Realm of the Ancestors: An Anthology in Honor of Marija Gimbutas*, edited by Joan Marler, 7–25. Manchester: Knowledge, Ideas & Trends, 1997.

Massey, Gerald. *Ancient Egypt: The Light of the World*. Sioux Falls: NuVision, 2008.

Matthews, Caitlin. "The Voices of the Wells: Celtic Oral Themes in Grail Literature." In *At the Table of the Grail: No one who sets forth on the Grail Quest remains unchanged*, edited by John Matthews, 3–25. London: Watkins, 2002.

Mayer, Janet. *Spirits…They Are Present*. Bloomington: AuthorHouse, 2011.

McErlane, Sharon. *A Call to Power: The Grandmothers Speak*. Net of Light Press, 2006.

–. *Casting the Net*. Net of Light Press, 2015.

–. *Our Love is Our Power: Working with the Net of Light That Holds the Earth*. Net of Light Press, 2009.

McTaggart, Lynne. *The Field: The Quest for the Secret Force of the Universe*. New York: HarperCollins, 2002.

Mead, G.R.S. *Fragments of a Faith Forgotten*. Whitefish: Kessinger, 1930.

Meyer, Marvin, ed. *The Gnostic Gospels of Jesus: The Definitive Collection of Mystical Gospels and Secret Books About Jesus of Nazareth*. New York: HarperSanFrancisco, 2005.

Meyer, Marvin, and Esther A. De Boer. *The Gospels of Mary: The Secret Tradition of Mary Magdalene, the Companion of Jesus.* New York: HarperSanFrancisco, 2004.

Michell, John. *Secrets of the Stones: New Revelations of Astro-archaeology and the Mystical Sciences of Antiquity.* Rochester: Inner Traditions, 1989.

—. *The New View Over Atlantis.* San Francisco: Harper & Row, 1983.

Naydler, Jeremy. *Shamanic Wisdom in the Pyramid Texts: The Mystical Tradition of Ancient Egypt.* Rochester: Inner Traditions, 2005.

Newberg, Andrew, Eugene D'Aquili, and Vince Rause. *Why God Won't Go Away: Brain Science and the Biology of Belief.* New York: Ballantine Books, 2001.

Nizamoglu, Cem. "The House of Wisdom: Baghdad's Intellectual Powerhouse." Muslim Heritage, accessed April 9, 2017. http://www.muslimheritage.com/article/house-of-wisdom.

—. "1001 Inventions: Discover the Golden Age of Muslim Civilization." Muslim Heritage, accessed April 9, 2017. http://www.muslimheritage.com/article/house-of-wisdom.

Novalis [pseud.]. *Henry von Ofterdingen.* Translated by Palmer Hilty. New York: Frederick Ungar, 1974.

Pagels, Elaine. *Beyond Belief: The Secret Gospel of Thomas.* New York: Random House, 2003.

—. *The Gnostic Gospels.* New York: Vintage Books, 1981.

Palia, Mamo. "Dialogue for the Restoration of the Original Seeds." The Mother Earth Restoration Trust, accessed April 2, 2017. http://www.themotherearthrestorationtrust.world/dialogue_for_the_restoration_of_the_original_seeds.

Pater, Walter. "Pico Della Mirandola." In *The Life of Pico Della Mirandola*, by Giovanni Della Mirandola, 4–11. Translated by Sir Thomas More. David Nutt in the Strand, 1890.

Pearce, Joseph Chilton. *The Biology of Transcendence: A Blueprint of the Human Spirit.* Rochester: Park Street Press, 2002.

Pert, Candace B. *Molecules of Emotion: The Science Behind Mind-Body Medicine.* New York: Simon & Schuster, 1999.

Potter, Charles Francis. *The Lost Years of Jesus Revealed: Newest Revelations of the Dead Sea Scrolls and the Nag-Hammadi Discoveries.* New York: Fawcett, 1962.

Querido, René. *The Golden Age of Chartres: The Teachings of a Mystery School and the Eternal Feminine.* Hudson: Anthroposophic Press, 1987.

Reeves, Minou. *Europe's Debt to Persia: Religion, Philosophy, Astronomy, Mathematics, Medicine and the Sciences.* Reading: Ithaca Press, 2013.

Rilke, Rainer Maria. *Briefe an einen jungen Dichter.* Leipzig: Insel-Verlag, 1932.

Ring, Kenneth. *Heading Toward Omega: In Search of the Meaning of the Near-Death Experience.* New York: William Morrow, 1985.

Roberts, Alison. *Hathor Rising: The Power of the Goddess in Ancient Egypt.* Rochester: Inner Traditions, 1997.

–. *My Heart My Mother: Death and Rebirth in Ancient Egypt.* Rottingdean: NorthGate, 2000.

Robinson, James M. *The Nag Hammadi Codices: A general introduction to the nature and significance of the Coptic Gnostic Library from Nag Hammadi,* 2nd rev. ed. Claremont: Institute for Antiquity and Christianity, 1977.

–, gen. ed. *The Nag Hammadi Library.* Translated by Members of the Coptic Gnostic Library Project of the Institute for Antiquity and Christianity. San Francisco: Harper & Row, 1977.

Rudgley, Richard. *Secrets of the Stone Age: A prehistoric journey with Richard Rudgley.* London: Century, 2000.

Schiffman, Lawrence H. "Judaism, Christianity and the Dead Sea Scrolls." University of California Television (UCTV). YouTube video, posted August 7, 2008. https://youtu.be/92hyhBXLaWE.

Shlain, Leonard. *The Alphabet Versus The Goddess: The Conflict Between Word and Image.* New York: Viking Penguin, 1998.

Silva, Freddy. *Secrets in the Fields: The Science and Mysticism of Crop Circles.* Charlottesville: Hampton Roads, 2002.

Slattery, Luke. "A Renaissance Murder Mystery." *The New Yorker,* July 22, 2015. https://www.newyorker.com/culture/culture-desk/a-renaissance-murder-mystery.

Smith, Huston. *Cleansing the Doors of Perception: The Religious Significance of Etheogenic Plants and Chemicals.* 3rd ed. New York: Jeremy P. Tarcher/Putnam, 2000.

Stace, Walter T., ed. *The Teachings of the Mystics: Selections from the Great Mystics and Mystical Writings of the World.* New York: Mentor Books, 1960.

Starbird, Margaret. *Magdalena's Lost Legacy: Symbolic Numbers and the Sacred Union in Christianity.* Rochester: Bear, 2003.

Starr, Chester G. *A History of the Ancient World.* 4th ed. New York: Oxford University Press, 1991.

Strachan, Gordon. *Chartres: Sacred Geometry, Sacred Space.* Edinburgh: Floris Books, 2011.

Strömberg, Gustaf. *The Soul of the Universe.* North Hollywood: Educational Research Institute, 1948.

Swimme, Brian. "Comprehensive Compassion, Part 1" and "The Divinization of the Cosmos, Part 2." *What is Enlightenment,* September–December 2006.

–. *The Hidden Heart of the Cosmos: Humanity and the New Story.* Maryknoll: Orbis Books, 1996.

Tarnas, Richard. *The Passion of the Western Mind: Understanding the Ideas That Have Shaped Our World View*. New York: Ballantine Books, 1993.

Thompson, William Irwin. *Beyond Religion: The Cultural Evolution of the Sense of the Sacred from Shamanism to Religion to Post-Religious Spirituality*. Great Barrington: Lindisfarne Books, 2013.

Torjesen, Karen Jo. *When Women Were Priests: Women's Leadership in the Early Church and the Scandal of Their Subordination in the Rise of Christianity*. New York: HarperSanFrancisco, 1993.

Vallee, Jacques. *The Invisible College: What a Group of Scientists Has Discovered About UFO Influence on the Human Race*. San Antonio: Anomalist Books, 2014.

van der Post, Laurens. *The Heart of the Hunter: Customs and Myths of the African Bushman*. San Diego: Harcourt Brace, 1989.

–. *A Mantis Carol*. Washington, DC: Island Press, 1975.

–. *A Story Like the Wind: An Epic Novel of Contemporary Southern Africa*. New York: Harvest/Harcourt edition, 1972.

Waite, Charles B. *History of the Christian Religion to the Year 200*. Chicago: C.V. Waite, 1908.

Walker, Barbara G. *The Woman's Dictionary of Symbols and Sacred Objects*. San Francisco: Harper & Row, 1988.

–. *The Woman's Encyclopedia of Myths and Secrets*. New York: HarperSanFrancisco, 1983.

West, John Anthony. *Serpent in the Sky: The High Wisdom of Ancient Egypt*. Wheaton: Theosophical Publishing House, 1993.

Weston, Jesse L. *The Quest of the Holy Grail*. London: Frank Cass, 1964.

White, Saryon Michael. "An Imaginal Journey of Peace," May 22, 2007, www.saryon.com.

Wilhelm, Richard, trans. *The I Ching or Book of Changes*. Translated into English by Cary F. Baynes. Princeton: Princeton University Press, 1975.

Wilkinson, Elizabeth M., and L.A. Willoughby. *Goethe: Poet and Thinker*. New York: Barnes & Noble, 1962.

Winkelman, Michael. *Shamanism: A Biopsychosocial Paradigm of Consciousness and Healing*. Santa Barbara: Praeger, 2010.

Winkelman, Michael, and John R. Baker. *Supernatural as Natural: A Biocultural Approach to Religion*. Upper Saddle River: Pearson Prentice Hall, 2010.

Wolf, Fred Alan. "Mind and the New Physics/Taking a Quantum Leap in Consciousness: An Interview with Fred Alan Wolf, Ph.D.," by Ronald S. Miller. *Science of Mind*, October 1985.

Yates, Frances A. *Giordano Bruno and the Hermetic Tradition*. Chicago: University of Chicago Press, 1964.

–. *The Rosicrucian Enlightenment*. Boulder: Shambhala, 1978.

Index

A

Abrams, M. H., *Natural Supernaturalism*, 394
Absolute Unitary Being, 297, 298–99
acorn, as symbol for psyche, 260, 442
Adams, Henry, *Mont-Saint-Michel and Chartres*, 132, 133
addiction to old story, 58, 59, 129–39
Adonis, 209
African Americans, 438, 444
Ahkenaten (Pharaoh), 334, 425
Akhmim, Egypt, survival of shaman-mystic tradition in, 342
Alaric (Gothic ruler), 145
Albigensians and Albigensian Crusade, 137
alchemy and alchemists, xviii, 26, 32, 82–83, 97, 98, 125, 254, 260, 334, 342, 343, 349, 351, 357, 359, 361, 377, 381, 385, 388, 394, 396, 397, 404, 408
Alexander the Great, 142, 143–44
alexithymia, 436
Allegorists, 181–83
alphabetic literacy, 164–65
Altamira caves, Spain, 268
altered states of consciousness
  in ancient Egypt, 330, 333
  archetype or symbol, as intersection of quantum field and matter, 293, 302–4
  biology of, 287–91
  Cosmic Consciousness and, xviii, 6–7, 15, 22, 26, 29, 33, 36, 48
  Cretan and Greek cultures' use of, 327, 338
  development of modern human consciousness and, 288–91
  evolutionary heritage of, 60, 71, 122–23, 125, 144, 159, 193
  five waves of awakening/remembering and, 358, 404, 405
  heart, integration of, 287–88, 290–91
  indigenous peoples and, 412, 414, 417
  Lewis-Williams' neuropsychological model of, 295–97, 299–300
  poetic expression and, 340
  reality of, arguments for, 297–304
  San Bushmen and, 318
  as shamanic practice, 286–90
  in Stone Age cultures, 279, 286–91, 294–97, 299–304
  therapist/professorial group working on, 448, 450
  viewed as illusion or mere neurobiological activity, 294–304
Aluna (film), 415–16
Aluna (Kogi name for Mind of the Universe), 416–17
King Amangon, 136, 444
Ammonias Saccas, 210
Anatolian presocratic Greek shaman-mystic tradition, xviii, 29–31, 124, 337–42, 404
animals, as aspects of "first spirit" or soul, 319–20
Annunciation, paintings of, 376–77
Anubis, 44, 45
Apollo, 339
Arabic culture. *See* Islamic world
archetype or symbol, as intersection of quantum field and matter, 293, 302–4
Aristotle and Aristotelianism, 373, 382
Armstrong, Karen, 100
King Arthur and the Round Table, 134, 351, 353, 373
Attis, 209
Augustine of Hippo, 210, 212
Augustus Caesar (Roman emperor), 142
Aurobindo, Sri, 41, 81, 192, 251
Autry, Gene, 94

B

Baba Yaga, 93, 95, 136, 162, 192, 197, 222, 260, 302, 353, 354, 446
baboons and Mantis, 320–21
Bache, Christopher, *Dark Night, Early Dawn*, 423, 424
Bacon, Francis, *New Atlantis*, 46–47, 247
Bamford, Christopher, 349, 387–89
  "The Meaning of the Rose Cross," 350, 388

495

Barber, William, II, 445
Baring, Anne, xi–xiii, 361
    The Dream of the Cosmos: A Quest for the Soul, 361, 381–82, 448–49
    The Myth of the Goddess (with Jules Cashford), 8, 22, 277, 278–79
Barker, Margaret, 9, 11, 27, 150, 154, 155–56, 158, 159, 162, 165, 167, 170, 179–80, 181, 186, 190, 207, 334, 471n13
basket of woman of the sky, 312–14
the Beast, 666 as number of, 189–90
Beatrice (Dante's love), 133, 375, 376
Beaumont, Peter, 474n8
Beguines, 349–50, 389
belief versus knowledge, 120–21
Bergson, Henri, 233
Bernbaum, Edwin, *The Way to Shambhala*, 91
Big Bang, 82, 304
biogenetic structuralism, 303
Black Lives Matter, 12, 444
Black Madonna, 355
black-figure vase with Paris, Hermes, and goddesses, Greek Archaic Period, 219
Blake, William, 393
Bleek, Wilhelm, 285, 314, 412
Blombos Cave, South Africa, 270, 271
blue, woman dressed in, 117, 197, 199, 200, 223, 224, 232, 243, 265
Böhme, Jakob, 9
Bohr, Niels, 66
Book of Enoch, 158, 162
Boshier, Adrian, 474n8
Botticelli, Sandro, *The Birth of Venus* and *Primavera (Spring)*, 375–76
Bubonic Plague, 374
Bucke, Richard Maurice, 70–71, 72, 73, 85, 88, 146, 252, 363–64, 410, 412
    Cosmic Consciousness, 70–71
Buddha, 66, 109, 251
burning bush, Lady in, 9, 162, 432
Byzantium, 378–81

C

Campbell, Joseph, 207–8, 272
    The Hero With a Thousand Faces, 428
Canyon de Chelly, 243
Capra, Fritjof, 403
    The Tao of Physics, 66–67
Casaubon, Isaac, 370

Cashford, Jules, and Anne Baring, *The Myth of the Goddess*, 8, 22, 277, 278–79
caterpillar metaphor for our evolutionary future, 423–24
Cathars, 350, 367, 389
cathedral construction in High Middle Ages, 355–65, 388
Catholic Church. *See* Christian Church
cave cultures of Europe and Africa, 7–8, 16, 17, 104, 107, 267–71, 277–87, 291, 293–97, 318, 322, 411–12, 474n8
Cave of the Three Brothers (Trois Freres), 283
Celsus, 210
Celtic cultures, 89, 106, 136, 265, 340, 356, 357, 360, 372–73, 442
censorship, 109–11
central pole, dancing/moving around, 272
Chaco Canyon, 243
chakras, 228, 329, 458
Charpentier, Louis, *The Mysteries of Chartres Cathedral*, 359
Chartres Cathedral and Cathedral school, 132–33, 196, 197, 199, 355, 357–63, 365–66, 372–74, 376, 382, 388, 429
Chaudhuri, Haridas, 82
Chief Bigfoot Memorial Ride, 421
chimpanzees, 271–72, 300
Chrétien de Troyes, 353
    Perceval: The Story of the Grail, 136
Christ, becoming, 190–94, 222
Christ Consciousness, 43, 52, 222, 252–53, 342, 355, 360, 361, 363, 364, 366, 373, 376, 377, 404, 432, 447
Christian Church
    Discovery/Domination, Doctrine of, 437–38
    establishment/legalization of, 205, 214
    feminine aspect of divine suppressed by, 119, 131–35, 188
    Grail story, Christianization of, 353, 367
    Inquisition, 367
    Betty Kovács' background and education in, 115–16
    myth of, 376
    Pseudepigrapha in, 212
    resistance to authority of, 392, 393
    shamanistic-mystic tradition, suppression of, 116, 124, 165–66, 205–15, 254, 342–44, 366–67, 372, 381, 382–84

Index   497

Christian world
  direct experience of Cosmic Consciousness, origins of Christianity in, 365
  feminine dimension of the divine in, 167–71, 186, 187–90, 194
  First Temple Jewish, early Christian, and Egyptian rituals compared, 333–34, 358
  historical versus cosmic Christ, 193, 195–96, 205, 208–12
  Judaism, roots in ancient mystical tradition of, 168, 185–87, 206
  leadership roles for women in, 188
  mystic Christianity, xviii, 9, 27, 71, 142, 167, 168, 179–80, 190–94, 206, 254, 333, 334, 341–42, 351, 373, 376, 383, 404, 408
Christmas, date of, 209
chullpas, 232
Church and State, resistance to authority of, 392, 393
Church of Rome. *See* Christian Church
civilization
  High Middle Ages and healing of, 362–64
  present duty to reclaim, 441–53
Clement of Alexandria, 190
Clottes, John, and David Lewis-Williams, *The Shamans of Prehistory*, 272, 296
CO_2 levels, NDEs attributed to, 75
coincidence, meaningful (synchronistic event), 312
collective unconscious, 261, 447
colonialism, 437–38
comet strike, Stone Age, 326
Communism, 120
conceptual language, 32, 103, 105–8, 204, 316–18
Constantine I (Roman emperor), 205, 379
Corbin, Henri, 173, 174–75, 177, 274, 394
Corpus Hermeticum, 125, 137, 369
Cosmic Consciousness, xiii, xvii–xix, 5–54, 435–53
  as Christ Consciousness, 43, 52, 222, 252–53, 342, 355, 360, 363, 366, 373, 377, 404, 432, 447
  civilization, present duty to reclaim, 441–53
  decay of Western worldview, emergence into consciousness of, 435–41

  evolutionary heritage, importance of remembering, xviii, 39–42, 57–62 (*See also* evolutionary heritage)
  as experience, 147–48, 151, 362
  five waves of remembering/awakening to, xix, 31, 455 (*See also* five waves of remembering/awakening)
  as foundation rather than goal, 192
  Gift of (*See* Gift)
  historical repression of, 9–11, 13–14
  indigenous/ancient cultures' awareness of, 7–9
  as knowledge of our immortality, divinity, and creativeness, xi, xiii, 6, 11, 39, 147, 231, 239–41, 246, 405
  Kovács' personal journey toward, 43–54
  kundalini energy and, 458
  Merchants of Light/ML and, 44–52, 246–48, 250, 252, 408, 432, 440–41
  modern rediscovery of, 11–13
  as net or web of light, xii, 77
  new science revolution and, 33–39
  pathology of Western worldview versus, xi–xii, xvii, xviii, 7, 13, 57–58, 95, 106, 109–11, 129–39, 163, 426–27, 440
  reframing of worldview to include, 14–15
  shaman-mystic-scientist cultures and, xi–xii, 14–33 (*See also* shaman-mystic-scientist cultures)
  techniques or rituals for experiencing, 6–7
Cosmic Tree of Life
  central pole, dancing/moving around, 272
  Christian denial of, 166
  Cosmic Consciousness as fruit of, xiii, 3, 6, 8–11, 13, 147, 231, 246, 435, 453
  in Cretan and Greek cultures, 327
  Divine Ostrich Egg as fruit of, for San Bushmen, 412
  dream/vision of, 239–41
  in Egyptian culture, 333, 335–36
  feminine aspect of divine and, 156, 157, 162, 179, 429, 432
  in five waves of awakening/remembering, 351, 391, 405, 407
  Garden of Eden story and, 10, 159–63, 337

the Gift, fruit as, 3, 10, 42, 52, 54, 190
Jesus and, 190
Kovács' personal journey toward, 43, 46, 52-54
Menorah equated with, 9, 432
in shaman-mystic-scientist cultures, 20, 22, 26, 28
the soul as fruit of, 239, 241
symbolic language and experience of fruit of, 190
Cota-Robles, Patricia, 248
Counterculture Movement, 14
Crete, cultures of, 20-21, 327
Critchlow, Keith, 17, 18, 326, 356, 358, 360, 362
crop circles, 37-38, 435
Crusades, 343, 344, 366, 379
Cusco, Catholic Cathedral in, 226

D

Dakota Access Pipeline, 444
Dalai Lama, 91, 177
Daly, Okasha El, 343
dance and dancing, 5, 8, 21, 22, 67, 147, 272, 279, 286, 287, 308-9, 327, 340
Dante Alighieri, *Divine Comedy*, 133, 353, 375, 382
D'Aquili, Eugene, 33, 303
Why God Won't Go Away (with Andrew Newberg), 297-99
Dark Ages, 215
Darwin, Charles, 66, 83, 109, 302, 304
de Quillan, Jehanne, *The Gospel of the Beloved Companion*, 457
Dead Sea Scrolls, 11, 27, 138, 141-42, 150, 151-54, 168, 179, 404
death ceremony (Inca), 226-30
Death Valley, 245, 422
Delgado, Jorge Luis, 232, 237
Demeter, 148
depth psychology, 206
Deuteronomists, 10, 11, 27, 28, 155-56, 158, 159, 162, 164, 165, 167, 170, 205, 207, 212, 254, 334, 337
Dionysius the Areopagite, 373, 382-83
Dionysos, 209
Discovery/Domination, Doctrine of, 437-38, 445
disk of radiant consciousness, 249, 451-52
Divine Matrix. *See* quantum field

double spiral, 122
Douno, Beinsa (Peter Deunov), 251-53
Dowson, Thomas, 296
dreams/visions, 173-80. *See also* symbolic/visionary mind; *specific subjects*
importance of, 323-24
incubation (Greek sleep cure/dream practice), 337-38
Martha Jaeger's Mantis dream, 309-10
Jesus on, 177
of Bradford Keeney, 410
of Betty Kovács (table), 456
of István Kovács, 44, 60, 104-6, 110, 245, 246, 247, 250, 253, 339-40, 450, 451
modern valuation of, 404
new story, as tools in becoming masters of, 90, 92, 97, 138
of Pisti Kovács' girlfriend, 130
in presocratic, Anatolian Greek shaman-mystic tradition, 338-39
of son of Patricia Cota-Robles, on ML, 248
Spanish man's dream of San Bushman in castle, 323, 413-14
in Sufi mystic tradition, 173
"terrible dream," 46, 52, 248, 352, 409, 430, 447, 453
Druids, 355, 372
dualism/non-dualism, 303, 350, 366, 388

E

Earthwalking Sky Dancers: Women's Pilgrimages to Sacred Places, 229
Edfu Building Texts, 48-49, 328
Egypt
Akhmim, survival of shaman-mystic tradition in, 342
First Temple Jewish, early Christian, and Egyptian rituals compared, 333-34, 358
Grail stories and, 351-52, 354
Hermetic texts and, 370
Jewish mysticism in, 150, 158, 188
kundalini in, 26, 119, 333, 336
shaman-mystic-scientist tradition in, xviii, 9-10, 22, 23-26, 29, 48-49, 119, 124, 147, 327-36, 404, 425-26
Therapeutae, 10-11, 150, 151, 165, 188, 206
El Miron Cave, Cantabria, Spain, 287

Eleusinian mysteries, 22, 144, 145–47, 194, 327
Eliade, Mircea, 9, 84–85, 123
Ellis, Richard, 416
emptiness/missingness, sense of, 63, 221–24, 319, 436
"empty" basket and woman of the sky, 312–14
Enlightenment (eighteenth century), 109, 110–11, 126, 390–92, 393–94, 402
Enlightenment (seventeenth century). *See* Rosicrucian Enlightenment
Erasmus, Desiderius, 380
Ereira, Alan, *The Elder Brothers*, 415
Essenes, 10, 150–54, 165, 205
Eusebius, 206, 210–11, 212–13
evolutionary future, 423–33
evolutionary heritage
  addiction to old story, 58, 59, 129–39
  blueprint for, 185–94
  importance of remembering, xviii, 39–42, 57–62
  individual mystical experience of, 121–27
  loss of, 205–15
  new story, becoming masters of, 87–101
  quantum field, experience and intellectual discovery of, 69–77
  sacred texts of our lives, discovering, 113–27
  shaman-mystic-scientist cultures, rediscovery/recreation of, 14–15, 63–68
  as "single energy event," 79–86
  symbolic and conceptual language and, 103–11
  timeline, 455
Exodus story, 207–8

F

Faiia, Santha, and Graham Hancock, *Heaven's Mirror*, 47
fairy tales, xvii, 6, 32, 89, 92–93, 95, 260, 431
fear, 165
feeling, importance of, 104, 335, 427, 441
feminine dimension of the divine. *See also specific aspects and names, e.g.* Wisdom, Our Lady, Queen of Heaven
  Beatrice (Dante's love) and Laura (Petrarch's love), 133, 375, 376
  in Christian history, 167–71, 186, 187–90, 194
  consequences of rejection of, 243–54, 427
  Cosmic Tree of Life and, 156, 157, 162, 179, 429, 432
  in Cretan and Greek cultures, 327
  as the Gift, 219, 223–24
  Grail stories and, 428
  in High Middle Ages, 349, 352–54, 355
  Holy Spirit, as feminine, 189
  in Italian Renaissance, 375, 376–77
  in Jewish history, 155–66, 187
  masculine principle and, 198–200, 234, 429, 449
  matrifocal cultures, 19
  net of light and, 449
  Peru, experiences of Betty Kovács in, 225–37
  prehistoric representations of, 270, 278–79
  rediscovering, 118–19, 131–36, 138–39, 185–94, 198–205
  returning to, 254–55
  Romantic movement, feminine visionaries in, 395, 396, 399–400
  song of, 249–50
  as the soul, 262–64
  symbolic/visionary mind, as organizing principle of, 259–60
Fenwick, Peter, 75
FFF (Forever Family Foundation), 420
Ficino, Marsilio, 125, 137, 369–70, 377, 382
Fisk, Robert, *The Great War for Civilisation*, 100
five waves of remembering/awakening, xix, 31, 455. *See also* High Middle Ages; Italian Renaissance
  masculine Western worldview creatively interrupted by, 427–28
  Romantic movement, 31, 345, 393–402
  Rosicrucian Enlightenment (Northern Renaissance), 31, 125–26, 137, 247, 366, 387–92, 395
  twentieth and twenty-first centuries (present time), 403–9, 435
fluke of nature, human beings viewed as, 13, 50, 82, 248, 263
Forever Family Foundation (FFF), 420
Fourth Crusade, 379

Fra Angelico, 377
Fraser, Sir Ronald, 358, 359
Freke, Timothy, and Peter Gandy, *The Jesus Mysteries*, 185–86, 194, 209, 343
French Enlightenment (eighteenth century). *See* Enlightenment
Freud, Sigmund, 31–32, 118
fruit of Cosmic Tree of Life. *See* Cosmic Tree of Life
Fry, Christopher, 447
Fulcanelli, *The Mysteries of the Cathedrals*, 357

G

Garden of Eden/Adam and Eve, 10, 159–63, 337
gematria (number symbolism), 186, 189–90
Genesis, Tree of Life in, 10
the Gift
  consequences of rejection of, 243–54
  of facing our true stories, 219, 221–24
  feminine aspect of the divine as, 219, 223–24
  fruit of Cosmic Tree of Life as, 3, 10, 42, 52, 54, 190
  as initiation into larger vision of life, 146
  Betty Kovács' reception of, 239–41
  Peru, experiences of Betty Kovács in, 225–37, 298
Gimbutas, Marija, 18–22, 327, 371, 443
Ginsberg, Bob and Phran, 420
gnosis, Gnostics, and Gnosticism, xviii, 10, 26, 28, 32, 97, 116, 125, 137, 138, 147, 151, 165, 168, 188, 190, 211–13, 215, 240, 254, 260, 329, 334, 354, 365, 369, 381, 408, 447
Göbekli Tepe, Turkey, 17, 325
Goddess/Great Goddess, 3, 8–9, 20, 93, 219, 227, 338, 339
Goethe, Johann Wolfgang von, 82–83, 99, 199, 394–402, 448, 483n8
  The Chemical Wedding of Christian Rosenkreutz, 395
  Faust, 398–401, 439, 483n8
  Das Märchen, 395–96
Gooch, Stan, 474n8
Goodall, Jane, 272
Goodchild, Veronica, *Songlines of the Soul*, 90–91
Goodenough, Erwin R., *By Light, Light*, 149
Gospel of Mary/Gospel of Mary Magdalene, 169, 170, 177, 179, 187, 457, 469n13
Gospel of Philip, 167, 169, 170, 176–77, 190, 191, 203
Gospel of Thomas, 87, 91, 116, 168, 169, 191, 263
Goswami, Amit, 34, 76, 443
Gothic cathedrals, 355–63
Grail legend, 43, 133–37, 169, 311, 349, 350–55, 363, 367, 372, 428
Great Council of the Grandmothers, 449, 451
great hunger, (San) dance of the, 279, 308
Great Mother, 21, 93, 203, 227, 228, 231, 245, 248, 264, 281, 415
"great time gap" in human development, 288–90
Greater or Inner Mysteries, 209–10, 211
Greek Key motif, 432
Greek world
  Classical period, philosophy, and rationalism, 144–45
  Cretan and Minoan cultures, 20–21, 327
  epic poetry of, 340, 379
  Hellenistic period, 142–48
  incubation (sleep cure/dream practice), 337–38
  Mysteries and Mystery Schools, 22, 32, 44, 74, 116, 144–48, 209–10, 214, 327, 425
  presocratic, Anatolian Greek shaman-mystic tradition, xviii, 29–31, 124, 337–42, 404
Ground of Being, 76, 110, 111, 136, 304, 350, 352. *See also* quantum field
Gunung Padang (Mountain of Enlightenment), Indonesia, 17, 325

H

Hancock, Graham, 288, 299, 314, 326
  Heaven's Mirror (with Santha Faiia), 47
  Magicians of the Gods, 47, 48, 49
  Supernatural, 270, 285
hand-axes, Stone Age, 269
Hapsburgs, 126, 385, 389
Harner, Michael, 66
Harrison, Jane Ellen, 219
hartebees, 320, 321

Harvey, Andrew, 458
Hathor, 330-33, 335, 425, 426
Healing Hearts at Wounded Knee, 421-22
heart
    as feminine energy, 449
    integration of, 287-88, 290-91, 317, 350, 404, 408, 443
    violence, overcoming, 422
    wisdom of the, 288, 290, 334-35, 354, 392, 399, 426, 443, 447
heart consciousness, xviii, 366, 388, 408, 450
The Heart of the World: Elder Brother's Warning (film), 415
HeartMath Institute, 33, 287-88, 290, 317
Heisenberg, Werner, 66
Hellenistic period, 142-48
Hermes, 219
Hermes Trismegistus, 370
Hermes-Tat, 149
Hermeticism/Hermetic arts, xviii, 26, 32, 97, 125, 137, 254, 260, 329, 334, 357, 369-71, 381, 384, 385, 387-88, 389, 404, 408
Herodotus, 143, 194
heroic impulse in Western worldview, 427-31
Herrin, Judith, *Byzantium: The Surprising Life of a Medieval Empire*, 378-79, 380
hidden or secret tradition, 11, 27, 31, 116, 142, 145, 165, 168, 188, 190-92, 210-11
Higgins, Godfrey, 212
High Middle Ages/twelfth century Renaissance, 349-67
    addiction to old story and, 131, 133, 134, 136-37
    cathedral construction in, 355-65, 388
    civilization, healing of, 362-64
    Cosmic Consciousness in, 363-66
    Courts of Love in, 133, 349
    feminine dimension of the divine in, 349, 352-54, 355-56
    Grail stories of, 43, 133-37, 169, 311, 349, 350-55, 363, 367, 372, 428
    Islamic world and, 349, 350, 354, 362
    Italian Renaissance and, 350, 370, 376
    mundus imaginalis in, 177
    reemergence of wisdom tradition in, 349-51

Rosicrucian Enlightenment and, 387-89
    suppression of, 366-67
Hitching Post of the Sun (Intihuatana), Machu Picchu, 226-27
Hoeller, Stephan A., 27, 138
Holotropic Breathwork, 417
Holy Grail, 43, 133-37, 169, 311, 349, 350-55, 363, 367, 372, 428
holy of holies
    in First Temple Judaism, 52, 177-78
    the Gift and, 239, 241, 242
    Jesus and, 190
    labyrinth designs and, 21, 38
    at Lascaux cave, 279
    symbolic language and, 190
    union of male and female in, 183, 339
    within us, 201
    Wisdom/Queen of Heaven and, 9, 52, 179, 183, 202, 432
Holy Spirit, as feminine, 189
Homer, *Iliad* and *Odyssey*, 379
Horus, 209, 331, 332, 352
House of Wisdom, Baghdad, 343
Huayna Picchu, 228, 239, 240, 298
Hubble Telescope, 449, 451
humanism, 374-75, 378
Hungarian Revolution, 197
hunters and hunting
    prehistoric hunters, initiation of, 279-82, 283
    in San culture, 308, 309, 315, 323
Huxley, Aldous, *The Doors of Perception*, 233, 234, 318

I

I Ching or *Book of Changes*, 18th Hexagram, 44-46, 51, 53, 246, 433, 440
Ignatius, *Letter to the Philippians*, 471n13
Imaginal cells, 51-52, 195, 201, 247, 408, 423
imagination as ground of soul, 310-11
Inca death ceremony, 226-30
incarnation of Jesus, 179-80, 207
incubation (Greek sleep cure/dream practice), 338
indigenous cultures, 409-22
    Cosmic Consciousness, awareness of, 7
    Discovery/Domination, Western Doctrine of, 437-38, 445
    Kogi (Colombia), 414-17

modern awareness of, 404, 405
Native Americans, 253, 287, 409, 421–22, 437–38, 444
Peru, experiences of Betty Kovács in, 225–37, 298
San Bushmen, xviii, 7–8, 15, 16, 279, 284–86, 291, 294–96, 307–24, 404, 409–14
Yanomami (Amazon rainforest), 417–20, 482n26
individual nature of mystical experience, 121–27
Indra, 451
Inner or Greater Mysteries, 209–10, 211
Inquisition, 367
instincts, 273–74
Integral Yoga, 251
Internet, 409, 482n26
Intihuatana (Hitching Post of the Sun), Machu Picchu, 226–27
Invisible College, 35, 247
invisible spirit world, visible world rooted in, 318
Ipupiara, 418–20, 482n26
the "irreducibly real," 84
Isis, 149
Islamic world
  Constantinople, fall of (1453), 369
  High Middle Ages and, 349, 350, 354, 362
  Italian Renaissance and, 378
  Muslim Spain, 350
  Ottoman conquest of Byzantium (1453), 369, 379–80
  Sufi mystic tradition, 173, 174, 289, 329, 344–45, 350, 351, 357, 389
  survival of shaman-mystic tradition in Persia, 342–44
  translations from Arabic to Latin, 349
Island of the Sun, Lake Titicaca, Peru, 231–32
Italian Renaissance, 369–85
  art of, 375–77
  Byzantium and, 378–81
  classical/pagan world, rediscovery of, 377
  Cosmic Consciousness awakened during, 371–74, 381–82
  economic and political changes affecting, 371
  feminine dimension of the divine in, 375, 376–77
  hermetic texts rediscovered in, 369–71, 381, 384, 387–88
  High Middle Ages, origins in, 350, 370, 376
  humanism in, 374–75, 378
  Islamic cultures and, 378
  Pico della Mirandola, synthesizing work of, 382–84
  Rosicrucian Enlightenment and, 126, 387
  suppression of, 372, 381, 382–85

J

jackals/jackal healers, 44, 45, 46, 51, 93, 246, 439
Jaeger, Martha, 309
Jeremiah (biblical prophet), 158
Jesuits, 126, 389
Jesus, 13, 28, 73, 87, 91, 115, 116, 124, 139, 152–54, 167–71, 176, 177, 179–80, 187–96, 202, 205–7, 366. *See also specific entries at* Christ *and* Christian
Jesus mysteries, 147, 150, 185–87, 209
Jewish world
  Babylonian invasion and exile, 142, 154, 156, 158
  Christianity and ancient mystical tradition of, 168, 185–87, 206
  Crusades, Rhineland massacres of Jews in, 366
  Deuteronomists, 10, 11, 27, 28, 155–56, 158, 159, 162, 164, 165, 167, 205, 207, 212, 254, 334, 337
  Egyptian, First Temple Jewish, and early Christian rituals compared, 333–34, 358
  feminine dimension of the divine in, 155–66, 187
  First Temple Judaism, shaman-mystic tradition of, xviii, 9–11, 27–28, 141–42, 150, 152, 155, 158, 159, 168, 177–80, 181, 201, 337, 349
  Garden of Eden/Adam and Eve, distortion of story of, 10, 159–63, 337
  Greek Mystery tradition influencing, 149–54
  Hellenistic Judaism, 149–54
  Josiah, king of Judah, reforms of, 10, 27, 141–42, 155–56, 158, 212, 254, 334

reemergence/rediscovery of mystical Judaism, 181–83, 186–87
Zohar, 349, 377
Johnson v. M'Intosh (US Supreme Court, 1823), 437
Joseph of Arimathea, 355
Josephus, 150
Joshua (Torah/Old Testament figure), 185
Josiah, king of Judah, reforms of, 10, 27, 141–42, 155–56, 158, 212, 254, 334
The Judgment of Paris, 219
Jung, Carl Gustav, 31–32, 96–99, 107, 108, 117, 118, 120, 147, 259–62, 303, 312, 371, 396, 410, 441–42, 447, 448
Modern Man in Search of a Soul, 96, 138
The Undiscovered Self, 96

K

Kabbalah and Kabbalists, xviii, 11, 32, 97, 125, 151, 165, 187, 254, 260, 329, 334, 351, 357, 377, 381–82, 384, 385, 388, 404, 408
Kalahari Bushmen. *See* San Bushmen
Keeney, Bradford, 409–11, 414
The Bushman Way of Tracking God, 411
Shamanic Christianity, 411
Way of the Bushman As Told by the Tribal Elders (with Hillary Keeney), 16, 307, 411
Keeney, Hillary, 409, 411
Way of the Bushman As Told by the Tribal Elders (with Bradford Keeney), 16, 307, 411
Kerényi, Carl, 43, 145, 146, 147, 148, 327
Dionysos: Archetypal Image of Indestructible Life, 21
Kidd, Sue Monk, *The Secret Life of Bees*, 57
Killstraight, Birgil, 421
King, Martin Luther, Jr., 444–45
King Amangon, 136, 444
King Arthur and the Round Table, 373
Kingsley, Peter, 124, 143, 145, 221–23, 337–38, 340–42, 344, 401, 436
In the Dark Places of Wisdom, 29–30, 145, 338
Klasies River Cave, South Africa, 271
Klettenberg, Susanne von, 395, 396
Knight and Our Lady, dream/vision of, 131–32, 134–35, 157, 164, 165, 170, 196–200, 224, 265, 294, 314, 429–30
Knights Templar, 356, 362, 367

knowledge versus belief, 120–21
Kogi (Colombia), 414–17
Köhler, Wolfgang, *The Mentality of Apes*, 271–72
Kovács, Betty
Chartres Cathedral and, 132–33, 357, 361, 362–63, 429
Christian background and early education of, 115–16
dreams/visions, table of, 456
emptiness/missingness, sense of, 63, 223
graduate work of, 46, 117, 120, 197, 225
Jung, study of, 96–99, 107, 108, 117, 120
mantis and, 311–12
marriage and birth of son, 197
The Miracle of Death, xi, xv, xvii, 44, 53, 60, 104, 244
new story, on becoming master of, 95–100
personal journey toward Cosmic Consciousness, 43–54, 159 (*See also* Gift)
Peru, experiences in, 225–37, 298
sacred texts of life, discovery of, 115–21
WWII, experience of, 94–95
Kovács, István (husband), 43–47, 51, 59, 60, 71–72, 104–6, 110, 197, 237, 244–47, 250, 253, 339, 446, 450–52
Kovács, Pisti (son), 43–44, 52, 59, 60, 71–72, 104–5, 110, 130, 197, 237, 243–44, 246, 248, 253, 439, 446, 448–52
Krippner, Stanley, 92
Kübler-Ross, Elisabeth, 69, 72–73
Kuhn, Alvin Boyd, 203, 206, 208, 209, 212, 213, 214
Kühn, Sophie von, 396
kundalini energy, 16, 26, 71, 119, 161, 333, 336, 337, 413, 458

L

labyrinths, in medieval cathedrals, 364–65
labyrinth/spiral, 8, 21–22, 38, 43, 89, 95, 97, 107, 115, 118–19, 121, 132, 133, 147, 162–63, 327, 338, 353, 364–65, 371, 395–98, 432
"Lady in the burning bush," 9, 162, 432
Lady of the Sycamore, 335
Lakota Sioux, 421–22
Lang, Walter, 357
Lascaux cave, 279

László, Ervin, 76, 431
Laughlin, Charles D., 293, 302-3
Laura (Petrarch's love), 375, 376
Laussel rock shelter, 278
Lavinia, in Shakespeare's *Titus Andronicus*, 229-30, 472n2
left brain versus right brain, 164-65, 196, 198, 204, 234
Legaux, Chanoine François, 365
Leloup, Jean-Yves, 141
  The Sacred Embrace of Jesus and Mary, 170
Leonardo da Vinci, *Vitruvian Man*, 384-85
Lesser or Outer Mysteries, 209, 211
Levi-Strauss, Claude, 303
Levy, Paul, 447
Lewis-Williams, David, 284-85, 295-97, 299-300, 301, 302, 412
  The Mind in the Cave, 296, 297
  The Shamans of Prehistory (with John Clottes), 272, 296
little hunger, (San) dance of the, 279, 308
Lloyd, Lucy, 285, 314
Logos, 181, 183, 186
Loom of Polarity, 118, 138, 429
Lorimer, David, 252
Louie, Kenway, 272
love
  Courts of Love in High Middle Ages, 133, 349
  higher consciousness through, xii, 26, 72-73, 106, 192, 334, 335, 366, 389, 440
  meaning and purpose in, 95, 96
  NDEs and experience of, 73-74
  net of light and, 450-53
  respect and, 446
Luxor, Temple of, Egypt, 25, 329

M

Machu Picchu, 226-30, 239
Mal'ta, Lake Baikal, mammoth tooth with labyrinth carving, 8
mammalian symbolic activity, 271-73
Mann, Thomas, 120
Mantis, 309-12, 315, 318-22, 323, 371, 413
Märchen, German Romantic concept of, 395-402
Martini, Simone, *The Annunciation*, 376
Mary, mother of Jesus, 136, 167, 169, 186, 355, 360, 366, 376-77

Mary, sister of Jesus, 167, 169, 186, 366
Mary Magdalene, 28, 167, 169, 173-74, 186, 189, 194, 202, 215, 311, 366, 457
Mary Mysteries, 360, 372-73
masculine principle, 189-90, 198-200, 204-5, 231-32, 427-31
Masters, Robert, 25
matrifocal cultures, 19
Mayan oracle, 114, 425
Mayer, Janet, 417-20, 482n26
  Spirits ... They Are Present, 417
McErlane, Sharon, 449
McTaggart, Lynne, 34, 65, 66, 75, 263
  The Field: The Quest for the Secret Force of the Universe, 34
Me Too movement, 12, 444
Mead, G. R. S., *Fragments of a Faith Forgotten*, 213
meaningful coincidence (synchronistic event), 312
Medici, Cosimo de', 125, 369-70, 377
Medici, Lorenzo de', 383
Medici, Pietro de', 383
medieval period. *See* High Middle Ages/twelfth century Renaissance
Megalithic builders and monuments, xviii, 16-18, 37, 38, 325-27, 358-59, 388
Menorah, 9, 432
Mephistopheles, 399-401, 438-39, 483n8
Merchants of Light/ML, 44-52, 246-48, 250, 252, 408, 432, 440-41
mescaline, 234
Mesolithic. *See* Stone Age
Meyer, Marvin, 28, 168, 191
Michelangelo, *The Birth of Adam* (Sistine Chapel), 375
Michell, John, 190
Middle Ages. *See* High Middle Ages/twelfth century Renaissance
mind-body connection, 175
mind-body dualism, 303
Minoan culture, 20-21, 327
missingness/emptiness, sense of, 63, 221-24, 319, 436
Mithras, 209
ML/Merchants of Light, 44-52, 246-48, 250, 252, 408, 432, 440-41
modern human consciousness, 52, 53, 61, 67, 287-89, 301, 310, 341, 385, 405, 412, 458
Montagu, Ashley, 20

Mont-Saint-Michel, 132–33
morphogenetic field, 458
Moses/Moses Mysteries, 149, 156, 181–83, 185–86, 207
mundus imaginalis (subtle or intermediate world), 174–78, 182, 192–93, 200, 206, 212, 215, 261, 289
mustard seed, 190
Mysteries and Mystery Schools in ancient world, 22, 32, 44, 74, 116, 144–48, 209–10, 214, 327, 425
mystic Christianity, xviii, 9, 27, 71, 142, 167, 168, 179–80, 190–94, 206, 254, 333, 334, 341–42, 351, 373, 376, 383, 404, 408
mystical experience, 173–80
myth of meaning, 8, 11, 12, 250, 279, 290–91, 308–9
myth of soul, 263–65
myth of survival, 8, 279, 290–91, 308

N

Nag Hammadi texts, 11, 12, 27–28, 87, 138, 139, 142, 152, 154, 167–71, 193, 222, 371, 404, 430, 441, 469n13
narcissistic personality disorder, 436
Native Americans, 253, 287, 409, 421–22, 437–38, 444
nature
  indigenous peoples' concern for, 414–20
  living in harmony with, 7, 20, 21, 40–41, 51, 53, 82–83, 92, 97–99, 161, 198–99, 205, 208–9, 264, 332
  Romantic approach to, 394
Naydler, Jeremy, *Shamanic Wisdom in the Pyramid Texts*, 25, 26, 330, 331, 342, 352, 370, 426
NDEs (Near/Actual-Death Experiences), 14, 33, 69–70, 72–75, 76, 147, 193, 233, 235, 301, 334, 404
Neanderthals, 271
Near/Actual-Death Experiences (NDEs), 14, 33, 69–70, 72–75, 76, 147, 193, 233, 235, 301, 334, 404
Neolithic. *See* Stone Age
Neoplatonism, 210, 377, 381
net or web of light, xii, 448–53
Never Again movement, 12, 444
New Chartres Academy, 361
New Science Revolution, 33–39, 407, 442
Newberg, Andrew, 33

Why God Won't Go Away (with Eugene D'Aquili), 297–99
Newcomb, Steven, 437
Newgrange, Ireland, 17, 325
N|om, 413, 458
North Pole, jackals stirring cauldron at, 93–94, 439
Northern Renaissance. *See* Rosicrucian Enlightenment
Novalis, 113, 222, 395–98, 442
  Heinrich von Ofterdingen, 396
nuclear weapons, xi, 11
number symbolism (gematria), 186, 189–90
Nut (Egyptian goddess of night), 332–33, 339, 428

O

OBEs (out-of-body experiences), 72, 301
ocher, symbolic use of, 270–71, 474n8
Odysseus, 131–32
"Old Europe," shaman-mystic tradition of, 18–22, 32, 61, 327, 371, 404, 443
Opener of the Way, 44, 360
organized religion, 101
Orpheus, 149, 209
Orphic mysticism, 144–45
Osiris, 194, 209, 331, 332, 352
Ostrich Egg, Divine, 412
Ottoman conquest of Byzantium (1453), 369, 379–80
Our Lady
  evolutionary heritage of, 131–36, 156, 160, 162, 163, 164, 169, 179, 196–200
  five waves of awakening/remembering and, 350, 353, 355–58, 361–66, 372, 388, 391
  the Gift and, 224–27, 232, 236
  Knight and Our Lady, dream/vision of, 131–32, 134–35, 157, 164, 165, 170, 196–200, 224, 265, 294, 314, 429
  retrieving/recovering, 264, 265, 294, 349
Outer or Lesser Mysteries, 209, 211
out-of-body experiences (OBEs), 72, 301

P

Pachamama/Pachamama Stone, 227–28, 236, 239, 241
Pagels, Elaine, 168
Paleolithic. *See* Stone Age

Paris, Judgment of, 219
Parmenides, 29, 30, 145, 338, 341
Parsifal/Perceval, legend of, 58, 136, 311
Paul (apostle), 71, 363–64, 373
Pauli, Wolfgang, 66
Pearce, Joseph Chilton, *The Biology of Transcendence*, 289–91
Pearl Harbor, 94
Persephone, 148, 339
Persia, 342–44
Pert, Candace, *Molecules of Emotion*, 175
Peru, experiences of Betty Kovács in, 225–37, 298
Petrarch, 374–75, 377
Philip of Macedon, 142
Philo Judaeus, 10, 149, 150, 153–54, 165, 181–83, 186, 187
Picasso, Pablo, 268
Pico della Mirandola, Giovanni, 382–84
  Conclusions, 382–83
  Oration on the Dignity of Man, 382
Pietism, 395
"pious frauds," 212–14
Pistis Sophia, 173
plants, sacred/healing/psychoactive, 232–37, 271, 286–87
Plato and Platonism, 26, 30, 49, 125, 144–45, 341, 369–70, 373, 377, 379, 381, 382, 389
Pletho, Gemisthus, 377, 379
Pliny the Elder, 150
Plotinus, 125, 210, 369–70, 377
poetic expression, 340, 442
Polarität, 398
Poor People's Campaign, 12, 444–46
Potter, Charles Francis, *The Lost Years of Jesus Revealed*, 153–54
prefrontal lobes, 289–91
prehistory, concept of, 268
present time (twentieth and twenty-first centuries), as fifth wave of remembering/awakening, 403–9, 435
presidential elections of 2016, 420, 440, 444–45
presocratic, Anatolian Greek shaman-mystic tradition, xviii, 29–31, 124, 337–42, 404
Pseudepigrapha, 212
pseudo-Dionysius, 373
pure clay, 245–47, 401, 435
pure spirit, world of, 174, 175–76

Pyramid Texts, 331, 370, 426
Pythagoras, Pythagoreans, and Pythagorean mysticism, 18, 29, 144–45, 150, 151, 188, 338

Q

quantum field, 5–6, 34, 69–77, 82, 101, 163, 175, 178, 261, 262, 287, 293, 302–4, 407
quantum physics, xii–xiii, 12, 15, 33–34, 65, 82, 302, 403, 407, 435, 443, 446
Queen of Heaven
  Cosmic Consciousness and, 9, 20, 52–53
  as Cosmic Tree of Life, 429, 432
  evolutionary heritage of, 118, 155–59, 162–64, 170, 179, 182, 183, 187, 190, 196, 199, 202
  five waves of awakening/remembering and, 355, 391
  the Gift and, 223, 225–28, 232, 234, 241, 244, 248–50, 253, 254
  kundalini energy and, 458
  net of light and, 449
  retrieving/recovering, 260, 262–65, 311, 314, 333
  San Bushmen and, 412
  as Wisdom, 9, 52–53, 155, 157–59, 162, 163, 170, 202, 223, 262, 429
Querido, René, *The Golden Age of Chartres*, 360–61, 362, 373, 376
Qumran community. *See* Dead Sea Scrolls; Essenes

R

Re (Egyptian sun god), 330–34, 339
Reeves, Minou, *Europe's Debt to Persia*, 344
religion, 101. *See also* Christian Church; Christian world; Islamic world; Jewish world
Renaissance. *See* High Middle Ages; Italian Renaissance; Rosicrucian Enlightenment
respect, 444, 446, 447
resurrection of Christ, 190–91
retrieving soul, xix
Reymond, E. A. E., *The Mythical Origin of the Egyptian Temple*, 48–49
ricorso, 107, 121, 316, 317, 397
right brain versus left brain, 164–65, 196, 198, 204, 234

Rilke, Rainer Maria, 14, 228–29
Ring, Kenneth, 69–70, 74
Robert de Boron, 353
Roberts, Alison, 25–26, 330, 331, 334, 342, 352, 370, 425–26
  Hathor Rising, 25, 330
  My Heart My Mother, 425
rock art
  cave cultures of Europe and Africa, 7–8, 16, 17, 104, 107, 267–71, 277–87, 291, 293–97, 318, 322, 411–12, 474n8
  of San Bushmen, 16, 284–86, 294–96, 299, 411, 413
Romantic movement, 31, 345, 393–402
Rosicrucian Enlightenment (Northern Renaissance), 31, 125–26, 137, 247, 366, 387–92, 395
Rosicrucians/Rosicrucian Brothers, 247, 395
Royal Society, 126, 247, 390
Rudgley, Richard, 269–71, 274
  Secrets of the Stone Age, 269

S

Sacred Science, 24–25, 329
sacred texts
  cave paintings as, 322
  discovering our own sacred texts, 113–27
samadhi, 30
San Bushmen, xviii, 7–8, 15, 16, 279, 284–86, 291, 294–96, 307–24, 404, 409–14
San Pedro (sacred cactus drink), 232–37
Sanz de Sautuola, Don Marcelino, 268
Savonarola, 383–84
Schiffman, Lawrence H., 152
school shootings, 438, 444
Schrödinger, Erwin, 66
Schwaller de Lubicz, R. A., 23–25, 49, 328, 329
science. *See also* shaman-mystic-scientist cultures
  developing out of shaman-mystic experience, 124–27
  Rosicrucian Enlightenment and scientific revolution, 388
secret or hidden tradition, 11, 27, 31, 116, 142, 145, 165, 168, 188, 190–92, 210–11
Sed Festival, Egypt, 331–33, 351–52, 354
Sermon on the Mount, 153
serpents/serpent deities/serpent energy, 3, 25–26, 47, 119, 161, 163, 332, 334, 336, 426
Seth (Egyptian deity), 332
Seti I (Pharaoh), 334
Shakespeare, William, *Titus Andronicus*, 229–30
shaman-mystic-scientist cultures, xi–xii, 14–33. *See also* altered states of consciousness; *specific cultures*
  archetypal patterns underlying, 424–26
  defining shaman/shamanism, 6, 283–91, 340–41
  dual need for shaman and scientist, 63–68
  major principles of, 318–24
  modern shaman-mystic revolution, 31–33, 404, 407, 424, 435, 442
  origins of shamanism in cave cultures, 283–91, 293–97
  rediscovery/recreation of, 14–15, 63–68
  science developing out of shaman-mystic experience, 124–27
Shambhala, 91, 177
Shanidar cave, Iraq, 271
Shekhinah, 73, 163, 264
shit, cauldron of, 93–94, 439
Shiva, dance of, 67
Shlain, Leonard, *The Alphabet Versus the Goddess*, 164–65
Silk Road, 143
Sillustani, Peru, 232–37
Silva, Freddy, 37, 38
"single energy event," evolution as, 79–86
Sistine Chapel, 375
skeptical dismissals of spiritual phenomena, 482n26
small, power of the, 318–19
social and political movements, emergence of, 12, 435, 444–45
Solomon (biblical ruler), 356
Solon, 49
Sophia (Wisdom figure), 149, 181, 182, 187, 388
soul
  acorn as symbol for, 260, 442
  archetypes of, 196
  feminine dimension of the divine as, 262–64
  as feminine energy, 449

as fruit of Cosmic Tree of Life, 239, 241
Hermes as guide of, 219
imagination as ground of, 310–11
major principles of San/shaman culture regarding, 318–24
myth of, 263–65
as organ of perception, 176, 193, 274, 277, 394
recovering, 259–66
spirit, relationship to, 100–101
soul of the world
evolutionary heritage of, 131, 132, 134–37, 156, 163
five waves of awakening/remembering, 350, 353, 355, 357, 361, 363, 364
the Gift and, 222, 227, 230, 236, 237, 239, 243
recovering, 265, 294
Specificationstrieb, 398
SPECT camera, 297
spine, base of, as root of spiritual consciousness, 119, 200, 458
spiral. *See* labyrinth/spiral
spirit and soul, relationship between, 100–101
spirit dimension. *See* quantum field
spirit voices of Yanomami people, 417–20, 482n26
Stace, Walter T., 298
Standing Rock, 444
Star of David, 183
Starbird, Margaret, *Magdalene's Lost Legacy*, 189–90
Steigerung, 398
Stone Age cultures, 15–16, 103–4
cave cultures of Europe and Africa, 7–8, 16, 17, 104, 107, 267–71, 277–87, 291, 293–97, 318, 322, 411–12, 474n8
hand-axes, 269
major principles of human culture from, 318–24
Megalithic builders and monuments, xviii, 16–18, 37, 38, 325–27, 358–59, 388
San Bushmen, xviii, 7–8, 15, 16, 279, 284–86, 291, 294–96, 307–24, 404, 409–14
Stonehenge, England, 17, 325, 359
Strachan, Gordon, *Chartres: Sacred Geometry, Sacred Space*, 358–59

strange attractors, 432
Strömberg, Gustaf, 178, 247
Sufi mystic tradition, 173, 174, 289, 329, 344–45, 350, 351, 357, 389
Sumerian Cylinder Seal, Goddess and God of Tree of Life offering sacred fruit, 3, 6
supramental manifestation, 251
Swimme, Brian, 79, 81, 82, 85–86, 222–23, 304, 472n4
symbol or archetype, as intersection of quantum field and matter, 293, 302–4
symbolic language, 32–33, 103–11, 190, 193–94, 206–7, 275, 289, 316–17, 436
symbolic/visionary mind
defined and described, 259–65
development of, 267–75, 289
modern human consciousness and, 52, 53, 61, 67, 287–89, 301, 310, 341, 385, 405, 412, 458
synchronistic event (meaningful coincidence), 312

T

Tammuz, 209
Tarnas, Richard, *The Passion of the Western Mind*, 424, 427
Teilhard de Chardin, Pierre, 81
Templars, 356, 362, 367
"terrible dream," 46, 52, 248, 352, 409, 430, 447, 453
Theodosius I (Roman emperor), 116, 145, 214
Theoharis, Liz, 445
Therapeutae, 10–11, 150, 151, 165, 188, 206
Thirty Years War, 126, 387, 389, 403
Thompson, William Irwin, *Beyond Religion*, 251
three worlds (material world, *mundus imaginalis*, world of pure spirit), 174–79
Titus Andronicus (Shakespeare), 229–30
Tomkins, Peter, 25
Torjesen, Karen Jo, *When Women Were Priests*, 188
Tree of Life. *See* Cosmic Tree of Life
trinity of goddesses, 219
Trois Freres (Cave of the Three Brothers), 283
twelfth century Renaissance. *See* High Middle Ages/twelfth century Renaissance

twentieth and twenty-first centuries (present time), as fifth wave of remembering/awakening, 403–9, 435

U
UFO phenomenon, 34–39, 407, 435
Unas, pyramid of, 331
underworld
  archetypal myth of hero descending into, 207–8
  Betty Kovács' dream/vision of, 245
United States government, 437–39
unity of vision, 18, 24, 32, 123
Universal Mind, 76, 82, 101, 231, 233, 235, 394. *See also* quantum field

V
Valentinian (emperor), 146
Vallee, Jacques, *The Invisible College*, 35–37
van der Post, Laurens, 307–15, 317–23, 409–10, 413
  The Heart of the Hunter, 315, 323
  A Mantis Carol, 309
Vedas, 448, 451
Velia, Italy, 29
Vico, Giambattista, 32–33, 106–9, 121, 178, 315, 316–17, 390–91, 397
  The New Science (1725), 109
violence. *See* war/violence
Virgo constellation, 355–56, 364
visions. *See also* dreams/visions; symbolic/visionary mind
Vivekananda, 188, 206
Voice in the desert, 245, 248, 254
Voices of/at the Wells, 136, 137, 138, 177, 265, 294, 311, 351, 444
von Klettenberg, Susanne, 395, 396
von Kühn, Sophie, 396

W
Waite, Charles B., *History of the Christian Religion to the Year 200*, 213–14
Walters, Dorothy, *Unmasking the Rose*, *The Kundalini Poems*, and *Kundalini Rising*, 458
war/violence. *See also specific events*
  ability of heart to overcome, 422, 443
  consequences of, 243–46
  knowledge and ability to change, 80–81
  modern propensity toward, xi, 11–13
  older cultures without, 8, 19, 443
  Western culture and, 438
Watts, Alan, 82
Way to the Light, 8, 21, 168, 182, 191, 206, 327, 338, 395
web or net of light, xii, 448–53
West, John Anthony, *Serpent in the Sky*, 24, 25, 329
West Tofts hand-axe, 269
Western worldview
  consequences of, 243–46, 263
  decay, emergence into consciousness of, 435–41
  Discovery/Domination, Doctrine of, 437–38, 445
  heroic impulse in, 427–31
  as masculine phenomenon, 427
  our complicity in, 164, 227, 248, 254
  pathology of, xi–xii, xvii, xviii, 7, 13, 57–58, 95, 106, 109–11, 129–39, 163, 426–27, 440
  superiority and privilege embedded in, 380–81
  as "terrible dream," 46, 52, 248, 352, 409, 430, 447, 453
Weston, Jesse, 354
White, John, 11
White, Saryon Michael, 195
  An Imaginal Journey of Peace, 51
wholeness of mind
  reality of, 293
  Romantic movement and, 393, 398
  San Bushmen culture and, 307–24
Wilhelm, Richard, 440
Wilson, Matthew, 272
Winkelman, Michael, and John R. Baker, *Supernatural as Natural*, 287, 300–302
Wisdom
  as Cosmic Tree of Life, 162, 429
  feminine side of Yahweh, loss/recovery of, 155–66, 167, 170–71, 179, 200–202, 205, 215, 223, 254, 262, 391
  Imaginal cells and, 201
  Jesus walking with, 194, 202
  kundalini energy and, 458
  as "Lady in the burning bush," 9, 162, 432
  as name for archetypes of the soul, 196
  Philo's rejection of femininity of, 187

as Queen of Heaven, 9, 52-53, 155, 157-59, 162, 163, 170, 202, 223, 262, 429
rediscovery of, 195-202, 205
Sophia, 149, 181, 182, 187, 388
Wisdom of Sirach, 162
Wisdom of Solomon, 53, 195, 201
wisdom of the heart, 288, 290, 334-35, 354, 392, 399, 426, 443, 447
wisdom tradition, loss and recovery of, 334-35, 342-45, 349-51
witches and witch-hunting, 126, 390
Wolf, Fred Alan, 34, 76, 83, 274
Wolfram von Eschenbach, 353
World Child, 243-44
World War I (Great War), 99-100
World War II, 11, 12, 94, 99, 100, 115, 130-38, 196
Wounded Knee, 421-22

Y

Yahweh
in ancient Judaism, 170
Jesus as, 170, 171, 187, 189, 207
Wisdom as feminine side of, loss/recovery of, 155-66, 167, 170-71, 179, 200-202, 205, 215, 223, 254, 262, 391
Yanomami (Amazon rainforest), 417-20, 482n26
Yates, Frances A., 370, 371, 385, 387-90
Giordano Bruno and the Hermetic Tradition, 369
The Rosicrucian Enlightenment, 46-47, 124-26, 247, 387
Yeats, William Butler, 9
yoga, 251

Z

Zeus, Archaeological Museum, Athens, 204
Zohar, 349, 377

About the Author

Betty J. Kovács received her Ph.D. from the University of California, Irvine, in Comparative Literature and Theory of Symbolic/Mythic Language. She has studied and taught in Europe and the United States. She taught Literature, Writing, and Symbolic/Mythic Language for twenty-five years. She served many years as Chair and Program Chair on the Board of Directors of the Jung Society of Claremont in California and sits on the Academic Advisory Board of Forever Family Foundation. She is author of *The Miracle of Death: There is Nothing But Life*. Contact Betty Kovács at bjkovacs@earthlink.net. Visit www.kamlak.com for a complete list of her work.

The Miracle of Death: There is Nothing But Life
Betty J. Kovács, Ph.D.

A Companion to *Merchants of Light*

The Miracle of Death is an interweaving of the story of a profound loss of a child and at once a remarkable insight into the mystical experience of that mystery. Dr. Kovács brings in both ancient and modern philosophy and spiritual teaching together with her own visions and insights and shows us not only how we can better cope with death of a child or loved one, but, because of it, find the opportunity to profoundly change our whole world view. Readers will find this both deeply moving and clearly informative.

— Fred Alan Wolf, Ph.D. Theoretical Physicist, National Book Award-winning author of *Matter into Feeling, Mind into Matter, The Spiritual Universe, Taking the Quantum Leap,* and *Time Loops and Space Twists*

Betty Kovács gives us not just one but two messages that are vital for our lives and times. First, that our individual mortality is an illusion, for death and birth are a cycle through which life, the sole reality, continues transformed, but unbroken. Two, that as more and more people are turning inward and experiencing the true dimensions of their inner self, a new consciousness is being born on this planet—a consciousness that we are all part of each other and of the cosmos, and that together we can heal the Earth—that we can dance, as Betty Kovács says, the Round Dance. Few things could be more important for us both individually and collectively than understanding these messages.

— Ervin László, Ph.D. Author, Systems Theorist, Founder of the Club of Budapest, twice Nobel Peace Prize nominee

Excerpt from Review of *The Miracle of Death*

Both love and healing run powerfully through the book, expanding into an inspiring collective vision. In these turbulent times we are the earth dreaming to heal herself as we long for a world of love and peace. "This longing is the thread that connects us to our deepest nature.... Now, out of this very longing, we were creating new worlds." So the earth can now "dream its future to itself through us" — what a sign of hope!

As the reader will realise, this is much more than a book about death, it is a book about life and a powerful call to connect with deeper orders of reality, to live our lives as consciously as possible, and to play our part in the healing of humanity and of the earth.

— **David Lorimer,** *Network: The Scientific and Medical Network Review Magazine* **(UK), Director of The Scientific and Medical Network (1986-2000), Programme Director, author and editor of over a dozen books**

Excerpt from Foreword to *The Miracle of Death*

The passionate longing of the human heart has always been to press beyond the boundaries of the known, to break through the limitations of our understanding. This is perhaps our most fundamental and essential freedom. Now, more than ever, we need to honor that longing and welcome those pioneers who can unveil new horizons, new possibilities of understanding our nature, our potential and our destiny.

This moving, courageous book, written with great sensitivity and intelligence and forged in the fiery crucible of personal experience, bears witness to the fact that there is only Life beyond death, that there is nothing *but* Life. Its powerful and compelling story, rich in insight, wisdom and astonishing revelation, offers us a new understanding of ourselves and our unacknowledged needs that can carry us beyond the present limit of our sight.

— Anne Baring, Jungian analyst and author and co-author of seven books, including *The Dream of the Cosmos: A Quest for the Soul*, *The Myth of the Goddess: Evolution of an Image* (with Jules Cashford) and *Soul Power* (with Dr. Scilla Elworthy)

Excerpts from *The Miracle of Death*

Death is as Divine as Life.
Hold them in both hands.
Play with them. Balance them.
This is the Divine Game.

—István

As we reconnect, full circle, to the roots of our existence in the Mind of the universe, we experience the deep unity of birth and death, and we experience the radical creativity of both. We understand that "Death is as Divine as Life" because it *is* Life—because "There is nothing *but* Life."

Death is the fundamental mystery of life, just as life is the fundamental mystery of death. It is not possible to experience one without experiencing the other, but it is possible to be born and to die without participating in the mystery of either. When we do not participate in this mystery, it is usually because we hold a worldview that there is no mystery to experience. Such a worldview has been part of the heritage of Western culture, but now, within this same culture, there is emerging a new "wave of organization" that is radically transforming that worldview.

Birth and death are events in time and space. There is nothing but life.

—Pisti

Excerpts from *The Miracle of Death*

All life is in danger when we hold a worldview that is not *inclusive*. We know this, yet we fear change and transformation. And it is this *fear* and the *belief in our limitations* that prevent us from knowing who we are. In our mostly unconscious effort to maintain our collectively constructed model of reality, we often refuse to validate viable evidence, and we often condemn those who dare to explore these excluded realities. We fear losing the only reality we know when, truly, only the limitation of that reality is threatened.

> *Dad, do you see that horizon? Even that is not the limit.*
> —Pisti

Excerpts from *The Miracle of Death*

*I didn't go anywhere. I'm right here, everywhere, and nowhere. I'm simply in another dimension. Let the body go. I'm not in that body.
I don't need it anymore.*
—István

Live each moment fully. Then let it go.
—Pisti

For the whole mind to be captivated and engaged in our perception and conception of reality, we must allow both symbolic language and conceptual language the dignity and respect of equal positions where neither language can control, dominate, or exclude the other. The healthy brain requires that we value our dreams, our life stories, our visions and our feelings as much as we value our ability to think about ideas.

*Let the Bard in each of us ignite artistic consciousness,
create new angles of perceiving reality, and
inspire the Round Dance of infinite possibilities.*

Available from bookstores and from the publisher

Putting Birth & Death Back Together Again
www.kamlak.com

www.ingramcontent.com/pod-product-compliance
Lightning Source LLC
Chambersburg PA
CBHW060908300426
44112CB00011B/1387